Tropical Versailles

Tropical Versailles

EMPIRE, MONARCHY, AND THE PORTUGUESE
ROYAL COURT IN RIO DE JANEIRO, 1808–1821

KIRSTEN SCHULTZ

ROUTLEDGE
New York London

A volume in the series New World in the Atlantic World, edited by
Jack P. Greene and Amy Turner Bushnell. Volumes in this series to date include
*Tropical Versailles: Empire, Monarchy, and the Portuguese Royal Court in Rio de Janeiro,
1808–1821* and *Creole Gentlemen: The Maryland Elite, 1691–1776.*

Published in 2001 by
Routledge
29 West 35th Street
New York, NY 10001

Published in Great Britain by
Routledge
11 New Fetter Lane
London EC4P 4EE

Routledge is an imprint of the Taylor & Francis Group.

Library of Congress Cataloging-in-Publication Data

Schultz, Kirsten
Tropical Versailles : empire, monarchy, and the Portuguese royal court
in Rio de Janeiro, 1808–1821 / Kirsten Schultz.
p. cm.
Includes bibliographical references and index.
ISBN 0-415-92987-3 (hb.) — ISBN 0-415-92988-1 (pb.)
1. Brazil—History—United Kingdom, 1815–1822.   2. Brazil—History—1763–1822.
3. Rio de Janeiro (Brazil)—History—19th century.   4. Monarchy—Brazil—History—19th century.
5. Monarchy—Portugal—History—19th century.   6. Brazil—Relations—Portugal.
7. Portugal—Relations—Brazil.   I. Title.
F2534.S324 2001
981'.53033—dc21   00-068741

CONTENTS

ACKNOWLEDGMENTS

THIS BOOK BEGAN AS A DISSERTATION AND RESEARCH FOR THAT DISSERTATION BEGAN at The John Carter Brown Library, Providence, Rhode Island, in the Summer of 1994. Along with generously providing funding to do so, the library also furnished a forum where I first formally shared ideas about this project. Funding for research in Rio de Janeiro, Brazil was provided by the Comissão Fulbright, Brasília, and funding for additional research in Lisbon, Portugal was provided by the Joint Committee on Western Europe of the American Council of Learned Societies and the Social Science Research Council with funds from the Luso-American Development Foundation. I would also like to acknowledge the generous assistance provided by the archivists and librarians at the various institutions in the United States, Portugal, and Brazil where I conducted research: in the United States, The John Carter Brown Library, The New York Public Library, and the Interlibrary Loan Office at Bobst Library, New York University; in Portugal, the Arquivo Nacional da Torre do Tombo, the Arquivo Histórico Ultramarino, and the Biblioteca Nacional, Lisboa; in Rio de Janeiro, the Arquivo Nacional, the Biblioteca Nacional, and the Arquivo Histórico Itamaraty. In particular, the staff of the Rare Book and Manuscript Divisions at the Biblioteca Nacional, Rio de Janeiro did their best to ensure access to their collections at a time when building maintenance and reforms meant that the conditions for attending to researchers were far from ideal. At the Arquivo Nacional in Rio de Janeiro Satiro Nunes always enthusiastically shared his understanding of the intricacies of the archive's early nineteenth-century collections. In São Paulo, I would like to thank José Mindlin for allowing me access to the *Biblioteca José Mindlin*, and Cristina Antunes for making research there truly a pleasure. The Biblioteca includes not only the invaluable collection of José Mindlin, but also the extensive holdings from Rio de Janeiro's Royal Press collected and studied by the late Rubens Borba de Moraes.

My research would not have been possible without the guidance and encouragement I received before I reached the archives. Barbara Weinstein, Ronnie Hsia, Maria Lígia Prado, Kenneth Maxwell, Nelson Schapochnik, Jeffrey Needell, Thomas Cohen, Richard Graham, David Higgs, and Roderick Barman generously provided comments on initial outlines for this project and made suggestions about sources, related scholarship, and Brazilian archives. Professor Barman's support was particularly encouraging, as it was after reading his work that I first began to consider the questions raised by the transfer of the court. Above all, however, it was Warren Dean's supportive criticism during the various stages of defining a dissertation topic that helped me to find a more analytical focus for the numerous questions about the transfer of the court that initially surfaced. Warren is not here to see the results in published form. His tragic death in 1994 was an insurmountable loss for his family and friends and for scholars of Brazil. For me it was both a personal loss and, as a graduate student, a loss that left me in a difficult position professionally. I would not have persevered in the endeavor of graduate school or research for this project had it not been for the support I subsequently received. Antonio Feros, Ronnie Hsia, Maria Lígia Prado, and Barbara Weinstein all went beyond the call of duty, beyond the boundaries of their own institutions in some cases, and beyond their fields of expertise in others, providing examples of the kind of collegiality that sustained Warren's own faith in academic life.

In Rio de Janeiro, Gladys Sabina Ribeiro pointed me in the direction of a collection of documents at the National Archive that became crucial sources for this book. Alessandra Silveira, Tania Salgado Pimenta, and Brodwyn Fischer made the most excellent research companions both in the archive and during debriefing sessions on the *calçadão*. Back in New York, funding for writing was provided by the Warren Dean Fellowship, Department of History, New York University—a fellowship created with the support of Elizabeth Dean—and by the Graduate School of Arts and Sciences, NYU, and the American Association of University Women. The Society of Fellows in the Humanities at Columbia University provided me with the resources and the time to do additional research and writing. While writing various drafts of this book, I benefitted from the comments and criticism of Antonio Feros, Ada Ferrer, Ronnie Hsia, and Barbara Weinstein; from Teresa Meade's careful reading of my dissertation; from Bonnie Wasserman's help with language and orthography and Mary Steiber's assistance with an important classical reference; and from the encouragement from and exchange of ideas and sources with Pedro Cardim, António Manuel Hespanha, Jurandir Malerba, David Higgs, Fátima Gouvêa, and Iara Lis Carvalho e Souza. Iara's recent *Pátria Coroada* has undoubtedly enriched my understanding of late eighteenth- and early nineteenth-century Brazilian political culture.

At various stages of writing this book I also benefitted greatly from those who commented on presentations of parts of this project in a number of venues, including The Cooper Union for the Advancement of Science and Art; the College of Charleston, South Carolina; the Society of Fellows in the Humanities, Columbia University; the Graduate Student History Workshop and the Atlantic History Workshop, New York University; the Conference on Latin American History; the Columbia University Brazil Seminar; the Latin American Studies Association Conference; and the Society of Spanish and Portuguese Historical Studies Annual Conference; and especially Timothy Anna and A.J.R. Russell-Wood. I thank as well those who reviewed parts or all of this work for the *Luso-Brazilian Review* and Routledge, especially Neill Macaulay. Portions of this work appeared as "Royal Authority, Empire and the Critique of Colonialism: Political Discourse in Rio de Janeiro, 1808–1821," *Luso-Brazilian Review* 37(2) (2000), and I thank the University of Wisconsin Press for granting permission to include that material here. I also thank Brendan O'Malley at Routledge for sharing both his enthusiasm and expertise.

Of course, I would have never completed this project without the support of family and friends. I thank Louis Anthes, Duane Corpis, Alejandro Cañeque, Julia Miller, Alejandra Osorio, and Daniella Santos for their collegiality, for reading drafts and listening to presentations and sharing their insights and skepticism, for their friendship, and for their sense of humor about academic life. Trudy Levy has, on a number of occasions, provided her characteristic optimistic encouragement when my own enthusiasm was on the wane. Jehan, Mahdi, Neveen, and Shrouk Abedrabbo; Summer, Sammer, and Reem Mustafa; and Suher and Dena Alsurakhi, perhaps more than anyone else besides myself, have had the most constant and immediate contact with this project, as drafts became scratch paper that they then transformed with their creativity and penchant for writing and drawing pictures. The constant support of my parents, John and Nancy Schultz, and of Erick Schultz and Julie Caspersen Schultz, in turn, has taken many, many forms, including travel to far away places, making it easier for me to be away from home. No one, however, has so intensely shared with me both the burdens and rewards of writing this book more than my husband, Nasir Abdellatif. Some time ago, he opened his life to both me and my pursuit of writing this book and the book and I are better for it.

A Note on Portuguese Orthography

José Joaquim Lopes de Lima, the author of a sardonic Portuguese political lexicon entitled *Diccionario Carcundatico* (1821) and its *Supplemento* (1821), defined orthography as the "only matter in which Portugal had an ample liberty to write." Early nineteenth-century Portuguese-language writers and printers indeed used a broad range of orthographic practices. Although there have been efforts to effect global standards for written Portuguese, publishers in Portugal and Brazil often follow distinct conventions. Here I have attempted to standardize the orthography of manuscript sources. I have transcribed printed sources as they were published and as they have been cited by other scholars, preserving the range of conventions used in Brazil and Portugal throughout the nineteenth and twentieth centuries. Thus, in spite of Lima's droll admonishment, orthographic inconsistencies remain.

Abbreviations

ABN, *Anais da Biblioteca Nacional,* Rio de Janeiro

AHI, Arquivo Histórico Itamaraty, Rio de Janeiro

AHU, Arquivo Histórico Ultramarino, Lisbon

ANRJ, Arquivo Nacional, Rio de Janeiro

BNRJ Ms., Biblioteca Nacional, Rio de Janeiro, Seção de Manuscritos

DHI, *Documentos para a história da independência* v. 1. Rio de Janeiro: Biblioteca Nacional, 1923

RHI, *Revista de História das Idéias,* Coimbra

RIHGB, *Revista do Instituto Histórico e Geográfico Brasileiro,* Rio de Janeiro

INTRODUCTION

IN NOVEMBER 1807, WITH A NAPOLEONIC ARMY AT THEIR HEELS, THE PORTUGUESE prince regent Dom João and thousands of courtiers and functionaries left behind their "beloved motherland" and set sail for Brazil.[1] For the next thirteen years Rio de Janeiro, Brazil's viceregal capital, replaced Lisbon as the center of the Portuguese world. Such events were unprecedented in the history of European empires. Never before had a European ruler visited, let alone taken up residence in, a colony. Long-standing political, cultural, and economic hierarchies of empire were dramatically challenged. Indeed, as Brazilian historian José Honório Rodrigues explained, the transfer of the court "denaturalized" Brazil's colonial status[2] and, consequently, what contemporaries called the "old colonial system" appeared to come to an end. Yet, it was not only the empire and the old colonial system that were at stake in the transfer of the court. The expansion of Europe and, more specifically, what had come to be called the Portuguese empire, were inseparable from the institution of monarchy. The monarchy embodied the laws and loyalties that joined all of its disparate "conquests" and, as a consequence, the monarch himself, or herself, was identified as constituting a political center. While the monarchy thus could account for the possibility of moving the royal court—because the monarch transcended all of the parts of his dominion, Portuguese memorialists explained, he could reside in any one of them—by momentarily decentering the monarch and by casting doubt on whether he could protect his dominions, such a move also called into question the legitimacy of Portuguese royal authority itself. This book examines the ways in which contemporaries in the new royal court of Rio de Janeiro defined in political discourse and practice the meaning of these events and responded to the challenges that they posed.

To frame this inquiry into the politics of monarchy and empire in early nineteenth-century Rio de Janeiro, I have borrowed the image of a "tropical Versailles" as a metaphorical point of departure. Brazilian historian Manuel de Oliveira Lima first used this phrase to describe Dom João's New World residence in his now classic account of the transfer of the court, *Dom João VI no Brasil*.[3] His generous comparison between the Sun King's palace and the Portuguese prince regent's *Quinta da Boa Vista* conjured up the splendor and magnificence that the presence of the royal court supposedly bestowed on the former colonial capital. Here, however, I have approached this image differently, as an evocation of both the larger political–cultural context in which these events unfolded and the contradictions that resulted from the encounter of an exiled sovereign with his vassals in the New World. Thus, on the one hand, the image of a "tropical Versailles" raises the question of the relationship between political power and representation. Versailles, after all, stands as a symbol of the grand effort to define Louis XIV's reign: to ritualize both extraordinary and quotidian events in the king's life and to assert persuasively and spectacularly an image of royal authority that was at once absolute, fearsome, magnanimous, and accessible.[4] From the perspective of the turn of the nineteenth century, Versailles also recalls a monarchical past torn asunder by a revolution that challenged both certain representations of political leadership and sovereignty, as well as the nature of representation itself.[5] In the wake of the transfer of the court, royal officials and residents in Rio de Janeiro too recognized the relationship between power and spectacle and grappled with the turn-of-the-century crisis in representation, reasserting the image of a virtuous and powerful sovereign and a unified empire, both of which were jeopardized by the retreat from Lisbon, in their efforts to transform the city into a royal court and capital of a new American empire.

On the other hand, such a transformation was shaped by certain realities that Oliveira Lima summed up euphemistically with the adjective "tropical": cultural and color differences and the institution of slavery. While Oliveira Lima imagined that the "exotic" nature of his New World residence enchanted Prince Regent Dom João, contemporaries repeatedly expressed concerns about the "colonial" obstacles to "civilization" and Europeanization in the New World, processes that, they argued, the transfer of the court both depended upon and ensured. Their ensuing efforts to eradicate the vestiges of a colonial past were, however, shaped and limited by the crown's commitment to the colonialism of slavery in the imperial present. As a tropical Versailles, Rio de Janeiro thus would be a place where the hierarchy of sovereign and vassal, threatened, vindicated, and then redefined, met the persistent and violent hierarchy of owner and slave.

MONARCHY AND EMPIRE IN AN AGE OF REVOLUTION

While the transfer of the court to Rio de Janeiro was unique, it was both part of and a particular response to an age of revolution. The North American, French, and Haitian Revolutions, and the movements for independence in Spanish America together challenged the principles and practices of hereditary rule as well as hierarchies of status, color, and culture, involuntary servitude, and the subordinate place of America within European empire.[6] For early nineteenth-century Portuguese royal officials, while all of these developments threatened their own old and imperial regime, the French Revolution and its apparent propensity to influence and inspire had proven to be the most calamitous. As revolutionaries in Paris assembled to dismantle an absolute monarchy that Portuguese kings and statesmen so admired, African and African-Caribbean slaves and people of color in the French colony of Saint Domingue seized the revolution as an opportunity to rebel against and then effectively destroy both French colonial rule and the institution of slavery, providing, as owners came to dread, an example for slaves in Brazil. Back in France, the National Assembly, the Committee of Public Safety, and the Directory then gave way to the rise of Napoleon and his own imperial ambitions for Spain and Portugal that led to the transfer of the court itself. In spite of efforts in the 1790s to isolate the dominions of the Portuguese sovereign from the consequences of revolution and what royal minister Rodrigo de Souza Coutinho characterized as the "French Nation's" embrace of "excesses" and "absurdities," with the French invasion of Portugal the profound impact of these consequences in the Portuguese empire could no longer be denied.

As these excesses appeared to have produced the conditions that eventually demanded the prince regent's departure from Europe in 1807, they also greatly influenced how contemporaries in Brazil and Portugal defined the meaning of the transfer of the court. Although Portuguese royal officials, memorialists, and chroniclers obsessively and equivocally decried the Revolution and its extensive and devastating effects as the results of treachery, immorality, impiety, and "philosophy," they also sought to provide systematic and circumspect responses that would at once defend the institution of monarchy and account for the new demands of the revolutionary conjuncture they experienced.[7] Indeed, the "political exigencies and public discourse generated by the French Revolution," as Marilyn Morris has argued of Britain, "helped lay the foundations for the . . . monarchy's character and ideology of justification" in the years that followed.[8] In the process, conservative, counterrevolutionary attempts to efface the possibility of change were transformed by a response to revolution that itself appeared to be revolutionary. For if a New World empire had been envisioned by a number of imperial officials, the transfer of the court was nevertheless, like the French Revolution, unprecedented and likewise identified by contemporaries as defying conventional politics and modes of expression. As José Acúrsio das Neves, the first Portuguese historian of the Peninsular War, argued, the "extraordinary" nature of the prince regent's departure from Lisbon made objective analysis difficult and rendered the "simple style" of historical writing inadequate. "Who," he asked, "could separate [the actual events] from the colorful pathos that characterized them?"[9] In the 1810s the task for Portuguese on both sides of the Atlantic then became to overcome this crisis of politics and its representation by discerning the meaning of these changes and the opportunities they presented.

Indeed, there were Portuguese in both Portugal and Brazil who came to see the transfer of the court itself as an event that paradoxically promised what one observer defined as "the greatest of all revolutions of the general political system" in defense of both monarchy and empire.[10] Accordingly, they sought to articulate an ideology of justification, to use Morris' term, that accounted for this predicament. In other words, they recognized that as both part of and a particular response to a larger rapidly changing context in which both the bases for political legitimacy and the intersecting histories of Europe and America were redefined, the prince regent's move to Brazil required a politics that both could subsume the divisions created by geography, history, and culture that had proved to be such fertile ground for insurgency elsewhere and reinterpret the categories of the metropolitan and the colonial once the hierarchical structure they had sought to describe was foregone; a politics that could, as well, reassert both royal authority and the unity of vassalage throughout the monarchy's dominions.

For some vassals and servants of the Portuguese crown this politics was one that privileged a renewal of the political old regime and its traditions. The monarchy, it seemed, was destined to be American because America was destined to provide the monarchy with the defeat of corruption and the triumph of absolutism and political virtue that Europe no longer could. Thus, in writing *memórias* and in negotiating the scope of royal patronage in the new royal court, exiles and long-standing residents in Rio de Janeiro both affirmed the undivided authority of the monarch and envisioned the transformation of what one courtier called a "vast but yet uncultivated continent"[11] into a powerful bulwark against threats to the Portuguese crown's independence.

There were, however, also Portuguese in Europe and America who saw in the transfer of the court an opportunity to embrace the very "ideas of the century" that elsewhere had challenged the established hierarchies on which the monarchy and empire were based. On the one hand, these ideas also allowed for a reinvention of tradition. Thus, the destruction of the old colonial system of mercantilist monopoly in favor of free trade that followed the prince regent's arrival at Brazil was not the end of the empire, but rather a return to the more just and lucrative imperial enterprise celebrated in sixteenth-century Portuguese chronicles. On the other hand, the "ideas of the century" inspired efforts to achieve more fundamental change. Indeed, by the end of the decade, in response to the political and imperial crisis produced by the transfer of the court, the ancient institution of the Cortes had been reinvented in the name of national sovereignty and representative government. Although the defenders of what contemporaries referred to as both a "regeneration" and a "revolution" sought the "salvation" of monarchy, they also recognized the principles of equality and liberty and the authority of *pátria*. Thus, as Dom João's reign in Brazil came to an end, the politics of representative government and national citizenship displaced the politics of absolute monarchy and vassalage. These early articulations of liberalism were fraught with contradictions, particularly in the ways in which contemporaries both identified empire and slavery as violations of the universal princi-ples of liberty and equality and then posited differentiated and increasingly racialized understandings of their consequences. Indeed, as products and parts of an age of rev-olution, the transfer of the court and the ways in which its meaning was defined also harbored and imparted that age's ambivalence.[12]

THE LOCAL POLITICS OF A NEW IMPERIAL CAPITAL

In spite of its dramatic and remarkable nature, and its place within the history of the old regime's demise, the politics and political culture of the transfer of the court have not been the subject of systematic or detailed analysis. Indeed, Oliveira Lima's *Dom João VI* was written almost a century ago. As the most comprehensive history of the Portuguese court in Rio, however, Lima's work has also been most influential. Fol-lowing Lima, subsequent narratives of Brazil's national history have contended that the arrival of the prince regent was the beginning of the larger process of Brazilian independence. In making independence a foregone conclusion, the presence of the court in Rio then determined its conservative result: the creation of an empire and a nation under the aegis of the Portuguese monarchy itself.[13] In other words, the meaning of the transfer of the court has been summed up as the answer to the ques-tions of why Brazil became independent, and why, more specifically, nineteenth-cen-tury Brazil was not a republic, as were the other newly independent states in the Americas. Thus, the remarkable nature of the transfer of the court also explains the remarkable absence of scholarly inquiry into its history. For a sui generis event, it is assumed, simply produced sui generis results.[14]

More recent scholarship of nineteenth-century politics has both challenged this unequivocally nationalist narrative and sought to avoid the often teleological linkage between the eighteenth century and independent empire as well as the limits of the continuity-rather-than-change paradigm by examining the contradictory reconfigu-rations of power in both Portugal and Brazil. In exploring contemporary manifesta-tions of and answers to "the national question" on both sides of the Portuguese Atlantic, the work of Roderick Barman, Iara Lis Carvalho Souza, and Valentim Alexandre reveals a process of independence that while undoubtedly linked to the experience of the transfer of the court, was neither transparent nor inevitable. There was, as Carvalho Souza explains, no relation of cause and effect.[15] Nor, as José Murilo de Carvalho has asserted, did "the presence of the Portuguese court in Rio . . . make a monarchy a necessary outcome in Brazil."[16] The monarchy, like in-dependence itself, as Murilo sustains, was an "option." This book contributes to an understanding of such an option by examining how local politics and political culture in Rio de Janeiro were shaped by, diverged from, and then reshaped imperial, transatlantic, and transregional agendas during Dom João's Brazilian reign. Its aim, however, is not to explain *why* an independent Brazil retained not only the institution of monarchy but also the same dynasty that had governed it as a colony since the seventeenth century, but rather to suggest a more complex answer to the question of *how* Brazil became a monarchy and an empire.

Restating this question more broadly, how was the exercise of power rendered legitimate or illegitimate to those both within and beyond officialdom in the wake of the transfer of the court? In conceptual terms answering this question has meant going beyond a narrow model of power emanating exclusively from the state to consider what Lynn Hunt has described as "the values, expectations and implicit rules that expressed and shaped collective intentions and actions." Thus, whereas Barman and Alexandre analyze political culture as it was articulated in official discourse and policy, I have approached the political culture of early nineteenth-century Rio in the various ways in which the dimensions of power and the grounds for legitimacy were expressed, and in which sovereignty, monarchy, and empire were understood, in a multiplicity of sites within the city. This political culture of the transfer of the court "did not just reflect social and political reality," but rather emerged out of contemporaries' efforts to transform that reality, a process in which officials, exiles, and long-standing residents self-consciously elaborated certain visions and practices of empire and monarchy, rebuilt a political framework that appeared to be crumbling before their eyes, and proposed alternative frameworks. This does not mean, however, that the political displaces the economic, social, and material "as the most global instance of the organization of society" in the history of early nineteenth-century Rio. While politics and political culture have their own logic or, as Hunt suggests in her work, textuality, they do not exist in a realm separate from society, culture, and economy. Thus, the history of the politics and political culture of the transfer of the court is also the history of the ways in which changing social and economic as well as political realities were rendered meaningful, within both new and old discourses, institutions, and practices.[17]

In practical terms, writing this history has meant reading official sources (correspondence and policy statements) in conjunction with sources that have not traditionally informed Brazilian political history. I examine, for example, police records, personal correspondence, sermons, theater, literature, travel memoirs, and iconography, some of which have been used to write comprehensive social and cultural histories of marriage, kinship, and slavery, of women and people of color, which both expose the contours of economic, social, and cultural structures (slavery and patriarchy) and explore resistence to these structures.[18] Here I have sought to examine further the understandings of public authority and legitimacy that these sources posit. Thus, while I consider policing as a larger process of social control, I have also analyzed the specific ways in which it was used to define the relationship between sovereign and vassal and the boundaries of political community. The process of reconstructing the royal court that emerges from the intendancy sources is a contested one, the product of royal administration and the police intendant's pronouncements and interventions, as well as alternative understandings of political legitimacy expressed in private and in public, in the relationships between slaves and owners, wives and husbands, sons and fathers, and among neighbors.

Such an examination of policing, as recorded in daily logbooks, correspondence, and more thorough and formal inquiries, also suggests that the city's elites and popular classes experienced politics in ways that not only diverged but also formed common ground. Thus, this book proposes the possibility of a shared, local political culture formed within the city of Rio de Janeiro in the 1810s, suggesting an alternative to the understanding of the politics of the transfer of the court and independence, presented by both Oliveira Lima and his critics, as the product of elite aspirations and agendas alone.[19] Although the intendant claimed to represent an official, elite politics, both elites and the popular classes experienced, and at times resisted, his scrutiny and interventions. Within the city of Rio, the immediate presence of the monarch also formed a common ground upon which residents advanced their agendas and claimed their "rights" as vassals, calling on the crown to provide opportunities for royal service and then reward that service, as well as to resolve disputes. Indeed, although formally denied these rights, slaves exploited their new proximity to the king to seek manumission and to redefine their particular relations with their owners. Thus, although royal officials sought to prescribe how all of the city's residents experienced politics, their interventions were only part of a political culture that encompassed both common and divergent understandings of the implications of sovereignty, alliances and divisions, different ways of understanding the consequences of these alliances and divisions, as well as attempts to efface them, all variously expressed in discourse and practice. In this sense, what the city's residents shared was not one single understanding of authority and legitimacy, but rather the opportunity to exploit the tension between the professedly universal character of empire, sovereignty, and vassalage and the recognizable hierarchies created within them.[20]

This history of the politics and the political culture of the transfer of the court begins before the prince regent left Portugal for Brazilian shores. In Chapter 1, I examine representations of monarchy and empire in early modern Portugal and, more specifically, how America became central to an evolving ideal of imperial renewal. The decision to transfer the court, made in the midst of an immediate, and seemingly chaotic, diplomatic crisis, was predicated on a vision of Brazil's potential that had been brought into sharper focus in the eighteenth century in the context of both

European rivalry and the profitability of Brazilian resources. Chapter 2, in turn, introduces the dimensions of empire and monarchy in the local context of the city of Rio de Janeiro. By the end of the eighteenth century, residents and colonial officials both beheld the rewards of economic prosperity and of their political preeminence within Portuguese America and contended with the consequences of the city's integration into an Atlantic world that was increasingly and "dangerously" revolutionary.

Metropolitan and viceregal efforts to isolate Rio and its residents from the effects of revolution ended with the arrival of the exiled royal court. The ways in which contemporaries sought to overcome this crisis and to account for the royal court's move to the New World and the war it left behind are examined in Chapter 3. In Rio de Janeiro, within a rapidly expanding culture of print, the city's residents and the newly arrived royal servants read pamphlets published by a new Royal Press, listened to sermons, and attended theatrical performances that sought to define the meaning of recent events as well as the future of monarchy, empire, and the Portuguese nation. In the context of the Peninsular War, Portugal remained a primary point of reference and the New World court was seen as enabling Portugal's political regeneration and "national" renewal. As the war came to an end, however, the status of Portugal and of a heroic royal exile were redefined and the future of an imperial monarchy appeared to be American.

In transforming Rio de Janeiro into the royal residence and the capital of the empire, royal officials sought to make manifest this "new order of things" in the New World. Chapter 4 examines the remaking of the city as "the court." In the 1810s Rio's infrastructure was greatly expanded to include new aristocratic neighborhoods, a royal theater, printing press, and academies. The crown established a new general intendancy of the police to ensure social order and political allegiance and to "civilize" the city's built environment and its residents. The re-creation of the Portuguese court in America also demanded the exhibition and the reaffirmation of the sovereign's authority and of the nature of the political community over which he presided. Chapter 5 examines the politics of monarchy in Rio de Janeiro, how certain political discourses and practices sought to define sovereignty and vassalage, and the alternative definitions offered by the city's residents. Although this reconstruction of the royal court meant that, as Maria Odila Silva Dias has argued, Brazil "interiorized" the metropolis,[21] the imperatives of the colony, particularly manifest in the maintenance of the institution of slavery, remained. Indeed, although officials in Rio de Janeiro reflected upon a local and international critique of slavery, negotiated British efforts to end the trade in the Atlantic, and envisioned a brighter and "whiter" future without slaves, they nevertheless fostered an intense dependence on slavery in the new royal court and the surrounding region. Thus, both Chapters 4 and 5 also examine how royal officials and residents of the city sought to reconcile a colonial past and present with an imperial future as the city became the court, and how the quest to Europeanize and eradicate differences between the metropolitan and the colonial both redefined and reaffirmed existing social, cultural, racial, and political hierarchies.

On a larger scale, Rio de Janeiro's new status as the court and Brazil's new status as "metropolis" demanded a reconfiguration of the empire. Chapter 6 explores the ways in which the boundaries and ideals of the Portuguese empire were redefined in the 1810s. The creation of a "United Kingdom" offered a conservative vision of the new American empire. Yet, this empire was also marked by a longer process in which, as Anthony Padgen has argued for the eighteenth-century Spanish empire, imperial statesmen had begun to privilege an enlightened "calculation of benefits" over providentialism in defining an imperial ethos.[22] Called on to account for both a glorious history of Portuguese trade and a future of commerce embodied by the British, the discourse of political economy suggested new ways of imagining political and imperial unity and the prospects for prosperity. Within an empire of open ports, Rio's residents then used political economy and the new principles of empire to defend local interests and sovereignties undercut by new imperial practices.

The remaking of the Portuguese empire in the New World and criticism of this effort took shape at a time when politics and political identities were being redefined by increasingly powerful appeals to universal rights and the generalized practice of citizenship.[23] In Chapter 7 I examine the early trajectory of liberal political practice and discourse in Rio de Janeiro that took shape as a response to, and in dialogue with, a constitutionalist movement that emerged in August 1820, when a diverse group of property owners, merchants, and low ranking military officers in Porto, Portugal successfully staged a rebellion in favor of convoking the formerly consultative Cortes for the deliberative task of writing a constitution. The proclamation of national sovereignty was accompanied by a request that Dom João return to Portugal and together, as defenders of the movement claimed, they represented steps toward rectifying the political and economic afflictions that the Peninsular War and the removal of the royal court from Portugal had created and that the crown had failed to address. In Rio, as residents speculated about how the crown would respond, and about what constitutionalism would mean for them, for the future of monarchy in Brazil, and for the new empire of the United Kingdom, a rebellion of Portuguese troops, with local support, succeeded in winning the crown's recognition of the legitimacy of the new "constitutional system." In the weeks and months that followed, constitutionalism then became a transatlantic discourse, forged in pamphlets published in both Portugal and Brazil. Yet it also had a particular resonance within Rio de Janeiro. Its promise of a political "regeneration" recalled the vision of political renewal that defined the New World empire and the New World court after 1808. As the end of absolute royal power appeared to follow from the end of "the old colonial system," constitutionalism represented the guarantee of a new status quo in which the rights and interests of Rio's residents were fully recognized. This understanding of constitutionalism diverged from constitutionalism in Portugal, which sought to end what was perceived to be Portugal's "colonial" condition created by the transfer of the court and an empire of open ports.[24] As these different interpretations of constitutionalism took shape, the transatlantic political community that rebels in Portugal and Brazil had set out to "regenerate" was challenged, leaving Rio de Janeiro's residents to choose between the newly sovereign nation and the ancient Portuguese empire. In the 1820s the choice made in Rio de Janeiro and across Brazil was for the nation, the *pátria*, redefined in American terms and "protected" by a European monarch called an "emperor." The maintenance of monarchy, many historians have argued, set a conservative Brazil apart from its republican neighbors in the Americas. Yet, the monarchy that presided over Brazil's independence was not the monarchy that left Portugal in 1807. If the transfer of the court allowed for the possibility of a transition from colony to empire based on political and institutional continuities and traditions, it also challenged those institutions and traditions and, ultimately, changed their meaning.

NOTES

1. Dom Manuel de Meneses to the [viceroy of Brazil] Conde dos Arcos, January 27, 1808, ANRJ Códice 730, f11; Thomas O'Neill, *A concise and accurate account of the proceedings of the squadron under the command of Rear Admiral Sir William Sidney Smith . . .* (London: R. Edwards, 1809), 24; and Alan K. Manchester, "The Transfer of the Portuguese Court to Rio de Janeiro," in *Conflict and Continuity in Brazilian Society,* eds. Henry H. Keith and S.F. Edwards (Columbia, SC: University of South Carolina Press, 1969), 154. Estimates of the total number of refugees vary between 10,000 and 15,000. The title of prince regent was given to Dom João, heir to the Portuguese throne, in 1792 when his mother Maria I was found to be unfit to exercise her own sovereignty.

2. José Honório Rodrigues, *Independência: revolução e contra-revolução* v. 1 (Rio de Janeiro: Francisco Alves, [1975–76]), 7.

3. Manuel de Oliveira Lima, *Dom João VI no Brasil (1808–1821)* (1908) v. 1 (Rio de Janeiro: José Olympio, 1945), 129. The image of a Versailles and of a "tropical Versailles" has had a sustained resonance within visions of urban Brazil. The French urbanist Agache's plans for reform in early twentieth-century Rio included, as David Underwood has noted, the transformation of one promontory into "an elegant image of a tropical Versailles," a "spacious, palm-lined, French formal garden with a reflecting pool." Explicating his plans for Brasília, Lúcio Costa also referred to the Praça dos Tres Poderes as a "Versailles of the People." See David Underwood, "Alfred Agache, French Sociology, and Modern Urbanism in France and Brazil," *Journal of the Society of Architectural Historians* 50, n. 1 (March 1991), 156, 163.

4. Peter Burke, *The Fabrication of Louis XIV* (New Haven: Yale University Press, 1992).

5. Lynn Hunt, *Politics, Culture and Class in the French Revolution* (Berkeley: University of California Press, 1984); idem, *The Family Romance of the French Revolution* (Berkeley: University of California Press, 1992); Ronald Paulson, *Representations of Revolution (1789–1820)* (New Haven: Yale University Press, 1983); and Antoine de Baecque, "The Allegorical Image of France, 1750–1800: A Political Crisis of Representation," *Representations* 47 (Summer 1994), 111–143.

6. The possibility of an Atlantic revolutionary political culture was proposed by R.R. Palmer in *The Age of Democratic Revolution: A Political History of Europe and America, 1760–1800* 2 v. (Princeton: Princeton University Press, 1959–64). Palmer argued that the late eighteenth century witnessed a critical moment in the history of "Atlantic Civilization" manifest "in different ways and with varying success in different countries" all marked by "a new feeling for a kind of equality, or at least a discomfort with older forms of social stratification and formal rank." Within a different chronological and conceptual framework, the political, economic, and cultural dimensions of an age of revolution were also outlined in E.J. Hobsbawm, *The Age of Revolution, 1789–1848* (New York: Signet, 1962). While both privileged the revolutionary experience in Europe and British North America, recently Lester Langley has offered a more thorough integration of Latin America, especially Spanish America and Haiti, into such a synthesis. See his *The Americas in the Age of Revolution, 1750–1850* (New Haven: Yale University Press, 1996). None of these accounts, however, considers the Luso-Brazilian experience in this age of revolution. For the period prior to the transfer of the court this experience is analyzed in Fernando Novais, *Portugal e Brasil na Crise do Antigo Sistema Colonial (1777–1808)* (São Paulo: Hucitec, 1979); Carlos Guilherme Mota, *Atitudes de Inovação no Brasil, 1789–1801* (Lisbon: Livros Horizonte, n.d.); and István Jancsó, "A sedução da liberdade: cotidiano e contestação política no final do século XVIII," in *História da Vida Privada no Brasil* v. 1, eds. Fernando Novais and Laura de Mello e Souza (São Paulo: Companhia das Letras, 1997), 389–437.

7. Rodrigo de Souza Coutinho to Fernando José de Portugal, August 25, 1798, BNRJ Ms. II-33,29,70.

8. Marilyn Morris, *The British Monarchy and the French Revolution* (New Haven: Yale University Press, 1998), 1.

9. José Acúrsio das Neves, *História geral da invasão dos franceses em Portugal e da restauração deste reino* (1810) v. 1 (Porto: Afrontamento, n.d.), 224, 229.

10. Conde de Ega cited in Ana Cristina Bartolomeu de Araújo, "O 'Reino Unido de Portugal, Brasil e Algarves' 1815–1822," *RHI* 14 (1992), 235. See also Heliódoro Jacinto de Araújo Carneiro to Tomás António Vila Nova Portugal, [London], March 3, 1818, AHI Lata 180 Maço 1, who argued that with the transfer of the court "the politics of Europe and perhaps of the Universe changed. . . ."

11. Visconde de Anadia to Sua Alteza Real, December 14, 1808, in Ângelo Pereira, *Os filhos de el-rei D. João VI* (Lisbon: Empresa Nacional de Publicidade, 1946), 136.

12. On "the inclusionary pretension of liberal theory and the exclusionary effects of liberal practices" see Uday Singh Mehta, *Liberalism and Empire: A Study in Nineteenth-Century British Liberal Thought* (Chicago: University of Chicago Press, 1999), 46. On the need to understand the trajectory of liberalism in Latin America in relation to the real and contradictory

experiences of liberalism elsewhere rather than the idealized version of its triumph in North America, see Jeremy Adelman, *Republic of Capital: Buenos Aires and the Legal Transformation of the Atlantic World* (Stanford: Stanford University Press, 1999), 12.

13. Published in 1908, the centennial of the arrival of the court at Brazil, Oliveira Lima's account is unequivocally celebratory. He defended Dom João as the founder of "Brazilian nationality" and the creator of a "real political unity" based on "a uniformity of sensations that captured and determined a uniformity of wills." See Oliveira Lima, *Dom João VI*, 17–19, 74, 268, 1173. Pedro Calmon's *História do Brasil* also celebrates the reign of Dom João as a "golden age." See v. 4 (Rio de Janeiro: José Olympio, 1963), 1382, 1446, 1459, 1475. In subsequent, and decidedly less triumphalist and nationalist, accounts of Brazilian independence, its conservative nature is nevertheless sustained and also attributed to the court's presence. See Caio Prado Jr., *Evolução Política do Brasil, Colônia e Império* (1933) (São Paulo: Brasiliense, n.d.); Sérgio Buarque de Holanda, "A herança colonial-sua desagregação," in *História geral da civilização brasileira* t.1, v. 1, ed. Buarque de Holanda (1960) (São Paulo: DIFEL, 1985); Maria Odila Silva Dias, "A Interiorização da Metrópole," in *1822: Dimensões*, ed. Carlos Guilherme Mota (São Paulo: Perspectiva, 1972), in English as "The Establishment of the Royal Court in Brazil," in *From Colony to Nation, Essays on the Independence of Brazil*, ed. A.J.R. Russell-Wood (Baltimore: The Johns Hopkins University Press, 1975); Emilia Viotti da Costa, *The Brazilian Empire: Myths and Histories* (Chicago: University of Chicago Press, 1985); Carlos Guilherme Mota and Fernando Novais, *A Independência Política do Brasil* (São Paulo: Moderna, 1983); and more recently, Lúcia Maria Bastos Pereira das Neves, "Corcundas, constitucionais e pes-de-chumbo: a cultura política da Independência, 1820–1822" (Ph.D. dissertation, University of São Paulo, 1992) and Jurandir Malerba, "A corte no exílio. Interpretação do Brasil joanino (1808–1821)" (Ph.D. dissertation, University of São Paulo, 1997). Within comparative discussions, Brazilian independence also exemplifies a conservative transition. See, for example, Brian R. Hamnett, "Process and Pattern: A Re-Examination of the Ibero-American Independence Movements, 1808–1826," *Journal of Latin American Studies* 29, pt. 2 (May 1997), 298–299.

14. As Roderick Barman has recently noted, compared with the independence of Spanish America and the United States, Brazilian independence remains relatively understudied. See Barman, *Brazil: The Forging of a Nation, 1798–1852* (Stanford: Stanford University Press, 1988), 65–66. This lack of scholarship can also be attributed to the influence of Marxist formulations of Brazil's historical development in which the transfer of the court and independence figure not as moments of political conflict per se, but rather as a resolution of the internal contradictions within capitalism in which the mercantilist pact was broken and the continuation of Brazil's "dependent" integration into a capitalist world economy was ensured. See Caio Prado Jr., *Evolução*, 44–52, and Mota and Novais, *Independência*, 5. In the 1960s and 1970s this economic explanation for independence suggested disappointingly little consequences for social and economic structures in Brazil as these very structures became privileged subjects for historians and political history in general waned. On the waning of political history, see Lynn Hunt, "Introduction: History, Culture, and Text," in *The New Cultural History*, ed. Lynn Hunt (Berkeley: University of California Press, 1989), 1–4. On the same trend in Brazilian history see Viotti da Costa, *Brazilian Empire*, xvii; Marieta de Moraes Ferreira, "A nova 'velha história': o retorno da história política," *Estudos Históricos* 10 (1992), 265–271;

Angela Castro Gomes, "Política: história, ciência, cultura, etc.," *Estudos Históricos* 17 (1996), 59–84; and Stuart B. Schwartz, "Somebodies and Nobodies in the Body Politic: Mentalities and Social Structures in Colonial Brazil," *Latin American Research Review* 31, n. 1 (1996).

15. Along with Barman, *Brazil*, Iara Lis Carvalho Souza, *Pátria Coroada: O Brasil como Corpo Político Autônomo, 1780–1831* (São Paulo: Editora UNESP, 1998); and Valentim Alexandre, *Os sentidos do império: questão nacional e questão colonial na crise do antigo regime português* (Porto: Afrontamento, 1993), see also Maria de Lourdes Viana Lyra, *A Utopia do Poderoso Império, Portugal e Brasil: Bastidores da Política, 1798–1822* (Rio de Janeiro: Sette Letras, 1994).

16. José Murilo de Carvalho, "Political Elites and State Building: The Case of Nineteenth-Century Brazil," *Comparative Studies in Society and History* 24, n. 3 (July 1982), 382, 397.

17. Hunt, "Introduction," in *The New Cultural History*, 17. On politics, culture, and "the new political history" see also Hunt, *Politics, Culture and Class*, 10–13; Dror Wahrman, "The New Political History: A Review Essay," *Social History* 21, n. 3 (October 1996), 343–354; Victoria E. Bonnell and Lynn Hunt, "Introduction," and William H. Sewell, Jr., "The Concept(s) of Culture," in *Beyond the Cultural Turn: New Directions in the Study of Society and Culture*, eds. Victoria E. Bonnell and Lynn Hunt (Berkeley: University of California Press, 1999). On language and political discourse see J.G.A. Pocock, "Introduction: The state of the art," in Pocock, *Virtue, Commerce, and History: Essays on Political Thought and History, Chiefly in the Eighteenth Century* (New York: Cambridge University Press, 1985); and Gareth Stedman Jones, *Languages of Class: Studies in English Working Class History, 1832–1982* (Cambridge: Cambridge University Press, 1983). On the question of Brazil's political history see Viotti da Costa, "Introduction," in *Brazilian Empire*; and Barbara Weinstein, "Not the Republic of Their Dreams: Historical Obstacles to Political and Social Democracy in Brazil," *Latin American Research Review* 29, n. 2 (1994), 262–273.

18. Mary Karasch, *Slave Life in Rio de Janeiro, 1808–1850* (Princeton: Princeton University Press, 1987); Leila Mezan Algranti, *O feitor ausente: estudos sobre a escravidão urbana no Rio de Janeiro—1808–1822* (Petrópolis: Vozes, 1988) and idem, *Honradas e devotas: mulheres da Colônia: Condição feminina nos conventos e recolhimentos do Sudeste do Brasil, 1750–1822* (Rio de Janeiro/Brasília: José Olympio/EDUNB, 1993); Maria Beatriz Nizza da Silva, *Cultura e sociedade no Rio de Janeiro (1808–1821)* (São Paulo: Companhia Editora Nacional, 1977); idem, *Sistema de casamento no Brasil colonial* (São Paulo: T.A. Queiroz, 1984); and idem, *Vida Privada e Quotidiano no Brasil. Na época de D. Maria e D. João VI* (Lisbon: Estampa, 1993).

19. In Oliveira Lima's work politics are constituted in either the conflicts and intrigues of the royal cabinet or diplomacy and administration, while Rio's residents appear as part of an exotic "environment" with which Dom João had "an intimate correspondence." See Lima, *Dom João*, v. 1, 17–19, 74. For a similar critique of Oliveira Lima's *O Movimento da Independência* (1922), see Nanci Leonzo, "Oliveira Lima: O Dramaturgo da Independência," *Revista da Sociedade Brasileira de Pesquisa Histórica* (São Paulo) 2 (1984/85), 55. The marked absence of a popular dimension of early nineteenth-century politics is also asserted in subsequent work that both sustains and departs from Oliveira Lima's nationalist framework. Although José Honório Rodrigues, for example, characterized Oliveira Lima's work as a "conservative thesis" that privileged the role of the monarch, in his own account of independence Rodrigues also reaffirmed that "the people resigned themselves to a chain of events that

emanated from a few individuals." See Rodrigues, *Independência,* v. 4, 124–25, 130, and v. 5, 255–256. See also Tobias Monteiro, *História do império. A elaboração da Independência* (Rio de Janeiro: F. Briguiet, 1927), 313; Viotti da Costa, *Brazilian Empire,* xix, 7; and Barman, *Brazil,* 6. Francisco Falcon and Ilmar Roloff Santos qualify this argument characterizing the urban popular classes as "permeable to certain revolutionary words," whereas the "great rural masses, the slave labor force, in its immense majority, remained anonymous and mute." See their "O Processo de Independência no Rio de Janeiro," in *1822: Dimensões,* ed. Mota, 316–317. More recently, Lúcia Maria Neves has argued that the politics of independence resembled a "a theater without an audience" and "a dialogue between segments of the Brazilian and Portuguese elite." See Neves, "Corcundas," v. 1, 10–11.

20. William Roseberry has argued for a similar understanding of local political culture using the concept of hegemony. "What hegemony constructs," he writes, "is not a shared ideology but a common material and meaningful framework for living through, talking about, and acting upon social orders characterized by domination." Such a "common material and meaningful framework is," he further explains, "in part, discursive: a common language or way of talking about social relationships that sets out the central terms around which and in terms of which contestation and struggle can occur." See William Roseberry, "Hegemony and the Language of Contention," in *Everyday Forms of State Formation: Revolution and the Negotiation of Rule in Modern Mexico,* eds. Gilbert Joseph and Daniel Nugent (Durham: Duke University Press, 1994), 361.

21. Silva Dias, "Interiorização," 171.

22. Anthony Pagden, *Lords of All the World: Ideologies of Empire in Spain, Britain and France, c. 1500–c. 1800* (New Haven: Yale University Press, 1995), 157.

23. Ann Laura Stoler and Frederick Cooper, "Between Metropole and Colony: Rethinking a Research Agenda," in *Tensions of Empire: Colonial Cultures in a Bourgeois World,* eds. Ann Laura Stoler and Frederick Cooper (Berkeley: University of California Press, 1997).

24. See, for example, Jacome Ratton, "Lettres de Jacques Ratton a António de Araújo de Azevedo, Comte da Barca (1812–1817)," *Bulletin des Etudes Portugaises* (nouvelle série) 25 (1964), 219–228.

ONE

"Brighter Glory in the Western Sphere":
MONARCHY, EMPIRE, AND THE NEW WORLD

IN 1803 THE PORTUGUESE STATESMEN RODRIGO DE SOUZA COUTINHO, CHIEF OF the Royal Treasury, offered Prince Regent Dom João an evaluation of the European "political situation." In the current war between France and Great Britain, he warned, the Portuguese monarchy's own "independence" was at stake. The maintenance of neutrality appeared increasingly illusive and, as a result, Portugal and other small European states were on the verge of being lost within the "monstrous colossus" of Napoleon's empire. In contrast to the treacherous diplomacy and belligerence within Europe, however, "the interior situation" of the prince regent's "vast dominions" beyond Europe was characterized by "public prosperity and tranquility." Indeed, Souza Coutinho observed, "Portugal alone" was "no longer the best and most essential Part of the Monarchy." Consequently, he then proposed, if a war were to leave Portugal devastated, "its Sovereign and its People could still go and create a powerful Empire in Brazil." This new empire would serve as a base from which Dom João could both reconquer "all that had been lost in Europe" and punish "the cruel enemy" who had refused to recognize his honorable attempt to remain outside such ignoble wars.[1]

Although, at the time, such a dramatic proposal was rejected, less than four years later Souza Coutinho's vision of an American empire became the basis of a new imperial politics in the Portuguese world.[2] In 1807 the crown decided to transfer the royal court to Rio de Janeiro and an extraordinary inversion of the political, economic, and cultural hierarchies that had guided three centuries of European expansion began to take shape. The meanings and consequences of this inversion will be examined throughout this book. Here, I begin with a survey of the ideological and historical foundations for the ideal of an American empire. Souza Coutinho indeed was neither the first nor the last to promote the establishment of a New World court and capital. Initially proffered in the sixteenth century, the vision of Brazilian potential both prompted and shaped an eighteenth-century critique of the Portuguese imperial ethos. While in the 1790s Souza Coutinho strove to transform this critique into a long-term program for imperial reform, it was in the first crisis-ridden years of the nineteenth century that he and other Portuguese statesmen made the ideal of American empire a reality.

RENOVATION, COMMERCE, AND THE AMERICAN CONTINENT: EIGHTEENTH-CENTURY IMPERIAL DISCOURSE

The idea of creating a Portuguese royal court in the New World appears to have emerged first in the 1580s. After the Spanish King Philip II successfully claimed his right to a vacant Portuguese throne, a counselor to the Prior do Crato, Philip's Portuguese challenger, identified Brazil as a possible haven for an exiled court. France, however, was chosen instead.[3] This same recommendation then was restated in the 1640s, as the Union of Crowns that Philip had created came to an end. Concerned with the continuing threat that Spain posed to the new, independent Portuguese monarchy of the House of Braganza, royal counselors, including the Jesuit missionary António Vieira, advised the crown to go and establish a new kingdom in America.[4] In this case, however, the creation of an American court figured not as a short-term solution to crisis, as it had in the 1580s, but rather as the foundation for an entirely new imperial era.

To explain this foundation Vieira appealed to the ideal of imperial renewal. "The image of the empire as the object of successive 'renovations' over time," as Anthony Pagden has explained, was central to the political identity of modern empires who saw their origins in Rome. Empire was, in this sense, the means to a Providential end: a true, universal Christendom, the culmination of a series of passages through spiritual and historical stages. Although within Europe, Spain was most frequently the subject of this at times prophetic "translation of empire,"[5] Vieira invoked Portugal's own local messianic tradition to reveal that the Portuguese monarchy was the universal Fifth Empire of the Book of Daniel. Drawing on the work of a popular prophet named Bandarra and on the political culture of Sebastianism, the belief that King Sebastião, reportedly killed in the disastrous battle at El-Ksar el-Kebir (Morocco) in 1578, would return to liberate Portugal from Spanish rule, Vieira claimed that it was the Duque de Braganza, Dom João IV (1640–1656), rather than a resurrected Sebastião, who represented the foretold messianic incarnation. The new king was, as Vieira explained, the head of an everlasting empire that could be brought to fruition in America.[6] Indeed, for Vieira, as Thomas Cohen has argued, the New World, where he had lived as a missionary, represented nothing less than "a locus of prophecies that the Portuguese ha[d] been uniquely chosen to reveal," a blessed place where the renovation of empire and both the temporal and spiritual triumph of the monarchy finally could be achieved. It was a vision that followed from what Cohen argues Vieira had earlier recognized as "a fundamental truth": that the cherished and hierarchical "distinctions between the metropolitan center and the colonial periphery" were "an impediment to the imperial enterprise" rather than its solid foundation. Following the death of his patron João IV, however, Vieira's endorsement of popular prophecy and his insistence on the New World's privileged place in postbiblical history went the way of his other controversial counsel (such as tolerance for New Christians), as both he and the king were investigated by the Inquisition (the king posthumously). Years later, in 1667, Vieira then was censured by both the Pope and the Holy Office of Coimbra.[7]

Although Vieira's predictions were discounted and the victory of a messianic Portuguese monarch appeared more and more remote, the geopolitical vulnerability of Portugal within Europe that had supported Vieira's vision remained a matter of particular concern for royal counselors as the seventeenth century drew to a close. Wars fought during the Iberian Union had left the empire in disarray and Portuguese statesmen now faced the sad fact that, as one advisor to the British crown noted, after the Dutch drove Portugal out of the East Indies, its "figure" in Europe collapsed. Portugal, in other words, had ceased to be a symbol of imperial glory to become instead, as Pagden has argued, a negative example of the close association between the maintenance of "reputation" and the maintenance of power.[8] In facing imperial crisis, however, the Portuguese crown was not alone. The seventeenth-century conflicts with the Dutch had taken a toll on the Spanish monarchy as well. With the end of the War of Succession (1701–1714), Spain lost its European imperial possessions and, as Pagden notes, its ideological claims to a universal empire. Without its European empire Spain's position as a metropolis was also jeopardized. As Montesquieu observed in his *The Spirit of the Laws* (1748), while "the Indies and Spain [were] two powers under the same master," the Spanish crown, "the Indies [were] the principal one to a secondary one." Indeed, Spain and Portugal together formed a case study of the causes and effects of the demise of imperial power, one that by the end of the eighteenth century had drawn the attention of not only Montesquieu, but also Diderot, David Hume, and Adam Smith.[9]

Spanish statesmen responded to this imperial crisis by advancing many of the observations made by their critics. Along with their British and French counterparts, as Pagden has shown, Spanish theorists articulated what amounted to a move away from honor to public welfare in imperial discourse and practice, "a shift from the considerations of rights and legitimacy to a concern with interests and benefits." In the process, they came to see commerce, rather than conquest, as the source of modern world power. To increase the empire's potential, the Spanish minister of finance, Pedro Rodríguez Campomanes (1723–1803), argued that it was necessary to redefine the scope of commercial relations within the Spanish territories. Opening trade to all subjects of the Spanish crown, he explained, would not only expand commerce and therefore lead to an increase in profits, but also, in the process, bring the empire's constituent parts closer to one another. A new commercial equity, in other words, would promote a new sense of unity. However, neither equitable commercial relations nor economic unity implied the end of fundamentally imperial purposes. Thus, Campomanes also reconfigured "the Kingdoms of the Indies" as "ultramarine provinces" and "colonies," communities that existed to serve the commercial interests of the metropolis above all. "[F]or the first time," Pagden writes, "Spanish Americans began to be defined in terms which made them clearly part of a periphery." The defense of a universal monarchy (*monarchia universalis*) had been supplanted by a hierarchical "calculation of benefits."[10]

Eighteenth-century Portuguese statesmen faced their empire's crisis with similar attempts to redefine its ethos. However, in their case, prevailing over loss (of much of their Asian enterprise) and restoring the Portuguese crown's prestige were facilitated by the late seventeenth-century discovery of gold and diamonds in Brazil. Indeed, in the first half of the eighteenth century these new sources of revenue financed a splendorous renovation of the monarchy's "figure" both within the Portuguese empire and beyond: João V's self-styled reign (1706–1750) as a Portuguese "Sun King." As Portuguese historian Rui Bebiano explains, the rhetorical aim of João V's official state art was "to reflect a new image of the kingdom that would celebrate the prestige and glory of the absolutist monarchy." The monarch's undivided authority, unrivaled piety, and sublime "magnificence" were displayed emblematically not only in Portugal, but in the rest of Europe as well, as royal marriage contracts were celebrated outside Portugal with the construction of monuments to the Portuguese king. Rome, in particular, became the focus of a "spectacular diplomacy" that culminated in the lavish ambassadorial entry of the Marquês de Fontes in 1716. In Lisbon, as Angela Delaforce notes, the procession of gilded allegorical carriages was reported as Dom João's "Roman triumph."[11]

João V's intense relations with and emulation of the Vatican harkened back to an older, providentialist translation of empire. Lisbon was recast as a "New Rome" and an explicitly messianic idiom figured prominently in panegyric accounts of his reign.[12] Yet, like their counterparts elsewhere in Europe, mid-eighteenth-century Portuguese statesmen and memorialists began to privilege commerce in redefining the empire. As Spanish theorists rejected the "spirit of conquest" that had inspired early territorial expansion, the Portuguese too ceased to write their empire as a crusade. They celebrated the mercantile dimensions of empire that, as Richard Helgerson has argued, the great sixteenth-century poet Luiz de Camões had sought to suppress in favor of epic aristocratic achievement. Thus, as one panegyrist insisted, the reign of João V was a time when the nobles of Portugal "lived in peace within their palaces, when, without threats, commerce flourished within the Kingdom and its Colonies . . . when Portuguese fleets navigated the globe undaunted, and brought to the Court the riches of Brazil and the fruits of Asia."[13] In this case, however, proffering the image of the origins of Portuguese commercial wealth as equally Brazilian and Asian, Dom João V's panegyrist produced another suppression of imperial reality. As Brazil had become both literally and figuratively the jewel in the Portuguese crown, the remaining eastern dominions waned. Indeed the Portuguese faced the same dilemma that Montesquieu attributed to Spain: the empire was so overwhelmingly American that the rest, including the metropolis itself, appeared increasingly insignificant.

To one Portuguese diplomat this American preeminence was evident even before the bulk of Brazilian mineral wealth had been reaped. In a secret memorandum that prefigured Montesquieu's own claim of an inversion within the early modern empires, Luiz da Cunha, ambassador to Paris and delegate to the negotiations of the Treaties of Utrecht, noted that while Brazil was virtually a continent, Portugal was but an "ear of land." The solution to this problem, Cunha then proposed, was to move the Portuguese court to Brazil, where João V could take the title of "Emperor of the West."[14] Although Cunha defended his claims by citing a similar proposal made to Philip V by the Spanish Duque de Medina Sidonia during the course of the Utrecht negotiations, he also anticipated that such a plan would be of greater interest in Portugal, considering the Portuguese crown's more acute predicament within Europe. The Methuen Treaty (1703), Cunha noted, gave the English command of the Port wine industry, a fact, he argued, that meant that if the crown remained in Europe it would "always be dependent on England." And for Cunha, such a relegation of the Portuguese to the domain of another empire was a fate far worse than an inversion of hierarchies within the dominions of the Portuguese crown. His "empire of the west" thus represented an attempt to arrest this trend and counter the idea that, as Louis XV's minister, the Duc de Choiseul, declared a few years later, "Portugal must be regarded as an English colony." As Cunha also argued, however, Portugal's problematic relationship with Great Britain was not the crown's only concern. Historically, the Portuguese monarchy had been the victim of Spanish imperial expansion and, although the House of Braganza had enjoyed over half a century of independence, it was still the case, as Cunha warned, that "the conquest of this Kingdom [Portugal]" by Spain was but a campaign away. It was a fact, he insisted, that meant that even with an increase in revenue and a larger army and navy in Portugal the king would "never sleep in peace and security."[15]

While Cunha's vision of a New World empire thus began with an analysis of Portugal's problematic position within Europe, it also depended on more than a simply defensive understanding of imperial politics. For, as Cunha also claimed, harkening back to Vieira, a move to the New World amounted to a providential translation of empire. Rather than the fruition of an imminently perfect spiritual empire, however, a royal court in Brazil would establish a translation of imperial ethos and geography from European conquest to American prosperity. Providence, Cunha explained, had provided for the "reciprocal lack of certain products in one and the other hemisphere, so that nations would communicate and form . . . the Universal Republic" and provide for the spread of Christianity to "those no less [God's] creatures than those of Europe." This first moment of empire, nevertheless, had come to an end and, as Cunha argued, there now seemed to be nothing produced in Portugal that could not be produced in Brazil. At the same time there was "no application or industry" sufficient to produce in Portugal the resources of Brazil. It was therefore "safer and more convenient," he concluded, "to be where one has everything in abundance, than where one has to wait for what one lacks."[16] History triumphed over exegesis in the endeavor to define the monarchy's imperial destiny. And although the American court as the capital of the empire was an element of Providential design, its legitimacy derived from the reasoned practice of commerce that such a reorganization of empire would allow.[17]

As Cunha sought to solve Portugal's predicament within a shifting European imperial discourse, his proposal of a new western empire also reflected his understanding of the specific nature of the Portuguese empire and of the important ways in which it differed from that of the Crown of Castile. The early modern Spanish empire was, like the ancient empires that served as its inspiration, land based, forged through expansion from a political and geographic center within the Iberian peninsula and beyond. Across the Atlantic, this pattern was reproduced, as Spanish settlements radiated outward from colonial capitals in Mexico and Peru. In contrast, the Portuguese empire was, as António Manuel Hespanha and Maria Catarina Santos have argued, oceanic, a global network of sea routes, commercial outposts, and missions that stretched from Macau to Brazil. Travel and trade, rather than extended settlement, shaped an imperial enterprise that while initially inspired by the spirit of crusade and beheld as the source of honor and glory, nevertheless was driven by "the logic of pragmatism" rather than "the splendor of power."[18] While the Spanish monarchs, "kings of a sedentary majesty," ruled their empire from "a powerfully constituted center," the nexus of the Portuguese empire was not a city, but the sea itself; and the political capital of the empire was necessarily a port.[19]

To defend an empire in which the sea constituted its "very body," Portuguese imperial discourse sought to establish the right of dominion over navigation, rather than of settlement per se. This doctrine of *mare clausum* was put forth systematically in the 1620s by Frei Serafim de Freitas, a professor of canon law at the University of

Valladolid, who challenged the attack on Portuguese interests made by Grotius in *Mare Liberum* (1608), and the general notion that according to natural law the seas were common, by asserting the right of original possession, the divinely sanctioned legitimacy of papal donation and conquest through just war, as well as the more tenuously sustained idea that a prince was not subject to natural law. The practical counterpart of this ideological justification for imperial expansion, in turn, was an "architecture of empire," the nautical sciences, that strove to guarantee the viability of sea routes rather than control of expansive territories.[20] This relative lack of concern with effective territorial occupation was also evident in imperial administration. Rather than reproducing traditional European modes of organizing an expanding exercise of power, such as an overarching network of officials with more or less clearly defined duties, the Portuguese empire comprised various ad hoc and in some cases relatively autonomous administrative arrangements (town councils, factory-fortresses, as well as even more indirect rule established in peace treaties). Even in Brazil, where the Portuguese presence most resembled the kind of settlement found in Spanish America, imperial administration was piecemeal, tenuous, and sparse. While the Spanish monarchy attempted to centralize royal authority within the New World at the beginning of its American enterprise by extending the institution of the viceroyalty, used first in the Kingdoms of Catalunya and Aragon, the governor-general of Brazil came to be called "viceroy" only in the eighteenth century and even then his authority over the other captains-general remained considerably more limited than his Spanish counterpart.[21] Such administrative plurality, as Hespanha and Santos have argued, amounted to a flexible imperial structure that allowed for the exploitation of local circumstances. As a consequence, the Portuguese crown could build and maintain an extensive empire in spite of the limited resources of the Kingdom of Portugal itself.[22]

For eighteenth-century statesmen, such as Luiz da Cunha, the oceanic and plural nature of the Portuguese empire also meant that its political capital could be located in any of its constituent parts without jeopardizing commercial or political interests. As Cunha explained, "the union of the two Portuguese dominions," in this case Europe and America, was made by "the interests of commerce." Thus, moving the royal court to Brazil would not imply a change in the relationship between the crown and the other parts of the empire because trade routes between the Americas, Africa, Asia, and Europe would remain the same. Cunha, in other words, saw that, as Valentim Alexandre has recently argued, although Portugal was historically "the center around which all political and economic activity turned," its position was not "the result of the definitive triumph of the nation," but rather represented "a reversible option, dependent upon geo-strategic considerations."[23] The principal political goal of such strategic considerations, in turn, was the enhancement of the power of the crown, the figure in which all differences and pluralities were resolved. This understanding of empire was a significant departure from that of the eighteenth-century Spanish. While Campomanes, for example, challenged the ideal of a transatlantic community "embodied in the legal person of the king,"[24] the Portuguese reconfiguration of empire relied precisely on a defense of not only the historic transoceanic monarchy but also the transoceanic community of vassals and the network of commercial interests over which it presided.

Yet, if Cunha's "empire of the west" provided continuity with the historic, oceanic Portuguese empire, making the latter's commerce "safer" and more "convenient," it also represented a rupture in Portuguese imperial history. Moving the empire's political center to Brazil, Cunha claimed, would serve as a point of departure for the transformation of the crown's American dominions, for a more rational administration of Brazil's economy, and a more thorough exploitation of its resources through additional "discoveries." As Cunha also foresaw, territorial losses in Europe could be compensated with territorial expansion in the New World. Rio de la Plata could replace Portugal, Cunha explained, whereas Chile could replace the Algarve, a "not impractical exchange," he added, that would serve the interests of both Iberian crowns.[25] American potential thus both responded to and displaced European vulnerabilities. An empire centered in the New World, once simply imagined as a refuge from the conflicts and intrigues of sixteenth-century Europe, now not only furthered the principle of oceanic commerce (both Atlantic and, considering interest in Chile, Pacific) but also promised to bequeath the land-based empire of "continental" dimensions that the Portuguese crown had been denied in Europe.

THE EIGHTEENTH-CENTURY PRACTICE OF EMPIRE

Although in the 1730s as Cunha was writing there was, of course, no transfer of the court, his idea that the key to a renewal of the Portuguese crown's global power was the development of America's potential became the basis for forging a new imperial politics in the second half of the eighteenth century. In part, these politics focused on the establishment of the borders between the territories of the Portuguese and Spanish crowns in South America and featured the "resurgence of controversy," as Demétrio Magnoli has described it, "over the phantasmagoric Meridian of Tordesillas." The Portuguese crown, inspired by the discovery of gold within its American territories, began to defend and further its interests there with on-the-ground reconnaissance and cartographic study. According to Magnoli, these superior efforts, when compared to those of the rival Spanish crown, then culminated in 1750 in the Portuguese diplomatic victory of the Treaty of Madrid, negotiated by Alexandre de

Gusmão. The Treaty of Madrid displaced the Treaty of Tordesillas (1494) by uphold-ing the principle of *uti possidetis* (occupation) in Africa and Asia as well as in the New World. Thus, the size of Portuguese territory in America doubled to include the vast basin of the Amazon River, while an exception to the principle of occupation was applied in the Rio de la Plata: the Portuguese relinquished claims to the Colônia do Sacramento in exchange for the Territory of the Seven Missions. Although this exception and the southern borders of Portuguese America continued to generate disputes, the new western borders endured.[26]

It was then left to João V's successor, José I (1750–1777), to respond to the ad-ministrative imperatives created by the treaty. This task was pursued energetically by his Prime Minister, Sebastião José de Carvalho e Melo, future Marquês de Pombal, with a systematic reform of the empire's administration and economy. Pombal, like Cunha, was a former diplomat and his political abilities had been noted by Cunha himself in his political testament.[27] Although he did not foresee Portugal relinquish-ing its metropolitan status, Pombal shared Cunha's concern with Portugal's vulnera-bility within Europe. To end what Cunha had characterized as dependency on England, Pombal promoted manufacturing to reduce imports and established the Alto Douro Company to curtail the English control of the wine industry, contradict-ing conventions established in earlier treaties.[28] Beyond Europe, Pombal similarly sought to develop local colonial economies in the interest of both security and impe-rial trade. Under the administration of Francisco Innocencio de Souza Coutinho (1764–1772), for example, attempts were made to diversify Angola's economy be-yond the narrow function of slaving depot. Yet it was Brazil, above all, that became the focus of Pombal's imperial reforms. To replace the income from a once lucrative yet now diminished American mining economy, and to establish in practice the sov-ereignty guaranteed in principle by the Treaty of Madrid, he furthered the settlement of the American territories beyond the coast and of the Amazon River region in par-ticular. There, to diversify and commercialize an agriculture that was comprised pri-marily of extractive and subsistence activities, the crown promoted the expanded use of African slave labor; the creation of trading companies; the settlement of Azorean immigrants; reforms of government, education, and building within indigenous vil-lages (*aldeias*); and the foundation of new towns based on standards of planning that evinced an enlightened spacial and administrative order.[29]

Fiscal and administrative reforms that Pombal initiated in Portugal were also ex-tended to Brazil as a whole. In recognition of the growing economic and strategic importance of the Brazilian south and to further shore up Portuguese control of its frontier territories there, the capital was moved from Salvador, Bahia to Rio de Janeiro. Auxiliary cavalry and infantry regiments were raised throughout Brazil, *jun-tas da fazenda* (exchequer boards) were established in each captaincy, and additional administrative reforms were achieved by enlisting Brazilian-born elites. The Lisbon *junta de comércio* (commercial board) also began to aid local manufactories in Brazil: a foundry, a leather factory, and the cultivation of silk. Ships were no longer obligated to sail within the fleet system, giving merchants more flexibility in accommodating supply and demand. In response to the British seizure of Havana in 1762, Pombal also sponsored a series of projects aimed at fortifying the neglected Brazilian coast. Foreigners, furthermore, were strictly barred from Brazil's ports, a move consistent with Pombal's quest to minimize the role of "foreign," principally English, commercial middlemen within the empire's economy.[30]

Pombal guaranteed the legacy of his imperial administration by reforming Portuguese education. In the 1770s the curricula at the faculties of law and medicine of the University of Coimbra were revised and additional faculties of mathematics and philosophy, which included the natural sciences, were created. Natural science, in particular, as a tool for understanding the laws and economy of nature, became a crucial matter of state, the basis for further reasoned reform that would promote "public prosperity" and the "good of society." In 1764, to ensure access to the learning required for such inquiries in the Portuguese world, Pombal appointed Domenico Vandelli (1735–1816), an Italian medical doctor and correspondent of Linnaeus, to the University of Coimbra.[31] Vandelli recruited several students and when the crown founded a Royal Academy of Sciences in 1779 natural science was featured in its correspondence and proceedings. As the author of a congratulatory prologue to the Academy's *Memórias* posed the question of its members' inspiration: "In a century in which more than ever, Nature has rewarded its studious observers with riches previously hidden on the surface, below the surface and in the atmosphere of the Earth, how could the Portuguese remain idle?"[32]

Such a rhetorical question not only celebrated the potential achievements of the Academy, but also alluded to the local scientific status quo against which its members struggled. Investigation limited by religious and political orthodoxies had left, and still threatened to leave, the Portuguese removed from the currents of innovation and enlightenment that the scientists of other imperial powers were freer to pursue. Accordingly, while some statesmen denounced the confluence of subversive political thought and science, the Academy's members responded by arguing that the viability of the Portuguese imperial enterprise rested upon their inquiries. As the Academy's founder, the Brazilian-born abbot José Correa da Serra, explained, "the sad experience of the past" showed "the need to study, because for many years we saw the substance and riches of the nation go to others in exchange for foodstuffs, which could either be grown in our territories or acclimatized with little effort."[33] In the wake of Pombal's fall from power, José Luiz Cardoso explains, the Academy, evincing the complex legacy of Pombaline reform itself, also fostered a systematic reflection on the Portuguese economy based on an engagement with physiocratic theory that included an emerging critique of royal intervention in markets and regimes of property and production associated with Pombaline mercantilism, making this mercantilism, as Fernando Novais has argued, "enlightened."[34] The Academy's members' interest in identifying the conditions necessary for the development of agriculture also coincided with efforts to promote a more comprehensive exploitation of the Portuguese empire's natural resources. The "first step that a nation must make in order to take advantage of its resources," Correa da Serra advised, "is to get to know its territory and its potential, what it contains, what it produces."[35] As was the case with Cunha and Pombal, for natural scientists in late eighteenth-century Portugal the imperial territories of most consequence were beyond Europe, in Africa and, above all, in America. "If from Brazil we could take useful resources," asked the Academy's correspondent Joaquim de Amorim Castro, "what advantages would the state not gain and what amount of trade would not be generated?"[36] To achieve what Vandelli characterized as "an exact Natural History of such a vast continent," the crown then sponsored a series of scientific expeditions led by Vandelli-trained Coimbra graduates.[37] With these expeditions, known as *viagens filosóficas*, the crown promoted experimental cultivation and the first systematic acclimatization of tropical plants, an enterprise that already had proven to be lucrative for the Dutch, French, and British, Portugal's rivals in Asia and America.[38]

Furthering the diversification of the imperial economy initiated earlier by Pombal, together with other inquiries and correspondence between students of natural science in Portugal and Brazil, the scientific expeditions also reinforced Cunha's vision of Brazil's continental dimensions and economic potential among the Portuguese imperial elite. This indeed was the case of Rodrigo de Souza Coutinho, statesman, theorist of empire, and student of natural science. As a diplomat, and later as Minister of the Navy and Overseas Affairs (1796–1801), he picked up where Pombal left off and promoted the Prime Minister's plan to counter Portugal's political weakness within Europe by developing the territories of Portuguese America. Convinced of the need to exploit Brazil's uncharted resources, Souza Coutinho sought to secure and protect royal sponsorship for botanical studies and inquiries into new modes of cultivation and production. He established a new printing house, *A Casa Literária Arco do Cego*, to edit and translate work on tropical agriculture. Its director, a Brazilian-born priest named José Mariano da Conceição Velloso, was entrusted with the task of creating a compendium of botanical products in the Portuguese territories in order to promote a productive integration of the empire's resources.[39]

As Souza Coutinho was aware, a more expansive and thorough exploitation of the crown's American territory also required dedication to the kind of administrative and political reforms initiated by Pombal. To this effect, in an address delivered in 1797 he proposed a series of innovations in the administration of Brazil. Administrative and judicial checks and balances, together with higher standards and better salaries for colonial officials, he argued, would facilitate a more efficient and impartial royal governance. A better educated and more closely supervised colonial clergy, he further suggested, would also be necessary if the crown intended to complete the royal mission of bringing Brazil's indigenous people into the fold of Catholicism and civilization and so fulfill the monarchy's desire to consolidate the "greatness of its dominions."

What amounted to a second effort to colonize Brazil, however, would be useless, Souza Coutinho insisted, without other reforms that integrated America and the rest of the empire. To achieve this integration and what he described as a "mutual and reciprocal defense," Souza Coutinho focused on military and administrative personnel. In a plan that recalled the seventeenth-century Spanish statesman Olivares' "union of arms," he argued that soldiers for the metropolitan armies should be recruited from all overseas territories so that "the monarchy [would] be defended equally by all the parts that constituted the whole." While a more thorough military presence would also ensure Brazil's defense, the "naturalization" of metropolitan recruits stationed there through marriage to local women, he further speculated, then would promote "even more the consolidation, and reunion of all of the parts of the monarchy." These and other forms of unity and integration, Souza Coutinho asserted, would guarantee that "a Portuguese born in the four parts of the world see himself only as Portuguese."[40] This new version of Spain's older union of arms, however, also depended on a crucial divergence from Spanish imperial politics. Whereas the Spanish had excluded American-born Spaniards from higher office, Souza Coutinho sought to integrate Brazilians into senior levels of imperial administration. Indeed, while he served on the royal cabinet, a number of Brazilians, including some who earlier had shown signs of political disaffection, were given administrative responsibilities not only within Brazil, but in Africa and Portugal as well. This, Souza Coutinho argued, restored the empire's initial design. While Portugal, he explained, was the "natural" "place of reunion" for the empire's scattered constituent parts, it was not geographic and political hierarchy, but rather the original, "inviolable and sacrosanct principle of unity," expressed here in an imperial elite, upon which both the monarchy and the empire were based.[41]

Souza Coutinho's quest to restore the empire's vitality made him Pombal's preeminent late eighteenth-century heir. Like Pombal, Souza Coutinho recognized the role of commerce in establishing and maintaining the monarchy's power and he sought to enhance imperial commerce using scientific inquiry and a reasoned exploitation of American resources above all. Faced with the limits of the Kingdom of

Portugal and with the continental dimensions of Brazil, they both strove to bring Portugal and its "most essential colony" closer than ever before. Perhaps they surmised that marginalizing and alienating Brazilian-born elites or creating a federation, as the Conde de Aranda proposed for the territories of Spain, were luxuries that the Portuguese could not afford.[42] Indeed, Portugal, it seemed, when compared with the other European states had most to lose. Although England had survived the loss of the thirteen North Atlantic colonies, Souza Coutinho explained, without its American empire Portugal would not be so fortunate. If with Brazil Portugal could enjoy wealth of continental dimensions, "reduced to itself," he concluded in an often-quoted ministerial address, it "would soon be a province of Spain."[43]

CRISIS AND THE CONSUMMATION OF AN IDEAL

Even as Souza Coutinho's reformist vision established continuities with Pombal's attempts to reinvigorate the Portuguese imperial enterprise, Souza Coutinho also faced new challenges to the empire. By the end of his term as Minister of the Navy and Overseas Affairs he had witnessed not only the achievement of North American independence, but also the French and Haitian Revolutions. Consequently, the challenge for Portuguese imperial statesmen had become not only to revitalize the empire but to preserve it within a now revolutionary Atlantic world. This task, as Souza Coutinho knew, was further complicated by Portugal's well-known geopolitical vulnerability.

The Portuguese crown initially responded to the political crises provoked by Europe's revolutionary wars by establishing neutrality, an active neutrality achieved by cultivating relations with various European monarchies. A precedent for this turn-of-the-nineteenth-century neutrality had been set during the North American war of independence, when the Portuguese crown had supported neither the British nor the North American cause. A series of marriages among Portuguese and Spanish royalty in the course of the eighteenth century, including that of Dom João with the Spanish Fernando VII's sister, Carlota Joaquina, also served to mitigate potential hostilities within the Iberian peninsula and undermined the inevitability of an alliance with Spain's enemy, Great Britain. In both 1796 and 1803 the Portuguese crown also made formal pledges to maintain a position of neutrality with regard to escalating conflicts between the British and the French.

The maintenance of neutrality, however, depended on more than the will of the Portuguese crown. In 1801 Napoleon demanded that the Portuguese close the empire's ports to the British. When the Portuguese did not comply, relations with Spain were undermined altogether, as Spanish troops invaded Portugal on Napoleon's behalf. The short and humiliating conflict known as the "War of the Oranges" resulted in the loss of Olivença and in a treaty that stipulated, among other things, the closing of Portuguese ports to the English. Additional negotiations with the French led to the signing of a treaty the same year that reaffirmed the future closure of Portuguese ports, prohibited the Portuguese from aiding France's enemies, enlarged French Guiana at the expense of territory in northern Brazil, and stipulated a regular payment to Napoleon's regime.[44]

It was in this context that Portuguese statesmen began to reconsider the creation of the kind of American empire proposed by Luiz da Cunha. During negotiations with the French, the Marquês de Alorna recommended to the crown that it announce its intentions to remove itself to Brazil. As Alorna speculated, if the Portuguese monarch merely threatened to go and be emperor of his vast territories in America, which, he added, could easily be extended to include the colonies of Spain, the French might withdraw their demands. If on the contrary the bluff failed to work, considering the European state of affairs he concluded that the prince regent might just as well establish his residence abroad.[45] The Conde de Ega also sustained that the time had come to move the royal court. It was not only the Kingdom of Portugal, he explained, but the empire itself that was at stake. "Either Portugal closes its ports to the English and risks the temporary loss of its colonies," he wrote, "or the Prince Our Lord . . . will go and establish a new monarchy in the New World." In this case, he argued, the prince regent would not only avoid a disastrous servitude to the French, but could himself become "an emperor of much greater stature."[46] Only two years later, Souza Coutinho issued his own endorsement of the transfer of the court, similarly insisting, as we saw at the beginning of this chapter, that the creation of a New World empire would allow the Portuguese crown to punish Napoleon for his refusal to honor its noble position of neutrality.[47]

The notion that the transfer of the court to Brazil was a brilliant move to remove the crown from European conflict and forge a greater and more independent empire was, however, not shared by the Portuguese court as a whole. While the idea alienated members of the nobility without interests in Brazil, it was also perceived as catering to British concerns and, hence, as jeopardizing whatever possibility of neutrality that remained. Indeed, the proponents of the transfer of the court often acknowledged their sympathies for an Anglo-Portuguese alliance in the war. Ega suggested that if forced to choose it was better to be an ally than an enemy of Great Britain, the monarchy most capable of encroaching on Portugal's empire. Souza Coutinho also reportedly acted in favor of a pro-British faction at court. This apparent alignment between those supporting the transfer of the court and Britain then was confirmed when the British crown itself announced its support for the plan to establish the Portuguese capital in Brazil. In 1806 and 1807, acting to avoid a Napoleonic annexation of the Iberian Peninsula, the British stepped up diplomatic efforts to promote this position in Lisbon, instructing the British representative Viscount Strangford to give weight to the faction at court that supported both the British and a transfer of the court. An anonymous pamphlet, written in French and published in London in 1807, reiterated earlier remarks attributed to William Pitt in support of a Portuguese-American empire.[48] And, by mid-November 1807, Sir Sidney Smith was stationed off the port of Lisbon with a squadron, a force of 7,000 men, and orders to either escort the royal family to Brazil or blockade the port and save the Portuguese fleet if Lisbon were to fall to the French.

In the meantime, the French also pressured the Portuguese crown to dismantle its policy of neutrality. If the British would not sign a treaty, Napoleon pledged, French troops would occupy Portugal. In response, Portuguese royal counselors both continued to pursue negotiations with the French and maintained conversations with Strangford about a possible departure from Lisbon. In one final attempt to avoid war with France, the Portuguese attempted to comply with Napoleon's demands by simulating hostilities with Britain. Strangford's passport was revoked and the British were denied access to Portuguese ports, while secret negotiations with the British crown established compensation for any confiscations. These intense and, at times, convoluted diplomatic efforts were, however, then abandoned altogether in late November 1807, when news reached Lisbon that French armies under the leadership of Junot had crossed the Spanish-Portuguese border. Opposition to a transfer of the court crumbled and by the time Strangford returned to Lisbon, only days after leaving, the royal family and nobility had boarded their ships.[49] The prince regent established a regency, counseled against armed resistence to the French, and assured his vassals that Portugal would endure his absence only "until the general peace" was attained.[50] Then, together with their British escort, he and the courtiers set sail for Rio de Janeiro, the Brazilian viceregal capital.

With the transfer of the court, Brazil thus became the short-term haven for a beleaguered Portuguese monarchy foreseen in the late sixteenth century. Yet, the departure of the prince regent was inspired as well by more recent imperial discourse and practice. As envisioned and fostered by Souza Coutinho, the move to America was predicated on an optimistic appraisal of the possibilities of reorganizing imperial space and redefining the empire's ethos. And this imperial renewal depended, above all, on the crown's perception of Brazil as an essential and central part of the monarchy's dominions; a continent of resources that, as eighteenth-century statesmen had sustained, reasoned and scientific inquiry could transform into a great empire of commercial wealth and utility. Less than a year later, the Portuguese crown's "Declaration of War against the French," drafted by Souza Coutinho in his more powerful position as Minister of Foreign Affairs and War, reflected the force of this promise of imperial renovation in the New World. With it the prince regent addressed

D.A. de Sequeira I.Pint. da Cam. de S.M. Fid. inv.   G. F. de Queiroz sculp. Lx.ᵃ 1817.

EXEGIT MONUMENTUM ÆRE PERENIUS.

FIGURE 1: Domingos António de Sequeira, "Exegit monumentum aere perenius," from José António Sá, *Defeza dos Direitos Nacionaes e Reaes da Monarquia Portugueza* (Lisbon: Impressão Régia, 1816). Copy and permission obtained from the General Research Division, The New York Public Library, Astor, Lenox and Tilden Foundations. With the epigraph "He has produced a monument more everlasting than bronze," borrowed from Horace, *Carmina* III, 30.1, and modified so as to suggest Dom João as the heir of Augustus, Sequeira invoked the imperial renewal that the transfer of the court promised.

Napoleon and the monarchs of Europe not from a humiliating exile, but rather, as the declaration described it, from the "bosom of a new Empire, that [he] was going to create."[51]

Yet, as we shall see, even as the prince regent and his courtiers celebrated the salvation of the independent monarchy and the empire, they also began to consider that the transfer of the court represented more fundamental and potentially threatening change; what Ega had described as "the greatest of all revolutions of the general political system."[52] For the Portuguese crown to achieve what one British observer hailed as a "brighter glory in the Western sphere,"[53] the legitimacy of the monarchy and the empire would have to be redefined in ways that accounted for recent developments. The new court of Rio de Janeiro became a crucial site in which these redefinitions were forged.

NOTES

1. Rodrigo de Souza Coutinho, "Quadro da Situação Política da Europa . . ." (August 16, 1803), in Ângelo Pereira, *D. João VI, príncipe e rei* v. 1 (Lisbon: Empresa Nacional de Publicidade, 1953), 127–136.

2. Souza Coutinho's proposal was rejected by Portuguese courtiers, nobles, and merchants who, without extensive properties in Brazil, saw nothing to be gained by moving the Portuguese capital to the New World. Soon after Souza Coutinho resigned from his post. See Kenneth Maxwell, "The Generation of the 1790s and the Idea of Luso-Brazilian Empire," in *Colonial Roots of Modern Brazil*, ed. Dauril Alden (Berkeley: University of California Press, 1973), 141; and Andrée Mansuy Diniz Silva, "Introdução," in Rodrigo de Souza Coutinho, *Textos políticos, económicos e financeiros (1783–1811)* t. 1 (Lisbon: Banco de Portugal, 1993), xlviii.

3. See Luiz da Cunha, *Instrucções inéditas de D. Luiz da Cunha a Marco António de Azevedo Coutinho* (1736) (Coimbra: Imprensa da Universidade, 1930), 208–209; and Joaquim Veríssimo Serrão, *Do Brasil filipino ao Brasil de 1640* (São Paulo: Companhia Editora Nacional, 1968), 13–15.

4. Ana Cristina Bartolomeu de Araújo, "O 'Reino Unido de Portugal, Brasil e Algarves' 1815–1822," *RHI* 14 (1992), 234; Maria de Lourdes Viana Lyra, *A Utopia do Poderoso Império, Portugal e Brasil: Bastidores da Política, 1798-1822* (Rio de Janeiro: Sette Letras, 1994), 107–108, 120–124; C.R. Boxer, *The Dutch in Brazil, 1624–1654* (Oxford: Clarendon, 1957), 204–207; and Luiz Norton, *A côrte de Portugal no Brasil* (São Paulo: Companhia Editora Nacional, 1938), 18–19. According to Norton, Vieira made references to these recommendations in a letter written in Bahia in 1691.

5. On the translation of empire in early modern discourse see Anthony Pagden, *Lords of All the World: Ideologies of Empire in Spain, Britain and France, c.1500–c.1800* (New Haven: Yale University Press, 1995), 15, 27, 42–43; idem, *Spanish Imperialism and the Political Imagination: Studies in European and Spanish-American Social and Political Theory, 1513–1830*

(New Haven: Yale University Press, 1990), 37–63; and Frances A. Yates, *Astraea: The Imperial Theme in the Sixteenth Century* (London: Ark Paperbacks, 1975), 4.

6. Lyra, *Utopia*, 108. Portuguese medieval messianic legends were strengthened by the apocalyptic literature of Kabbalists who emigrated to Portugal after their expulsion from Spain in 1492. The legend of a hidden king (*o Encoberto*) residing on a mysterious western island, destined to return to create an everlasting empire, was embellished by the sixteenth-century popular poetry of a reportedly New Christian shoemaker known as Bandarra. See Gonçalo Annes Bandarra, *As trovas do Bandarra* (Porto: Imprensa Popular de J.L. de Souza, 1866); Carole A. Myscofski, *When Men Walk Dry: Portuguese Messianism in Brazil* (Atlanta: Scholars Press, 1988), 48, 52, 55–57; and António Pires Machado, *D. Sebastião e o Encoberto* (Lisbon: Fundação Calouste Gulbenkian, [1969]), 78, 84–87. On António Vieira's messianism, see Luiz Reis Torgal, *Ideologia política e teoria do estado na restauração* v. 1 (Coimbra: Biblioteca Geral da Universidade, 1981), 306–310; and Vieira, "Sermão dos Bons Anos," in *Obras Escolhidas* v. 10, eds. António Sergio and Hernâni Cidade (Lisbon: Livraria Sá da Costa, 1954), 166. Vieira elaborated these ideas in *Esperança de Portugal, Quinto Império do Mundo* (1659), *História do Futuro* (1664), and *Clavis Prophetarum* (1677).

7. Thomas Cohen, *The Fire of Tongues: António Vieira and the Missionary Church in Brazil and Portugal* (Stanford: Stanford University Press, 1998), 1, 119–129, 145–146, 157; and Myscofski, *When Men Walk Dry*, 108–109.

8. Pagden, *Lords*, 111; John Oldmixon cited in idem.

9. Pagden, *Lords*, 70, 122, 152, 164–167; Charles de Secondat, Baron de Montesquieu, *The Spirit of the Laws* (1748) (New York: Cambridge University Press, 1989), 396 (part 4, chapter 22). For Adam Smith's understanding of the Iberian empires see his *An Inquiry into the Nature and Causes of The Wealth of Nations* (1776), Chapter 7, "Of Colonies." Smith's work, as we shall see in Chapter 6, had a particular resonance for Portuguese statesmen following the transfer of the court.

10. Pagden, *Lords*, 116, 124–125, 157. For a recent analysis of Spanish imperial reform in America see Jeremy Adelman, *Republic of Capital: Buenos Aires and the Legal Transformation of the Atlantic World* (Stanford: Stanford University Press, 1999).

11. Rui Bebiano, *D. João V: poder e espectáculo* (Aveiro: Livraria Estante: 1987); Angela Delaforce, "Lisbon: 'This New Rome': Dom João V of Portugal and Relations between Rome and Lisbon" and Marco Fabio Apolloni, "Wondrous Vehicles: the Coaches of the Embassy of the Marquês de Fontes," in *The Age of the Baroque in Portugal*, ed. Jay Levenson (Washington, DC/New Haven: National Gallery/Yale University Press, 1993); António Filipe Pimentel, "Absolutismo, Corte e Palácio Real—Em torno dos palácios de D. João V," in *Arqueologia do Estado, Jornadas sobre Formas de Organização e Exercício dos Poderes na Europa do Sul. S.XVII–S.XVIII* (special issue of *História e Crítica*) (Lisbon, 1988). See also António Caetano de Souza, *História Genealogica da Casa Real Portugueza* t. 8 (1749) (Coimbra: Atlantida, 1951), 1–178. Under the aegis of the newly created Royal Academy of History, João V solicited and then sponsored the publication of Caetano's monumental history of the Portuguese monarchy, which includes a description of the Viennese commemoration of the king's engagement to the Hapsburg princess Maria Anna, as well as of her arrival at Lisbon.

12. See Delaforce, "Lisbon: 'This New Rome.'" For images of João V as messiah see also António da Costa, "Sermão nas Sumptuosas Exéquias do Serenissimo Senhor D. João V . . . ,"

and António de Oliveira, "Estatua de Ouro, que o Muito Alto e Muito Poderoso Rey . . . Erigio nas Immortaes e Gloriosos Acções," in João Jorge de Barros, *Relação Panegyrica das Honras Funeraes que as Memórias do Muito Alto Poderoso Senhor Rey Fidelissimo D. João V consagrou a Cidade da Bahia, Corte da América Portuguesa* . . . (Lisbon: Régia Officina Sylvaniana, e da Academia Real, 1753). On João V's uses of liturgical ceremony to renovate the image of royal power, see also Pimentel, "Absolutismo," 693, 694.

13. João Jorge de Barros, "Relação Panegyrica das Honras Funeraes," in *Relação Panegyrica*, 14–16, 22. On Camões, see Richard Helgerson, *Forms of Nationhood: The Elizabethan Writing of England* (Chicago: Chicago University Press, 1992), 155–163.

14. Cunha, *Instrucções*, 211–212.

15. Cunha, *Instrucções*, 207, 211, 219; Duc de Choiseul cited in Kenneth Maxwell, *Pombal: Paradox of the Enlightenment* (New York: Cambridge University Press, 1995), 111.

16. Cunha, *Instrucções*, 213–214; 218. Cunha's claims concerning the role played by trade in the advancement of a spiritual empire are similar to observations made by Vieira. See Vieira, *Livro anteprimeiro*, cited in Cohen, 162: "for if God in his providence had not enriched those lands with those many treasures, no amount of religious zeal would have been sufficient to bring the faith to them."

17. As Norbert Kilian notes, residents of the British colonies in North America expressed a similar sense of American preeminence; a recognition that, as one speculated, "this vast Country will, in Time, become the greatest Empire that the world has ever seen." John Adams similarly imagined that "After many more centuries when the colonies may be so far increased as to have the balance of wealth, numbers and powers in their favor, the good of empire [shall] make it necessary to fix the seat of government here; and some future GEORGE . . . may cross the Atlantic, and rule Great Britain by an American parliament." Nor did the commercial dimensions of this American empire preclude understanding its history in providential terms. "Westward the course of empire takes its way," wrote Bishop Berkeley, "The first four Acts already past, . . ." See Adams and Berkeley cited in Norbert Kilian, "New Wine in Old Skins? American Definitions of Empire and the Emergence of a New Concept," in *Theories of Empire, 1450–1800*, ed. David Armitage (Brookfield: Ashgate/Variorum, 1998), 315, 317.

18. António Manuel Hespanha and Maria Catarina Santos, "Os poderes num império oceânico," in *História de Portugal: O Antigo Regime* v. 4, ed. António Manuel Hespanha (Lisbon: Estampa, s.d.), 395, 398; Helgerson, *Forms of Nationhood*, 160; and Sanjay Subrahmanyam, *The Portuguese Empire in Asia, 1500–1700, A Political and Economic History* (London: Longman, 1993), 47, 50–51, 107–112. The King of Portugal ruled over not only his "conquests," but also the "navigation and commerce of Ethiopia, Arabia, Persia, and India." In a report written in Pará Francisco de Souza Coutinho also noted the "different system" of the Spanish territories and, in particular, that the Viceroy of New Granada lived in Santa Fé de Bogotá "very far from sea ports." "I judge," he continued, "that that which is superior should exist on the coast, and not in the interior, and it is not in the interior that they [the Spanish] encounter dangers, nor there that they need forces except those necessary to keep the peace. . . ." See F. de Souza Coutinho to R. de Souza Coutinho, September 20, 1797, BNRJ Ms. I-28,25,30.

19. Pagden, *Lords*, 45; Hespanha and Santos, "Os poderes," 395; Fernando Bouza Álvarez, "Lisboa *Sozinha, Quase Viúva*. A cidade e a mudança da corte no Portugal dos Filipes," *Pené-*

lope: Fazer e Desfazer a História 13 (1994), 86–87.

20. See Frei Serafim de Freitas, *Do justo império asiático dos portugueses* (1625) 2 v. (Lisbon: Instituto Nacional de Investigação Científica, 1983); Hespanha and Santos, "Os Poderes," 396–397; Ana Maria Ferreira, "'Mare Clausum, Mare Liberum': Dimensão doutrinal de um foco de tensões políticas," *Cultura e História* 3 (1984): 315–357; C.H. Alexandrowicz, "Freitas Versus Grotius" and G.D. Winius, "Millenarianism and Empire: Portuguese Asian Decline and the 'Crise de Conscience' of the Missionaries," in *Theories of Empire*, ed. Armitage, 239–259, 261–174.

21. The viceroy, according to Heloísa Liberalli Bellotto, was a "viceroy without a viceroyalty." See her "O Estado Português no Brasil: Sistema Administrativo e Fiscal," in *Nova História da Expansão Portuguesa. O Império Luso-Brasileiro, 1750–1822* v. 8, ed. Maria Beatriz Nizza da Silva (Lisbon: Estampa, 1986), 276; Guy Martinière, "Implantação das estruturas de Portugal na América, (1620–1750)," in *Nova História da Expansão Portuguesa. O Império Luso-Brasileiro, 1620–1750* v. 7, ed. Frédéric Mauro (Lisbon: Estampa, 1991), 172–177. James Lockart and Stuart Schwartz have explained the different approaches to the administration of empire by characterizing Brazil's early colonization as similar to that of the Spanish American periphery. See their *Early Latin America: A History of Colonial Spanish America and Brazil* (New York: Cambridge, 1983), 181.

22. Hespanha and Santos, "Os Poderes," 398.

23. Valentim Alexandre, *Os sentidos do império: questão nacional e questão colonial na crise do antigo regime português* (Porto: Afrontamento, 1993), 810.

24. Pagden, *Lords*, 125.

25. Cunha, *Instrucções,* 215, 217.

26. Demétrio Magnoli, *O corpo da pátria: imaginação geográfica e política externa no Brasil (1808–1912)* (São Paulo: UNESP, 1997), 71–77; Andrée Mansuy-Diniz Silva, "Imperial Reorganization, 1750–1808," in *Colonial Brazil*, ed. Leslie Bethell (New York: Cambridge University Press, 1994), 244–269.

27. Maxwell, *Pombal*, 1.

28. With the Methuen Treaty in 1703 Portugal agreed to admit British woolen cloth and other woolen manufactures free of duty. In exchange England was to admit Portuguese wine at one-third less than the duties on French wine. See Alan K. Manchester, *British Preëminence in Brazil, Its Rise and Decline. A Study in European Expansion* (1933) (New York: Octagon, 1964) 24, 43–44.

29. C.R. Boxer, *The Portuguese Seaborne Empire, 1415–1825* (London: Hutchinson, 1969), 194; Manuel Nunes Dias, "Política Pombalina na colonizção da Amazónia (1755–1778)," *Studia* 23 (April 1968), 7–32; Alexandre Lobato, "A Política Ultramarina Portuguesa no Século XVIII," *Ultramar* (Lisbon) 30, v. 8 (1967), 81–113; Roberta Marx Delson, *New Towns for Colonial Brazil: Spatial and Social Planning of the Eighteenth Century* (Ann Arbor: University Microfilms International/Dellplain Latin American Studies, 1979). The presence of royal officials in indigenous villages replaced the recently expelled Jesuits.

30. Maxwell, *Pombal*, 88–89, 114, 118–130.

31. Maxwell, *Pombal*, 96–100; William J. Simon, *Scientific Expeditions in the Portuguese Overseas Territories (1783–1808)* (Lisbon: Instituto de Investigação CientíficaTropical, 1983), 5; Warren Dean, *With Broadax and Firebrand: The Destruction of the Brazilian Atlantic Forest*

(Berkeley: University of California Press, 1995), 118.

32. [Anonymous], "Prologo," *Memórias da Academia Real das Sciencias de Lisboa* 1 (1797). The Academy's motto, *Nisi utile est quod facimus, stulta est gloria* (If what we do is not useful then our glory is foolish), also reflected its members' dedication to the scientific promotion of "public utility."

33. José Correa da Serra, "Discurso Preliminar," in *Memórias Econômicas da Academia Real das Sciencias de Lisboa para o adiantamento da Agricultura, das Artes e da Indústria em Portugal e suas Conquistas* 1 (1789), viii; Dean, *With Broadax*, 120.

34. José Luiz Cardoso, "Economic thought in late eighteenth-century Portugal: physiocratic and Smithian influences," *History of Political Economy* 22, n. 2 (1990), 432-2; idem, *O Pensamento económico em Portugal nos finais do século XVIII, 1780–1808* (Lisbon: Estampa, 1989); Fernando A. Novais, *Portugal e Brasil na Crise do Antigo Sistema Colonial* (São Paulo: Hucitec, 1979), 228–230.

35. Correa da Serra, "Discurso," viii.

36. Joaquim de Amorim Castro, "Memória sobre a cochonilha do Brasil," *Memórias Econômicas* 2 (1790), 143. Vandelli shared this enthusiasm for the potential resources of "the overseas territories." See Vandelli, "Memória sobre algumas producções das conquistas, as quaes são pouco conhecidas, ou não se aproveitão," *Memórias Econômicas* 1 (1789), 206.

37. Vandelli to Martinho de Melo e Castro (Minister of Navy and Overseas Affairs), June 22, 1778, in Simon, Appendix I. Alexandre Rodrigues Ferreira surveyed the Amazon region (1783–1792), collecting specimens and experimenting with the collection of hemp. Manuel Galvão da Silva served as secretary of government of Mozambique (1783–1793) while also traveling and collecting mineral specimens. The naturalist Joaquim José da Silva served as secretary of government in Angola (1783–1808), where he assembled an herbarium and collected plants and animals to be shipped to Lisbon. During this time, other less structured inquiries were made regarding Brazilian mineralogy and agriculture as well. To standardize its correspondents' ad hoc participation and collection of specimens, the Academy published guidelines, *Breves instrucções aos correspondentes da Academia das Sciencias de Lisboa sobre as remessas do produtos, e noticias pertencentes a História da Natureza para formar hum Museo Nacional* (Lisbon: Régia Officina Typografica, 1781). On the expeditions see Simon, *Scientific Expeditions*. On natural science reports see the Academy's *Memórias*; José Joaquim Roiz, *Documentos dos Arquivos Portugueses que Importam ao Brasil* (Lisbon) n. 5 (January 1945), 2–3; and "Carta muito interessante do advogado da Bahia, José da Silva Lisboa, Para Domingos Vandelli . . . ," *ABN* 32 (1910), 494–505.

38. This effort was enthusiastically championed by Correa da Serra who argued that surveying Brazil's resources and acclimatizing new plants was the Academy's "patriotic" duty. See his "Discurso," viii. To gain further knowledge of the empire's resources, Vandelli organized a botanical garden at the Ajuda palace that was to serve as a clearing house. See Dean, *With Broadax*, 118. The scientific endeavors of men born in Brazil and then educated in Europe are analyzed in Maria Odila da Silva Dias, "Aspectos da Ilustração no Brasil," *RIHGB* 278 (January–March 1968), 105–170.

39. As the son of a high-ranking imperial official, Souza Coutinho enjoyed the personal blessings of Pombal, his godfather, as well as access to an education that reflected the Prime Minister's vision of a well-educated, well-trained, and reform-minded nobility. His father

served as governor of Angola during Pombal's administration. His dedication to natural science was reflected in his charter membership of the Linnaean Society of London. See Ângelo Pereira, *D. João VI, príncipe e rei* v. 3 (Lisbon: Emprensa Nacional de Publicidade, 1956), 86; Kenneth Maxwell, "The Generation of the 1790s," 133; Dean, *With Broadax*, 118–121; Lyra, *Utopia*, 83–88; and Guilherme Pereira das Neves, "Del Imperio Luso-Brasileño al Imperio del Brasil (1789–1822)," in *De los Imperios a las Naciones Iberoamerica*, et. al. A. Annino (Zaragoza: Ibercaja, 1994), 169–193.

40. Rodrigo de Souza Coutinho, "Memória sobre o Melhoramento dos Domínios de Sua Magestade na America" (1797), *Brasília* (Coimbra) 4 (1949), 407–422. Also in 1797, Francisco de Souza Coutinho submitted a proposal for similar reforms in "the governments of the North of our America." See Francisco de Souza Coutinho to Rodrigo de Souza Coutinho, September 20, 1797, BNRJ Ms. I-28,25,30. See also Rodrigo de Souza Coutinho, "[Discurso feito] na abertura da Sociedade Real Maritima, em 22 de Dezembro de 1798," in Marquês do Funchal, *O Conde de Linhares* (Lisbon: Typografia Bayard, 1908), 105–115. On Olivares and the union of arms see J.H. Elliott, *Imperial Spain, 1469–1716* (New York: Meridian, 1963), 326–328. I thank Antonio Feros for calling my attention to the similarity between Olivares' and Souza Coutinho's proposal.

41. Souza Coutinho, "Memoria sobre o Melhoramento dos Dominios," 406. On the Bourbon administrative elite's disdain for American-born Spaniards see David Brading, *The First America: The Spanish Monarchy, Creole Patriots, and the Liberal State, 1492–1867* (New York: Cambridge University Press, 1991), 477; and John Lynch, "The Origins of Spanish American Independence," in *The Independence of Latin America*, ed. Leslie Bethell (New York: Cambridge University Press, 1987), 24–27. On the Brazilian-born imperial elite see Maxwell, "Generation," 138–144; Roderick Barman, *Brazil: The Forging of a Nation, 1798–1852* (Stanford: Stanford University Press, 1988), 119; and José Murilo de Carvalho, "Political Elites and State Building: The Case of Nineteenth-Century Brazil," *Comparative Studies in Society and History* 24, n. 3 (July 1982), 395.

42. Pagden, *Lords*, 124–125, 194.

43. Souza Coutinho, "Memoria sobre o Melhoramento dos Dominios," 406. See also a report by Francisco de Souza Coutinho to Rodrigo de Souza Coutinho, September 20, 1797, BNRJ Ms. I-28,25,30. The report was inspired by the need to promote "the conservation of the colonies" in spite of "opposing efforts by foreign enemies" and "internal disorder" by way of a "regular administration of civil and criminal justice, with public economy, and by maintaining political relations in accordance with the established system."

44. Manchester, *British*, 55.

45. On the Marquês of Alorna, José Manuel de Souza, see Lyra, *Utopia*, 109.

46. See Ega cited in Araújo, "O 'Reino Unido,'" 235.

47. Souza Coutinho, "Quadro da Situação Política," in Pereira, *D. João VI* v. 1, 127–136.

48. British support for a transfer of the court dated back at least to 1762 when British forces helped the Portuguese repel a Spanish invasion. At that time, commentary suggested that in the event that Spain and France occupied Portugal's capital the British could escort the Portuguese king "his treasures, and all that of his family and faithful subjects" across the Atlantic and in doing so themselves gain direct access to Brazil. See *Punch's Politicks* (London, 1762) cited in Maxwell, *Pombal*, 112. The anonymous pamphlet of 1807 proclaimed that it

was "in Brazil that Portugal is a power." There the Prince Regent would build "the inexpugnable bulwark against the tyranny of Europe. . . ." See the citation in Tobias Monteiro, *História do império. A elaboração da independência* (Rio de Janeiro: Briguiet, 1927), 54. According to Monteiro, this pamphlet, *Reflexions sur la conduit du Prince Regent de Portugal* (London: F. Harper, 1807), was published in June. Monteiro notes that its language recalled earlier formulations attributed to William Pitt, as well as Strangford's subsequent account of the royal family's departure. Monteiro, however, does not cite a Portuguese version of the tract published in Coimbra after the Prince Regent's departure, apparently as an apologia. See *Reflexões sobre a Conducta do Principe Regente de Portugal* (Coimbra: Real Imprensa da Universidade, 1808). At that time the author was identified as the Portuguese Francisco Soares Franco. See pp. 7–8 for identical passages. Pitt's plan for Portuguese America was also integrated into Joaquim Rafael do Valle's *Manifesto Juridico, e Político a Favor da Conducta do Principe Regente N.S., e dos Direitos da Caza de Bragança, contra as usurpações Francezas desde a Epoca da injusta invasão de Portugal* (Rio de Janeiro: Impressão Régia, 1811), 18.

49. One contemporary account of the debates among Portuguese courtiers in 1807 is found in Anonymous, "Jornada do Sr. D. João 6º ao Brazil em 1807," in Ângelo Pereira, *Os filhos de el-rei D. João VI* (Lisbon: Empresa Nacional de Publicidade, 1946), 101–116. On the diplomatic context of the transfer of the court see Alan K. Manchester, "The Transfer of the Portuguese Court to Rio de Janeiro," in *Conflict and Continuity in Brazilian Society*, eds. Henry H. Keith and S.F. Edwards (Columbia, SC: University of South Carolina Press, 1969) and idem, *British Preëminence*, 54–68; Ana Cristina Araújo, "As Invasões franceses e a afirmação das ideias liberais," in *História de Portugal: O Liberalismo* v. 5, eds. Luiz Reis Torgal and João Lourenço Roque (Lisbon: Estampa [n.d.]), 17–24; David Francis, *Portugal, 1715–1808, Joanine and Rococo Portugal as Seen by British Diplomats and Traders* (London: Tamesis, 1985), 245–286.

50. "[Cópia do] Decreto que o Principe Regente de Portugal foi servido deixar em Lisboa para a boa direção do Governo na sua ausência para o Rio de Janeiro," November 25, 1807, BNRJ Ms. I-3,19,69.

51. "Manifesto de Declaração de Guerra aos Francezes," May 1, 1808, ([Rio de Janeiro]: Impressão Régia, [1808]). Also published as *Manifesto, ou Exposição Fundada, e Justificativa do procedimento da Corte de Portugal a respeito da França desde o principio da Revolução até a epoca da Invasão de Portugal . . .* (Rio de Janeiro: 1808), reprinted in Souza Coutinho, *Textos*, t. 2, 335–343. The counsel received regarding this document is transcribed in Pereira, *D. João VI* v. 1, 19–34. The implications of this language were apparent to the Marquês de Angeja who advised that "it would be convenient to omit on the first page the words 'from the new Empire that he will create'; because I am persuaded that this expression denotes few hopes of His Royal Highness returning to possess Portugal."

52. Ega cited in Araújo, "O 'Reino Unido,'" 235.

53. [John Wolcot], *The Fall of Portugal; or The Royal Exiles, A Tragedy in Five Acts* (London: Longman, Hurst, Rees and Orme, 1808), 20.

TWO

Preeminence and Its Price:
EIGHTEENTH-CENTURY RIO DE JANEIRO

IN MARCH 1808, AFTER TWO MONTHS AT SEA AND A STOP AT SALVADOR, BAHIA, Portuguese Prince Regent Dom João and his convoy sailed into Guanabara Bay, an exceptional natural harbor known for both its "capaciousness and security" and spectacular natural environs. As the ships passed through a narrow entrance between two hills, the bay suddenly widened into what appeared to be "an extensive lake." From a distance, the royal exiles could behold the rugged mountains that surrounded the bay and the white sandy beaches and transparent blue water that lay at their feet. As they drew closer, passengers could discern the city of São Sebastião of Rio de Janeiro itself, nestled among rocky hills and lush vegetation. The city's border closely followed the bay's winding coastline, with building extending to nearby hills that left, as one late eighteenth-century visitor noted, "[a]lmost every eminence in the vicinity of the town . . . crowned with a castle or a fort, a church or a convent." The resulting contrast of whitewashed fortifications and churches, with the stony, brown hills and green foliage was striking.[1]

It was here, in this pleasantly incongruous setting, that the prince regent and his courtiers would set out to make their visions of political salvation and imperial renewal a reality. And it was with Rio de Janeiro's residents that they would negotiate the terms for constructing the new royal court and a new imperial politics. While a few of the statesmen who accompanied the prince regent had served previously in Brazil, most of the royal exiles knew little of Rio de Janeiro, apart from a general perception of life in the colonies as inferior.[2] For the exiles their arrival at the city thus was a discovery, one which, as the cleric Luiz Gonçalves dos Santos claimed in an epigraph to a history of his native Rio de Janeiro, recalled that most emblematic Portuguese discovery, Vasco da Gama's voyage to Asia in 1498. Just as the earlier Portuguese mariners, Gonçalves dos Santos pointed out with words borrowed from the poet Luiz de Camões (c. 1524–1580), the exiled courtiers came "from the far off Tagus." Writing in a similarly triumphant tone, the exiled Marquês de Bellas also found the comparison of da Gama's voyage and the royal journey to Brazil to be compelling and likened the prince regent to da Gama's sponsor, King Manuel.[3]

Yet if, as the courtiers had learned from Camões, Vasco da Gama was greeted by the residents of India ostensibly eager both to trade and to learn of the God who had "certainly brought him," when the courtiers themselves prepared to disembark, and begin their lives in the New World, they could only wonder: what and who would *they* encounter? This chapter provides answers to this question with an overview of the eighteenth-century city of Rio de Janeiro. For Rio de Janeiro's residents the eighteenth century was a time of new political preeminence and economic prosperity, based on plantation agriculture, an expanding international and internal trade, and the traffic in and use of African slaves. Politics and commerce also linked the newly named capital of Brazil to the larger Atlantic world. By the end of the eighteenth century, this world had become revolutionary. Living and governing in Rio thus meant grappling with the consequences and experiencing what one resident described as "dangerous times."

THE CAPITAL OF PORTUGUESE AMERICA

In contrast to its spacious natural environment, the city of Rio de Janeiro was small; an intimate, densely constructed setting about one and one-half miles long and three-quarters of a mile wide. The eighteenth-century urban environment began at the *Terreiro do Palácio*, a large and reportedly "handsome square" that opened up onto the bay. To the right of its docks, the terreiro was bordered by the arches of Teles, the remains of an elite residence destroyed in a fire that was now home to a tavern keeper and reputed to be a haven for petty thieves and prostitutes. To the left was the simple, rectangular, two-story building that housed the viceroy and served as the seat of government. Nearby, completing the square's perimeter, were the Carmelite convent and the city's jail. The terreiro also contained the *pelourinho*, a stone pillar used for public whippings. At its edge near the quay stood a "luxurious" public fountain.[4]

Disembarking at the terreiro's docks, visitors confronted a host of activities and glimpsed both the city's economic and political dimensions as well as its social and cultural hierarchies. During the day, the busy square was filled with African and African-Brazilian slaves. Some loaded and unloaded goods at the docks and carried them back and forth from stores and warehouses. Others, under the watch of guards, waited in long lines for water from the fountain to be carried back to their owners' houses. The administrative responsibilities that the city encompassed were evident in the presence of magistrates and other royal officials, making their way along the sidewalks that criss-crossed the square to and from meetings with the viceroy. The guarantee of order and the consequences of justice then were further revealed in the daily scene of shackled prisoners begging for alms at the prison's door, as well as in the occasional acts of exemplary corporal punishment at the pelourinho.[5]

Leaving the terreiro from the left, the Rua da Misericórdia wound back toward the bay, along the foot of Castle Hill, to a compound of fortifications and buildings that were part of the city's original mid-sixteenth-century settlement. There both a *colégio* and the church of Bom Jesus dos Perdões stood as reminders of the Society of Jesus, the powerful religious order that had built them and indeed dominated the church and missionary effort in Brazil until its expulsion in the middle of the eighteenth century. The Church of São Sebastião was there as well, demonstrating that saint's long-standing patronage of the city and its residents. Nearby, among other churches and barracks, was the Santa Casa da Misericórdia (The Holy House of Mercy), the local chapter of the most prestigious lay brotherhood in the Portuguese world.[6] The Misericórdia's careful selection of its members, based on lineage, wealth, and profession, provided the city's elite with an institutionalized measure of status. The Rio de Janeiro chapter was over two hundred years old and by the eighteenth

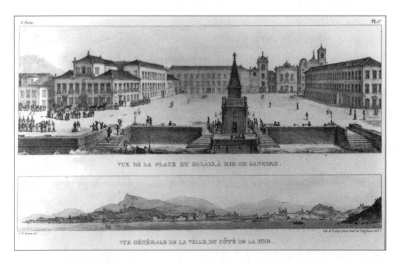

FIGURE 2: Jean Baptiste Debret, "Vue de la Place du Palais à Rio de Janeiro" and "Vue Générale de la Ville, du Côté de la Mer," from Debret, *Voyage Pittoresque et Historique au Brésil, sejour d'un Artiste Français au Brésil* v. 3 (Paris: Firmin Didot Fréres, 1839). Copy and permission obtained from the Print Collection, Miriam and Ira D. Wallach Division of Arts, Prints and Photographs, The New York Public Library, Astor, Lenox and Tilden Foundations. In the view of the *largo do paço* (above), the viceregal palace is to the left. In the middle of the docks stands the public fountain.

century it included a hospital and a *recolhimento* (retreat) that functioned as an orphanage, as a place of seclusion for married women whose husbands were temporarily absent from the city, and, at times, as a penitentiary for elite women who had
strayed from their families' moral demands. Modeled after their counterparts in Lisbon, both the Misericórdia and the recolhimento together signified the ability of the
city's elites to reproduce not only metropolitan institutions but also metropolitan
virtues: piety, charity, sobriety, and purity.[7]

Returning to the northwest corner of the terreiro, the Rua Direita, one of the
city's busiest streets, led away from the older nuclear settlement toward São Bento's
hill and the Benedictine Monastery atop, where within its seventeenth-century
chapels ornate, gilded altars, painted images, and intricate *jacarandá* wood grates
and furniture displayed the mastery of European and local artists.[8] Beyond both the
Rua Direita and the terreiro, a grid of narrow, "well-paved," but often dirty, streets
and *largos* (squares) extended northwest to the foot of Conceição hill, southwest to
the hills of Santo António and Santa Teresa, and west to the Campo de Santa Anna,
a large meadow surrounded on three sides by houses and gardens. Most streets were
both commercial and residential. Many were named after prominent nearby land-
marks, such as the Rua da Cadeia (jail), or the Rua do Rosario, which began at the
Rua Direita and ended in front of the Church of the Rosary, home of the city's
largest black brotherhood. Other street names, such as Rua do Sabão (soap) and Rua
dos Ourives (goldsmith), evincing what Angel Rama described as the "metonymic
displacement" typical of colonial Latin American city streets, indicated the primary
object of exchange or service offered. The Rua do Ouvidor (magistrate), in turn, was
named after its most famous resident, the local circuit judge, who since the mid-
eighteenth century enjoyed a residence on the corner of the Rua da Quitanda (grocer). Such residential buildings were reportedly "of good appearance." Most were
two-storied, stone houses and many featured latticed-covered balconies that provided both shelter from the tropical summer sun and more famously, according to
visitors to the city, a place from which women of distinction could discreetly greet
passersby.[9]

In the eighteenth century this built environment had greatly expanded. Fortification, in particular, became a priority, as the century that opened with the French
sack of Rio in 1711 also witnessed the British capture of Havana in 1762. Reforms
of existing structures were accompanied by a series of new projects supervised by the
Swedish military engineer Jacob Funck. An expansion of the city's civilian infrastructure also began in the 1730s with the construction of a two-tiered aqueduct, extending from the hill of Santa Teresa to the city's center, completed under the supervision
of the Conde de Bobadela (Governor, 1733–1763) and the Portuguese architect and
engineer José Fernandes Pinto Alpoim, whose other projects in Rio included a hos-

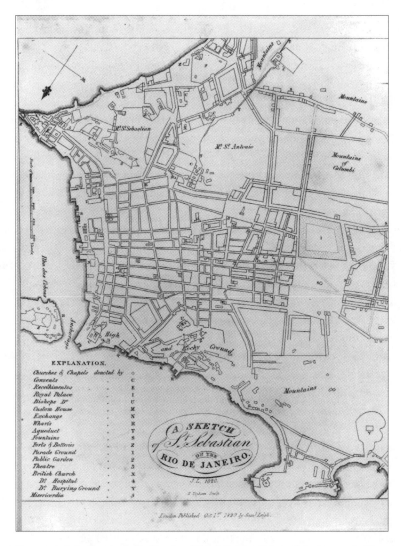

FIGURE 3: John Luccock, "A Sketch of San Sebastian," from John Luccock, *Notes on Rio de Janeiro and the southern parts of Brazil* . . . (London: Samuel Leigh, 1820). Copy and permission obtained from the General Research Division, The New York Public Library, Astor, Lenox and Tilden Foundations. The map runs from south to north. Before the arrival of the court, Luccock noted, the city was contained within narrow boundaries.

pital and residences for the governor and bishop. Major urban reforms then followed in the administrations of the Marquês de Lavradio (Viceroy, 1769–1779) and his successor, Luiz de Vasconcellos e Souza (Viceroy, 1779–1790). By the end of the eighteenth century, Rio de Janeiro featured new public fountains, roads, bridges, corrals, and slaughtering facilities.[10]

Another addition to the cityscape, the newly reformed customs house, demonstrated the link between the fertile Brazilian countryside and the world beyond its shores that Rio de Janeiro provided.[11] Indeed, life in the eighteenth-century city revolved around its bustling port. Beginning in the late seventeenth century, proximity to the new mining region of Minas Gerais gave the city strategic importance. In the second half of the eighteenth century Rio's port then surpassed Bahia's in volume to become firmly established as both the principal entrepot between Brazil and other parts of the empire and a major center of distribution for other regions of the colony.[12] The increasing importance of Rio's port also meant that the city became the focus of metropolitan attentions. In 1763 the Portuguese crown formally recognized the city's preeminence by moving the capital of Portuguese America there from Salvador. In the last decades of the eighteenth century, although the mining economy waned, trade remained lucrative. Rio's merchants exported to Portugal rice, sugar, cotton, coffee, hides, wood, and whale oil. From Lisbon arrived wine, wheat, flour, olives, salt, and manufactures to be sold in the city and, in many cases, reexported to other areas of Brazil. The economic growth generated by transatlantic trade was also accompanied by an expansion of production for internal consumption and interregional trade. Manioc from Bahia and Santa Catarina and *charque* (jerked beef) from Rio Grande do Sul were imported to Rio to be both consumed locally and distributed to nearby plantations.[13]

The wealth generated by trade was reflected in the city's steadily expanding marketplace and notable commercial vitality.[14] Rio's streets reportedly were lined with "shops of every kind" and crowded with pedestrians and slave-borne sedan chairs. By 1799 the city had over 1,300 registered commercial establishments, including *boticas* (pharmacies), *casas de café* (coffee houses), *casas de pasto* (eating houses), and tobacco shops. Taverns were found along the Rua São José. Wholesalers were concentrated on the Rua dos Pescadores and the Rua Direita, where in 1794 almost one hundred stores were located. In these "large and commodious" shops the city's residents could find regional products, as well as both legally and illegally imported European manufactures, including linens, silks, and silverware.[15] By the turn of the nineteenth century, the city's prosperity and well-being were even more dramatically manifest in an attractive *Passeio Publico* (public promenade). Built and maintained with African labor, it featured tile-covered benches, decorated pavilions, granite fountains, and marble statues designed by the famous Afro-Brazilian sculptor known as Mestre Valentim.[16] Its gardens boasted numerous examples of European and indigenous commercial crops and its main pavilion was lined with murals which, one English visitor explained, displayed "the principal productions to which that country was indebted for its opulence." There, he noted, "the gay society of Rio, after taking exercise in the evenings in the walks, often after hearing songs and music, [sat] down to partake of banquets, accompanied, sometimes, by music and fireworks."[17]

Those who partook of such moments of leisure and who, more generally, reaped the benefits of commerce were, however, the fortunate and the few. Indeed, although artisans, soldiers, and servants managed to avoid indigence, the majority of the city's residents were poor. An "enormous economic differentiation," Florentino and Fragoso explain, existed even among the propertied of Rio de Janeiro. As their recent study of *postmortem* inventories shows, at the end of the eighteenth century only 11 percent of the city's and nearby region's property owners controlled 75 percent of its wealth. This narrowly distributed wealth, in turn, depended on an expanding use of slave labor. Between 1790 and 1808 an average of almost 10,000 Africans, primarily from the regions of the Congo and Angola, arrived per year at the port of Rio de Janeiro.[18] By the second half of the eighteenth century the existing slave market near the city's center could scarcely accommodate new arrivals. In response to this increase, and so that the city's residents might avoid what he construed to be demoralizing encounters with the growing number of "disease-ridden and naked" Africans arriving to Brazil after a brutal transatlantic voyage, the Marquês de Lavradio had moved the market to Valongo, a more isolated northwestern district beyond Conceição Hill. There Africans were kept in warehouses until they were sold.[19] While most African slaves were then sent outside the city to work as agricultural laborers or miners, many remained in Rio as personal servants, dock workers, vendors, and artisans. As a result, by the end of the eighteenth century the growing population of Rio de Janeiro was as African as it was European. Indeed, in 1780 almost half of the captaincy's 200,000 inhabitants were enslaved. The other half comprised Portuguese and Brazilian-born whites, and people of color, a category that could include people of African and mixed ancestry born free as well as freed slaves.[20] Of the 45,000 to 60,000 people who lived in the city of Rio itself, 45 percent were identified as "white," 35 percent were slaves, and 20 percent were "freed *pardos*" (of mixed African and European ancestry) and "freed blacks."[21]

For royal officials in the city and its hinterland, this diverse and growing population meant increased threats to the maintenance of order and royal authority. More slaves meant more incidents of slave rebellion, flight, and the consequent formation of runaway communities—*quilombos*—on the margins of Portuguese settlement. In these cases, royal government in Rio, local municipal governments in the region, and slave owners turned to *capitães do mato* (bush captains), bounty hunters drawn from the ranks of white settlers and free people of color, paid for retrieving runaways dead or, preferably, alive. According to one report, the Conde de Bobadela was particularly zealous of these matters, seeking to provide regulation and local auxiliary forces for the expeditions. To maximize the exemplary effects of punitive expeditions against quilombos, slaves who died resisting a return to slavery were beheaded and "these heads were placed on posts in the principal towns" for all to behold "until time consumed them."[22]

While waging this war against runaway slaves, royal officials also trained their attentions on the specter of vagrancy (*vadiagem*). As one royal official explained his perception of the threat in 1798, vagrants "rob[bed] from the public the services that all vassals" owed to the king.[23] The problem of vagrancy, however, was not unique to the eighteenth century. From its inception the Portuguese empire was, as Russell-Wood has characterized it, "a world on the move"; it demanded the "constant flux and reflux of people" that resulted from both voluntary and involuntary journeys to missionize, to trade, and to settle. Consequently, as Laura de Mello e Souza has argued, the Portuguese crown promoted and depended on itinerancy even as it marginalized and criminalized itinerants. Often, the indigent in Portugal were recruited forcefully for military service that entailed a series of transitory assignments, while those associated with criminal activity, including vagrancy itself, were sentenced to punitive exile in one of various destinations in the *ultramar*.[24] Officials in eighteenth-century Rio de Janeiro, nevertheless, overlooked these historic and imperial dimensions of vagrancy, and the poverty of those accused of being vagrant, in favor of what they perceived to be particularly local and Brazilian circumstances. Although the *juiz de fora* (district crown judge) Balthazar da Silva Lisboa claimed the "luxury, limitless prostitution and vagrancy" in Rio were symptomatic of a reigning climate of moral decadence found in eighteenth-century Portugal as well,[25] royal officials more often conflated the category of vagrant, legally defined as anyone without a "master" or an "office," with people of color in general. "Judgments of indolence," as Mary Louise Pratt has noted of Spanish America, "remained quite compatible with the labor-intensive forms of servitude," which, in this case, sustained both Brazil's and the empire's economy.[26] Thus, Viceroy Vasconcellos e Souza and his successor the Conde de Resende (Viceroy, 1790–1801) warned of the connections among vagrancy, "unspeakable, extravagant acts," and "mulattos and blacks." The "innumerable Individuals who come here [Rio de Janeiro] without occupation," Resende reported in 1798, "are poor people and mostly Mulattos and Blacks" who "abuse their liberty indulging in every sort of vice and passing their lives in complete inaction, either because they do not have any means to earn their living or because they are not subjected to anyone who looks after their conduct."[27] Other administrative reports in turn focused on what were perceived to be the structural dimensions of vagrancy and stressed that it was the excessive number of slaves that produced both an idle and corrupt elite and a population of unoccupied slaves, held as symbols of wealth, rather than as productive labor. Slaves who had acquired skills, it was also argued, contributed to vagrancy by taking jobs away from free men with the same training.[28]

To solve what they perceived to be the mounting problem of vagrancy and to curtail the range of threats to the city's social and political hierarchies ostensibly posed by people of color, royal officials limited "gatherings" of "blacks and mulattos" and met infractions with incarceration and forced service to the crown. Vasconcellos boasted that the funds generated by the labor of vagrants provided for the maintenance of public works.[29] His predecessor Lavradio also had promoted the institution of the *terços dos homens pardos* (regiments of men of color). These regiments not only contributed to security and defense, argued Lavradio, but also provided members with necessary examples of discipline, obedience, and respect. Indeed, Lavradio advised his successor in 1779, the establishment of effective royal authority among the region's poor and itinerant inhabitants was a matter deserving particular attention and "the greatest care." For "an anxious spirit" may appear among these people, he warned, and "talking to them in a language that they find more appealing, and coaxing them into insolence, they [will] quickly forget what they owe to follow his flag."[30] Thus, for royal officials Rio de Janeiro's eighteenth-century growth and prosperity brought a sense of vulnerability and an increasing awareness of the challenges of governance. As we shall see below, as the eighteenth century drew to a close these potential threats to the city's political and social order would only increase.

"Trêmulo Jardim, Cidade Erratica": Eighteenth-Century Rio de Janeiro as Spectacle

Both the cityscape and the commercial and social routines of Rio de Janeiro's residents were momentarily transformed by public commemorations.[31] Together with annual religious festivals and processions, residents celebrated the arrival of new royal and ecclesiastical authorities with the appropriate displays of pomp. In 1747, for example, for the ceremonial entrance of the new bishop, Frei António do Desterro Malheiro, residents staged an elaborate procession along flower-lined streets, past windows decorated with silk and tapestries, through seven triumphal arches, each one invoking a classical virtue. The celebration culminated at the city's cathedral, where a mass was held and the bishop formally assumed his new post. Festivities then continued into the night with luminaries and music.[32] Similar commemorations marked the beginning of a new viceregal government. Like the bishop, the viceroy formally "took possession" of his office in the cathedral before religious officials, members of the city's town council, distinguished residents, and "the people of this City" who all gathered to witness a reading of the orders that nominated the crown's new representative in Brazil.[33] Although both the bishop and the viceroy had powers that extended beyond the city of Rio de Janeiro, such commemorations were primarily local affairs. Consequently, they heightened the city's residents' sense of living together in the capital of Portuguese America.

In contrast, public commemorations of the royal life cycle, of the sovereign's birth, his or her Acclamation to the throne, marriage and death, sought to reaffirm the existence of a larger imperial political community to which the city's residents also belonged. The commemorations of a royal birth, for example, staged simultaneously throughout the Portuguese dominions, were intended to reveal an essential relationship between the empire's parts and its whole. As one memorialist in Rio suggested, unity and relations of reciprocity were expressed in both collective and individual gestures. While the residents prayed for the distant "king and kingdom," they also "congratulated each other," he explained, "as if each one of them contained all of the happiness of the State."[34] The lavish celebrations of the royal life cycle, in this sense, allowed the city's residents both to witness the splendor of royalty as it was revealed in processions and festive ephemera, and to participate in a performance intended for an imagined imperial audience. Rio de Janeiro, in other words, became what one memorialist described as the "extraordinary spectacle . . . a brilliant garden, impassioned City" that the whole empire could behold. As accounts of such celebrations were published subsequently in Lisbon, recognition of the city's allegiance, wealth, and status among the crown's other dominions was guaranteed.[35]

This transformation of Rio de Janeiro as spectacle into text often implied bringing both local and imperial tensions to the surface. While, as was the case in local festivals, royal commemorations encompassed a careful display of the hierarchies that existed among Rio's residents, as a text they also established the city's status within the empire with boasts of an ostensibly collective luxury and opulence. This collectivity, in turn, was expressed as an imminent transcendence of social boundaries. As one resident-memorialist described the commemoration of the birth of Maria I's first-born son in 1762, all of Rio's residents appeared "to be so well-dressed that the nobles were distinguished from the common people only by their faces and by their names, rather than by their attire." Even the impoverished Franciscan friars became emblems of luxury and, as the memorialist further explained to his distant readers with a reversal of imperial geography, it "appeared as if Rome had been left with only the sovereignty of its land, as the attentions of the Vatican were transferred to Rio de Janeiro."[36] Thus, the celebration of an all-encompassing imperial monarchy was eclipsed by the celebration of the city itself.

The tension between the staging of local allegiances and the metropolitan discourse of imperial unity, described in Chapter 1, intensified in the early 1790s as residents witnessed an extraordinary counterpoint to their lavish commemorations of monarchy, empire, and Rio de Janeiro: the ritual punishment of political dissidence. In 1789 officials discovered a plot to overthrow Portuguese royal government in Brazil in the name of "liberty" and republicanism. Although the center of the conspiracy, apparently inspired by French philosophy and North American tracts, was the nearby region of Minas where the accused conspirators lived, it was the city of Rio de Janeiro, as the viceregal capital, that hosted the royal *alçada* (special court) convened to adjudicate the case and where the final spectacle of judgment took place.[37] For Rio's residents, as one royal judge surmised, it was a tense and uncertain time. After initial inquiries, the scope of the investigation had expanded to include the city, as officials pursued their suspicions of local collaboration. Fear and the desire to avoid costly entanglements also reduced the intense trade between the city's merchants and the Minas elite. Indeed, in 1792, with the alçada drawing to a close, it became impossible, as an anonymous memorialist recalled, "to hide the oppression" that was felt. "Many retired to the countryside," he reported, "communications diminished," and the city's streets were emptied.[38]

When the day of sentencing finally arrived, those who remained in Rio awoke to find a well-orchestrated show of force in auxiliary and European regiments stationed throughout the city. The ceremony of judgment, a veritable drama in three acts, began with the reading of the sentence over the course of eighteen hours within the tribunal's chambers, where the viceroy, judges, defendants, priests, and guards were gathered. The figure of an army lieutenant, Joaquim José da Silva Xavier, known as *Tiradentes* (tooth-puller), took center stage. Tiradentes was the most admittedly republican of the defendants and, according to royal officials, he had confessed to playing a central role in both the plotting and spreading word of the rebellion. For him, full and exemplary punishment was the order of the day. Tiradentes was to be hanged and quartered. His head would be displayed in Minas Gerais, his body parts placed at the entrance to the captaincy, and his home would be destroyed. The other defendants, the judge then explained, were to be given punishments that were similarly severe.[39] The second act then began with the defendants' pleas for reconsideration and culminated, as one resident recalled, with an orchestrated surprise. With the accused and other royal officials gathered once again in the tribunal's chambers, the judge proceeded to the podium and produced a previously drafted letter of royal clemency that he had brought with him from Lisbon. The merciful monarch, the letter revealed, would spare the lives of ten defendants and banish them to Africa instead. Tiradentes alone would be hanged. News of such a magnanimous act reportedly was received throughout the city with both relief and euphoria.

As Kenneth Maxwell has argued, Tiradentes provided the crown with a helpful scapegoat. On the one hand, because he was neither as wealthy nor as socially prominent as the other defendants, revealing him as the leader "minimiz[ed] and ridicul[ed] the objectives of the movement." On the other hand, his public punishment provided the crown with an opportunity to reaffirm the nature and scope of royal authority and to suggest that similar plotting would produce a similar response. Thus, royal officials seized on the opportunity presented by the tribunal and provided a lesson in political loyalty that aimed to deflect any feelings of sympathy for the defendants that Rio's residents may have harbored.[40] Accordingly, the final act of the spectacle of judgment began with a swift execution only two days later, followed by commemorative festivities that lasted almost a week. A mass was held to give thanks that Rio had been spared from the ignoble plans for revolution and, as a friar who had witnessed the proceedings explained, "to persuade the people to be faithful and loyal to their pious and merciful sovereign and to pray that God would protect both her life and the empire." Allegory then made the lessons of the Minas conspiracy even clearer. During one commemoration participants beheld the image of a forceful, just, and merciful monarch, flanked by Hercules and Astrea, confronting the figure of "America" who, kneeling at the foot of the throne, "reverently" offered a platter of hearts that "signified the love and fidelity of Americans." Completing the scene were the conspirators themselves represented by the figure of a naked, kneeling Indian, "pledging allegiance to the sovereign and begging for mercy." A savage, treasonous America thus was rendered helpless by the powerful Portuguese crown. And just as early Portuguese settlers and missionaries had instructed the Brazilian coastal Indians, this spectacle of adjudication and punishment taught that although disobedience could lead to death, in contrast, humiliation, sacrifice, and allegiance paved the way to reconciliation and redemption. Rio de Janeiro, having weathered the threat of treason, was saved. Once again consumed by images of an invincible monarchy and a unified empire, its residents were bestowed with the knowledge that, as the anonymous memorialist explained, the pardon of the Minas conspirators derived from both "absolute power and absolute piety" and the sovereign vision of clemency that "extended itself . . . from sea to sea, embracing finally the extremities of the earth."[41]

"Dangerous Times"

The pardon for the conspirators was not, the memorialist also claimed, "the effect of ordinary and common causes." It was, on the contrary, an extraordinary "act of absolute power" for extraordinary and "dangerous times."[42] The independence of the United States had challenged both the nature of the relationship between Europe and America and the virtue of monarchy, leaving Portuguese royal officials to wonder whether, or simply when, the residents of Brazil would find their experiences to be analogous to those of the thirteen British colonies, as the Minas conspirators reportedly had. After all, although the *Inconfidência Mineira*, as the conspiracy came to be known, was squarely defeated, by the time Tiradentes was hanged and the rest of the conspirators banished, similar claims to "liberty" had inspired a successful revolution in France. And, even as revolutionaries there began the process of constructing a new republican government, in the French colony of Saint Domingue slaves began an ultimately successful campaign to rid that island of both the institution of slavery and the population of white landowners. Indeed, by the turn of the nineteenth century the Atlantic had become a world where empire, monarchy, and slavery, the once apparently durable foundations of politics, society, and economy in Rio de Janeiro and Brazil, had been forsaken.

Although between the inconfidência in Minas and arrival of the court in 1808, Rio de Janeiro witnessed no serious threat to the authority of the Portuguese crown, events in the United States, France, and Haiti did begin to reshape the city's political culture. For royal officials it was time that called for shoring up defenses. Rio de Janeiro's busy port, they feared, made the city particularly vulnerable to revolutionary ideas. As the city had neither a printing press nor a vigorous book trade through which such ideas could be disseminated,[43] officials focused on the people suspected of endorsing insurgent agendas. Existing restrictions on foreigners—visitors to the city from beyond the Portuguese empire—were strictly enforced. As the British diplomat John Barrow reported of a visit to Rio de Janeiro in the early 1790s, the viceregal government did not to allow "any stranger to remain on shore after sunset" or "walk the streets in the daytime, without a soldier at his heels."[44]

The most energetic response to the threat of revolution, however, focused on vassals of the Portuguese crown: an invasive inquest of suspected local dissidence led by the Viceroy Conde de Resende. Resende had arrived in Rio as the Minas investigations were beginning and had presided over the execution of Tiradentes. As these events unfolded, correspondence received from his advisors in Lisbon informed him of French advances in Europe.[45] Convinced that the city was vulnerable to a now clearly expanding sphere of revolutionary influence, Resende decided that rather than wait for an insurrection he would go on the offensive. Thus, in 1794 he ordered a broad investigation to determine who "with scandalous liberty, had dared to include in his discourse subjects offensive to religion, and to speak of European public affairs with praise and approbation for the present French system" and who "beyond such scandalous discourses had taken steps to form or suggest a seditious plot."[46] The unstated targets of the investigation were the members of a local literary society, established in 1786 with the assistance of the Viceroy Vasconcellos e Souza so that its members might "not forget . . . what they had learned in other countries" and share new knowledge of "public interest" and "utility." Its members had stopped meeting during the investigation into the Minas conspiracy, but in 1794 they were instructed by Resende himself to reconvene.[47] The fact that Resende gave these orders only a few months before the formal investigation began later led to speculation that he had set a trap. It was also the case, however, that the society's members were less than grateful for his gesture, for Resende and his administration were the preferred subjects of their often satirical commentary.[48] Shortly after making contact with informants, Resende had heard enough rumor and accusation to make arrests.

The most prominent defendants in the investigation were Mariano José Pereira da Fonseca and Manuel Inácio da Silva Alvarenga. A native of Rio de Janeiro, Fonseca was sent at the age of eleven to study at the Royal College at Mafra in Portugal. From there he went on to receive degrees in mathematics and philosophy at the University of Coimbra. When he returned to Rio, only a few years before the investigation began, he took with him a well-established reputation and the friendship of several courtiers. Upon resettling in the city, he established a business using the inheritance received from his father, a successful merchant. At the same time, hoping to continue his intellectual pursuits, he sought out Silva Alvarenga and urged him to reconvene the city's literary society.[49] Silva Alvarenga, in turn, was born in Minas, and identified as the son of a musician and a woman of color. In spite of his more modest origins, he also studied at Coimbra, where he received a degree in canon law. Before returning to Brazil he distinguished himself as a poet and established alliances with people close to the Marquês de Pombal. Back in Minas as captain-major of a militia of men of color, he also began to work as a lawyer in the region's capital. In 1782 he then left Minas to take a position as Royal Professor of Rhetoric in Rio de Janeiro. There his residence became an intellectual focal point, providing a venue for informal discussions as well as the more structured meetings of the literary society.[50]

Among the other nine defendants were a professor of Greek, a doctor, a surgeon, a property owner, a goldsmith, and several artisans. Almost half of the accused were Portuguese, while most of those born in Brazil were from the region and city of Rio. Beyond their interest in the literary society, they appear to have had little in common, with the possible exception being, as David Higgs has observed, that most were older, unmarried men, with fewer domestic responsibilities that would impinge on their opportunities to both attend meetings and at other times "stand about engaged in speculative chat." The investigation also involved sixty-five witnesses, including Resende's informants. They too had mixed professional backgrounds and birthplaces. The overwhelming majority of all those involved in the investigation (defendants, spies, and voluntary and involuntary witnesses) were male and white. Although few were near the top of the local social hierarchy, few were at the bottom.[51] Among these men who fueled Resende's sense of impending peril, many were well read and well informed about events on both sides of the Atlantic. Fonseca's not surprisingly well-stocked library featured a selection of dictionaries, grammars, and atlases, as well as works on medicine, natural science, theology, law, economy, travel literature, and poetry. Testimony also revealed that European newspapers and pamphlets, together with works by Raynal and Mably and Rousseau's *Emile,* circulated among the defendants, and their letters, confiscated along with their possessions, shared speculations about the future and made clever references to forbidden authors.[52]

Along with reading books and worldly correspondence, the men under investigation had kept up on current affairs and debates by attending the meetings of the literary society, held in Alvarenga's house, where "discourses in the French language" were read aloud and where, as a clandestinely drafted charter stipulated, no one would enjoy "superiority" and discussions would be "conducted in a democratic mode."[53] There lawyers joined shopkeepers and soldiers with, as Higgs has noted, little if any "systematic separation between the world of the rich and poor, of loyal and disloyal, of long-established and newly arrived."[54] Interest in discussing politics was not, however, confined to the formal society itself. Other private residences as well as public and semipublic places also served as venues for conversation and debate: "the house of Dr. José da França and his pharmacy on the Rua Direita," "the docks by the [viceregal] Palace," "the stairs of the church of the hospice," "Dom Manuel's beach, behind the boiler," and the Amarante pharmacy which, as one informant reported, was regularly transformed into "an assembly house."[55] New inquiries into the nature of politics thus were associated with emerging forms of sociability and new delineations of social space. The meaning of the house itself, István Jancsó explains, "the privileged locale of private life" was "enriched" by gatherings of literary societies while the city's poorer residents appropriated public spaces, such as street corners and shops, for their private discussions of public affairs. In this range of private places made public and public places made private, residents exchanged ideas and considered books they had read as well as those about which they had only heard, creating a continuum of literacy and orality that accounted for, as Jancsó argues, the printed text, the written and copied text, and the spoken word.[56]

Among the preferred topics of conversation and debate were the French Revolution and the revolutionary wars. Consequently, foreign-language newspapers and the city's few French residents were regarded as important sources of information.[57] In passionate discussions of French actions, Resende's defendants reportedly appealed to both general principle and history. A tailor recalled a conversation in which several of the accused argued that "the law of the French is just and sacred because it is taken from Holy Scripture, that as a king can kill men, so can men kill the king." Along these lines, the goldsmith, António Gonçalves dos Santos, has offered another defense of the regicidal French. "The death of the king of France was just," he explained, "because his oath to the assembly was false." The master-carpenter, João da

Silva Antunes, in turn, down-played the revolutionary regime's injustices as actions common to other governments as well. Those "who the assembly had punished," he argued, "were traitors who didn't want to respect the new laws, and if [the revolutionaries] had confiscated sacred vessels and lamps from the churches, this was nothing new, because the [Portuguese] King Dom Sebastião had done the same thing when he went to Africa."[58]

Comments on the French revolution and the revolutionary wars also led to criticism of other European governments. Jacob Miliete, a Frenchman residing in Rio, insisted that French aggression was just because "the kings of Europe were all thieves," an argument that others reportedly found convincing. Francisco António, in turn, argued that the fight against France was unjust because it was motivated only by royal self-interest. "The war that the other kings were waging against [France]," he claimed, "was not motivated by devotion [to their vassals]," but rather by the will "to rid themselves of what sooner or later they would experience." The Portuguese monarchy too faced similar charges of self-interest and wrongdoing, as memories of the Minas conspiracy were fresh. Antunes was known to have said that the conspirators' sentences were unjust. The plot, he claimed, had been invented by the government as a ploy to confiscate the property of the wealthy defendants.[59] Members of the literary society, including Alvarenga and Fonseca, speculated on potential support for the conspiracy as well, suggesting "that the Minas conspiracy defendants were treated like rebels because they were unsuccessful, but if they had succeeded, they would have been heroes."[60]

Many of the most heated and uneasy debates involved the question of religion. In one such discussion, the pharmacist Dr. França provocatively claimed that "there were no such things as miracles and that not even the saints could perform them." According to Resende's informants, it was this kind of transgression, linked to a dangerous exposure to foreign ideas, that led some to unequivocally support the arrests. Indeed, a Franciscan friar close to the viceroy, reportedly angered by Alvarenga's satire of the clergy, provided the first denunciation of the literary society's members.[61] Yet Alvarenga and the literary society's members did not focus their attacks on religious faith or dogma per se. Rather they challenged what they perceived to be the excessive influence of the church in government and education as well as embarrassing examples of fanaticism. At one of their meetings, Silveira Frade reported to Resende, "after having read some discourses in French against the Sovereignty of Monarchs, they said that the kingdom had been given over to friars." Several members also denounced the prince regent's disgracefully superstitious act of sending for holy water from the Jordan River so that the princess would conceive, and on another occasion, in Frade's house, João Marques, a professor of Greek, attacked Portuguese King João V as "a bad king, fanatic and ignorant."[62]

Marques' remark also revealed an interest in the nature of monarchy and the question of political authority in the wake of the French Revolution and French republicanism. Indeed, one defendant claimed, the French Revolution had shown that "bad governments should be shaken and cast off."[63] The "laws of the French were good," the wood carver Francisco António asserted, "because of the equality that they introduced among men," adding "that only when the French arrived here would such things be set straight."[64] Silva Alvarenga, in turn, was accused of having argued similarly that "the plan of the French was the best that one could believe and that no one had the obligation to obey only one man."[65] The lieutenant José da Costa Cravador had gone further and "praised republics" saying that they were better than monarchies,[66] while another, Frade reported, had said that soon "there would be no more crowned heads because the people had opened their eyes and discovered their rights."[67]

Reflections on political authority in the Portuguese world, however, did not always conclude with unqualified endorsements of republicanism. Frade, the informant, made self-serving claims that in conversations with the accused he had always maintained that "the liberty implied in republics is [not in harmony with] the customs of our nation, which has always been accustomed to obey one sovereign. The sovereigns of Portugal," he testified he had insisted, "had always been fathers of the country and they loved their people like children."[68] For most, however, no longer reassured by such a simple paternalism, to defend monarchy meant both to attack specific instances of tyranny and corruption and to recognize the popular origins of the Portuguese crown's sovereignty and the limits of paternal authority. Francisco António, for example, praised the French because their actions could be seen as just within the framework of the old regime. Because kings received their power from the people, he explained, "a tyrannical king should die on the gallows, as any other wrongdoer."[69] Kingship, in other words, could be just but it was no longer sacred. The cross was sacred but "the king is like anyone of us," Francisco António had responded to the carpenter Manuel Pereira Landim's claim that kings were "earthly gods." Alvarenga too was overheard declaring that "liberty had been given by God to men," rather than to kings.[70] Thus, as the soldier Joaquim Cardoso had explained, the "rights of a nation were superior to those of any king, because upon the nation were based the rights of the king and not the rights of the nation upon the king."[71] In a discussion near the docks, the *caixeiro* (clerk) Manuel da Costa Santos had given the most detailed analysis of the crisis of the old regime. "All kingdoms," he explained, "had statutes, and so the Kingdom of Portugal has the Laws of Lamego and when [kings] took possession of [the throne], they took an oath to conserve peace among the people." But "after time had passed," Santos continued, "their intent became to be the lords over all of the vassals' property, because of the bad counselors they had, because all that nobles want is to have everything for themselves." For the monarchy the challenge presented to kingship by the French Revolution, therefore, was not insurmountable. Kings simply needed to respect popular sovereignty, to rid their councils of the corrupt, and, as Francisco António insisted, to learn how to govern.[72]

Years of confinement, interrogation, and cross-examination thus yielded evidence of curiosity about the French Revolution and European affairs, at times irreverent discussion of the church and royal government, and understandings of monarchy decidedly more complex than those offered by official commemorations. There was, however, no proof of conspiracy. In the meantime letters from Fonseca's influential friends in Lisbon protested and pleaded for royal intervention on his behalf. Finally, in 1797, the new Minister of Overseas Affairs, Rodrigo de Souza Coutinho, wrote to Resende and instructed him that the defendants should be either released or sent to Lisbon. In response to this ultimatum, the presiding judge ended the investigation and, after restating his accusations, his discoveries, and the gravity of the subject at hand, he reluctantly recommended their release. After all, he conceded in a carefully worded reassertion of the merits of his case, the alternative to release, sending the defendants to Lisbon, would lead to a more public affair, and it was not in the crown's best interest, he reminded his superior, to allow the French to discover that their "abominable principles" had sympathizers in Brazil.[73]

At a time when "'speaking about' was as disconcerting as 'speaking against,'"[74] it is not surprising that the image of heady discussions that emerged from the witnesses' and defendants' depositions alarmed royal officials in Rio. For even considering the inevitable fabrications and exaggerations of sycophantic informants, as well as the ultimate absence of a conspiracy, both the radical proposals as well as the commentary on monarchy challenged the image of a simply loyal populace upon which, Portuguese royal officials believed, the maintenance of empire depended. Within Rio de Janeiro there were people of varying rank and status who wanted to talk about politics and, more specifically, about the revolutionary transatlantic context and the future of monarchy. Such discussions, reinvigorated by incoming news from Europe, amounted to what David Higgs has characterized as "layers and forms of disrespect for the status quo at a time when the reverberations of the Jacobin experiment in France sounded throughout the Atlantic world."[75] And as the Minas conspiracy suggested, discussions and disrespect could lead to systematic criticism and to a questioning of the very "organization of power" by those who, as Jancsó argues, having glimpsed "the politics of the future in the interstices of the present," were prepared to endorse new forms of government even when this implied sedition.[76]

Indeed, within one year after the Rio defendants were released, the possibilities of a well-articulated and revolutionary challenge to the imperial regime had extended into the core of colonial society itself. This time, however, the stage for insurrection was Salvador, Bahia, where in 1798 popular rebels, including slaves and free people of color, openly inspired by the French Revolution, called for both independence from Portugal and the end of "discrimination between white, black and mulatto."[77] Punishment was exemplary and, in this case, four of the leaders were executed. Yet the message of the rebellion, now institutionalized as the colony of Saint Domingue became an independent Haiti, could not be suppressed. Although slave owners in Rio de Janeiro were spared a similar rebellion, in the city the significance of these events was manifest. Just one year after Haitian independence, in 1805, the image of the Haitian General Jean Jacques Dessallines appeared on the medallions of several members of Rio's black militia. It was "notable," wrote a horrified local magistrate in an order to have the portraits "ripped from their chests," that such an image should be worn by *cabras* and freedmen who were skilled at handling artillery. Equally notable, as the historian Luiz Mott has argued, was the speed with which news of Haiti's independence reached Brazil. Alongside, and perhaps at times in conjunction with, the formal and informal channels through which members of Rio de Janeiro's literary society had debated the merits of revolution, slaves and free people of color had formed their own networks to exchange ideas about a changing Atlantic world.[78]

The eighteenth century had brought Rio de Janeiro growth, prosperity, and political preeminence. Yet, by the 1790s it had become clear to colonial officials and elites that this prosperity and further integration into the Atlantic had come at a price. Rio de Janeiro was now part of a world in which empire, monarchy, and slavery had been successfully challenged. Although the decade leading up to the prince regent's arrival at the city saw no overt challenge to royal government, the city's residents did seek to understand what these developments meant for their lives. As we shall see in the following chapters, in the 1810s their debates then were both reinvigorated and transformed. Their increasingly urban yet intimate Rio de Janeiro, the residents learned in the first days of 1808, would serve as the Portuguese prince regent's new royal court.[79] Upon receiving "the unexpected news," as one resident recalled, "everything here changed."[80]

NOTES

1. For descriptions of arrival at Rio de Janeiro in the late eighteenth century see George Staunton, *An authentic account of an embassy from the King of Great Britain to the Emperor of China . . .* (London: Robert Campbell, 1799), 78; James Wilson, *A missionary voyage to the southern Pacific Ocean, performed in the years 1796, 1797, 1798, in the Ship Duff, commanded by Captain James Wilson, Compiled from journals of the officers and missionaries . . .* (London: Chapman, 1799), 34; and John Barrow, *A Voyage to Cochinchina, in the years 1792 and 1793 . . .* (London: Cadell and Davies, 1806), 77. "If the Portuguese of Rio have done but

little towards improving nature," Barrow arrogantly commented, "they are entitled at least to the negative merit of not having disfigured her."

2. In the early eighteenth century, Luiz da Cunha attempted to counter prevailing notions of American inferiority and difference with claims that Brazil's cities were settled by "many and good Portuguese" who relied on slave labor only as the people of Lisbon did, while Brazil's indigenous people (*tapuyos do sertão*) "differed only in color from the rustic people of [Portugal's] provinces." See Luiz da Cunha, *Instrucções inéditas de Dom Luiz da Cunha a Marco António de Azevedo Coutinho* (Coimbra: Imprensa da Universidade, 1930), 217–218.

3. Luiz Gonçalves dos Santos, *Memórias para servir à História do Reino do Brasil* t. 1 (1825) (Belo Horizonte/São Paulo: Itatiaia/EDUSP, 1981), 167. Gonçalves dos Santos cites the sixteenth-century epic poem by Luiz de Camões, *Os Lusíadas* (1572), Canto VII, est. 30–31; [José Vasconcellos e Souza], the Marquês de Bellas, [parecer (plan for reforms)], n.d. [ca. 1808], transcribed in Ângelo Pereira, *D. João VI, principe e rei* v. 3 (Lisbon: Empresa Nacional de Publicidade, 1956), 40. Sérgio Buarque de Holanda also argued that the arrival of the court inaugurated a "new discovery of Brazil" produced by foreigners rather than by the Portuguese exiles. See his "A herança colonial—sua desagregação" in *História geral da civilização brasileira* t. 2, v. 1, ed. Sérgio Buarque de Holanda (São Paulo: DIFEL, 1985), 13.

4. Barrow, *Voyage*, 77, 79; Gilberto Ferrez, *O Paço da Cidade do Rio de Janeiro* (Rio de Janeiro: Fundação Nacional Pró-Memória, 1985), 15, 25; Brasil Gerson, *História das ruas do Rio de Janeiro* (Rio de Janeiro: Editôra Souza, n.d.), 33, 38–39; Luiz Edmundo, *O Rio de Janeiro no tempo dos vice-teis* (Rio de Janeiro: Editôra Aurora, 1951), 18, 504; and Clarival do Prado Valladares, *Rio, análise iconográfica do barroco e neoclássico remanentes no Rio de Janeiro* v. 1 (Rio de Janeiro: Bloch Editores, 1978), 39 and figure 378. See also the letter of an anonymous crew member in the royal convoy to Brazil, transcribed in Ângelo Pereira, *Os filhos de elrei D. João VI* (Lisbon: Empresa Nacional de Publicidade, 1946), 127. The terreiro is also referred to as the Largo do Carmo, Terreiro do Carmo, and Largo do Paço. The residence of Francisco Barreto Teles de Meneses burned in a fire in 1790.

5. Staunton, *An authentic account*, 79; J.H. Tuckey, *An Account of a voyage to establish a colony at Port Philip in Bass's Strait, on the south coast of New South Wales, in his Majesty's Ship Calcutta, in the years 1802–3–4* (London: Longman, Hurst, Rees and Orme, 1805), 50. Inmates were maintained by their families. Those who had no nearby family or who were too poor to count on such maintenance were allowed to beg. See Edmundo, *Rio de Janeiro*, 472.

6. The Misericórdia, founded in Lisbon at the end of the fifteenth century, assisted orphans, widows, prisoners, and the infirm. See C.R. Boxer, *The Golden Age of Brazil, 1695–1750, Growing Pains of a Colonial Society* (Berkeley: University of California Press, 1962), 135–137. The classic work on the Misericórdia at Salvador, Bahia is A.J.R. Russell-Wood, *Fidalgos and Philanthropists: The Santa Casa da Misericórdia da Bahia, 1550–1755* (Berkeley: University of California Press, 1968).

7. One eighteenth-century English visitor described the recolhimento as a place where "the incontinent fair weep for, and atone for their faults." See Tuckey, *An Account*, 48. On recolhimentos in late colonial Brazil see Leila Mezan Algranti, *Honradas e devotas: mulheres da Colônia: Condição feminina nos conventos e recolhimentos do Sudeste do Brasil, 1750–1822* (Rio de Janeiro: José Olympio, 1993). On the city's growth beyond the original settlement, see Gerson, *História das ruas*, 11–15; and Nestor Goulart Reis Filho, *Contribuição ao estudo da*

evolução urbana do Brasil (1500–1720) (São Paulo: Livraria Pioneira/EDUSP, 1968), 117.

8. Valladares, *Rio*, figures 10–62. The jacarandá is a dark-wooded tree indigenous to Brazil.

9. Angel Rama, *The Lettered City*, trans. and ed. John Charles Chasteen (Durham: Duke University Press, 1996), 25–26. The *largo* refers to a widening of a thoroughfare, James Holston explains, and reflects the "street system of public spaces" in urban colonial Brazil. See James Holston, *The Modernist City: An Anthropological Critique of Brasília* (Chicago: University of Chicago Press, 1989), 109. On Rio de Janeiro's streets and other features of the urban environment see *Planta da Cidade de S. Sebastião do Rio de Janeiro levantada por ordem de Sua Alteza Real o Principe Regente Nosso Senhor no anno de 1808* . . . (Rio de Janeiro: Impressão Régia, 1812); Staunton, *An authentic account*, 79; Tuckey, *An Account*, 45, 64–65; Edmundo, *Rio de Janeiro*, 11–12, 26; Gerson, *História das ruas*, 46–48, 56–57, 64–65, 83, 192; J.M.P.S., *Definição da amizade* . . . (1816), in *O Rio de Janeiro na literatura Portugueza*, ed. Jacinto Prado Coelho (Lisbon: Comissão Nacional das Commemorações do IV Centenário do Rio de Janeiro, [1965]), 113; G.M. Keith, *A voyage to South America, and the Cape of Good Hope in His Majesty's Gun Brig, The Protector* (London: Richard Phillips, 1810), 21; Wilson, *A missionary voyage*, 33; Barrow, *Voyage*, 84, 92–93, 95; and Dauril Alden, *Royal Government in Colonial Brazil, with Special Reference to the Administration of the Marquis of Lavradio, Viceroy, 1769–1779* (Berkeley: University of California Press, 1968), 48. English visitors to Rio often speculated about the function of the lattices and many commented on women's habit of tossing flowers from their balconies, a custom that was apparently in decline in the early years of the nineteenth century.

10. Carlos Lemos, José Roberto Teixeira Leite, and Pedro Manuel Gismonti, *The Art of Brazil* (New York: Harper & Row, 1983), 86–88; Staunton, *An authentic account*, 79; Luiz de Almeida Portugal, Marquês de Lavradio, "Relatório . . . entregando o governo a Luiz de Vasconcellos e Souza, que o succedeu no vice-reinado," *RIHGB* 16 (January 1843), 414; Luiz de Vasconcellos e Souza, "Officio . . . com a cópia da relação instructiva e circunstanciada, para ser entregue ao seu successor," *RIHGB* 14 (July 1842). On fortification projects see correspondence from Jacob Funck and his assistant, Francisco João Rossio, in "Capitania do Rio de Janeiro, Correspondência de varias authoridades e avulsos," *RIHGB* 65, pt. 1 (1902), 183–204; Alden, *Royal Government*, 52, 222–223, 428; and David Kendrick Underwood, "The Pombaline Style and International Neo-classicism in Lisbon and Rio de Janeiro" (Ph.D. dissertation, University of Pennsylvania, 1988). Underwood places Rio's reform projects within the context of urban reform in Pombaline Portugal that gained momentum after the earthquake of 1755.

11. See the report on the customs house project in Vasconcellos e Souza, "Officio," 164. On this and other aspects of the port's infrastructure that were frequently reformed, see Corcino Medeiros dos Santos, *Relações comerciais do Rio de Janeiro com Lisboa (1763–1808)* (Rio de Janeiro: Tempo Brasileiro, 1980), 92–102.

12. Between 1796 and 1807 the port of Rio accounted for 38 percent of all imports and 34 percent of all exports. See João Fragoso and Manolo Florentino, *O Arcaísmo como Projeto: Mercado Atlântico, Sociedade Agrária e Elite Mercantile no Rio de Janeiro, c. 1790–c.1840* (Rio de Janeiro: Diodorim, 1993), 38–39. Fragoso and Florentino base their analysis on data furnished by José Jobson Arruda, *O Brasil no comércio colonial* (São Paulo: Ática, 1980), as well as

on their respective monographs: João Luiz Ribeiro Fragoso, *Homens de Grossa Aventura: Acumulação e Hierarquia na Praça Mercantil do Rio de Janeiro (1790–1830)* (Rio de Janeiro: Arquivo Nacional, 1991); and Manolo Garcia Florentino, *Em Costas Negras: Uma História do Tráfico Atlântico de Escravos entre a África e o Rio de Janeiro (Séculos XVIII e XIX)* (Rio de Janeiro: Arquivo Nacional, 1993).

13. Fragoso and Florentino, *Arcaísmo*, 41; Eulalia Maria Lahmeyer Lobo, *História do Rio de Janeiro (do capital comercial ao capital industrial financeiro)* v. 1 (Rio de Janeiro: IBMEC, 1978), 55, 60–61.

14. Staunton, *An authentic account*, 79. Staunton observed that the economy was "thriving," dwellings were in "good condition," the markets were well stored, and many buildings were new. Contemporary statistics compiled by António Duarte Nunes, a lieutenant in an artillery regiment, also indicate economic and commercial vitality. In 1792 there were 110 wholesale establishments and 1,007 *lojas de varejo e oficinas* (retailers and workshops). In 1794 the number of wholesale establishments rose 13 percent to 126, and retailers were up 8 percent to 1,098. In 1799, although the number of registered wholesalers declined 23 percent to 97, the number of registered retailers and offices rose 16 percent to 1,311. See [António Duarte Nunes], "Almanaque da cidade do Rio de Janeiro para o ano de 1792," *RIHGB* 266 (Jannuary–March 1965), 207–209; idem, "Almanaque da cidade do Rio de Janeiro para o ano de 1794," *RIHGB* 266 (January–March 1965), 276–279; idem, "Almanaque da cidade de S. Sebastião do Rio de Janeiro [1799]," *RIHGB* 267 (April–June 1965), 194–198. An earlier, less detailed, report stated that in 1789 there were 2,107 commercial establishments registered in the city. See "Memórias públicas e econômicas da cidade de São Sebastião do Rio de Janeiro para o uso do vice-rei Luiz de Vasconcellos, por observação curiosa dos annos de 1779 até o de 1789," *RIHGB* 47, pt. 1 (1884), 44–45.

15. Wilson, *Missionary Voyage*, 35; Barrow, *Voyage*, 85, 96; Nunes, "Almanaque . . . para o ano de 1794," 219–250, 276–279; J.M.P.S., *Definição* 113; Staunton, *An authentic account*, 89; and Tuckey, *An Account*, 86–87. According to Tuckey trade was good in spite of what he identified as numerous obstacles, including no legal direct trade with foreigners and the lack of a bank. On the commercial district see also Gerson, *História das ruas*, 42. One Portuguese informant complained that the port of Rio was inundated with English textiles. See Amador Patricio de Maia to Martinho de Melo e Castro, Rio de Janeiro, February 15, 1794, in "Capitania do Rio de Janeiro, Correspondência de varias authoridades," 272. Although some English textiles were legally imported by Portuguese merchants, many were not, and the crown's efforts to curtail contraband apparently had limited success. Jobson estimates that between 1796 and 1808 17 percent of all imports were contraband. See José Jobson de Andrade Arruda, "A circulação, as finanças, e as flutuações económicas," in *Nova História da Expansão Portuguesa. O Império Luso-Brasileiro, 1750–1822* v. 8, ed. Maria Beatriz Nizza da Silva (Lisbon: Estampa, 1986), 168. For a more recent analysis of contraband in the colonial economy, see Ernst Pijning, "Controlling Contraband: Mentality, Economy and Society in Eighteenth-Century Rio de Janeiro" (Ph.D. dissertation, The Johns Hopkins University, 1997).

16. Valladares, *Rio*, figures 584–591; and Lemos et al., *Art in Brazil*, 93–95.

17. Staunton, *An authentic account*, 82–83; Barrow, *Voyage*, 81–84.

18. Fragoso and Florentino, *Arcaísmo*, 42, 51, 72–75; Florentino, *Em Costas Negras*, 52. Fragoso's and Florentino's estimates are similar to those of Dauril Alden, who, synthesizing a

variety of sources, concluded that between 1796 and 1790, 8,900 Africans arrived per year, while between 1801 and 1805 that number increased to 10,500. See Dauril Alden, "Late Colonial Brazil, 1750–1808," in *Colonial Brazil*, ed. Leslie Bethell (New York: Cambridge University Press, 1987), 294. For comments on poverty see also Wilson, *A missionary voyage*, 35; and Tuckey, *An Account*, 55.

19. Lavradio. "Relatório," 450–451. Commenting on the spectacle of arriving Africans, Lavradio wrote: "Honest persons did not dare approach their windows; and those who were innocent learned there what they did not, and should not, know."

20. Estimates of the population of Brazil at the turn of the nineteenth century vary between 2.5 and 4 million inhabitants. See *Estatísticas Históricas do Brasil* (Rio de Janeiro: IBGE, 1990), 30–31. According to Alden between 1772 and 1782 the captaincy of Rio de Janeiro had 215,678 inhabitants, 14 percent of Brazil's total population of 1,555,200. In 1780 approximately 50 percent of the population in the captaincy of Rio was enslaved, a ratio that also was exhibited in the city, where around 25 percent of the captaincy's inhabitants lived. See Dauril Alden, *Royal Government*, 46, 497. To one British visitor in Brazil in 1805 the region appeared overwhelmingly African. He estimated that the captaincy's population included 37,000 white persons and 629,000 "blacks," a category that included both slaves and free persons of color. See Keith, *A voyage*, 22.

21. These estimates are from a 1799 census. See Mary Karasch, *Slave Life in Rio de Janeiro, 1808–1850* (Princeton: Princeton University Press, 1987), 61–62. Barrow estimated that in the early 1790s the city's population was 60,000, including slaves. Barrow, *Voyage*, 85. Alden gives the figure of 51,000. See *Royal Government*, 46. Elsewhere Alden points out that the city of Rio, growing at a rate of 9 percent per year, along with several other cities in Brazil, was larger than most North American cities. Regarding categories used to describe the population, it is important to note that both formal and informal racial categories in Brazil have been historically fluid and that official estimates have seldom employed categories consistently. Furthermore, few contemporary population estimates mention the indigenous population, which, according to Alden, comprised 2 percent of the captaincy's population at the end of the colonial period. See Alden, "Late Colonial Brazil," 289–290.

22. Paulo Fernandes Viana [police intendant], "Ofício expedido ao Ministro de Estado dos Negócios do Reino," November 11, 1818, ANRJ Códice 323 v. 5, f68v. On runaway communities see Flávio dos Santos Gomes, *Histórias de Quilombolas: Mocambos e Comunidades de Senzalas no Rio de Janeiro Século XIX* (Rio de Janeiro: Arquivo Nacional, 1995). On official perceptions of the threat posed by runaways and the bush captains enlisted to capture them see also A.J.R. Russell-Wood, "Ambivalent Authorities: The African and Afro-Brazilian Contribution to Local Governance in Colonial Brazil," *The Americas* 57, n. 1 (July 2000), 17, 26–31. As Russell-Wood explains, the requirement that bush captains return from their expeditions with the heads of dead slaves also ensured against the collection of payment based on false claims.

23. José Feliciano da Rocha Gameiro [da Mesa da Inspecção] to Rodrigo de Souza Coutinho, Rio de Janeiro, April 28, 1798, in "Capitania do Rio de Janeiro, Correspondência," 277–281.

24. A.J.R. Russell-Wood, *The Portuguese Empire, 1415–1808: A World on the Move* (Baltimore: The Johns Hopkins University Press, 1998), 59–122; Laura de Mello e Souza, *Desclassificados do ouro: a pobreza mineira no século XVIII* (Rio de Janeiro: Graal, 1982), 57–66. In the

early eighteenth century, for example, gypsies, for centuries stigmatized as wanderers regardless of whether they lived in communities, were expelled forcefully from Portugal and banished to Africa and Brazil where they pursued both itinerant activities and formed settled communities. See Bill M. Donovan, "Changing Perceptions of Social Deviance: Gypsies in Early Modern Portugal and Brazil," *Journal of Social History* 26, n. 1 (Fall 1992): 33–53.

25. Balthazar da Silva Lisboa to Martinho de Mello e Castro [Minister of Overseas and Navy], Rio de Janeiro, January 1, 1788, in "Capitania do Rio de Janeiro, Correspondência," 228–230. Silva Lisboa complained that in Brazil inadequate jurisdictional boundaries made law and order difficult to establish.

26. Mary Louise Pratt, *Imperial Eyes: Travel Writing and Transculturation* (New York: Routledge, 1992), 153.

27. Vasconcellos, "Offício," 34; [Resende] cited in Patricia Ann Aufderheide, "Order and Violence: Social Deviance and Social Control in Brazil, 1780–1840" (Ph.D. dissertation, University of Minnesota, 1976), 88; Mello e Souza, *Desclassificados*, 58.

28. Aufderheide, "Order and Violence," 85–87. Guild rules applied only to free men.

29. Vasconcellos, "Offício," 35.

30. Lavradio, "Relatório," 423–424, 430. The *terços* were first organized in 1766, during the administration of the Conde da Cunha. See Elysio de Araújo, *Estudo histórico sobre a polícia da capital federal de 1808–1831* v. 1 (Rio de Janeiro: Imprensa Nacional, 1898), 8. On the black militia experience in Brazil see also Hendrik Kraay, "The Politics of Race in Independence-Era Bahia, The Black Militia Officers of Salvador, 1790–1840," in *Afro-Brazilian Culture and Politics, Bahia, 1790s–1990s*, ed. Hendrik Kraay (New York: M.E. Sharpe, 1998), 30–56. As Russell-Wood explains, the service of Africans and Afro-Brazilians in law enforcement also responded to a dearth of white settlers willing or able to assume such duties. See "Ambivalent Authorities," 24.

31. Barrow, *Voyage*, 96. English travel accounts often describe the religious and political commemorations in Rio as excessive. According to Barrow, the lives of Rio's residents seemed "divided between sleep and ceremony."

32. *Relação da entrada que fez o excellentissimo, e reverendissimo D.F. António do Desterro Malheyro, bispo do Rio de Janeiro* (Rio de Janeiro: António Isidoro da Fonseca, 1747).

33. The last "Auto da posse do Governo Geral e Vice Reinado deste Estado do Brasil" occurred only three years before the prince regent's arrival, when the Conde dos Arcos, Marcos de Noronha e Brito (1771–1829) assumed the post. Between 1763, when the capital was moved to Rio, and the arrival of the court, there were seven changes of viceregal government. See "Autos de posse. . . ," ANRJ Códice 774, v. 1.

34. *Epanafora festiva, ou relação summaria das festas, com que na cidade do Rio de Janeiro, capital do Brasil se celebrou o Feliz Nascimento do Serenissimo Principe da Beira . . .* (Lisbon: Miguel Rodrigues, 1763), 4. There are several notices of local commemorations of the House of Braganza. See *Relaçam da Aclamação que se fez na capitania do Rio de Janeiro do Estado do Brasil . . . ao Senhor Rey Dom João IV. . .* (Lisbon: Jorge Rodrigues, 1641), facsimile published in *Boletim Internacional de Bibliografia Luso-Brasileira* 6, n. 2 (1965): 433–447, and transcribed in *RIHGB* 5 (1843), 319–327. Based on official sources, Baltazar da Silva Lisboa's history of Rio also recounts a number of royal commemorations. See his *Annaes do Rio de Janeiro* (Rio de Janeiro: Seignot-Plancher, 1834–5).

35. *Epanafora*, 16: "insólito espectáculo de trêmulo jardim, Cidade erratica." On the rise of printed accounts of commemorations see Roy Strong, *Art and Power: Renaissance Festivals, 1450–1650* (Berkeley: University of California Press, 1984), 21–22.

36. *Epanafora*, 6, 9.

37. Kenneth R. Maxwell, *Conflicts and Conspiracies: Brazil and Portugal, 1750–1808* (New York: Cambridge University Press., 1973), 115–140, 190. As a friar who accompanied the adjudication of the conspirators reported, one of the proposed emblems for the new republic bore the slogan *libertas quae sera tamen*. See "Ultimos momentos dos Inconfidentes de 1789, Pelo Frade Que os assistio de confissão," *Anuário do Museu da Inconfidência* (Ouro Preto) ano II (1953), 237.

38. Anonymous, "Memória do exito que teve a Conjuração de Minas e dos fatos relativos a ela. Acontecidos nesta cidade do Rio de Janeiro Desde o dia 17 até 26 de Abril de 1792," *Anuário do Museu da Inconfidência* (Ouro Preto) ano II (1953), 228; Maxwell, *Conflicts*, 192.

39. "Memória," 231. The scene is also described in Maxwell, *Conflicts*, 190, 198.

40. "Ultimos momentos," 234, 239; "Memória," 227–229; Maxwell, *Conflicts*, 192.

41. "Ultimos momentos," 243; "Ceremônias religiosas em regozijo de se ter descoberto a conjuração," in *Autos de Devassa da Inconfidência Mineira* v. 6 (Rio de Janeiro: Ministério da Educação, 1937), 407–408; "Memória," 223.

42. "Memória," 223–224.

43. In 1747 António Isidoro da Fonseca, a Lisbon printer, established a press in Rio de Janeiro. Fonseca managed to print as many as three pamphlets and a broadside before the crown ordered that the press be returned to Portugal. The most notable work published was the *Relação da entrada que fez . . . D.F. Antonio do Desterro Malheyro*, cited above. "Fonseca secured permission from the Bishop himself," Laurence Hallewell explains, "who granted it in the mistaken belief that further sanction was not needed in the case of an insubstantial work (*obra volante*)." See Laurence Hallewell, *Books in Brazil: a History of the Publishing Trade* (Metuchen, NJ: Scarecrow, 1982), 15–16. See also the royal decree of July 6, 1747, reprinted as "Prohibição do uso da imprensa no Brasil nos tempos coloniais," *RIHGB* 47, pt. 1 (1884), 167–168.

44. Barrow, *Voyage*, 85–86; Wilson, *A missionary voyage*, 33; Tuckey, *An Account*, 51. "Idlers," Tuckey reported, "were either sent to the Ilha das Cobras, or to Lisbon as prisoners.

45. David Higgs, "Unbelief and Politics in Rio de Janeiro During the 1790s," *Luso-Brazilian Review* 21, n. 1 (1984), 13–14.

46. *Autos da Devassa—prisão dos letrados do Rio de Janeiro* (Niterói/Rio de Janeiro: Arquivo Público do Estado do Rio de Janeiro/UERJ, 1994), 36.

47. Manuel Inácio Silva Alvarenga, *Autos da Devassa*, 127.

48. Higgs, "Unbelief," 15.

49. Afonso Carlos Marques dos Santos, *No rascunho da nação: inconfidência no Rio de Janeiro* (Rio de Janeiro: Secretaria Municipal de Cultura, 1992), 86, 92–93.

50. Marques dos Santos, *Rascunho*, 85, 90, 95; Alvarenga, *Autos da Devassa*, 128–29.

51. Marques dos Santos, *Rascunho*, 85–88, 95; Higgs, "Unbelief," 22–23.

52. See "Rellação dos livros aprehendidos ao bacharel Mariano José Pereira da Fonseca," *RIHGB* 63 (1901), 15–18; and confiscated letters in *Autos da Devassa*, 116–120, including an anonymous letter dated "Constantinople, February 20, 1791" in which the author waxed

philosophical on Mercier's *L'An deux mille quatre cent quarante*: "in the year 2,440, a time when the rights of man and of the citizen will be respected . . . in which all of the new hemisphere will divide into two republics, one encompassing all of the north, and the other all of the middle." José Honório Rodrigues claimed that Mercier was well known in Brazil and indeed another of his works was found in Fonseca's library. See Rodrigues, *Independência: revolução e contra-revolução* v. 1 (Rio de Janeiro: Francisco Alves, 1975–76), 5. On Mercier, including an excerpt of *L'An* in English, see also Robert Darnton, *The Forbidden Best-Sellers of Pre-Revolutionary France* (New York: Norton, [1995]). Although a definitive history of the book trade, libraries, and reading in colonial Brazil has yet to be written, a number of studies have begun to provide a more detailed understanding of these practices. See Eduardo Frieiro, *O diabo na livraria do cónego* (Belo Horizonte: Itatiaia, 1957); E. Bradford Burns, "The Enlightenment in Two Colonial Brazilian Libraries," *Journal of the History of Ideas* 25, n. 3 (July–September 1964), 430–438; Nancy Naro, "Leitores e reformadores: alguns aspectos comparativos da cultura do livro em relação à independência do Brasil e da américa inglesa," *Revista da Sociedade Brasileira de Pesquisa Histórica* 3 (1986–87), 17–28; and a special edition of *Acervo* 8, n. 1–2 (January–December 1995).

53. The handwritten notes on the charter, apparently drafted by Silva Alvarenga, are cited in István Jancsó, "A sedução da liberdade: cotidiano e contestação política no final do século XVIII," in *História da Vida Privada no Brasil* v. 1, eds. Fernando Novais e Laura de Mello e Souza (São Paulo: Companhia das Letras, 1997), 413.

54. Higgs, "Unbelief," 24.

55. *Autos da Devassa*, 38, 40–41. Taverns were also notorious places of gathering. After 1790, keepers were ordered by the town council to keep their doors closed to avoid "public scandal." Edmundo, *Rio de Janeiro*, 67–68, 86.

56. Jancsó, "Sedução da liberdade," 394, 403.

57. Foreign residents may have served as occasional translators. As Janscó notes, as there were few Portuguese translations of eighteenth-century works originally written in French and English, men without knowledge of these languages, such as Tiradentes, were known to seek amateur translations, which, in turn, were copied and circulated. See Janscó, "Sedução da liberdade," 406.

58. Delgado, *Autos da Devassa,* 42, 45, 51.

59. Delgado, *Autos da Devassa,* 44–45, 49; Manuel Pereira Landim, *Autos da Devassa,* 53.

60. Frade, *Autos da Devassa,* 47. This observation can be seen as particularly insightful when one considers that a century later Tiradentes became the symbol of the new Brazilian republic. Interest in the crown's affairs further encompassed questions of imperial diplomacy and politics. Sending Portuguese troops to assist the Spaniards in a battle against the French, for example, was judged by Alvarenga to be folly. See Delgado, *Autos da Devassa,* 41.

61. Rodolfo Garcia, "Introdução à Edição de 1941," in *Autos da Devassa,* 28; Marques dos Santos, *Rascunho,* 85.

62. Frade, *Autos da Devassa,* 38; Delgado, *Autos da Devassa,* 42.

63. Jacinto Martins Pamplona Corte Real, *Autos da Devassa,* 61.

64. António Lopes, *Autos da Devassa,* 60.

65. José Bernardo da Silveira Frade, *Autos da Devassa,* 40.

66. António Fernandes Machado, *Autos da Devassa,* 69.

67. Frade, *Autos da Devassa*, 41.

68. Frade, *Autos da Devassa*, 46.

69. Landim, *Autos da Devassa*, 53–54.

70. Delgado, *Autos da Devassa*, 44; Landim, *Autos da Devassa*, 54.

71. Corte Real, *Autos da Devassa*, 61.

72. Delgado, *Autos da Devassa*, 43.

73. Marques dos Santos, *Rascunho*, 103, 105. David Higgs has uncovered connections between the investigation of the Rio academy and an inquisitorial investigation in 1796 focused on a "conventicle of impious men" who met in the pharmacy of José Luiz Mendes on the Rua Direita. Perhaps not coincidentally, the Inquisition acted on a denunciation received two years earlier, just as Resende's investigation was getting under way. In fact, Mendes had previously provided the royal judge with testimony that established that his pharmacy was a place where "European affairs" were discussed. Unlike the judicial inquiry, however, the inquisitorial investigation was carried through to a prescribed end. In 1799, confronted with his references to French materials and his criticism of superstition and fanatical piety, Mendes appeared in an expiatory ceremony and promised that his shop would no longer serve as a place of gathering. See José Luiz Mendes, *Autos da Devassa*, 93; Higgs, "Unbelief," 15–16, 18–20; idem, "Nota sobre um documento acerca da história político-religiosa do Rio de Janeiro no período da revolução francesa," *RHI* 9 (1987), 439–449; and idem, "'A Luceferina Assembleia': Rio de Janeiro nos anos 1790 [Sumário contra José Luiz Mendes, boticário, morador na cidade do Rio de Janeiro e outros]," (manuscript, April 2000).

74. Arlette Farge, *Subversive Words: Public Opinion in Eighteenth-Century France*, trans. Rosemary Morris (University Park: The Pennsylvania State University Press, 1992), viii.

75. Higgs, "Unbelief," 26.

76. Janscó, "Sedução da liberdade," 390.

77. João de Deus do Nascimento, a conspirator in the so-called Tailors' Conspiracy of 1798, cited in Roderick Barman, *Brazil: The Forging of a Nation, 1798–1852* (Stanford: Stanford University Press, 1988), 36. For a narrative of the rebellion see Luiz Henrique Dias Tavares, *História da sedição intentada na Bahia em 1798: ("A Conspiração dos Alfaiates")* (São Paulo: Pioneira/Ministério da Educação e Cultura, 1975).

78. See Luiz R.B. Mott, "A revolução dos negros do Haiti e o Brasil," *História: Questões e Debates* (Revista da Associação Paranaense de História, Curitiba) 3, n. 4 (June 1982), 57–58. For the history of these networks in the North Atlantic see Peter Linebaugh and Marcus Rediker, *The Many-Headed Hydra: Sailors, Slaves, Commoners, and the Hidden History of the Revolutionary Atlantic* (Boston: Beacon Press, 2000), especially Chapter 7. "The mobility of sailors and other maritime veterans," they observe, "ensured that both the experience and the ideas of opposition carried fast." The term *cabra*, which means goat, is a derogatory reference to a person of color of mixed ancestry.

79. Brought by the ship "Voador" that arrived at Rio on January 14, 1808. See Gonçalves dos Santos, *Memórias*, 167.

80. *Relação das festas que se fizerão no Rio de Janeiro quando o Príncipe Regente Nosso Senhor e toda a sua Real Familia chegarão pela primeira vez a'quella Capital . . .* (Lisbon: Impressão Régia, 1810), 4–5.

THREE

Tragedy and Triumph:
THE POLITICS OF ROYAL EXILE

EMBODYING BOTH THE EIGHTEENTH-CENTURY PROMISE OF IMPERIAL RENEWAL AND the crown's failure to remain neutral and protect Portugal, the transfer of the Portuguese court to Rio de Janeiro was at once a "providential" and "tragic" moment, a moment in which the nature of the monarchy, of the empire, and of the Portuguese nation were all called into question and then reconfigured as part of a quest to define a new and, according to many contemporaries, post-European era.[1] The process was complex. In Portugal, as one historian of the Peninsular War has argued, following the prince regent's departure from Lisbon, fear and incomprehension crystallized into "a durable sense of political orphanage." In response to the French invasion, the creation of an imperial capital in America, and the less than favorable consequences of the subsequent negotiations at Vienna, an analysis of the causes of Portugal's decadence served as a point of departure for reasserting the supremacy of peninsular interests within the Portuguese world. The Portuguese nation was revealed as a privileged community defined by history, lineage, and geography. This emerging "nationalist discourse," as Valentim Alexandre has argued, then supplanted earlier pluralist visions of monarchy and empire in which the scope of political identity and public well-being transcended Europe's borders.[2]

The other dimension of this reconfiguration of monarchy and empire—the meanings and consequences of the transfer of the court within the New World—will be examined throughout this book. Here, I begin by exploring the politics of royal exile in Rio de Janeiro as they were articulated by two groups: the Portuguese exiles and the city's elite residents. The exiles, those who accompanied the prince regent to Rio or joined him there during the course of the Peninsular War, included members of the Portuguese nobility, royal advisors, confessors, servants, and attendants.[3] The city's elites, in turn, were similarly diverse: clerics, government officials, merchants, and landowners, some who were born in Rio, some who had made the city their long-term residence. The exiles and Rio's residents shared cultural and political allegiances, cultivated, in some cases, through study in Portugal, royal service, and marriage.[4] They were all distinguished vassals of the Portuguese crown and their appearance together at public commemorations in Rio was construed readily, as one observer noted, to be a perfect and transformative aggregation of power and prestige. Beginning in 1808, the observer explained, they formed "a Body so respectable that Rio de Janeiro seemed to be a New City."[5]

Yet, in spite of sharing distinctions and honors within Rio de Janeiro, the exiles and residents represented both the royal exile and their experience in the new court in dramatically different ways.[6] The exiles faced a tragic separation and an empathetic sense of the loss that their own departure had created in Europe. They lamented their life in Rio de Janeiro, judging Luiz da Cunha's early eighteenth-century plan to establish the court in Brazil to be "a childish error."[7] The residents, in turn, hailed the transfer of the court as the beginning of a new era of happiness and prosperity ordained by Providence itself. These differences were at times expressed as the product of political identities. Even as they were all loyal to the Portuguese monarch, the exiles were his "European vassals" while the residents were his "American vassals." Such divergent identities were not based as much on place of birth, as on the claim of distinct interests, defined and redefined within particular contexts. Indeed, both the exiles and Rio's residents self-consciously represented themselves as European Portuguese and American Portuguese, respectively, as part of their quest to define the meaning of the transfer of the court and, consequently, the future of the Portuguese monarchy and empire. In other words, as Europeans and Americans they struggled to offer a definitive answer to the question: Should the prince regent's residence in Rio, and the new empire it created, be permanent? As we shall see, although for both the exiles and the residents Portugal remained an important point of reference, ultimately it was the New World court that appeared to enable "national" renewal. Whether tragic or heroic, the royal exile redefined the imperial monarchy as American.

THE PENINSULAR WAR AND REIMAGINED COMMUNITY: EXILE, MORALITY, AND VICARIOUS PATRIOTISM ABROAD

By all accounts, the royal convoy's departure from Lisbon was chaotic. It was only three days before that the prince regent had announced his decision to go to Brazil, advising that all those disposed to "share his reverse of fortune" had his royal permission to follow. News of the decision spread rapidly through the city and "the utmost confusion and distress prevailed." As one eyewitness described the experience, hopes and fears gave way to "visions of horror and calamity." A caravan of over seven hundred coaches brought the royal family and their effects from their residence outside the city to the quay, while thousands headed to the beach with hopes of joining them. Many were overwhelmed by panic and to secure a place aboard one of the departing ships some resorted to extreme measures. The struggle, as one observer noted, cut through rank and reduced the most illustrious members of Portuguese society to a pitiful state of desperation. "Ladies of distinction," he recalled, drowned as they waded toward anchored boats. To add to the commotion, a restless crowd of those forced to stay behind filled the port area and Lisbon's streets and hills.[8]

With boarding completed and weather permitting, the convoy of over thirty ships then departed Lisbon, sailing past the Tower of Belem to join a British naval escort for what proved to be a grueling transatlantic crossing. The difficult journey was made even more perilous, as those aboard complained, by the congestion, the lack of provisions, and the "total disarray" and "poor administration" that prevailed on most of the convoy's ships.[9] Along the way to Brazil, taking stock of precious objects left behind—"a much admired tea pot that made the best tea in the world" or "a trunk that contained many necessary things"—passengers also confronted the unexpected and now bitter nature of their exile. To make matters worse, less than two weeks after departing Lisbon, a storm left the fleet irreparably scattered; some sailed directly to Rio, and others, including the prince regent's ship, in need of provisions and repairs, took a shorter course to northeastern Brazil. The consequent confusion and miserable conditions fueled criticism and, in some cases, panic. To stifle "the certain conclusion that the decision to make that journey was a very poor one" passengers were forbidden to complain or discuss "political affairs." As one of those who joined the royal family explained, the only acceptable subject of conversation was "the sea."[10]

Once ashore, the deprivation and deplorable conditions of the Atlantic crossing appeared to foreshadow the suffering and estrangement the exiles experienced in their new place of residence. With the rupture of family ties, a royal counselor assured his wife who remained in Lisbon, those in Brazil were beset by a "painful *saudade*" (nostalgic longing).[11] This sense of loss and of sentimental fragility was joined by fears of physical exposure. "The illnesses," complained one newcomer to Rio, were "innumerable."[12] Indeed, the toll of heavy rains, heat, and pestilence appeared to make the exiles' presence untenable. The city's churches "are continually announcing deaths," lamented Luiz Marrócos, a royal archivist who arrived at Rio in 1811. "Only in the Church of the Misericórdia of this City," he wrote to his father in Portugal, "they buried over 300 persons, natives of Lisbon."[13]

These physical challenges were quickly construed as moral tribulations. A range of new experiences, the exiles found, was to be explained by appealing to a topos of physical and moral degeneration in America, inaugurated in the sixteenth-century Jesuit indictment of Portuguese settlers "gone native" in Brazil and rearticulated in eighteenth-century assertions that in the New World nature and humankind were inferior (due to immaturity or degeneracy) as well as in claims about the relationship between climate, customs, and law that equated the tropics with servitude and barbarism.[14] As he complained in numerous letters to his father, in Rio Marrócos was overwhelmed by the dirt, the isolation, and the city's "indignant, arrogant, vain and libertine residents."[15] For others, life in "a sad and sickly land" became a "*degredo*" (punitive banishment), akin to those dispensed by the Portuguese Inquisition and civil courts. Rio de Janeiro became an "inferno," or, as one exile described it drawing on long-established images of Brazil as a land of vice, a modern day "Babylon," where slavery corrupted both slaves and their owners and where "indecency" and other "amusements" led to perdition.[16] "[T]his is a new world, but for the worst," reported the Marquês de Borba to a son who stayed behind; a world of "abomination and scandal" attributable, he concluded, only to an absence of "religion and the fear of God." Although he stopped short of such a withering indictment, the newly arrived bishop also joined in the exile lament, declaring that Rio de Janeiro was a place where the "infirmities of languor and weakness, from which few escape in a swampy country" precluded even the piety of Lent.[17] In a moment when the empire and Portugal itself faced ruin, the exiles thus reacted by reconstructing the relationship between Portugal and Brazil as what Mary Louise Pratt has described as "an essentialized relationship of negativity," one in which America necessarily defined Europe's afflictions.[18] Accordingly, lines of division were also dramatically drawn. As Marrócos vowed in a letter to his father, residing in Rio de Janeiro provoked in him such "hate and rage" that he suspected he cursed Brazil "even in his sleep."[19]

The exiles' disaffection and their self-representation as both apart from and threatened by the city in which they now lived sustained their overwhelming nostalgia for and loyalty to Portugal. And it was, above all, the moment of departure that marked this nostalgia and their exile, making them, as Amy Kaminsky has written of twentieth-century exile, "no longer present in the place departed, but not part of the new place either." As they looked back, the royal exiles' memories of sailing from Lisbon formed the basis for imagining the ordeal of those who remained on the peninsula to receive the French invasionary force: the leadership of the Regency, others who were physically unprepared for the transatlantic crossing, those unable to attain passage in the royal convoy, and Lisbon's popular classes. Even during the initial celebrations of arrival at Rio, one exile recalled, both Portugal's remembered past and its imagined present supplanted the newcomers' immediate experience in Brazil. The fleet that brought the royal family, he noted, became a symbol not of what it encountered and the future it promised, but rather of what it left behind: the Europe that cried for the absent prince.[20] Lisbonian scenes and displaced feelings of sorrow for the loss of the royal family similarly framed another account of the journey and arrival at Rio de Janeiro. As its author imagined the days following the prince's departure, the "sadness of the people of Lisbon in those days was indescribable: tears streamed from the faces of all." Because, he explained, the "person of the prince was extremely loved," to everyone in Lisbon "it seemed as if along with his presence a great fortune was leaving them."[21] The image of a sorrowful, abandoned, violated Portugal was also memorialized in an elegy published in Rio shortly after the arrival of the court. "And who," the author asked, "will dry the tearful, anguished eyes of the loving wife, / When suddenly they see their Father distant . . . Who will offer refuge to the innocent / Orphans, the progeny of Lusitania. . . ?"[22]

For the exiles this effort to reenact a presence in their absence depended, above all, on their ability to maintain current, and tangible, connections to Europe. Marrócos, who had participated in the defense of Lisbon during the second French invasion (1809), closely followed the remainder of the Peninsular war from Rio.[23] He eagerly awaited the arrival of ships, hoping for greetings from Portugal and "the political, military and rural news of the Continent" that letters might contain. Such interest, he further noted, was shared by others in the city who beheld the latest reports as "nuggets of gold."[24] As one resident reported, with similar hopes of news from Portugal "people of all classes" made their way to the post office, making it, as he complained, an increasingly crowded and at times disorderly place.[25] Gazettes, broadsides, and what Marrócos referred to generally as "public papers" were another much sought after source of information, for they "offered those far from the Old World comfort, amusement, and pleasure."[26] As a royal archivist, Marrócos had easy and regular access to "all the Periodicals . . . from different parts of the world," including those sent to Rio de Janeiro from expatriates in London, where more than one Portuguese-language newspaper was published.[27] Beyond the palace, book dealers also offered a selection of the two thousand books, pamphlets, flyers, proclamations, and engravings published in Portugal, including translations of Spanish, French, and English works on the Napoleonic conflict and, according to police reports, unauthorized works that slipped by censors at the customs house.[28] Engravings of Peninsular War heroes were particularly popular. As Marrócos wrote to his father in 1812, the arrival of a portrait of Beresford by the Portuguese Aguilar was eagerly awaited. The works of the Florentine engraver Bartolozzi, he also noted, "were also much esteemed," and those he did of Wellesley in particular "commanded a high price."[29]

In addition to materials from abroad, news of the state of affairs in Europe could be found in locally printed works. In 1808, for the first time in the history of Portuguese settlement in America, the crown reversed its ban against printing in Brazil and established the *Impressão Régia* on the Rua do Passeio, using presses that had been brought along from Lisbon. Although the Royal Press was founded "to print exclusively all legislation and diplomatic papers" generated by the crown, it also supplied news about the war. Twice a week in the *Gazeta do Rio de Janeiro* readers could find reports of battles and negotiations, translations from foreign newspapers, editorials, advertisements for pamphlets and engravings, and local letters and notices of patriotic Portuguese residing within and beyond the prince regent's domain.[30]

In keeping the exiles apprised of the national struggle against Napoleon, of defeats, victories, changing strategies, and their political implications, pamphlets and letters from Portugal allowed them, in effect, to experience the Peninsular War. Such an experience could be both private and individual, as much of Marrócos' personal correspondence with his family reveals, as well as public and collective. Posting pledges of support in the *Gazeta*, such as one announcement of November 1808 in which "a Sword of gold filigree" was offered to "the person who most distinguishes himself in the Restoration of Lisbon," allowed one to display patriotism and contribute to the war effort.[31] While the *Gazeta* provided a common forum for expression, just as pamphlets provided common reading, the act of procuring and reading these materials could also be collective. As was the case prior to the court's arrival, both private homes and public spaces served as sites for discussions and exchanges about military defeats, victories, and their consequences. Marrócos' own abundant supply of letters and "interesting papers" was "public" knowledge, he reported. Indeed, he wrote to his father in 1813, his house could "be called the second office of the *Gazeta*, for the intense interest with which I am sought."[32] "News about the French" also reportedly circulated at inns and shops. Such notices and reports could be read or, as the police intendant suggested, misread (*mal avaliada*) in a variety of ways. Indeed, talk of such disputable questions as treason, the legality of the transfer of the court, and the future place of the royal residence was, the intendant lamented, common. And, according to Marrócos, when reliable news from Europe was unavailable, those he referred to as "bar room politicians" filled the gap with rumor.[33]

The exiles' vicarious Peninsular War experience, afforded by reading pamphlets and debating the news, also included a sense of living through a national ordeal of both historic and epic dimensions, the product of the French invasion as well as its more disturbing underlying moral causes and effects. A discourse of disaster and moral vulnerability, of apocalypse and a diluvian "general calamity," featured in pamphlets, as well as in sermons and prayers preached and published in Rio, both recalled what one historian has called the "funereal memory" of the disastrous Lisbon earthquake of 1755, forged in Portuguese pamphlets in the second half of the eighteenth century, and described more recent misfortune. The punishing French occupation, critics in both Portugal and Brazil charged, followed from Portugal's own corruption and decadence, just as in the 1750s Portuguese beheld "vanity, arrogance, rage, and lust" as "the four vices, that compelled Divine Justice to enact [that] lamentable devastation."[34]

For the exiles in Rio, in particular, recalling this national history of physical peril and moral disorder not only sustained their solidarity, but also allowed them to see their own role in the ordeal. Just as the Portuguese in Europe struggled against "profane" conditions and the "impious politics" that had engendered, as the author of one pamphlet recalled, the "monstrous *Portugueses afrancesados*" (Frenchified Portuguese), they themselves contended with a similar threat to Portuguese political and moral integrity: Americanization. As Marrócos confirmed to both his own and his father's dismay, there were exiles who had become "hybrids of America."[35] And their transgressions, the Marquês de Borba often noted along with oblique references to physical excesses, were as horrifying as those of the city's long-standing residents.[36] In other words, the national ordeal of the Peninsular War was experienced in both Portugal and Brazil with what Anne McClintock, writing of British colonial bureaucrats, has described as the "dread of catastrophic boundary loss,"[37] fear of the loss of boundaries that once separated an allegiant Portugal from revolutionary France, Europe from America, and, as Borba suggested in a letter to his daughter-in-law in Portugal, moral integrity and selfhood from decadence and infantilization. Indeed, Borba insisted, that in Rio the Marquês de Alegrete was "swimming in happiness . . . with little decency" contradicted, and therefore threatened to undermine, "His Person."[38] Such examples of degeneration together with what Marrócos perceived as a condition of hybridity were at once products of the experience of empire—of the necessary physical presence of Portuguese in Brazil—and, as the exiles sustained, causes of the empire's demise. The failure to reproduce metropolitan decorum and "ways of thinking," they argued, undercut the restoration of Portugal's and its empire's political integrity as much as Napoleon and the French. As Marrócos explained, as long as "the Pseudo-Brazilians, commonly known as *Janeiristas*," promoted "the rumor that we will stay on here forever," metropolitan Portugal remained a thing of the past.[39]

As the exiles considered their experience in Rio as part of the nation's history of both physical and moral tribulation, however, they also discerned the possibility of redemption. Just as the people of Lisbon had begged for forgiveness following the earthquake's destruction of their once opulent city,[40] for the early nineteenth-century exiles, resistant moral rectitude promised to make living in Rio de Janeiro a brief purgatory. Recognized as a mode of suffering and atonement since the sixteenth century, the ordeal of the *inferno Atlântico*, displacement to the New World, provided, in this case, for a purification of Portuguese nationhood written as essentially pious, moral, and heroic.[41] Within the discourse of disaster, the exiles' renunciation of Rio and of its moral and physical infirmity thus became a political act; an act marked by what McClintock has called "an excess of boundary order."[42] Accordingly, the exile rejection of Brazil was not only justifiable, but also necessarily complete. As Marró-cos dramatically pledged: "I am so scandalized by the Country, that I want nothing from it, and when I leave here I will not forget to wipe my boots on the edge of the docks so that I do not take back even the smallest vestige of this land."[43]

For Marrócos and Borba, in particular, resisting Americanization and remaining an integrally "European" Portuguese was also achieved in the act of correspondence itself. "Each time I take up a pen to write to *Vossa Mercê*," Marrócos wrote to his father in 1811, "I feel a new spirit within myself, which brings me happiness and en-livens me." What Borba in turn described as "the relief of writing" restored senti-mental connections on which a unified moral and political identity and the faith in a return to the status quo ante could be based. Correspondence, as Borba wrote, gave "hope that Portugal existed."[44] Writing also promised to restore the distance that once safely separated the metropolitan exiles from the American colony. It realized what Kaminsky has described as the exile discourse of desire, intended "to recuper-ate, repair and return." Writing, Marrócos could assure both his father and himself that "no one is farther from America in customs and ways of thinking than I."[45]

Correspondence, like reading, also reconnected a collective experience in Rio de Janeiro to the experience of those who remained in Europe. Writing, sharing in the sentimental and spiritual consequences of the "general calamity" in Portugal, the ex-iles could seek to minimize the consequences of their physical removal to the New World and reestablish connections severed by the French invasion. They could share with Portuguese in Portugal, their letters suggested, the experience of fear and de-spair for "the poor state of affairs in Europe" as well as in the "great satisfaction of the prodigious general Pacification."[46] Out of their initial estrangement, the exiles thus defined their experience in Rio as part of the political and moral challenge of the Peninsular War. Whether in defeat or victory, reading, writing, listening to sermons, or sharing news, they sought, above all, to make the Portuguese nation, divided and besieged, once again whole.

A "PÁTRIA MISERA": THE LIMITS AND ALTERNATIVES TO PATRIOTIC EXILE

While letters to and from Portugal, pamphlets, and newspapers, restored connec-tions and allowed for a common experience as well as for the reconstruction of a moral and political Portuguese identity in the New World, they also revealed differ-ences and suggested the impossibility of a return to the former status quo. As months turned into years, the ideal of resistance to Americanization began to wither along with expectations of a prompt return to Portugal.[47] The toll of living in Rio de

Janeiro came to seem unavoidable. Having indicted certain newcomers for succumbing to the temptations of the New World, Marrócos himself recognized that, moral rectitude notwithstanding, simply living in a "land of vice and perdition" caused the *Lisboetas* (women native of Lisbon) to "degenerate." After a few years in Rio, he noted ironically, they earned the poor reputation that in Lisbon was given to women from Brazil.[48] Nor could he himself, he confessed, escape the consequences of the New World's "dangers and deprivations." Brazil, he wrote to his father, had "opened his eyes and taught him things not found in books," transforming his "figure and constitution." He was left, he despaired, "thin, tired, and old."[49]

The exiles' insistent bemoaning of Rio de Janeiro because it was dissimilar to Lisbon and despairing at the thought of remaining in Brazil, however, also had political-cultural limits. As they confronted their growing sense of the unavoidable and indelible nature of their experience in Rio, their peninsular correspondents proposed that it was for the very fact of the New World's difference that the exiles should be thankful. Those who accompanied the royal family to Brazil, one letter from Portugal suggested, did not realize their fortune and happiness. To be in Rio, the author imagined, was to escape "a continuous restlessness of spirit provoked by scenes of misery . . . plunder, death, robbery, scorn and violence." "Oh! my friend," he concluded, "how much better to suffer storms at sea for a few days, and after live peacefully!"[50] Furthermore, the exiles were reminded, having been delivered from the pillage of French soldiers, they also eluded the specter of collaboration, what Captain António Coutinho de Seabra e Souza characterized as the "suspicious" nature of his "reputation" and his subsequent misfortune that had resulted from the "sad" fact that he had not embarked with the prince regent.[51]

Indeed, Portugal's suffering, the exiles became aware, established their own future in Brazil. As refugees fleeing the disasters of war and occupation continued to arrive, a return to Europe seemed not only improbable but also ill-advised.[52] The marginal position of the Portuguese government in the war between the British and the French made any future in Europe seem bleak. As one Portuguese posed the problem to his correspondent in Rio, "after it is said what is happening in Europe, after [seeing] the total scorn with which the great powers deal with small states, is there anyone who can be persuaded that our prince should return to a corrupted Europe?"[53] Such a rhetorical question both confronted the exiles with the limits to their attempts to reinscribe themselves into a European Peninsular War experience and suggested an alternative to their longing to return: the transfer of the court should be permanent. After all, as the exile Miguel José Barradas suggested to his family in Portugal, "the example of our beloved Prince and Holy Family" outshone the "*Pátria misera*, isolated by the French tyrants."[54]

In this case, the exiles in Rio de Janeiro were not just far from the battlefields and the horrors of war, free from the desperation of abandonment and the stigma of collusion, but also close to the crown. In contrast to those who stayed behind, those in Rio confronted not the challenge of defending the besieged ancient court, but rather that of constructing a new one. These Portuguese were, in effect, custodians of the artifacts of governance, of what one historian has called "the paraphernalia of government" and "essential elements of a sovereign state": the Royal Treasury, the royal chapel's accouterments, the library, official documents, manuscripts, and a printing press. Although cast out from Europe, by having unpacked this most cumbersome cargo, the exiles were poised to broker royal power and patronage throughout the Portuguese empire.[55]

Indeed, as Marrócos' correspondence reveals, letters to and from Lisbon incessantly addressed the maintenance of royal patronage for those who remained in Portugal, requests which, as Marrócos complained to his father, grew overwhelming. "Those who live in Lisbon" were mistaken, he wrote, if they supposed that "the residents of this court have . . . wealth, influence, and time to attend to others' affairs."[56] Many Portuguese without family and reliable associates in the new court did perceive the limits of transatlantic brokerage and relocated to Rio to maintain their royal privileges. As one royal bureaucrat explained, living in Rio was appealing "because there payments are more prompt."[57] In other cases, "to remedy their misfortune" Portuguese in Portugal found themselves adopting strategies formerly reserved for residents of the *ultramar*: embarking on a costly journey "to present their petitions personally."[58]

As the Portuguese in both Europe and America recognized Rio de Janeiro as the new center of royal power, they also reinforced a sense of the Portuguese monarchy's renewal in the New World, a vision of a "Great Empire" in Brazil invoked by the exiled Portuguese statesmen Rodrigo de Souza Coutinho both before and after the transfer of the court.[59] Indeed, asserted the newly arrived playwright António Leite, the transfer of the court had produced a new imperial ascendancy based on a "fortunate union." The ancient Portuguese empire "given to [King] Afonso," he proposed in a one-act musical drama performed in Rio in 1811, joined a newer American empire. This union, as Leite further claimed, then brought to fruition an older colonial project: the transplantation of Portuguese civilization to Brazil. "What glory!" the allegorical figure of America exclaims upon the arrival of the prince regent, "My children, now we are *Lusos*." The indivisibility of the union, in turn, also appeared to enable its transcendence. Thus, as the drama ends, a tableaux of both Lusitanian and American figures ushers in a timeless period of peace, prosperity, and harmony.[60]

This ideal of imperial renewal and prosperity also framed a royal memorandum drafted during the transatlantic crossing by the Marquês de Bellas. Bellas argued that "to make the most of the disaster" the crown should renew the eighteenth-century project of imperial reform initiated by the Marquês de Pombal. The government of Brazil, he suggested, should be "simplified" and centralized, with expenditures efficiently limited to revenue. "Good economy," he claimed, could also be established by curtailing the creation of new offices and by detaining revenue generated by royal monopolies on wood and diamonds formally remitted to the metropolis in Brazil. In addition, foregoing new taxes would encourage local production. Above all, the Marquês argued, the Portuguese crown would benefit from the opening of Brazil's ports. "It is incredible," he insisted, "the utility that can result from the good principles today better known as a new science, which seems to be reserved for Your Highness, just as the discovery of India was for King Dom Manuel."[61]

For Bellas, recalling the monarchy's glorious Asian empire inspired confidence in its renewal in America, where the prince regent would be in a position to "endear himself even more with his vassals on both sides of the Atlantic, to make himself loved by men, to be a model prince, to gain a great reputation in this manner." A prosperous New World empire, he claimed, evoking arguments made before 1808, would also provide the firm base from which the crown could engage in continental negotiations. "It does not matter if the Kingdom [of Portugal] finds itself in need, [or] if it longs for your Royal Highness," Bellas explained, "as long as Brazil has a great fortune, and this is noticed throughout Europe with envy and admiration."[62] In a pamphlet published in Rio in 1811, the magistrate Joaquim do Valle came to a similar conclusion. Once freely wielding his "Iron Scepter" in America, he sustained, echoing Souza Coutinho and others, the prince regent could punish the impieties of the revolutionary French.[63]

This promise of American prosperity and potency was also manifest in the construction of the new royal court, a project that will be examined in more detail in Chapter 4. The crown began to host grand dinner parties, "as it had in Mafra," and sent for musicians and the rest of the royal library. The royal chapel was gilded and both a new Royal Theater and a private opera house for the princess regent were built.[64] By 1814 the construction of new public buildings and of a larger palace for the prince regent at São Cristovão was in full swing. At considerable expense, the courtiers also built houses and estates, signs, according to Marrócos, of their "stronger roots in this Country."[65]

Such affluence and vitality provided a stark contrast to what was increasingly construed in both Portugal and Brazil as the "undeniable fact that this Country [Portugal] is everyday more wretched." Together, the possibility of renewal in the new court and the truth of Portugal's demise led many newcomers to Rio to reconsider their initial understandings of the moral imperatives of their exile. As Marrócos explained, along with moral challenges, the city also presented an alternative to his own personal tribulations: celibacy and what he described as the "misanthropic" solitude and vulnerability to vice that followed such an option. The physiological nature of the experience of exile that Marrócos first lamented could be, he came to recognize, an opportunity for welcome transformation. "I came to this Court," he wrote to his father in 1813, "and changing climate, I also modified earlier decisions."[66] Referring to his commitment to marry a *carioca* (a native of Rio de Janeiro), Marrócos justified his decision with allusions to the reinvigorated potency of a paterfamilias, claims of a shared culture and standards, and the promise of moral renewal. Indeed, Marrócos argued, his wife, Ana Maria de São Tiago Souza, embodied virtue itself. The daughter of a Brazilian-born woman and a Portuguese-born merchant, Ana came from a family that was, as Marrócos described it, "clean, honest and wealthy." With her mother's supervision, he explained to his sister, Ana had escaped the laziness and ignorance that characterized the daughters of other Brazilian families. Consequently, "although Brazilian" she was, Marrócos wrote, "better than many Portuguese women." For her simplicity, he explained, freed her from the superficiality and decadence of European aristocrats who carelessly danced and played instruments or, "with a fan and handkerchief, served as window decorations."[67]

Having thus envisioned his own regeneration in the arms of his innocent, American bride, Marrócos stood for a renewal of paternal authority writ large, an authority that was jeopardized in Portugal by the separation of fathers and sons in exile and in war, and by the absence of the political father-figure of Dom João. Like that of feminine virtue embodied in his wife, this renewal was identified not with Portugal, but rather with Brazil. Indeed, founding a family in Rio de Janeiro resulted in a transformation of son into father that paralleled Brazil's own transformation from colony into the center of empire, what the city's residents came to refer to as an "emancipation." Although both transformations depended on a recognition of the cultural and moral authority of ancestry, they also implied a redefinition of allegiances and a repositioning of the locus of power. For Marrócos one such moment of redefinition and repositioning came in response to his father's scathing charge that in marrying Ana he had behaved "as a stupid African, and presumptuous American." Rather than resorting to his once defensively European identity, or his desperate pleas for reassuring news, Marrócos refused any compromise with his father's disappointment and defended his decision as "very serious, politic, and resolute."[68]

Marrócos's claim that Rio de Janeiro was a place where personal honor and paternal authority could be reestablished corresponded with a larger vision of Rio de Janeiro as a place that the exiles themselves could make. Reenacting earlier efforts to colonize and civilize the New World, the exiles cast aside their initial rejection of American degeneration in favor of American innocence and potential and came to recognize that they could rebuild the city in their own image. The new court would be both a model of civility and morality, as were its European antecedents, and, now, in the wake of the revolutionary and Napoleonic wars, a singular place within the Portuguese world in which a public and national virtue could be reasserted.[69] After all, as one playwright claimed, the "fall of despotism" (of Napoleon) followed not only from victories on the battlefields, but also from a rededication to "industry" and "the arts";[70] from a restoration of a quotidian morality now as manifest in Rio as it was seemingly unattainable in Portugal. Indeed, Marrócos explained to his father in 1819, Rio de Janeiro afforded a "solid, satisfactory, peaceful" life, a more "decent, dignified, and splendorous" life than was available in postwar Lisbon. Portugal, on the contrary, the "Pátria" for which Marrócos once had longed so desperately, now seemed to be, as he described it, a "frivolous pretext of the senile" that offered nothing but ingratitude.[71] And if, as Marrócos suggested in his letters, women marked the boundaries between civility and degeneration within the empire, the New World court of Rio de Janeiro then marked these same boundaries between the empire and beyond. It provided the Portuguese monarchy freedom from what the exiled bishop José Caetano da Silva Coutinho characterized as "the contagion that had debauched and lacerated Europe," just as living in Rio de Janeiro allowed the exiles to escape what their Peninsular correspondents decried as the corruption of Portugal.[72]

This vision of the new court as sustaining the Portuguese nation's regeneration and progress also drew on a new understanding of national character that had taken shape during the course of the eighteenth century. Within the Portuguese discourse of the nation, the idea that humankind was fundamentally equal had displaced the perception of national character as "natural." Manifest in a distinct tradition, Portuguese critics sustained, national character nevertheless was shaped by education, laws, and government, what contemporaries also described as *polícia*. With polícia, virtues could be preserved, and vices which, many argued, had contributed to the empire's decadence, could be amended. Accordingly, some years before the French invasion, in the interest of reform Portuguese statesmen set out to inventory the nation's vices as part of what Soares and Hespanha describe as "an encounter with *o estrangeiro*," in this case, other European nations recognized by the Portuguese as more "refined and enlightened" (*polidas e ilustradas*).[73]

Together with others inhabiting the Atlantic world, the Portuguese also appreciated that an enlightened refinement, as well as a public morality, required an engagement with classical antiquity and its disciples. As the exiled Conde de Aguiar noted in 1810 in the preface to his translation of Alexander Pope's *An Essay on Criticism* (1711), along with eighteenth-century translations of Horace and Aristotle, it was a "useful service" to make available Pope's "rules and precepts" of both writing and judging verse. Although Pope did not emerge as a symbol of republican virtue, as was the case in British North America, for those in the new court of Rio de Janeiro he offered a guide, as Aguiar noted the following year in his translation of *An Essay on Man* (1733–34), to "particular ethics, or practical morality; considered in all circumstances, orders, professions and exercises of human life."[74]

This recognition of "the origins of civilization in civility," as Gordon Wood has noted, marked much of eighteenth-century political discourse.[75] For the Portuguese exiles, in particular, the new court of Rio and the renewal of morality and civility that it was held to foster, also allowed for a reconciliation of their initial self-representation as "European" with what they increasingly construed to be the imperative of a post-European empire. Conceived as an endeavor to civilize Rio de Janeiro, to imbue the city with morality, their exile produced what Pratt has described as a "transatlantic appropriation" in which "European" was distinguished from "Europeanizing" in the quest to find "esthetic and ideological grounding" for a new imperial capital.[76] In other words, while the exiles' quest to restore the integrity of nationhood led to an initial rejection of the New World, their understanding of the nation's boundaries as above all moral and political also allowed them then to reenvision nationhood within a transformation of the New World based on the ideals of civilization and civility. The "relocation and renegotiation of oppositions and boundaries" that characterized the European colonial project had allowed Europeans, in this case, to forego Europe itself.[77] Once conceived of as a land of perdition, Brazil was now a haven from decrepitude; and America, as one exiled playwright proclaimed, would be the new "metropolis."[78]

AN "EPOCH OF HAPPINESS": THE TRIUMPH OF NEW WORLD EMPIRE

The Portuguese royal exiles were not alone in their quest to understand the consequences of the transfer of the court and the larger conflict of the Peninsular War. Those who received the prince regent and his court, natives of Rio de Janeiro, as well as others who had made the city their home before 1808, also sought to explain the meaning of the royal exile and to place their experience as residents of the new court within the history of the Portuguese empire and monarchy. The contrast between their representations of recent events and those offered by the newcomer-exiles is striking. Whereas for the exiles the transfer of the court initially produced a sentimental experience based on estrangement, for Rio's residents "it opened a horizon of fortune and happiness."[79] It inaugurated a "golden age," proclaimed Manuel Ignacio Silva Alvarenga, the former critic of royal government and target of Viceroy Resende's investigation in the 1790s. Or, as the Brazilian-born cleric Luiz Gonçalves dos Santos declared in his *Memórias*, the "extraordinary" and "prodigious" disembarkation of Dom João, the royal family, and his "faithful European vassals" on the city's beaches marked the beginning of "the Epoch of Happiness." Indeed, the "ecstasy" he experienced as he viewed the royal family's first procession through the city's streets was so overwhelming that it led him to wonder whether he beheld "an illusion rather than a reality."[80]

Such joy and "expressions of respect," as Gonçalves dos Santos and other residents carefully explained, were the product of political loyalties.[81] With the transfer of the court the crown's "American vassals" were finally close to their sovereign, able to actively show their love and allegiance, they insisted, and receive the prince regent's love in return. So preached Duarte Mendes São Payo, rector of one of the city's seminaries. After 1808, he proclaimed, Brazil could sing of its "much desired Triumph" because its inhabitants now held in their arms their "legitimate, and indispensable Lord, beloved, caring Father, faithful and true Friend."[82] This ideal of loving reciprocity between the prince regent and the city's residents then was translated from the realm of sentiment into a tangible monumentality shortly after the arrival of the court. Elias António Lopes, a Portuguese-born wholesaler on the Rua Direita, offered the prince regent the *Quinta da Boa Vista*, an estate located outside the city's center in São Cristovão, so that the royal family could have a palace on a grander scale than the existing viceregal residence near the quay. The donation and Lopes' "notorious disinterest and demonstration of faithful vassalage," according to one chronicler, made manifest the love and generosity of the residents of the new royal court. The prince regent's response, in turn, showed that such sentiment was not unrequited. On arriving for the first time at the estate, the chronicler reported, the prince regent exclaimed: "This here is a royal veranda! In Portugal I had nothing like this." Indeed, the chronicler further reassured his correspondent in Portugal, "[a]ll of the Royal Family [was] doing well here" in Rio de Janeiro.

Evoking a permanence and therefore the possibility of transcending Europe itself, the Quinta thus stood for both the future that Rio de Janeiro could provide the royal family and the future that the royal family could provide the city; for the potential of New World vassalage and, above all, for the prince regent's recognition of the greatness of his dominions in Brazil. Indeed, Lopes' donation and the prince regent's response showed that the transfer of the court both literally and figuratively ennobled Rio's residents. Along with monetary compensation and a monthly allowance for continuing to administer the estate, Lopes received the proprietary office of scribe of the town council of the Village of Paratí. In the years following the arrival of the court, in spite of his reportedly illegitimate birth, Lopes was also granted the title of *Fidalgo da Casa Real*; he served as a deputy to the Royal Board of Commerce and Agriculture, as a broker in the *Casa de Seguros* [Insurance Commission], and as a royal counselor. And, when he died in 1815, he was buried in the distinguished habit of *Cavaleiro da Ordem de Cristo* [Knight of the Order of Christ].[83]

In the 1810s similar gestures of American vassalage and royal commendation

Figure 4: Jean Baptiste Debret, "Améliorations progressives du palais de S. Christophe," from Debret, *Voyage Pittoresque et Historique au Brésil, sejour d'un Artiste Français au Brésil* v. 3 (Paris: Firmin Didot Fréres, 1839). Copy and permission obtained from the Print Collection, Miriam and Ira D. Wallach Division of Arts, Prints and Photographs, The New York Public Library, Astor, Lenox and Tilden Foundations. By 1816, Debret observed, a "simple, Brazilian country house" in a beautiful natural setting had been transformed by "European taste."

then followed this monumental exchange between Lopes and Dom João. Rio's residents provided the courtiers with food, lodging, and other necessities, as one of the exiled courtiers noted, and the prince regent responded to "these demonstrations with an extravagant offering of honors and compensations of which there was no previous example in the monarchy."[84] Indeed, to accommodate the burdens of both fighting a war and establishing a new court, Dom João dispensed more titles of nobility during the eight years of his residence in Rio than in the preceding one and one-half centuries of Braganza rule in Portugal, in addition to thousands of commissions in Portuguese military orders, *titulos de conselho* (titles of royal counselor) and ranking militia appointments.[85] To further expand the possibilities for royal *mercês* (favors), he instituted the *Ordem da Torre e Espada* (Order of the Tower and Sword) in May 1808.[86]

As British resident John Luccock remarked snidely, this "welcome" that wealthy residents received at court depended, above all, on their ability to "repay an empty honor with solid benefits" for the crown.[87] Yet, it was also the case that many of the honors themselves translated into "solid benefits" for the residents. The establishment of new and duplicated institutions in Rio de Janeiro, including the *Desembargo do Paço* (Tribunal of the High Court), the *Casa de Suplicação do Brasil* (Court of Appeals), the *Junta de Comércio* (Commercial Board), the *Erário Real* (Royal Treasury), and a Bank of Brazil facilitated the exercise of justice and commerce, brought the city prestige, and provided unprecedented opportunities for royal service. Although many exiles were given posts in recognition of the hardship of joining the prince regent in Brazil, the city's residents too enjoyed the dividends of a growing royal bureaucracy as well as royal grants of land.[88]

For Gonçalves dos Santos the crown's recognition of the city of Rio and its American vassals was part of what he described as a "new order of things" and a "new political system." Within the first years of his residence in Brazil, he explained, the prince regent worked to amend the less than ideal circumstances he encountered. The "royal hand" "regenerated" America by opening Brazilian ports and, according to Gonçalves dos Santos, so ushered in a period of increased trade and prosperity. By ending the prohibition of manufactures, he also claimed, Dom João "broke the chains that bound Brazilians and impeded them from using their hands." New royal academies, a school of medicine, the royal library, a military archive, and expanded "royal lessons" offered unprecedented opportunities for education and professional training in the city as well, while the establishment of the royal press, he further judged, "dissipated the darkness of ignorance, whose black and terrible clouds had covered all Brazil."[89] These gestures of royal "liberality" both showed that Dom João was "a true father of his vassals" in America[90] and, with resonance in the exile embrace of New World potential, revealed the transfer of the court as an opportunity to cultivate virtue in the royal court. Indeed, writing on the establishment of a military academy and the "great benefits that the August Presence of His Royal Highness brought to Brazil," Manuel Ferreira de Araújo Guimarães, the editor of the local periodical *O Patriota*, imagined that morality, "upon which public happiness depends," thus would be "refined." The people of Brazil, "newly conquered" by the sovereign's tenderness and love, he explained, would reap the rewards of a renewed effort to "propagate civilization."[91]

Yet, what Guimarães described as "the pleasing object of the increase in enlightenment" in Brazil came as a result of the "bloody scenes of war" that "terrorized humanity" in Europe.[92] In other words, the "happiness" justified by the material benefits of living in a royal court and by the recognition and the enhancement of status that royal grace implied was inevitably circumscribed by its undeniably unhappy origins. As one resident observed, as "[t]hose of the colonies" received the prince regent "with tender tears, those of Europe defend[ed] him with their lives."[93] The sanguine Gonçalves dos Santos himself similarly lamented that the intoxicating image of "the triumphant entry of the first European sovereign into the most fortunate city of the New World" was forever tarnished by the mournful memory of his departure from Portugal. Thus Rio's residents found themselves celebrating a tragedy. They experienced at once, Gonçalves dos Santos despaired, tranquility and fear, flattery and sadness, happiness and mourning, the consolation of peace and the horror of war, and pride together with insecurity and affliction. Even the marriage of Dom João's daughter, Infanta Maria Teresa to Spanish Prince Pedro Carlos, he explained, was marred by the knowledge that as "a proud and content Brazil celebrated the event with such happiness . . . Portugal cried out in agony."[94] Indeed, as one officer who attended the prince regent's entry into the city suggested, the contrast of the residents' feelings of "happiness and enthusiasm" with the "sadness and consternation of the People of Lisbon" formed the "indescribable" sentimental framework for the transfer of the court.[95]

To resolve these contradictions between a tragic royal exile and the joyous prospect of a New World court, Rio's residents sought to depreciate the link between the potential and progress of America and the destitution of Portugal that the exiles had come to embrace. Writing to his counterpart in Lisbon to request that he send skilled laborers, Rio's police intendant reassured him that "it was not because of the circumstances in Portugal" that he made such a request, for he and other residents of the new court had never had "better hopes." Rather, he explained, the requisition simply reflected the "need to improve the police of this country in which our prince and his royal family now reside, at the same time perfecting and improving agriculture."[96] Patriotism, in turn, then sustained the residents' less defensive efforts both to mend divisions and define their own place in the ordeal of war. Long-standing residents of the city joined the exiles in expressing their solidarity with the Portuguese who remained in Portugal, reading and writing about the war, pledging resources for its victims, listening to sermons, lamenting defeats, and, as the editor Guimarães pledged, feeling the joy of victory in "the tender expanses of [their hearts]."

On the one hand, Rio's residents explained the threat posed by the war as a personal one. As Gonçalves dos Santos noted, like the exiles, some residents were anxious for the fate of "their parents, their relatives and their friends" living in Portugal. Others worried about their children, while many with commercial interests in Europe sadly "judged that all was lost." On the other hand, Rio's residents described the war as a larger political challenge to be met, as the police intendant claimed, by all "good patriots." As vassals of the Portuguese monarchy they saw Napoleon's threat to its sovereignty as a threat to their own political integrity and honor. They were, as were the exiles and the Portuguese in Portugal, part of the heroic and virtuous Portuguese nation, a nation of soldiers, wrote Guimarães, invested with "the spirit of the ancient conquerors of Asia and Africa, and discoverers of America" now besieged by Napoleon's revolutionary impieties.[97] "[E]ach Citizen is a warrior," proclaimed the native royal preacher Januário da Cunha Barbosa in a commemorative sermon, "each warrior a Hero; each Hero a Distinguished Portuguese." As it then followed from this analogy, Barbosa challenged listeners and, following the sermon's publication, readers to consider, together with the valor of those fighting the French in Portugal and the virtue of the prince regent, Rio's residents' own patriotic interest formed a spiritual continuum that transcended diverse material experiences.[98]

Expressing the scope of this interest and wartime solidarity indeed became a privileged mission for Rio de Janeiro's preachers. Between 1810 and 1815 commemorative sermons and prayers repeatedly explicated the meaning of the Napoleonic conflict by articulating certain events and local circumstances with larger imperial imperatives. Resident preachers offered, Frei Francisco de São Carlos explained, "the domestic history of the Nation, that should be transmitted from fathers to sons."[99] They showed, more specifically, how different ordeals converged in the unified destiny of the Portuguese nation revealed in Providential design. As Barbosa proclaimed, while the prince regent's journey saved his Portuguese subjects from bloodshed, his absence then inspired the ultimately victorious popular resistence on the Peninsula. The Portuguese, he suggested, were like an angry lion who, on awakening to find an empty throne, defeated "the eagle" who usurped the prince regent's legitimate authority. Having recognized and confronted Napoleon's ambition, perversity, and illegitimacy, the end of the French occupation then came as a reward for their piety and faith.[100] Providence, in this sense, had both ordained the transfer of the court and chosen the Peninsula as the birthplace of Europe's freedom.[101] Thus the Portuguese were saved from revolutionary evil, as the Israelites had been deliv-

ered from the bondage of Egypt.[102] Or, as the royal chaplain João Pereira da Silva
proposed with an apocalyptic flourish, as Napoleonic France appeared to be the
monstrous Fourth Empire of Daniel's dream (Book of Daniel, Chapter 7), the victorious Portuguese monarchy would emerge as its everlasting successor.[103]

These eschatological understandings of the French invasion and the transfer of
the court contributed to a wave of messianic interpretations of monarchy that gained
currency throughout the Portuguese world in the context of the Peninsular War.[104]
Like anti-Napoleonic pamphlets, prophetic sermons and prayers served to form a
transatlantic discourse of nationhood that both explained the larger meanings of the
transfer of the court and linked the experiences of Portuguese and American vassals.
Yet, sermons and prayers in Rio also distinguished themselves from Peninsular visions of prophetic redemption and victory in important ways. While, in early nineteenth-century Portugal the prince regent was seen as having departed in order to
return and usher in a new and glorious reign with Europe at the center of imperial
transcendence, for the residents of Rio de Janeiro the end of the story was different.
As São Payo explained, with reference to the diluvian ordeal, Dom João was saved
from the turbulent waters that covered Portugal not to return, but rather to become
"the Father of the new world."

Indeed, for Rio's preachers, the transfer of the court marked the beginning of
the "great Empire of Brazil" that would stretch from "sea to sea . . . to the ends of
the earth." Within Providential design, Rio de Janeiro was the chosen imperial city.
"Oh brilliant Capital of Portuguese America," São Payo asked his listeners, "do you
not know your great and boundless happiness?" You are the first in the New World,
he reminded them, to experience "the glory of seeing a Sovereign Prince."[105] In coming to Brazil the prince regent had transformed both the empire and its new capital,
João Pereira da Silva similarly suggested. Rio, he proclaimed, was not only "a new
Court, a new Athens, a new Lisbon," but also "a new Jerusalem, comparable to the
one that John saw in his Apocalypse."[106]

This celebration of the monarchy's American destiny appeared to undermine
the residents' appeal to nationhood and the shared political and moral ordeal of the
French invasion of Portugal. Yet, as resident memorialists pointed out, it could also
serve as the basis for reasserting a now regenerated national unity and harmony. Invoking a cosmic "universal plan," they defended the New World court not only as
the source of local benefits in Brazil, but also as an inspired imperial imperative
upon which rested the well-being of the Portuguese nation as a whole. As Gonçalves
dos Santos explained, "the occupation of Portugal by the French was certainly a lamentable disaster, a general and public calamity; yet the salvation of His Royal Highness, his coming to Brazil to create a new Lusitanian Empire in America, was a

joyous event for all Brazilians" and "for all Portuguese."[107] In other words, even as the transfer of the court was a tragedy for Portugal, on the larger scale of the monarchy, empire, and nation, it was a triumph. Unrestrained by narrow geographic boundaries, an American empire promised a new historical era for the monarchy and for all of its vassals, for all "true Portuguese," who, as São Payo proclaimed, were "the same in all places."[108] Reflecting on the dimensions of "Brazilian Loyalty" and Dom João's arrival at Brazil, the Brazilian-born statesman and political economist José da Silva Lisboa reached a similar conclusion. Even as the "sentiments of the residents of Brazil" regarding the transfer of the court were free from the "terror of invasion," blessed with "the great benefit of the presence of their prince" and, Silva Lisboa surmised, therefore "better expressed," they were also, he noted, "in unison with those of the mother country." Like all good Portuguese, the residents not only reviled the injustice of Napoleon's acts, but also recognized that the "salvation of the reigning dynasty" was cause for "National Happiness."[109]

This ideal of national happiness rebuilt in the New World then was further bolstered by claims to history and political tradition. The transfer of the court to Rio de Janeiro was, as the resident preacher Pereira da Silva explained, a foundational act that both created something new and recalled something old, the Acclamation of Afonso, the first king of Portugal.[110] This history that Afonso had begun, one poet publicized during the royal family's disembarkation, then culminated with Dom João, "the sublime Founder of a new Empire" and in America, a place that guarded "Sacred Virtues" while "the rest of the world [was] all iniquities."[111] Indeed, as São Carlos imagined, Rio de Janeiro was the new Campo d'Ourique, site of the miraculous creation of Portuguese royal authority.[112]

As the residents' celebration of a tragic royal exile thus culminated in a complete vision of imperial renewal based on national unity, history, and allegiance to the monarchy, this vision then converged with the promise of political and moral regeneration defined by the royal exiles. For the exiles conceiving of this promise had meant redefining Brazil as a virtuous haven from a corrupted Europe, a place where a besieged civility could thrive. The residents, in turn, began where the exiles ended, with the new court as a privileged location for a resurgence of national and monarchical power and prosperity. For both, the novelty of an American empire was circumscribed by tradition: vassalage and Portuguese nationhood. Although, as we shall see in Chapter 4, the crown would also contend with skepticism and dissident understandings of the war and the transfer of the court, in the 1810s the embrace of a moral Portuguese nationhood and the discourse of imperial renewal and New World virtue sustained efforts to make a new American empire and a new royal court in Rio de Janeiro a reality.

Notes

1. See for example Domingos Sequeira's allegory of the departure reproduced in José António Sá, *Defeza dos Direitos Nacionaes e Reaes da Monarquia Portugueza* (Lisbon: Impressão Régia, 1816) and here Figure 1. For a British rendition of the departure see [John Wolcot], *The Fall of Portugal; or the Royal Exiles, A Tragedy in Five Acts* (London: Longman, Hurst, Rees and Orme, 1808).

2. On the experience of the Peninsular War and the transfer of the court in Portugal see Ana Cristian Araújo, "As Invasões franceses e a afirmação das idéias liberais," in *História de Portugal: O Liberalismo* v. 5, eds. Luiz Reis Torgal and João Lourenço (Lisbon: Estampa n.d.), 25–29; and Teresa Bernardino, *Sociedade e atitudes mentais em Portugal (1777–1810)* (Lisbon: Imprensa Nacional, n.d.). Raul Brandão, *El-rei Junot* (1912) (Lisbon: Imprensa Nacional/Casa da Moeda, 1982) provides both an impressionistic narrative and transcriptions of contemporary documents from the French invasion. For debates about Portugal's decadence and nationalism see Valentim Alexandre, "O nacionalismo vintista e a questão brasileira: esboço de análise política," in *O liberalismo na península ibérica na primeira metade do século XIX* v. 1, ed. Miriam Halpern Pereira (Lisbon: Sa da Costa, 1982), 287–307; and idem, *Os sentidos do império: questão nacional e questão colonial na crise do antigo regime português* (Porto: Afrontamento, 1993), 411–420. As Alexandre explains, the sense of discontent with the absence of the court was most acute after the war when the transfer of the court no longer appeared as a temporary wartime measure and as the negotiations at the Congress of Vienna did not result in substantial rewards for the Portuguese war effort.

3. "Relação dos Criados e mais Pessoas que Accompanhão Sua Alteza Real para o Rio de Janeiro," ANRJ Códice 730, f12; "Mappa do Estado Actual da Guarnição, Fragata Minerva. . . ," ANRJ Códice 730, f13. Those aboard included the Marqueses de Vagos, Angeja, Torres Nova, Lavradio, Bellas, Pombal, Alegrete, and the Viscondes de Barbacena and Anadia.

4. The relative lack of tension between colonial and peninsular elites within the Portuguese empire, especially compared with the Spanish empire, has been noted by a number of historians. On study in Portugal see José Murilo de Carvalho, "Political Elites and State Building: The Case of Nineteenth-Century Brazil" in *Comparative Studies in Society and History* 24, n. 3 (1982), 378–399; and Roderick Barman, *Brazil: The Forging of a Nation, 1798–1852* (Stanford: Stanford University Press, 1988), 33, 76–80. Both argue that the Coimbra experience determined alliances and agendas before, during, and after Brazilian independence.

5. "Preparativos no Rio de Janeiro para receber a Família Real Portuguesa," BNRJ Ms. II-35,4,1, f5.

6. On the discourse of nationhood and the practice of European self-representation and the New World see Richard Helgerson, *Forms of Nationhood: the Elizabethan Writing of England* (Chicago: University of Chicago Press, 1992).

7. Luiz Joaquim dos Santos Marrócos to his father [Francisco José dos Santos Marrócos], November 21, 1812, *Cartas de Luiz Joaquim dos Santos Marrócos* (Rio de Janeiro: Biblioteca Nacional/Ministério de Educação e Saude, 1939), 113.

8. Thomas O'Neill, *A concise and accurate account of the proceedings of the squadron under the command of Real Admiral Sir William Sidney Smith . . .* (London: R. Edwards, 1809), 19, 22–24; "Memórias de Eusebio Gomes, 1800–1832," and Anonymous, [ca. 1807–08], in

Ângelo Pereira, *Os filhos de el-rei D. João VI* (Lisbon: Empresa Nacional de Publicidade, 1946), 119n, 123–124. Pereira suggests that the latter was written by an officer aboard the ship *Rainha Portugal*. See also José Acúrsio das Neves, *História geral da invasão dos franceses em Portugal e da restauração deste reino* (1810) v. 1 (Porto: Afrontamento, n.d.), 218–219, 224–226; Alan Manchester, "The Transfer of the Portuguese Court to Brazil" in *Conflict and Continuity in Brazilian Society*, eds. Henry Keith and S.F. Edwards (Columbia, SC: University of South Carolina Press, 1969), 154; Araújo, "Invasões," 26; and David Francis, *Portugal, 1715–1808, Joanine and Rococo Portugal as Seen by British Diplomats and Traders* (London: Tamesis, 1985), 281. According to some reports, the crowd was openly hostile.

9. Dom Manuel Meneses to the Conde dos Arcos [Viceroy of Brazil], January 27, 1808, ANRJ Códice 730, f11; O'Neill, *A concise and accurate account*, 25, 37, 47.

10. For accounts of the crossing see António de Araújo de Azevedo [later Conde da Barca] to Prince Regent, n.d. [ca. 1808], transcribed in Pereira, *Os filhos*, 120–121; Anonymous, "Jornada do Sr. D. João 6° ao Brazil em 1807," reportedly written in 1812 and transcribed in *Os filhos*, 113–115; Anonymous in *Os filhos*, 124–125; and letters to the Prince Regent from Azevedo and José Egidio Alvarez de Almeida in Ângelo Pereira, *D. João VI, principe e rei* v. 1 (Lisbon: Empresa Nacional de Publicidade, 1953), 183–185.

11. José Correa Picanço to Caterina Picanço, March 10, 1808, AHU Caixa 306 Documento 81. The AHU's collection of passports contains numerous requests to rejoin family separated by the royal exile.

12. Marquês de Borba to the Condessa do Redondo [his daughter-in-law], Rio de Janeiro, February 20, 1809, in *Os filhos*, 140.

13. Marrócos to his father, February 27 and 29, 1812, *Cartas*, 60, 63–64.

14. The Jesuit Manuel da Nóbrega (1517–1570) was most prolific on this subject. See his *Cartas do Brasil (1549–1560)* (São Paulo/Belo Horizonte: EDUSP/Itatiaia, 1988). On eighteenth-century thought on America see Antonello Gerbi, *The Dispute of the New World, The History of a Polemic* (1955), trans. Jeremy Moyle (Pittsburgh: University of Pittsburgh Press, 1983).

15. Marrócos to his father, October 24, 1811, and Marrócos to his sister, March 31, 1812, *Cartas*, 38, 68.

16. Anonymous in *Os filhos*, 123; Borba to Condessa, in *Os filhos*, 140.

17. Borba to the Conde de Redondo [his son], [Rio de Janeiro], May 10, 1810, transcribed in *Os filhos*, 143. In a letter to his sister, March 31, 1812, Marrócos also complained of the residents' failure to abstain from eating meat during Lent. See *Cartas*, 68. The Bishop's dispensation, *D. José Caetano da Silva Coutinho, Por Mercê de Deos . . .* ([Rio de Janeiro]: Impressão Régia, [1811]), is cited in Ana Maria de Almeida Camargo and Rubens Borba de Moraes, *Bibliografia da Impressão Régia do Rio de Janeiro* v. 1 (São Paulo: EDUSP/Kosmos, 1993), 73–74.

18. Writing on eighteenth-century discourses on America, Mary Louise Pratt describes this relationship of negativity as "the pivot of colonial semantics." See her *Imperial Eyes: Travel Writing and Transculturation* (New York: Routledge, 1992), 140.

19. Marrócos to his father, November 21, 1812, *Cartas*, 112–113.

20. Amy K. Kaminsky, *Reading the Body Politic: Feminist Criticism and Latin American Women Writers* (Minneapolis: University of Minnesota Press, 1993), 30. As Kaminsky ex-

plains, the experience of exile "carries something of the place departed and of the historical circumstance of that place at the moment of departure. . . ." On exile remembrance see Anonymous in *Os filhos*, 127. A "painting of the ship in which His Royal Highness came" is noted as well in *Relação das festas que se fizerão no Rio de Janeiro quando o Principe Regente Nosso Senshor e toda a sua Real Familia chegarão pela primeira vez a'quella Capital . . .* (Lisbon: Impressão Régia, 1810), 9.

21. "Jornada," *Os filhos*, 114.

22. J.M., *Elegia á Sempre Saudosa e Sentidissima Auzencia de Sua Alteza Real de Lisboa para os seus estados do Brazil . . .* (Rio de Janeiro: Impressão Régia, 1808), 6: "E quem enxugará da esposa amante / Os olhos lacrimosos macerados, / Quando imprevista vir o Pai distante, / E os laços de Hymeneo em flor cortados?" "Quem abrigo dará aos innocentes / Orfãos sem Pai, renovos Lusitanos. . . ?" For images of exile and abandonment see also Gastão Fausto da Camara Coutinho, *Parabens ao Principe Regente Nosso Senhor, e á Patria pelos Presagios Felices da Restauração de Portugal . . .* (Rio de Janeiro: Impressão Régia, 1808), 6: "Dos Tropicos além, onde mais baixa / A gente misti-cor escalda, e cresta / Tocha Febrêa, que dissipa as sombras: / Pula em seus olhos cordial saudade / Dos ternos filhos, que sem Pai deplora."

23. Rodolfo Garcia, "Explicação," in *Cartas*, 7. On the invasion see David Gates, *The Spanish Ulcer: A History of the Peninsular War* (New York: Norton, 1986), 138–142.

24. Marrócos to his father, August 29 and November 21, 1812, *Cartas*, 97, 112.

25. Manuel Teodoro de Sa, March 15, 1813, ANRJ Ministério dos Negócios do Brasil (hereafter MNB) Caixa 6J 79.

26. Marrócos to his father, December 1, 1813, *Cartas*, 175.

27. Marrócos to his father, October 29, 1811, October 14, 1812, November 16, 1813, and July 2, 1814, *Cartas*, 42, 105, 172, 204. Portuguese language papers published in London included *O Investigador Portuguez* (1811–1819), *O Portuguez* (1814–1826), and the more well-known *Correio Braziliense* (1808–1822). See José Augusto dos Santos Alves, *Ideologia e Política na Imprensa do Exílio, "O Portuguez" (1814–1826)* (Lisbon: Imprensa Nacional/Casa da Moeda, 1992). *O Investigador Portuguez* was subsidized by the Portuguese crown to counter the initially more independent *Correio Braziliense*. By 1812, however, the *Correio's* editor, Hipólito José da Costa, was also receiving a royal subsidy. See Barman, *Brazil*, 52, and Chapter 4 here.

28. On Peninsular War publications see Nuno Daupias D'Alcochete, "Les Pamphlets Portugais Anti-Napoléoniens," *Arquivos do Centro Cultural Português* (Paris, Fundação Calouste Gulbenkian) 11 (1977); Araújo, "As Invasões," 42. On the commercial and personal importation of pamphlets to Brazil, see Maria Beatriz Nizza da Silva, *Cultura e sociedade no Rio de Janeiro (1808–1821)* (São Paulo: Companhia Editora Nacional, 1977), 216–219; and Laurence Hallewell, *Books in Brazil: A History of the Publishing Trade* (Metuchen, NJ: Scarecrow, 1982), 25–28. Hallewell records eight book dealers working in Rio between 1808 and 1815. On printed works in Rio see also Delso Renault, *O Rio antigo nos anúncios de jornais, 1808–1850* (Rio de Janeiro: Francisco Alves, 1984), 56–57; and Marrócos to his father, December 1, 1813, *Cartas*, 175. An 1810 shipment, for example, included 250 copies of *Coleção de escritos selectos publicados em Espanha depois da invasão aleivosa dos francezes, traduzida em português* and 250 copies of *Epistola em verso heroico, quintilhas, decimas, e sonetos, cujo assumpto é a nação franceza.* See packing list in ANRJ Antiga Seção Histórica Caixa 169, Doc. 112.

29. Marrócos to his father, March 7, 1812, November 8, 1812, and December 1, 1813, *Cartas*, 108, 130, 175. Manuel Marques Aguilar (b. 1767), a Portuguese engraver, studied in Porto and London. Francesco Bartolozzi (1728–1815), a Florentine engraver, arrived at the Portuguese Court in 1802. See "biografias" in Museu Nacional de Belas Artes, *Memória da independência 1808/1825* (Rio de Janeiro: Museu Nacional de Belas Artes, 1972). On engravings circulating in Rio, see also Nizza da Silva, *Cultura*, 151–152; and Renault, *Rio antigo*, 52.

30. "Decreto," May 13, 1808, BNRJ Ms. I-46,8,14. The press was under the jurisdiction of the Ministério de Negócios Estrangeiros e de Guerra. On the *Gazeta* see Tereza Maria Rolo Fachada Levy Cardoso, "A Gazeta do Rio de Janeiro: subsídios para a história da cidade (1808–1821)" (M.A. thesis, Federal University of Rio de Janeiro, 1988), 96–115. In 1813, an additional gazette appeared called *O Patriota*, "a periodical," as the editor Manuel Ferreira de Araújo Guimarães, a native of Bahia, announced, "which will avenge the accusations of our ineptness that foreign and, unfortunately, some national authors (*nacionaes*) make." *O Patriota* featured articles on science, literature, politics, commerce, agriculture, laws, treaties, and diplomacy. See "Prospecto" (Rio de Janeiro: Impressão Regia, 1812) and its twelve issues published in 1813 by the Royal Press.

31. *Gazeta do Rio de Janeiro*, November 23, 1808, cited in Cardoso, "Gazeta," 109.

32. Marrócos to his father, December 1, 1813, *Cartas*, 175.

33. The question of political debate and the police will be treated in more detail in Chapter 4. See "Auto de Perguntas feitas a Manuel Luiz da Veiga," October 23, 1810, f3v, ANRJ Devassas Caixa 2754; Paulo Fernandes Viana [police intendant] to Aguiar [Ministro de Negócios do Reino], November 27, 1809, ANRJ MNB Caixa 6J 78; Viana, "Registro do Ofício expedido ao Juiz de Crime do Bairro de Santa Rita," November 14, 1812, ANRJ Códice 329 v.2, f31; Marrócos to his father, December 1, 1813 and July 7, 1815, *Cartas*, 175, 234; and "Jornada," *Os filhos*, 115–116. Marrócos also noted that the dissemination of rumor led to arrests.

34. See Frei Francisco de Santo Alberto, *Estragos do terremoto* (1757) cited in Ana Cristina Araújo, "Ruína e Morte em Portugal no Século XVIII," *RHI* 9 (1987), 351. On the Portuguese recognition of the 1755 earthquake as "the wrath of God," see T.D. Kendrick, *The Lisbon Earthquake* (Philadelphia/New York: Lippincott, n.d. [1955]). As Kendrick notes, in the 1750s Portuguese preachers claimed that the earthquake was a moment of both punishment and redemption within the uniquely sacred destiny of Portugal first defined by the miraculous apparition of Christ that had led to the foundation of the Portuguese monarchy itself at Ourique in 1139. In the rest of Europe, preachers also propagated the idea that the earthquake was divine punishment. For associations between sacred foundations, decadence, and retribution as well as discourses of fear and repentance during the French invasion in Portugal and Brazil see Kendrick, *Lisbon Earthquake*, 129; and Bernardino, *Sociedade*, 220–222. For images of spiritual calamity and tribulation in sermons preached and published in Rio see Francisco de São Carlos, *Oração de Acção de Graças . . .* (Rio de Janeiro: Impressão Régia, 1809), 13; Duarte Mendes São Payo, *Oração Sagrada . . . pelo feliz transito de Sua Alteza Real . . .* (Rio de Janeiro: Impressão Régia, 1808), 12; Francisco de Paula de Santa Gertrudes Magna, *Sermão em Memoria do Faustissimo Dia em que Sua Alteza Real Dezembarcou . . .* (Rio de Janeiro: Impressão Régia, 1816); and Francisco Mãi dos Homens, *Oração que na Real Capella desta Corte Celebrando-se as Acções de Graças pelas Noticias do Armisticio Geral . . .* (Rio

de Janeiro: Impressão Régia, 1814). Writing in Portugal in the 1810s, José Daniel Rodrigues da Costa also employed images of decadence to describe postwar Portugal. See his *Portugal enfermo por vicios e abusos de ambos os sexos* (Lisboa: Impressão Régia, 1819).

35. José de Goes, *Vozes do Patriotismo, ou Falla aos Portuguezes* (Rio de Janeiro: Impressão Régia, 1809), 26; Marrócos to his father, August 8, 1813, *Cartas*, 153. On Goes, a native of Pernambuco, see Augusto Victorino Alves Sacramento Blake, *Diccionario bibliographico brazileiro* (1883) (Nendeln, Liechtenstein: Krause reprint, 1969), v. 4, 440–441.

36. Borba to Condessa do Redondo in *Os filhos*, 140. See also Borba's letter to his son in which he complained of the "most supreme acts of vulgarity" (*bregerice*), July 4, 181[0], in *Os filhos*, 146.

37. Anne McClintock, *Imperial Leather: Race, Gender and Sexuality in the Colonial Contest* (New York: Routledge, 1995), 24, 26.

38. Borba to Condessa do Redondo, in *Os filhos*, 140. On representations of exile as feminization, see also Kaminsky, *Reading the Body Politic*, 36.

39. Marrócos to his father, December 22, 1814, *Cartas*, 220.

40. Araújo, "Ruína," 332, 346, 353; and Kendrick, *Lisbon Earthquake*.

41. On images of the transatlantic journey and Brazil as a purgatory see Laura de Mello e Souza, *Inferno Atlântico: demonologia e colonização: séculos XVI–XVIII* (São Paulo: Companhia das Letras, 1993), 89–101.

42. McClintock, *Imperial Leather*, 26.

43. Marrócos to his father, November 21, 1812, *Cartas*, 112–113.

44. Marrócos to his father, July 3, 1811, *Cartas*, 33; Borba to Condessa de Redondo in *Os filhos*, 139; Borba to his son, May 11, 1810, in *Os filhos*, 145.

45. Kaminsky, *Reading the Body Politic*, 33; Marrócos to his father, August 8, 1813, *Cartas*, 153.

46. Borba to his son in *Os filhos*, 143; Marrócos to his father, July 2, 1814, *Cartas*, 207. For further comments on the war, see also *Cartas*, 101, 112, 210–212, 229, 231.

47. See Marrócos to his father, August 29, 1812, May 16, 1814, November 1, 1814, December 22, 1814, *Cartas*, 97, 199–200, 215, 220.

48. Marrócos to his sister, January 31, 1818, *Cartas*, 313–314.

49. Marrócos to his father, June 2, 1814, *Cartas*, 204.

50. José Luiz, [functionary of the *almoxarifado* of Royal Palaces] to Joaquim José d'Azevedo [*almoxarife* of the Royal Palaces], Lisbon, October 1, 1808, transcribed in Ângelo Pereira, *D. João VI, principe e rei* v. 3 (Lisbon: Empresa Nacional de Publicidade, 1956), 118.

51. António Coutinho de Seabra e Souza, October 24, 1808, AHU Documentos Avulsos–Rio de Janeiro Passaportes Caixa 306 Documento 47.

52. Requests for passports often cited the miserable conditions in Portugal. See, for example, AHU Caixa 308 doc. 103; Caixa 309 docs. 52, 54; Caixa 245 docs. 28, 61. On the continuing "exodus of Portuguese" and their arrival at Rio see Viana to Sua Alteza Real, August 27, 1810, in Marcos Carneiro de Mendonça, *Dom João VI e o Império no Brasil, a Independência e a Missão Rio Maior* (Rio de Janeiro: Biblioteca Reprográfica Xerox, 1984), 108. Within a year of the departure the Portuguese ambassador in London also expressed concern about the numerous Portuguese seeking refuge in England. See Domingos de Souza Coutinho to Rodrigo de Souza Coutinho, London, April 29, 1808 in Pereira, *D. João VI* v. 3, 50–51.

53. Manuel José Maria de Costa e Sá to José Anselmo Correa Henriques, n.p. [Lisbon], December 14, 1815, transcribed in Pereira, *D. João VI* v. 3, 221–222. Sá argued that those who wanted the prince regent to return to Portugal under any circumstances were only self-interested.

54. Miguel José Barradas to Joaquina Rosa [his sister], Rio de Janeiro, August 9, 1810, AHU Caixa 309 doc. 54.

55. Manchester, "Transfer," 156, 158–159.

56. Marrócos to his father, November 16, 1813, *Cartas*, 171. The letters of Jacome Ratton (1736–1820) and his family to the Conde da Barca and other royal servants also reveal the efforts and frustrations of royal favor seekers living far from the court in Rio. See "Lettres de Jacques Ratton a António de Araújo de Azevedo, Comte da Barca (1812–1817)," *Bulletin des Etudes Portugaises* (nouvelle série) 25 (1964), 137–256; and Jacome Ratton, *Recordações de Jacome Ratton, sobre occorrências do seu tempo em Portugal de Maio de 1747 a Setembro de 1810* (1813) (Lisbon: Fenda, 1992). The Ratton family arrived at Portugal from France in 1747 and in spite of success in commerce, agriculture, and manufacturing, as well as a record of royal service (Jacome Ratton was appointed to the Junta do Comércio in 1788), they were denounced for collaboration during the French invasion and exiled in London. Cleared of these apparently false accusations in 1816, Ratton's sons pursued careers in commerce and royal service.

57. Passport request for Romão José Pedroso, Oficial da Secretaria de Estado dos Negócios do Reino, November 23, 1809, AHU Caixa 307 doc. 99. Alan Manchester further describes requests both to move to Brazil and to send for family members remaining in Portugal, often at the expense of the crown. See Manchester, "The Growth of Bureaucracy in Brazil, 1808–1821," *Journal of Latin American Studies* 4, n. 1 (1972), 77–79. As one historian of Portuguese migration has noted, an estimated 24,000 Portuguese, including royal officials, merchants, laborers, and shopkeepers, arrived in Brazil between 1808 and 1817. See Maria Beatriz Rocha-Trinidade, "Portuguese Migration to Brazil in the Nineteenth and Twentieth Centuries: An International Cultural Exchange," in *Portuguese Migration in Global Perspective*, ed. David Higgs (Toronto: Multicultural History Society of Toronto, 1990), 32–33.

58. Passport request, Filipe Neri de Freitas, June 15, 1808, AHU Caixa 308 doc. 68; and passport request, António Feliciano d'Albuquerque, October 17, 1809, Caixa 307 doc. 85. See also Caixa 306 doc. 47; Caixa 308 docs. 47, 75; Caixa 309 docs. 3, 12; Caixa 314 doc. 22.

59. Rodrigo de Souza Coutinho, "Quadro da Situação Política da Europa . . . (1803)," in Pereira, *D. João VI* v. 1, 131; idem, *Manifesto, ou Exposição Fundada, e Justificativa do Procedimento da Corte de Portugal a respeito da França . . .* (1808) in Souza Coutinho, *Textos políticos, económicos e financeiros (1783–1811)* t. 2 (Lisbon: Banco de Portugal, 1993), 335–343. For references to imperial renewal and recognition of American potential see also "Soneto aos annos de Sua Alteza Real o Principe Regente Nosso Senhor . . . Remettido ao Lisboa por D. Mariana Antónia Pimentel Maldonado," in *O Patriota* 5 (May 1813), 44: "Foste do negro cahos arrancado, / Para esmalte de Lysia a ti foi dado / Fazer que a idade de ouro se renove"; and "Lettres de Jacques Ratton." While Ratton defended the interests of merchants in Portugal, he recognized nevertheless the geopolitical expediency of a capital in the New World. See especially letters of January 10, 1815 and January 3, 1816, written in London, and his article in the *Investigador Portuguez*, "Pensamentos Patrioticos Império Luzo" (1816), included in "Lettres," 219–228.

60. António B. Leite, *A União Venturosa, Drama com Musica* . . . (Rio de Janeiro: Impressão Régia, 1811), 10, 13, 18–19. For Leite's biography see Blake, *Diccionario*, v. 1, 117. For another celebratory image of Brazil by a newcomer, see Paulino Joakim Leitão, *Libambo. Metamorfose do Pão d'Assucar* (Rio de Janeiro: Impressão Régia, 1811).

61. [José Vasconcellos e Souza], the Marquês de Bellas [parecer (plan for reforms)], n.d., transcribed in Pereira, *D. João VI* v. 3, 38–40.

62. Bellas, [parecer], 38–39.

63. Joaquim Rafael do Valle, *Manifesto Juridico, e Político, A favor da Conducta do Principe Regente N.S., e dos Direitos da Caza de Bragança, contra as usurpações Francezas desde a Epoca da injusta invasão de Portugal* (Rio de Janeiro: Impressão Régia, 1811), 18. Here Valle cites William Pitt.

64. Anonymous in *Os filhos*, 128; Marrócos, *Cartas*, 160, 164. The new royal theater, modeled after Lisbon's Teatro São Carlos, opened in 1813.

65. See Marrócos to his father, November 17, 1812, November 1, 1814, June 29, 1815, February 23, 1816; and to his sister, April 10, 1815, September 21, 1816, *Cartas*, 111, 216, 222, 232, 260–261, 289. Pianos were also imported from London. See Renault, *Rio antigo*, 49.

66. Marrócos to his father, August 24, 1819, *Cartas*, 376; and Marrócos to his father, December 23, 1813, *Cartas*, 177.

67. Marrócos to his father, November 1, 1814, *Cartas*, 217–219; and Marrócos to his sister, November 1, 1814, *Cartas*, 213.

68. Marrócos to his father, November 23, 1815, *Cartas*, 249–253. On a similar embrace of paternal power in the colonies as it was "withering in the European metropolis," see McClintock, *Imperial Leather*, 70, 240.

69. That the royal court provided a civilizing process was recognized earlier, particularly in the seventeenth century as the Portuguese grappled with the absence of the royal court during the union of the Iberian crowns. As one contemporary observed: "no one can doubt that the nobility's brutishness and coarseness are polished and refined with the presence of the kings. . . ." See Diogo Gomes Carneiro, *Oração apodixica* (1641), cited in Diogo Ramada Curto, "Ritos e cerimónias da monarquia em Portugal," in *A Memória da nação*, eds. Francisco Bethencourt and Diogo Ramada Curto (Lisbon: Livraria Sá da Costa, 1991), 226. On the European court as civilizing, see Norbert Elias, *The Civilizing Process: The History of Manners* (New York: Pantheon, 1982).

70. See [Nuno Álvarez Pereira Pato Moniz], *A Queda do Despotismo: Drama Dedicado a Sua Alteza Real o Principe Regent Nosso Senhor* (Reprint) (Rio de Janeiro: Impressão Régia, 1810).

71. Marrócos to his father, August 24, 1819, *Cartas*, 377.

72. [José Caetano da Silva Coutinho], *Memória Histórica da Invasão dos Francezes em Portugal no Anno de 1807* (Rio de Janeiro: Impressão Régia, 1808), 83–84.

73. See Ana Cristina Nogueira da Silva and António Manuel Hespanha, "A identidade portuguesa," in *Historia de Portugal: O Antigo Regime* v. 4, ed. António Manuel Hespanha (Lisbon: Estampa, n.d.), 32. In the Portuguese-speaking world reformist thinking was akin to what Pagden has called the "defense of civilization" and in contrast to Rousseauian attacks on civilization as corrupting. See Anthony Pagden, "The 'Defense of Civilization' in Eighteenth-Century Social Theory" (1988), reprinted in Pagden, *The Uncertainties of Empire* (Norfolk,

GB: Variorum, 1994). This defense, as Pagden notes, was grounded to a certain extent in the work of political economists which, as we shall see in Chapter 6, was embraced by statesmen in Rio de Janeiro following the transfer of the court in their quest to analyze the empire's weaknesses and redefine its future. In Portugal a recognition that national character was not immutable is also evident in criticism of efforts at reform and change. The Marquês de Penalva, for example, argued that it was a vassal's duty to preserve the integrity of national character defined in terms of customs, the "moral will of the Sovereign, and of the People," "the result of much meditation," and "the consequence of climate, Religion, and the nature of the great family of the State. . . . " See Fernando Teles da Silva Caminha e Meneses, Marquês de Penalva, *Dissertação sôbre as obrigações do vassalo* (Lisbon: Régia Officina Tipographica, 1804), 134.

74. See *Ensaio sobre a Critica de Alexandre Pope traduzido em Portuguez pelo Conde de Aguiar* (Rio de Janeiro: Impressão Régia, 1810) and *Ensaios Moraes de Alexandre Pope em Quatro Epistolas a Diversas Pessoas Traduzidos em Portuguez pelo Conde de Aguiar* (Rio de Janeiro: Impressão Régia, 1811). The Conde de Aguiar, Fernando de Portugal, had served as governor of Bahia from 1788 to 1801. Pope, along with La Rochefoucauld and Bacon, also provided inspiration for a contemporary series of maxims published in a local periodical. See "Maximas, Pensamentos, e Reflexões Moraes Por hum Brazileiro," *O Patriota* (January–March and August 1813). A similar concern with the cultivation of the arts and sciences, with the "reestablishment of discipline" and "the obligations of the Citizen, and of Man" can be seen in a funeral prayer for the Marquês de Pombal published in Rio and regarded as a model of eloquence. See [Frei Joaquim de Sancta Clara], *Elogio do Illustrissimo e Excellentissimo Senhor Sebastião José de Carvalho e Mello . . .* (Rio de Janeiro: Impressão Régia, 1811) and Camargo and Moraes, v. 1, 76. For an analysis of the neoclassical idiom in early nineteenth-century theater, see Jurandir Malerba, "A corte no exílio. Interpretação do Brasil joanino, 1808–1821" (Ph.D. dissertation, University of São Paulo, 1997), 72–78. On the cultivation of classical virtue and Pope in the eighteenth-century English-speaking world see Gordon S. Wood, *The Radicalism of the American Revolution* (New York: Vintage, 1993), 101, 103. On Pope see also Laura Brown, *Alexander Pope* (Oxford: Blackwell, 1985), especially Chapter 2, "The 'New World' of Augustan Humanism." Brown's reading pays close attention to the ways in which Pope, within ambivalent commentary on bourgeois culture, connected the arts with imperial expansion, a connection that would have reassured Aguiar.

75. Wood, *Radicalism*, 194; Pagden, "The 'defense of civilization'."

76. Pratt, *Imperial Eyes*, 175.

77. Gyan Prakash, "Introduction," in Prakash, ed. *After Colonialism, Imperial Histories and Postcolonial Displacements* (Princeton: Princeton University Press, 1995), 3–4.

78. Gastão Fausto da Camara Coutinho, *O Triunfo da America, Drama para se Recitar no Real Theatro do Rio de Janeiro* (Rio de Janeiro: Impressão Régia, 1810). Coutinho was also a captain in the Portuguese navy. Although he was born and died in Lisbon, he apparently spent time in Rio during the 1810s. See Innocencio Francisco da Silva, *Diccionario bibliographico portuguez* v. 3 (Lisboa: Imprensa Nacional, 1860), 136 and J. Galante de Souza, *O Teatro no Brasil* t. 2 (Rio de Janeiro: Ministério de Educação, 1960), 197. Similar themes of monarchical power and tradition and redemption in the tropics can be found in Coutinho's *O Juramento dos Numes* (Rio de Janeiro: Impressão Régia, 1813).

79. Viana, "Registro da Informação expedida ao Ministro de Estado dos Negócios do

Reino," November [18], 1818, ANRJ Códice 323 v. 5, f75v.

80. Manuel Ignacio Silva Alvarenga, [verses to commemorate the arrival of the court] transcribed in "Preparativos," March 23, 1808, BNRJ Ms. II-35,4,1, f4v: "Vinde honrar a idade d'ouro / Pois é nosso este Thesouro / Que ninguem pode roubar"; Luiz Gonçalves dos Santos, *Memórias para servir à História do Reino do Brasil* (1825) t. 1 (Belo Horizonte/São Paulo: Itatiaia/EDUSP, 1981), 33, 178.

81. "Preparativos," f3–4.

82. Duarte Mendes de São Payo, *Oração Sagrada que em Acção de Graças pelo feliz transito de Sua Alteza Real, e Sua Serenissima Familia, da Europa Portugueza para os Seus Estados do Brazil, foi recitada na Santa Igreja Cathedral do Rio de Janeiro estando presente o mesmo Senhor* (Rio de Janeiro: Impressão Régia, 1808), preface (no page number), 10, 12. Gonçalves dos Santos records hearing the prayer. See *Memórias* t. 1, 186.

83. *Relação das festas*, 12–14; Gonçalves dos Santos, *Memórias* t. 1, 196; and Rui Vieira da Cunha, "A vida do Rio de Janeiro através dos testamentos: 1815–1822," *RIHGB* 282 (January–March 1969), 54.

84. "Jornada," in *Os filhos*, 114.

85. According to Manchester, in 8 years Dom João awarded 20 titles of Marquês, 8 Counts, 16 Viscounts, and 21 Barons. Titles of nobility were not hereditary and carried no explicit material advantage. He also granted 4,084 knighthoods, commissions, and titles of the Grand Cross in the Order of Christ; 1,422 in the Order of Avis; 590 in the order of Santiago. See Manchester, "Transfer," 171–172. For a historical perspective on the creation of titles of nobility see "Quadro 6: Casas titulares existentes em Portugal (1611–1820)," in Nuno Gonçalo Monteiro, "Poder senhorial, estatuto nobiliárquico e aristocracia," in *História de Portugal: O Antigo Regime* v. 4, ed. Hespanha, 364. According to Monteiro, 58 noble houses were created between 1791 and 1820, while between 1641 and 1790 42 were created.

86. Gonçalves dos Santos, *Memórias* t. 1, 208, 223. On the Ordem da Torre e Espada see Álvaro da Veiga Coimbra, "Noções de Numismática. Condecorações (III)," *Revista de História* 26, n. 53, ano 14 (1963), 219–264. Earlier in 1801 the Princess Carlota Joaquina had sponsored the creation of the Real Ordem de Santa Isabel, which continued to honor elite women throughout Dom João's Brazilian reign. See Coimbra, "Noções de Numismática. Condecorações (IV)," *Revista de História* 26, n. 56, ano 14 (1963), 457–471. Although these honors implied recognition of individual service, royal grace also acknowledged corporate deeds. Thus the city's town council, as Maria de Fátima Silva Gouvêa has noted, was granted the honorific title of *Senhoria* because its members attended the Acclamation in 1818 and, most importantly, took "oaths of loyalty in the name of the people of the city." Gouvêa's research also shows that between 1790 and 1822 there was an increasing tendency among the city's elite—*os homens bons*—to formally identify themselves, and justify their service in government, in terms of honorific titles, rather than, as they previously had, in terms of their commercial and proprietary concerns. See Maria de Fátima Silva Gouvêa, "Redes de Poder na América Portuguesa—O caso dos Homens Bons do Rio de Janeiro, ca. 1790–1822," *Revista Brasileira de História* 18, n. 36 (1998), 313.

87. John Luccock, *Notes on Rio de Janeiro and the southern parts of Brazil; taken during a residence of ten years in that country, from 1808–1818* (London: Samuel Leigh, 1820), 99, 246.

88. Gonçalves dos Santos, *Memórias* t. 1, 201–207, 219; Manchester, "Transfer,"

169–170; idem, "The Growth of Bureaucracy," 77–83; Riva Gorenstein, "Comércio e Política: O Enraizamento de Interesses Mercantis Portugueses no Rio de Janeiro (1808–1830)," in Lenira Menezes Martinho and Riva Gorenstein. *Negociantes e Caixeiros na Sociedade da Independência* (Rio de Janeiro: Secretaria Muncipal de Cultura, 1992), 189–204; Jurandir Malerba, "Instituições da monarquia portuguesa decisivas na fundação do Império brasileiro," *Luso-Brazilian Review* 36, n. 1 (Summer 1999), 33–48. Those formerly beheld with suspicion by the viceregal government apparently were not penalized. Mariano José Pereira da Fonseca, a target of the viceroy's investigation and the future Marquês de Maricá, was appointed to be a director of the royal press. See Hallewell, 27. In some cases, Rio's elite cultivated honor and royal patronage in marriage. Although marriages involving the nobility and the daughters of untitled vassals were rare, according to Riva Gorenstein, marriages of the daughters of local elite families and royal bureaucrats, as we have seen in the case of Marrócos, were common. For an overview of social status and occupation in Rio de Janeiro see Maria Beatriz Nizza da Silva, *Análise de estratificação social (o Rio de Janeiro de 1808 a 1821)* (São Paulo: Faculdade de Filosofia, Letras e Ciências Humanas da Universidade de São Paulo, 1975).

89. Gonçalves dos Santos, *Memórias* t. 1, 169, 194–195, 198–201, 229, 242. See also "Alvará [revogando a prohibição das Fabricas . . .]," April 1, 1808 ([Rio de Janeiro]: Impressão Régia, [1808]). The opening of ports was decreed from Bahia on January 28, 1808. Unlike neighboring colonies in Spanish America, colonial Brazil did not have a university. Although seminaries provided some degree of higher education, in the eighteenth century those who could not afford to study in Portugal relied on private tutoring and *aulas régias* [royal lessons]. Although the academies and schools founded after the arrival of the court helped to fill the gap, Brazil remained without a university. On education in eighteenth-century Brazil see Maria Beatriz Nizza da Silva, *Vida Privada e Quotidiano no Brasil. Na época de D. Maria e D. João VI* (Lisbon: Estampa, 1993), 24–29; 92–94; and idem, "A cultura," in *Nova História da Expansão Portuguesa. O Império Luso-Brasileiro, 1750–1822*, ed. Maria Beatriz Nizza da Silva (Lisbon: Estampa, 1986), 445–454.

90. Gonçalves dos Santos, *Memórias* t. 1, 184–185.

91. See *O Patriota* 1 (January 1813), 120–121; 4 (April 1813), 90; and 2 (August 1813), 66 (note that the periodical's numeration recurs). Manuel Ferreira de Araujo Guimarães' interest in promoting "moral" progress is evident throughout *O Patriota*. Along with "Maximas, Pensamentos, e Reflexões Moraes Por hum Brazileiro" (January–March and August 1813), he published, for example, an inquiry by the city's town council from 1798 on public health that included observations on moral causes of illness. See 1 (January 1813), 58–67; 2 (February 1813), 56–63.

92. Guimarães, *O Patriota* 4 (April 1813), 89.

93. Francisco de São Carlos, *Oração de Acção de Graças recitada no dia 7 de Março de 1809 na Capella Real, Dia Anniversario da Feliz Chegada de Sua Alteza Real a Esta Cidade* (Rio de Janeiro: Impressão Régia, 1809), 12. For the biography of São Carlos, born in Rio in 1763, see Benjamin Franklin Ramiz Galvão, "O Pulpito no Brasil," *RIHGB* 92, n. 146 (1922), 74–92; and "Fr. Francisco de S.Carlos," *RIHGB* 10 (1848), 524–546.

94. Gonçalves dos Santos, *Memórias* t. 1, 168, 175, 180, 270. It seemed as if the sun, he wrote, wanted to see "the triumphant entrance of the first European sovereign into the most

fortunate city of the New World" and "to participate in the joy and praise of a people drunk with the most poignant pleasure; when on the contrary everything mourned, and he hid, seeing this same sovereign on the verge of leaving his ancient Court and the consternation of Lisbon, so as not to witness such sadness and so many tears."

95. "Jornada," *Os filhos*, 114.

96. Viana, "Registro do Ofício expedido ao Ajudante da Intendência Geral da Polícia de Portugal," December 29, 1810, ANRJ Códice 323 v. 2, f52.

97. [Guimarães], "Estado Político da Europa," *O Patriota* 1 (January 1813), 112–113. See also his "Discurso sobre o Estado Político da Europa," *O Patriota* 5 (May 1813), 112–124. As Jurandir Malerba notes, during the war the city's merchants sponsored donations for war victims and for the rescue of prisoners of war. See Malerba, "A corte no exílio," 209–211. Together with sermons and prayers cited, for public Peninsular War commemorations in Rio see Joaquim de São José, *Sermão de Acção de Graças pela Feliz Restauração do Reino de Portugal Pregado em 21 de Dezembro de 1808 na Real Capella do Rio de Janeiro . . .* (Rio de Janeiro: Impressão Régia, 1809); Eduardo José Moira, *Oração que no dia 22 de janeiro do anno de 1809 recitou . . . Na solemne Acção de Graças pela feliz Restauração do Reino de Portugal. . . .* (Rio de Janeiro: Impressão Régia, 1809); Guimarães, "Política," *O Patriota* 2 (February 1813); Anonymous, in *Os filhos*, 128; Borba, in *Os filhos*, 147 (on victory at Badajoz); and Gonçalves dos Santos, *Memórias* t. 1, 168, 218–219, 224 (Vimeiro); 241, 279, 308 (Badajoz); 320, 324–325, 340–342 (arrival of Beresford).

98. Januário da Cunha Barbosa, *Sermão de Acção de Graças pela Feliz Restauração do Reino de Portugal Pregado na Real Capella do Rio de Janeiro na Manhãa de 19 de Dezembro de 1808* (Rio de Janeiro: Impressão Régia, 1809), 13. Barbosa's sermon was noted by Gonçalves dos Santos, *Memórias* t. 1, 226. For a short biography of Barbosa see Galvão, "O Pulpito no Brasil," 104–114.

99. São Carlos, *Oração de Acção de Graças*, 14.

100. Barbosa, *Sermão de Acção de Graças*, 9–12, 16.

101. Januário da Cunha [Barbosa], *Oração de Acção de Graças Recitada na Capella Real do Rio de Janeiro, Celebrando-se o Quinto Anniversario da Chegada de S.A.R. Com Toda a Sua Real Familia a Esta Cidade* (Rio de Janeiro: Impressão Régia, 1813), 10. Gonçalves dos Santos similarly describes the transfer of the court as "one of the great effects of Divine Providence, through which . . . were raised new earthly empires." See *Memórias*, t. 1, 33.

102. Barbosa's *Sermão* begins with Exodus, chapter 15, verse 2, and the *Oração* with Leviticus, chapter 23, verses 41–43. He urged his audience both to recognize the role of Providence in providing for the end of bondage and to commemorate the liberation regularly.

103. João Pereira da Silva, *Sermão de Acção de Graças, rendidas ao Ceo na Feliz Chegada de Sua Alteza Real . . .* (Rio de Janeiro: Impressão Régia, 1809), 8. The published sermon identified Silva as a native of Rio and chaplain of the royal chapel. For readings of the war in terms of scripture see also São Payo, *Oração Sagrada*, 10, 12; and São Carlos, *Oração de Acção de Graças*, 6, 13.

104. Messianism was a persistent, albeit suspect, influence in early modern political discourse. Although in the eighteenth century expressions of messianism surfaced only occasionally, after the transfer of the court prophetic interpretations of the Portuguese monarchy were reasserted. Between 1808 and 1811 at least thirty messianic tracts were published. See, for ex-

ample, Joaquim José Pereira Machado, *Promessas feitas ao Magnanimo e Sempre Invicto Rei o Senhor D. Affonso Henriques no Campo de Qurique, Realizadas nas trez vezes em que os Francezes tem sido expulsados de Portugal pelo Exercito Anglo-Luso* (Lisbon: Impressão Régia, 1811). See also Ana Cristina Araújo, "Revoltas e Ideologias em Conflito durante as Invasões Francesas," *RHI* 7 (1985), 7–90; and Araújo, "Invasões," 32–37, which includes reproductions of the Portuguese Peninsular War engravings: "O Grande Monstro de que trata S. João no Apocalipse" [The Great Monster that confronts St. John at the Apocalypse], in which a Napoleonic beast is about to be slain by a well-armed knight, protected by a shield bearing the Portuguese coat of arms and an image of the Virgin; and "Visão do profeta Daniel" [Vision of the Prophet Daniel], in which a departing ship, guided by angelic and Christ-like figures, evokes the messianic prophecy of the Book of Daniel. The appeal to Sebastianism was also scathingly criticized by José Agostinho de Macedo. See his *Justa Defesa do Livro Intitulado os Sebastianistas* . . . (Lisbon: 1810) (Rio de Janeiro: Impressão Régia, 1810). Sebastianists, Macedo argued, were "bad Vassals, bad Christians and big and great fools" because in passively waiting for a messianic kingdom they allowed the spread of revolutionary ideas. One subtle reference to the transfer of the court and Providential design was made by Bellas ca. 1808. See *Os filhos*, 133.

105. São Payo, *Oração Sagrada*, 3–4, 9, 12, 15, 17.

106. Pereira da Silva, *Sermão de Acção de Graças*, 13. This same vision of the transfer of the court as the foundation of a new empire was offered in commemorative texts preached or written outside Rio and then published and sold within the city. See Bento da Trinidade, *Sermão de Acção de Graças pela feliz vinda do Principe . . . Pregado na Igreja do Sacramento do Recife de Pernambuco em 1808 . . .* (Rio de Janeiro: Impressão Régia, 180[9]); and António José Vaz, *A Sua Alteza Real, o Principe Regent, Nosso Senhor, em o Faustissimo dia 7 de Março de 1810 . . .* (Rio de Janeiro: Impressão Régia, [1810]). Trinidade was born in Bahia and educated in Coimbra, before beginning a career as an Augustinian in Pernambuco. See Blake, v. 1, 403–404. Vaz was a native of São Paulo. See Raimundo de Menezes, *Dicionário Literário Brasileiro Ilustrado* v. 5 (São Paulo: Saraiva, 1969), 1295.

107. Gonçalves dos Santos, *Memórias* t. 1, 168.

108. São Payo, *Oração Sagrada*, 15–16.

109. José da Silva Lisboa, *Memoria dos beneficios politicos do governo de El-Rey Nosso Senhor D. João VI*, pt. 1 (Rio de Janeiro: Impressão Régia, 1818), 64–65.

110. Pereira da Silva, *Sermão de Acção de Graças*, 3, 13. The commemorative sermons and prayers properly echoed the slogans heard during the initial reception. As the royal family disembarked, the residents of Rio were said to have hailed not the prince regent of Portugal, but rather "the Emperor of Brazil." See "Preparativos," f3v; *Relação*, 8.

111. *Relação*, 9: "América feliz tens em teu seio / Do novo Império o Fundador Sublime: / Será este Paiz das Santas Virtudes, / Quando do resto do Mundo he todo crime. / Do grande Affonso a Descendencia Augusta, / Os Povos doutrinou do Mundo antigo: / Para a Gloria esmaltar do novo Mundo / Manda o Sexto João o Ceo amigo."

112. São Carlos, *Oração de Acção de Graças*, 6, 11. On Ourique see Ana Isabel Buescu, "Um mito das origens da nacionalidade: o milagre de Ourique," in *A Memória da nação*, eds. Francisco Bethencourt and Diogo Ramada Curto (Lisbon: Livraria Sá da Costa, 1991), 49–69.

FOUR

The New City of Rio de Janeiro:
Reconstructing the Portuguese Royal Court

Both residents and newly arrived courtiers, as we have seen, came to view Rio de Janeiro as an alternative to an impious and decadent Europe, a site in which morality, civility, and the monarchy's prestige could be restored. As exiles, residents, and royal officials then recognized, sustaining this vision of New World renewal required corresponding reforms. The greatness of an American monarchy would have to begin with the greatness of its new capital. Rio de Janeiro's transformation into a royal court began just two months before the prince regent's arrival when news of the royal exile, as "pleasurable" as it was "shocking," was received.[1] Although residents, the city's memorialists insisted, viewed the prospect of serving as the new royal residence with happiness and pride, accommodating the prince regent, the royal family, and the other exiles was nevertheless a daunting task that required large-scale mobilization and extraordinary expenditures. Preparations were immediately commenced. To provide adequate quarters for the prince regent, the viceregal palace was enlarged by annexing the adjacent jail and a garage for carriages was created. The palace exterior was painted and the interior walls were lined with silk.[2] The city's churches were cleaned and their altars were polished, and a canopy of the finest cloth was erected near the docks.[3] Further repairs and arrangements for a formal reception were authorized by the city's town council. As a result, one resident wrote of viewing the city's elite receive the prince regent and his retinue amid luxurious decorations and festive illumination, Rio de Janeiro became "a New City."[4]

As the city's residents discovered, however, their initial preparations to accommodate Dom João and the exiles marked only the beginning of Rio de Janeiro's transformation into the royal court. For the project to construct a "new city" and imperial capital lasted throughout the prince regent's Brazilian reign. This chapter examines the reconstruction of Rio de Janeiro following the prince regent's arrival, the discourses and practices of the emerging project to remake the city into "the court." The institution entrusted with much of this task was the general intendancy of police, created shortly after the prince regent's arrival. On the one hand, the intendant and other royal officials sought to reconstruct Rio de Janeiro based on eighteenth-century experiences of urban renewal in Portugal and Brazil in which both the projection of absolute royal power and the establishment of an enlightened order had served as primary objectives. On the other hand, however, even as reforms following the transfer of the court provided continuities with these earlier experiences, what Gonçalves dos Santos described as Rio's "political transformation" was also defined by the particular historical moment in which it occurred.[5] Policing thus entailed ensuring that the city provided a peaceful haven of political loyalty amid the turmoil of Napoleonic Europe and insurgent Spanish America. And, unlike earlier reforms of Lisbon or Rio de Janeiro, the construction of a new court in America depended on an explicit metropolitanization of the city. In other words, royal officials and Rio's residents recognized that because the transfer of the court undermined the dichotomy of metropolis/colony, the transformation of Rio de Janeiro into the royal court had to entail a marginalization of the aesthetics and the practices that failed to reflect this change. It was an undertaking that anticipated the paradox of post-Independence Latin America. To no longer be colonial meant embracing a colonial project: to "civilize."

"GROWING SPLENDOR" AND "SECURITY": MAKING RIO DE JANEIRO A ROYAL COURT

To construct a royal court was to construct an ideal city; a city in which both mundane and monumental architecture, together with its residents' social and cultural practices, projected an unequivocally powerful and virtuous image of royal authority and government.[6] Such an endeavor was undertaken by the eighteenth-century Portuguese on more than one occasion. During the reign of João V (1706–1750) the crown dedicated much of the revenue from the newly discovered Brazilian gold and diamond mines to what historian Russell-Wood has described as "an intellectual and cultural Europeanization" of the royal court. The society of courtiers and the city of Lisbon experienced an unprecedented opening to European manners and aesthetics. In an explicit emulation of both the court of Louis XIV and the Vatican, João V brought artists from France and Italy to serve in the creation of his own spectacle of royal power and piety. A royal palace-convent built outside Lisbon in Mafra and the sumptuous decoration of churches and chapels within Lisbon itself became emblems of what Portuguese historian António Pimentel has described as "the indissoluble connection of Royalty to God and of God to the Monarchy." Lisbon, indeed, was likened to "a new Rome."[7]

In the second half of the eighteenth century, the intimate correspondence between the Portuguese capital and the monarchy was sustained. During the reign of José I (1750–1777), however, Lisbon ceased to be a symbol of royal piety to become instead, as José Augusto França has described it, the stage on which the Prime Minister Pombal was to play out his drama of "reasoned" reform. While France continued to serve as a model of placing art in the service of politics and French architects provided the Portuguese crown with their expertise, the new reigning aesthetic was characterized, as França has noted, by a simplicity, proportion, and harmony that reflected what contemporaries perceived as a "modern" utilitarianism. Thus, Pombal's reconstruction of the city of Lisbon following the devastating earthquake in 1755 evoked the same efficient, pragmatic administration and commercial exchange that the Prime Minister's reforms sought to achieve.[8] As we saw in Chapter 2, Pombaline urban reform was also extended to Rio de Janeiro, where new military and civilian infrastructure reflected the power of a distant yet imperial crown as well as the viceregal capital's new political and economic preeminence.

The transformation of the city of Rio de Janeiro following the prince regent's arrival was predicated on a similar quest to project an image of royal power and similar notions of the relationship between order, enlightenment, and progress. As royal officials argued, governance itself was expected to exhibit the decorum and propriety "compatible with the residence of His Royal Highness in this City."[9] What officials referred to as the city's "perfection" also meant the creation and enforcement of an aesthetic and cultural uniformity and the redefinition of proper rules for public conduct for both elites and the popular classes that reflected hierarchy, virtue, and royal splendor. "The old Court dress was required," the British merchant and resident of Rio John Luccock reported, and the city's elites, those he described as "the private gentry," became "more attentive to propriety and taste in their modes of dress" as well as in the decoration of their homes, while "state livries were introduced similar to those of Lisbon." As Luccock also noted, however, it was not an absence of manners and deference among the colonial elite that the new courtly decorum supplanted, but rather a severity and austerity that evoked provincial isolation instead of the dynamic life of a royal residence. The "formality which had prevailed until then in the manners of the City," he explained, gave way to "an air of bustle and importance." Rio de Janeiro became, as he described it, "a showy and intrusive place."[10]

After the end of the Napoleonic Wars, as fervid anti-French patriotism began to wane, the Portuguese crown and the city's elite also began to look to France, as they had from Lisbon, for models of aesthetic refinement for the new court. French women's fashion and hairstyles began to compete with the traditional Iberian mantilla, and the opening of Rio's port also gave elites easier access to foreign luxuries, such as perfumes, fabrics, and, as one notice in the city's *Gazeta* announced, "wine from Champagne."[11] In 1815, the crown then moved to consolidate Rio de Janeiro's cosmopolitan elegance and "growing splendor" by recruiting and subsidizing a number of artists from France. Brazil, as the decree that formally announced these intentions explained, needed "great aesthetic assistance in order to take advantage of [its] resources, whose value and preciousness could come to make Brazil the richest and most opulent of Kingdoms." What came to be known as the "French Cultural Mission" included over a dozen artists and artisans: painters, sculptors, engravers, a composer, an engineer, and an architect, Auguste Henri Victor Grandjean de Montigny. While, as historians have noted, the so-called mission came to fruition somewhat later, with the creation of a national museum and a national school of fine arts in the 1830s, during the Brazilian reign of João VI these artists and artisans provided the crown with a vision of civilization, progress, and order inspired by French neoclassicism. Grandjean de Montigny and the painter Jean Baptiste Debret were responsible for much of the festive ephemeral architecture constructed for Dom João's Acclamation. More generally, they came to be identified as arbiters of artistic and architectural expression, designing public buildings and monuments, such as the neoclassical merchants' exchange building known as the *praça do comércio*.[12]

Beyond the implementation of current European aesthetic standards, the construction of a royal court in Rio de Janeiro also required the reestablishment of institutions identified with the particular culture of the Portuguese monarchy and its court in Lisbon. In 1808, for example, with the creation of a royal chapel near his own palace in Rio, the prince regent both reaffirmed a "most ancient custom" and the crown's historic patronage of sacred music and re-created an important venue for court gatherings and the reception of foreign dignitaries.[13] Two years later Dom João then provided for the construction of a new royal theater and appointed the well-established Portuguese composer Marcos Portugal as its director. As the royal decree explained, Rio needed "a decent theater proportionate to the population and greater degree of elevation and greatness" that Rio de Janeiro had come to enjoy "as a result of the [prince regent's] residence within it, and of the foreigners and other persons who come from the vast provinces of all [the crown's] States." Indeed, while the city's residents continued to frequent older, small-scale *casas de espectáculos*, the *Real Teatro de São João*, inaugurated in 1813 with the one-act drama entitled *O Juramento dos Numes* by the Portuguese playwright Gastão Fausto da Camara Coutinho, became an artistic and social focal point within the city. The inaugural drama itself sparked a lively debate in Rio's press on aesthetic standards and, as Luccock noted, the prince regent's patronage made "showing" oneself at the theater "fashionable for all, who wished to be thought persons of consequence." The city's popular classes, or, as Luccock remarked, "the multitude," also joined the prince regent and the courtiers in attending the theater's offerings.[14]

The institution entrusted with the supervision of the theater, and with public life in the court in general, was the *intendência geral da polícia* [general intendancy of the police], established in Rio shortly after the prince regent's arrival.[15] The general intendancy of Rio de Janeiro was modeled after the same institution created in Lisbon in 1760, which, in turn, resembled the *lieutenance générale de police* of Paris. Although the intendant's jurisdiction extended to all of Brazil, his attentions were focused primarily on the city of Rio and nearby areas. As was the case in Lisbon, within Rio the intendant had a wide range of responsibilities that made him, as historians of the Brazilian police have argued, akin to a modern-day mayor; one who, the statesmen Souza Coutinho explained by invoking "the best definition of the police" of Louis XIV, ensured the city's "cleanliness, abundance, security and [public] health." In other words, as were his European counterparts, Rio's intendant was responsible for the promotion of the "common good" and the city's residents' "well being." In practice, this included not only sponsoring and regulating public entertainment, such as the theater, but also supervising public works intended to improve living conditions.[16] To fulfill these duties, the crown chose the Coimbra-trained magistrate Paulo Fernandes Viana, a native of Rio de Janeiro with ties and allegiances to the city's most influential families that he then extended to the courtiers following the prince regent's arrival.[17]

Viana, who often framed his reports and recommendations to the royal cabinet with references to his native knowledge of the city, zealously embraced the task of meeting the needs and demands of the newly arrived courtiers and, most importantly, in so doing recasting Rio de Janeiro as an imperial capital, promoting, as he himself explained, the "decorum and perfection of the Court."[18] To this effect, the intendant worked to ensure the supply of foodstuffs and initiated projects to provide sidewalks, landfills, street lighting, new public fountains, an efficient sewer system, and additional roads and bridges that connected the city's center to nearby neighborhoods.[19] Among the most immediate undertakings with which the intendancy was involved was the provision and regulation of residential housing. Much of this task was achieved using *aposentadoria*, a royal requisition of urban property for crown officials. As one resident reported, such requisitions had begun even before the prince regent's arrival. "The ship that brought the news of the coming of His Royal Highness had barely arrived," he recalled, "[when] many houses were taken for the *Fidalgos* who accompanied him."[20]

Ensuring that the city's infrastructure accommodated both the residents and the exiles required almost constant negotiation with local institutions, the crown, and the city's residents; and, as Viana often complained, the realities of building a royal court were at times far from the circumstances envisioned in legislative precedent and by newly arrived cabinet ministers with less knowledge of the city.[21] An orderly response to the need for housing with requisitions, in particular, was thwarted by the extraordinary growth of Rio de Janeiro's population, which doubled to 80,000 between 1808 and 1821.[22] While, as we saw in the previous chapter, memorialists rendered the residents' accommodation of the exiles as acts of vassalage duly recognized by the crown, such emblematic loyalty and royal grace could not bear the costs of housing entirely. Within months the intendant was confronted with both the political and physical perils of the housing crisis and requisitions. Although owners were to receive rents for the houses they surrendered, many resented what they regarded to be the unsatisfactory terms of these rents. Aposentadoria was an oppressive and "feudal" regulation, charged the editor of the London-based *Correio Braziliense* in October 1808, a "direct attack on the sacred rights of property" that "could not but make the new Government of Brazil odious to the People."[23] Tenants, in turn, both residents and exiles alike, complained that accommodations were not only expensive but also poorly built.[24] Indeed, according to the royal architect José Joaquim de Santa Anna, new houses haphazardly constructed on Rio's mountains were improperly designed, failing to adequately allow for drainage.[25]

According to Luccock, resident property owners, some initially generous in providing housing, responded to the crisis and, more specifically, to the threat of requisition by developing strategies to minimize their losses. "A few," he recalled, "foreseeing that the display of wealth would render them . . . objects of continued peculation, became prudently poor, and passed into voluntary seclusion."[26] The intendant, in turn, suspected that the residents' resistance to the requisitions was even more elaborately designed. On the one hand, he reported, "frightened" by the possibility of having property requisitioned, Rio's residents were abstaining from building houses, "leaving unfinished even those buildings that they had started." On the other hand, those who proceeded to build not only ignored an earlier directive against the building of one-story houses, but they also "made public that they do so because such buildings were not of a nature as to be [subject] to aposentadoria." The situation was particularly lamentable, Viana explained, because "being now a Court" Rio de Janeiro needed "properties of another order, that ennoble and beautify it."[27] In other words, a concerted lack of compliance threatened to displace the official joyousness and happiness of the reception, and both undermine the prince regent's authority and jeopardize the creation of an imperial capital that his presence demanded.

In March 1811, after the crown had dismissed his earlier requests for exemptions and as refugees from Portugal continued to arrive, Viana proposed that a solution to the crisis could be found by focusing attention on an area outside the city's center known as the *Cidade Nova* (New City). Although rights to use the "beautiful" plots had been granted, the swamps that covered most of the area had kept building to a minimum. The residents, he suggested, should be encouraged to dry and fill the area and build houses. Thus, the city would be "beautified," more housing would be available, and rents would decrease. The enforcement of standards for building in the area, Viana further explained, could be mitigated, or "disguised," by exemptions. Most importantly, he argued, the crown's intervention would also bring to an end the "mistaken liberty" to build as one pleased and therefore reinforce the authority of the prince regent.[28] The plan apparently appealed to other members of the royal cabinet as well, for on April 26 a royal decree established that, while in the Cidade Nova the building of one-story houses was prohibited, all two-story houses there and in any other previously swampy areas built within two years would be exempt from the *décima dos prédios urbanos* (a tax on urban property) for 10 to 20 years depending on their size.[29] Subsequently, building in the new neighborhood expanded. Speculation followed, however, and caused other problems including, as Viana complained in 1818, property disputes. Amid what the intendant characterized as generalized "disturbances," the crown finally abrogated the practice of aposentadoria in the city that same year.[30]

For Viana and other royal officials, the housing crisis, and the growing population that produced the crisis, thus showed that with the transfer of the court what one royal alvará described obliquely as "former circumstances" had been displaced by not only new standards of public life but also new sources of social and political disorder produced, in part, by official efforts to reconcile these circumstances with new standards. Obstacles to courtliness, and to the "personal security and tranquility of loyal vassals," however, also included older and ongoing sources of disorder, including a broad range of actions defined as criminal. Accordingly, Rio de Janeiro's transformation into the court would be based on the first systematic effort at policing crime in Brazil. With a "broad and unlimited jurisdiction," the intendancy gathered together formerly disparate and limited constabulary efforts under the leadership of a *desembargador* (magistrate) with legislative, executive, and judicial powers.[31] Beginning in 1808, Viana routinely issued instructions on the enforcement and punishment of crime to *juizes do crime dos bairros* (neighborhood judges) in each of the city's four parishes, Santa Rita, São José, Candelária, and Se, including a call for the compilation of registries of all establishments and residents within their jurisdiction.[32] To eliminate public disorder and crime within the city, the intendant also had at his disposal the military division of the royal guard of the police, created in 1809.[33] Its four companies, distributed throughout the city, made night rounds, dispersed nighttime gatherings, verified that cafes and gaming houses closed at the appropriate time, and arrested anyone suspected of vagrancy and criminal activity. The guard could also furnish a less visible and strategically unpredictable presence with patrols hidden "in inconspicuous places, and in silence, so that they might hear whatever row, or racket, and then suddenly appear at the location of the disturbance."[34]

While relying upon the guard to repress disorderly acts on Rio's streets, the intendant also embraced his responsibility, as the memorialist Gonçalves dos Santos explained, "to prevent evil, before [having to] punish evil doers" and to discourage both the disruption of "civil order and the tranquility of families" and the corruption of "political morals." In practice, this meant attempts at transforming public life in Rio by defining through word and deed the standards of conduct, providing what Viana referred to as a "reflection" of "the good police that should be maintained."[35] The area around the palace in the city's center was cleared of "indecorous" taverns and fish stands that were known to provide havens for noisy, "disorderly" gatherings.[36] At the nearby docks, the guard was deployed to maintain "the public peace" following the disembarkation of crews,[37] and at the city's theaters troops were called on to curtail "the licentious liberty that the people had taken to clapping and whistling [during public spectacles] without decency and without any attention to the good order that they should maintain" and to publicize by way of posted edicts the "manner in which one should conduct oneself."[38] Gambling, displays of irreverence at local festivals, and other "lamentable spectacles that implied a lack of policing" were targeted for containment and eradication.[39] Preventing such occasions for disorder also motivated Viana to rigorously enforce antivagrancy laws, arresting deserters and those to whom he referred using the equivocal categories of "suspicious men" and "scandalous women," and to interdict "excessive prostitution." Teresa dos Moleques and Mathildes de Jesus, a *crioula* (an African woman born in Brazil), known as Talavêra, thus found themselves facing the intendant's charge that they had led husbands, fathers, and sons astray and, in the case of Mathildes de Jesus, expulsion from Rio de Janeiro.[40]

Yet, such responses to what Viana insisted were the daily challenges to the city's "public tranquility" required resources that the intendant did not always enjoy. Although the guard was authorized at 218 men, in 1818 it had only 75 members.[41] It was also the case that even when the guard could be deployed effectively, Viana continued to face, as he did in the provision of residential housing, conflicts between the ideals and realities of constructing a new royal court. Public commemorations and entertainments intended to promote well-being and to reflect Rio de Janeiro's new status as a royal court, Viana anxiously complained, could just as easily become occasions for crime and disorderly obstacles to achieving the decorum required of a royal residence. And while, in the case of the conflicts over building standards or disturbances at the theater, it was the resident's lack of obedience that jeopardized Rio's ennoblement, at other times what Viana characterized as the recent decline in "good morals" appeared to stem not from the residents' own shortcomings, but rather from living in the new city that Rio de Janeiro had become. Responding to the request of a recently arrived composer to stage a theatrical performance during Lent, for example, Viana explained that although the request seemed innocent enough, it represented a rupture of the city's tradition of Lenten piety and propriety that anteceded the transfer of the court. As "the people of Brazil are not accustomed to seeing anything but the stations of the cross," Viana wrote as he affirmed the prohibition of the production, "let it not be said that it was the arrival of the court that abolished such solitude, silence and privation."[42] In other words, the triumph of a courtly present over a provincial past, manifest in a more splendorous and expansive public life, could not corrupt the city and its residents and thus undermine the ideal of political and moral renewal that such a triumph was supposed to guarantee.

According to Viana, however, the moral dilemmas and perils of constructing a new royal court could be overcome by recognizing that "good police" was not limited to the enactment of a series of prohibitions and punishments. The splendor of a royal court, its larger population, and new public venues and entertainments could be reconciled with both security and virtue by providing what he referred to as "a moral education" for the city's residents, a responsibility that, as José Subtil explains, had been a central and, to a certain extent, innovative feature of the institution of the intendancy since its creation in the context of Pombal's enlightened reforms. To create what Gonçalves dos Santos and others referred to as "useful vassals," Viana counseled the crown to direct particular attention and moral force toward the free urban poor. If the prince regent provided an "education" for those who had been led down the road to "perdition" by their "poverty and lack of resources," Viana suggested, he would benefit from "vassals of all colors."[43] More specifically, he recommended that the crown intensify viceregal efforts to ensure that the free lower classes were dedicated to certain productive activities. "Poor boys," including "whites, mulattos, mestizos and blacks" were rounded up, most often forcibly, and brought to the intendancy "so that they might be employed in workshops where they [would] be dressed and supported" and paid according to their performance.[44] The incarcerated were sentenced to labor at public works and within the city and nearby region those accused of vagrancy or of leading lives devoid of moral rectitude were similarly targeted for "correction" and given "opportunities" for royal service in the army, the militia, and other activities deemed "useful to the State." Soldiers found gambling with "black and brown people" on the city's beaches, squares, and streets were removed from the city for service elsewhere. Recently arrived Portuguese with no prospects for productive activity were also relocated beyond Rio de Janeiro where, officials hoped, they would make their living in agriculture.[45]

These inclusions and exclusions both promoted the ideal of utility, which, as we will see in a subsequent chapter, was central to a new ethos of empire and provided expressions of royal authority as above all paternal. While "the people," as Viana complained to Vila Nova Portugal in 1818, responded to the crown's efforts to enforce standards of propriety like "children who cry when their parents wash them and correct them," moral education, the intendant noted elsewhere, also cultivated their deference to and "love" for the king, their political father. Indeed, just as it led children to obey their parents, "giving both rewards and punishments at the proper time" led men "to act properly and respect the wishes of the Sovereign."[46] This quest to achieve political allegiance within a framework of social control attests to what historian António Manuel Hespanha describes as a shift in eighteenth-century Portuguese understandings of the nature of social order, crime, and punishment in which "within the realm of the guiding ideas for political action" discipline displaced a symbolic exercise of justice that functioned politically to defend the supremacy of the king. This shift was not clear cut and, as we saw in the case of the Minas conspiracy, the late eighteenth-century and early nineteenth-century monarchy continued to provide symbolically enacted justice. Indeed, in his own political education Dom João had been counseled that "Kings terrify more than they punish."[47] Yet, the crown's sponsorship of a policing that sought to achieve social discipline on an increasingly broader scale, guided by the idea that, as the intendant argued in the case of prison labor especially, punishment would "correct" the particular subject of the sentence, signaled that it was not only the presence of the sovereign, the city's beautification, and the amplification of services and of its built environment that made Rio de Janeiro a royal court. Occurring within a moment of enlightened optimism about the possibility of reform, the "new city" encompassed the quest to create, with both force and education, a practical social-cultural order.

The "Most Peaceful" of Cities: Making Rio de Janeiro Loyal

The intendancy's mission to guarantee order and loyalty corresponded to Rio de Janeiro's duty to provide a haven for both the prince regent and the institution of monarchy itself. After all, the city's almanac reported, "His Majesty and all of His Royal Family chose this famous country for their repose amid the agitations that shook Europe."[48] Yet, in a century in which, as royal minister Vila Nova Portugal decried in 1814, "diverse peoples" had been touched by "certain metaphysical words"—"liberty," "pátria," "humanity,"—that spread "with electric force" to cause "the misfortune of others," formidable threats to this repose were never far from view.[49] Consequently, for royal officials the challenge of rebuilding a royal court in the New World and of ensuring that Rio remained the "most peaceful" of cities included responding to "the question of all questions," as one police informant described it, of how to maintain "a purely monarchical government" in an age of democratic revolutions.[50]

For Viana, this task of affirming "respect and vassalage" and diminishing "dislike and indifference for the government" was the "object" of what he called *alta polícia* (high police). Alta polícia, on the one hand, followed from the intendancy's mission of guaranteeing the residents' well-being. Along with promoting the idea that the sovereign attended to the needs of his vassals with good administration, it entailed the sponsorship of collective moments of allegiance, such as commemorations of the sovereign and his reign, in which "the people" were both "entertained" and instructed of their place in a political community founded on love and allegiance to Dom João. The maintenance of this political community, on the other hand, then depended on the repressive exclusion of anybody whose sentiments or conduct challenged established standards of propriety and loyalty. While, as we have seen, such persons could be those accused of violence, vagrancy, or indecency, officials perceived the greatest threat to be posed by the bearers of "revolutionary principles."Accordingly, alta polícia also included concerted efforts at political surveillance and repression.[51]

The intendant assumed these duties formerly remitted to Rio's viceroys who, as we saw in Chapter 2, sought to discover and eradicate political dissidence in the 1790s. By the 1810s, however, the political landscape of Rio de Janeiro had changed and Viana faced challenges that were quantitatively, if not qualitatively, greater. To begin with, the opening of Brazil's ports meant that foreigners, once categorically suspected of subversive activity, no longer were discouraged from visiting and taking up residence in the city. The royal court was necessarily an international crossroads, where the presence of representatives of other nations signified recognition of the prince regent's legitimate authority. Indeed, as we shall see in Chapter 6, the crown promoted European immigration and, together with ambassadors, foreign merchants, artisans, and artists in Rio were all identified with the city's new political status and prosperity. By choosing to relocate to Brazil rather than to the United States or England, Viana reported, they "made this court more opulent." Yet, Viana also warned, the presence of foreigners demanded a particular policing. While "the nations with the largest population owe this to an unlimited reception of all," he wrote, it was also the case that these nations "keenly watched over them, punishing them and expelling them when they violated public tranquility and the laws of the country." Consequently, the intendant instituted a series of safeguards, including a centralized inspection of passports and registries of all foreigners who visited or lived in the city.[52] The surveillance of foreigners and, most importantly, of any contacts that they had with the city's residents, was also accomplished through what the intendant characterized as counterespionage. For this task, Viana asserted in 1816, the intendancy needed trustworthy spies "who know [foreign] languages, frequent [foreigners'] dinner parties and accompany them on their strolls, to the theater and other public amusements." Indeed, by the end of the decade he had recruited at least two Frenchmen for the task. Although Viana defined this policing of foreigners as "vigilance without oppression," in practice it often led to arrest and indeterminant periods of incarceration.[53]

For the duration of the Peninsular War the primary goal of this policing was to discover the presence in Brazil of Napoleonic "emissaries" who sought to enlist Dom João's own vassals to overthrow his legitimate authority. As Portuguese representatives abroad exchanged information on an apparent network of conspirators in France, the United States, and South America, where, it was reported, Napoleon hoped to foment an insurrection against Spanish and Portuguese royal authority, Viana set out to uncover evidence of "revolutionary correspondence" at home.[54] This search for French spies was made difficult, however, by the fact that not everyone in Brazil knew that they would recognize a Frenchman when they saw him. "News spread that he was French," Viana reported in 1811, writing of a man who was later, and more conclusively, identified with certain documentation as a "Spaniard from Louisiana." However flippant, the accusation of being French could have irreparable effects nonetheless. As the intendant concluded in this case, the rumor, together with his origins in a territory once belonging to the French, and now within the domain of the United States, warranted that the Spaniard should continue to be surveiled.[55] Even when investigations yielded only the itineraries of Frenchmen attempting to make their way and some sort of living outside France, avoiding, perhaps, conscription in Napoleon's armies, Viana moved to deport them so that, as he explained, Brazil would be "cleaned of a race" that had "revealed itself" to be "very prejudicial."[56]

Within a few years of the transfer of the court, royal officials also began to consider the possibility that insurgency would spread into Brazil and to the new royal court from Spanish America. By 1818, as the Conde dos Arcos, governor of Bahia (1810–1818) concluded, the impending circumstances were grim. "The Spanish colonies," he predicted, "will end their business with Spain in the same way that the French and English colonies ended theirs with France and England, and then these neighbors naturally will be our enemies."[57] In the case of Rio de la Plata, in particular, while Viana both foresaw future diplomatic imperatives and recognized the region's intense commercial ties with Rio de Janeiro, as the revolution in Buenos Aires gained momentum Spaniards residing in the city who "rejoiced in the conduct of those who figured in the scandalous cause of Buenos Aires" were detained and, in some cases in consultation with the Spanish crown's representative, expelled from the city.[58] Alternately, those who sought to travel to the region could be stopped from leaving Rio de Janeiro, where the intendancy could observe their activities and therefore prevent them from promoting insurgency. As Viana explained in the case of the Spaniard Ascencio Claudio, who had been in Paris and now wanted to go to Buenos Aires with a "suspicious" French colonel, the passport could not be granted because all efforts were needed to avoid "enlarging that faction."[59]

Such fears that revolution, and the "bloodshed and devastation that in our days afflicted miserable France," would spread into the Portuguese monarchy's domain were then dramatically realized in 1817, as the province of Pernambuco and surrounding areas of the Brazilian northeast were engulfed by a republican insurrection that succeeded in displacing royal authority there for several months. The same year, across the Atlantic, in postwar Portugal, discontent with what one "good Portuguese" described as "the evils of his devastated pátria" led a group of officers to plot against the "tyranny" of the interim government of the British Marshal Beresford in favor of Portugal's "independence" and a constitutional monarchy. Both movements were squarely defeated and those suspected of involvement were left facing years of imprisonment and, in some cases, execution.[60] Yet, correspondence between the rebel government in Pernambuco and the United States, and news of a bizarre plan to launch a squadron from the Brazilian northeast to rescue Napoleon from Santa Helena, affirmed royal officials' sense of being besieged by the potential for revolution, of living through a time when, as the Conde dos Arcos lamented, "the most vile of crimes perpetrated by a half a dozen bandits or revolutionaries" was regarded by other governments as a movement worthy of protection.[61] Although the residents of Rio de Janeiro had remained allegiant, raising funds as well as troops to assist in the restoration of Dom João's authority in the Brazilian northeast, and had celebrated the rebels' defeat with fireworks, singing, and theatrical performances,[62] they were not spared the crown's vehement response. Two new army regiments were brought from Portugal and stationed in Rio de Janeiro, while Salvador and Recife received one each. Working with his *moscas* (flies), as he referred to his informants, Viana also moved to interdict masonic activities, linked to the insurgents on both sides of the Atlantic and then criminalized following the crown's proscription of "secret societies" in 1818.[63]

Yet although republicans and masons, and the movements that they formed, remained the crown's most dreaded opposition, in Rio de Janeiro in the 1810s political contestation more frequently appeared in less spectacular, if no less irksome, forms. As the intendancy's logbooks record, the intendant confronted people such as Fortunato de Brito Correa e Melo and "the mulatto" Padre Leonardo de Correa de Sa, who "spoke of government" and of royal officials, in bars, pharmacies, and inns with "indiscretion and impudence";[64] who "analyzed," as did one recently arrived lieutenant colonel in the royal navy, "different facts according to his opinion";[65] who, like the *pardo* tailor José Elisbão Ferreira, "had the custom of sending for gazettes and of reading them . . . making speeches and giving credit to the actions to which they referred";[66] and who, as the Conde de Aguiar fumed, drafted in purposefully disguised handwriting and then surreptitiously posted satirical pasquinades that circulated in subsequent transcriptions.[67] Together, these practices formed a response to what Arlette Farge has described, writing of eighteenth-century France, as the "permanently truncated information" that characterized the old regime. They "put words in the very place where nothing was supposed to be said."[68] In this case, these words presented an alternative understanding of the meaning of the transfer of the court: decadence and disaffection in place of imperial and monarchical renewal. Elisbão Ferreira, for example, along with voicing his disgust with the corruption of the papacy and the clergy, and his skepticism about the crown's granting of honors and offices to those "who didn't deserve it" while others who did went unpaid, concluded that "these colonies of Brazil were in great decadence and weakness because there was no one who looked after them and the development of their happiness . . . and if Napoleon were here this would flourish with other greatness."[69] The lieutenant, an innkeeper testified, similarly declared before his fellow visitors at the inn, including a sympathetic Portuguese surgeon, that not only was "the intendant an ass and a great fool who sat out at his house emptying bottles of wine instead of solving problems," but also that "all from this court was lost" and that the king "was a fool, that in Portugal they wanted a king even if he was made of wood and that if His Majesty did not return they wanted to make a republic, and that they did very well, and they were right."[70] Strikingly similar "expressions," the intendant noted in his report, had been rendered in the form of a pasquinade posted on the Rua do Fogo only a few days before the lieutenant made his declarations:

> The intendant in Andrahi
> And the king at Santa Cruz
> Only you, great Bonaparte
> You may enjoy a nascent reign
> and provide the needed measures
> But you are imprisoned in Santa Helena!![71]

In stark contrast to the vision of the crown acting to transform the city into the capital of a prosperous New World empire, the pasquinade, like Ferreira and the lieutenant, offered the image of indifference: an inattentive intendant and an indisposed monarch enjoying their respective retreats outside the city instead of attending to the needs of the crown's vassals. At the heart of the satirical insult was the juxtaposition of the impotence of royal power and the rule of an enemy rendered powerless. Like Napoleon, the pasquinade proposed, the promise of an new empire languished.

To such acts of dissidence the crown responded, as it did in the case of foreigners, with arrests, incarceration, and banishment. The lieutenant and the surgeon, categorized as disgruntled seekers of royal favor, were sent back to Portugal, where the surgeon would have to reckon with Viana's counterpart in Lisbon for an allegedly criminal past. Elisbão, in turn, repudiated by the intendant in his report as "a reader of gazettes, rumormonger (*falador do governo*) and enemy of priests," "one of those mulattos who in this country are called petulant charlatans (*capadócios pronósticos*) . . . who want to say everything without knowing what they say, and who want to pass among their own as the cleverest," was jailed until he could be banished to Angola.[72] Contestation, and the political message of this contestation, thus were negated and punished at once. Indeed, the intendancy's alta polícia was predicated on both the idea that the city's popular classes could not have political ideas—instead they were merely dissatisfied petitioners or, in the case of Ferreira, members of what Viana called a "class" disposed to impertinence—and the practice of ascertaining what their ideas about politics were so as to prevent the further expression of these ideas. As a French baker living in Rio thus discovered after a street fight led to his arrest, although he was found to be of "an abject class without the education and circumstances that would make him suspect of [revolutionary activities]," he was deported nonetheless.[73] This fundamental contradiction, as Farge has explained, meant that "popular speaking about current events dwelt in a kind of limbo; in politics it had no place, but its suspect nature was nothing if not a commonplace."[74]

There were, however, limits to the contradictory repression of dissent that was "both existent and nonexistent" and of the individuals whose reportedly subversive expressions were brought to the intendant's attention. As Viana and other royal officials came to recognize, expressions of contestation, like the potential for social disorder, were also associated with many of the innovations that made Rio de Janeiro a royal court, with what the intendant described in one report as the "frequent and easy communications" of the city's open port[75] and the unprecedented proliferation of print, realities that could not be denied or, as Viana often complained, completely controlled. With its small staff and reliance on overburdened and less exhaustive magistrates, he protested, the intendancy could scarcely provide for the inspection of all passports and the passenger lists from arriving ships. And as the lieutenant at the inn made clear, by the time a newcomer's disposition to "speak of government" was known, the damage had already been done. At the same time, royal censors, faced with mounting manuscripts to review for publication by Rio's Royal Press and an increasing number of pamphlets and books imported from abroad, had similar difficulties in fulfilling their duties. While, on the one hand, censorial zealousness meant that "because they [were] printed" a shipment of blank ledgers awaited dispensation alongside books on European philosophy and politics, on the other, a lack of personnel and an ad hoc application of standards left royal officials scrambling to interdict pamphlets whose "antipolitical" contents managed to go unnoticed in both Portugal and Brazil until after publication and distribution.[76]

Throughout the 1810s both censorship judges and the police intendant also struggled to contain one of the most bothersome inspirations for contestation in both Portugal and Brazil: the Portuguese-language press published outside the Portuguese empire, whose very existence was fueled, as the editor of the London-based *Correio Braziliense* noted, by the crown's insistence on proscribing press freedoms within its territories.[77] The crown's ability to interdict these publications apparently was limited, for the city's clerks read "pamphlets from London," one of Rio's residents observed, especially *O Portuguêz*, the periodical published in London between 1814 and 1826 and officially banned by the crown.[78] From London there also came copies of the banned *Campião, Ou Amigo do Rey e do Povo*[79] and the more well-known, and legal, *Correio Braziliense,* where readers could find the editor's attacks on the intendant's "despotism."[80] By the end of the decade, this unprecedented supply of oppositional printed matter showed signs of eroding, as Lisa Graham has observed of eighteenth-century France, the hierarchies on which political authority was based.[81] Indeed, in newspapers imported from abroad residents read of imperial crisis, a possible separation of Brazil and Portugal, and, as Viana lamented, plans for "constitutions."[82]

The knowledge that, as one observer warned, "conversations" were "founded upon what is read in the papers"[83] also encompassed what contemporaries referred to as "public opinion." Public opinion could be regarded, as it had been by Rousseau, as an expression of reason, a "collective judgment in matters of morality, reputation and taste" forged by the elite.[84] Thus, the statesmen and political economist José da Silva Lisboa surmised, Dom João had championed the advancement of arts and sciences in Brazil out of respect for "the Tribunal of Public Opinion, which esteems England and France as the *Eyes* of Europe and as the seats of the instruction in Science and refined Arts."[85] What Silva Lisboa referred to as "the century's opinions" could, however, also refer to a political force of elite and popular dimensions, the product of active discussion that deliberately countered, as Keith Michael Baker has argued, "the administrative secrecy and arbitrariness" of government of the old regime.[86] As Hipólito José da Costa, the editor of the *Correio Braziliense,* explained, the "character of public men is an object of public observation because this serves as a check, and even if one could repress the publication of these opinions in the press, one can never suffocate the voices [that express them]." The process through which public opinion took shape was, therefore, liberating and empowering. "When a people act as flock of sheep," Costa continued, "it is incapable of great things." On the contrary, when "men reason for themselves, when they have the faculties and the opportunity to judge public affairs, they acquire an energy of spirit that makes them aspire to fame, and to do the services necessary to attain it." And, he added, there was "nothing that is more conducive" to this process of reasoning than "reading of the successes that are occurring in the world."[87]

In Rio de Janeiro, according to Lúcia Neves, this understanding of public opinion as the product of the proliferation of print, limited increases in literacy, and a broader use of forms of sociability associated with reading that also encompassed speech led to "a tenuous amplification of the sphere of power beyond the limited circles of the court."[88] In the 1810s, however, the salience of public opinion may have depended less on its ties to the formation of a "public sphere" in the sociological sense of the term, whose creation, Neves also argues, was ultimately "frustrated" by an official political, economic, and social traditionalism, than on its status as what Baker has called a "political invention." Unable to stifle "the processes of political contestation," Baker explains for the case of eighteenth-century France, the monarchy "found itself under increasing pressure to participate in them." Consequently, by the last decades of the eighteenth century public opinion had become a "principle of legitimacy"; "an abstract category of authority" invoked by the monarchy as well as by its critics "to secure the legitimacy of claims that could no longer be made binding in the terms (and within the traditional institutional circuit) of an absolutist political order."[89]

For the Portuguese crown its own subjection to the "tribunal of public opinion" was strikingly evident during the Peninsular War. As royal officials were acutely aware, the transfer of the court was a controversial move whose legitimacy required explanation to constituencies beyond the circle of courtiers, both within and outside the empire. In Rio de Janeiro, as we have seen both here and in the last chapter, exiles and residents shared an avid interest in the war and in the current state of affairs in the new royal court and Portugal and gathered together to exchange information and debate. For the Portuguese monarchy the danger in these debates was that those involved might consider, and then assume, French claims that the move to Brazil was an act of cowardice and, worse yet, that in departing Portugal the prince regent forfeited "his Sovereign Rights within the Kingdom." As one of Junot's proclamations publicized, in Portugal the House of Braganza had "ceased to reign."[90] By way of its editor's criticism, readers of the *Correio Braziliense* were also apprised of additional arguments advanced by British pamphleteers, including one who claimed that the move to Brazil was designed by Bonaparte and dutifully executed by the Francophile ministers of the "feeble" Portuguese prince.[91] Faced with these accusations, variously expressed in incidents of dissident speech in the city's streets and shops, royal officials recognized, as had their counterparts in France, that a response had to entail not only the suppression of these tracts and the repression of those who dared to debate, but also a concerted, and more persuasive, rebuttal in kind: pamphlets that would, as the intendant suggested, contradict the "falsehoods and lies of the French."[92]

For this task the crown had its Royal Press. Indeed, in the early 1810s the majority of Royal Press publications encompassed tracts that attacked Napoleon and affirmed the Portuguese crown's position and alliances.[93] These included the crown's own official justification of its conduct, the *Manifesto, ou Exposição Fundada*, written by Souza Coutinho and published in 1808 in both Portuguese and French, which focused on French diplomatic treachery and belligerence. A year later, the Royal Press then made available similar arguments advanced by the first Portuguese historian of the Peninsular War, José Acúrsio das Neves, in his *Manifesto da Razão Contra as Usurpações Francezas*. Written in Portugal and first published there in 1808, the pamphlet asserted that the declaration of war and the departure from Lisbon were justified by recalling the captivity of the Spanish Fernando VII. For the Portuguese prince regent, a choice between a similar fate and removing the court to Brazil was, Acúrsio das Neves explained, no choice at all. Indeed, he argued, far from an act of cowardly abandonment, as the crown's enemies had charged, the transfer of the court was a noble sacrifice, intended to spare the Portuguese from a bloody resistance to the invaders.[94]

Pithier accounts of present circumstances, including reprints of pamphlets published first in Portugal, were also issued by the Royal Press, such as the satirical *Recipe for Making Napoleons*: "a handful of corrupt dirt," "a garden of refined lies" and "a barrel of impiety." Together, these short, inexpensive pamphlets formed a transnational and transatlantic wartime genre in which, on the one hand, a Black Legend of Napoleon and the French was constructed through similarly concise and repeated references to opportunism, artifice, and perfidy, and on the other, Portuguese heroism and patriotism were celebrated. The prince regent and his vassals were revealed to be precisely what Napoleon and the French were not: God-fearing, moral, and heroic. To defend their independence, pamphleteers reminded their readers, the Portuguese defeated the Romans, the Moors, and the Castilians. Resistance to the French and loyalty to Dom João thus were additional examples of their deep-rooted willingness to defend the old regime; or, as one pamphleteer explained, "To defend our Fathers' Homes, / To give one's life for the King, / Is for the valiant Lusitanians, / Character, Custom and Law."[95]

This effort to shape public opinion in the crown's favor within the medium of print also extended beyond the Royal Press to London, where, as we have seen, many of the critical works that made their way to Rio de Janeiro were published. As Roderick Barman has noted, along with interdicting publications deemed offensive or seditious, the crown encouraged the publication of pamphlets that refuted arguments made in the expatriate press and subsidized the periodical *O Investigador Portuguêz* founded in London in 1811. More efficiently, the crown then went after the most influential source of attacks. By 1812 royal officials reached a secret agreement

with Costa, the editor of the *Correio*, that included subsidies and compulsory purchase and distribution in exchange for less pointed commentary on royal officials
and the crown's affairs, the end of "dissertations on Cortes" and of comparisons of
what Costa had repeatedly referred to as "the ancient Portuguese Constitution" to
the "current English constitution," as well as, one letter from Costa suggests, the
publication of articles on subjects recommended by the intendant. Although there
were royal counselors who criticized the crown's dealings with the acerbic Costa, the
arrangement apparently satisfied officials in the new court. As the intendant reported to Dom João in 1818, from Costa the crown "received good service" and
could "expect even better."[96]

The crown's decision to meet printed criticism with printed praise and, more
concretely, its financial support for this endeavor may have served, as Barman suggests, the unintended consequence of accelerating the emergence of a Portuguese-
language periodical press; in the 1810s there were eight periodicals published in
London, Lisbon, and Rio de Janeiro. These measures also attested to royal officials'
recognition of both the inevitability of contestation and the political function of
public opinion. Consequently, they sustained what Farge has described as "an
emerging sense of the right to know and to judge."[97] In Rio de Janeiro, such judgments focused on the meaning of the war and the removal of the royal family from
Lisbon. They signaled that while Viana furthered his efforts at alta polícia, staging
celebrations of approbation, guarding against conspiracy, and investigating dissidence, the transformation of Rio de Janeiro into the royal court was not, and could
not be, based on passive consent. As royal officials themselves acknowledged, safe-
guarding the institution of the monarchy in a city that was open to foreigners and
increasingly apprised of the politics of war and revolution on both sides of the Atlantic required engagement with opinions that now more than ever before in the
city's history were purposefully formed in public.

"Perfeita Civilização": Making Rio de Janeiro a Metropolis

Although the transformation of Rio de Janeiro into a royal court was inspired by an
earlier urban reformism and by contemporary efforts at policing both actions and
opinions in other national contexts, the project nevertheless, like the transfer of the
court itself, was unprecedented. As the capital of what one diplomat called an *império florescente*, the new city of Rio de Janeiro could not be simply orderly, decorous,
and politically allegiant. It also had to exhibit explicitly the demise of what the
memorialist Gonçalves dos Santos referred to as "the old colonial system" and the
penury that it produced.[98] As the Portuguese physician Manuel Vieira da Silva

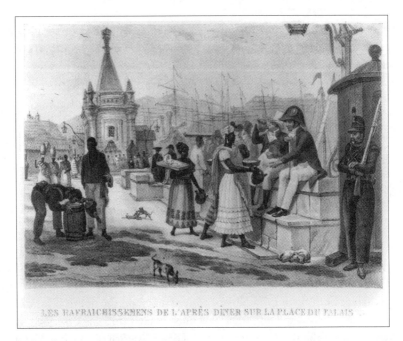

FIGURE 5: Jean Baptiste Debret, "Les rafraichissemens de l'après diner sur la place du palais," from Debret, *Voyage Pittoresque et Historique au Brésil, sejour d'un Artiste Français au Brésil* v. 2 (Paris: Firmin Didot Fréres, 1835). Copy and permission obtained from the Print Collection, Miriam and Ira D. Wallach Division of Arts, Prints and Photographs, The New York Public Library, Astor, Lenox and Tilden Foundations. In the late afternoon, Debret reported, men of "modest means" gathered to take in fresh air, to chat, and to purchase sweets and refreshments from African and African-Brazilian street vendors.

argued in one of the first works published by the Royal Press, for the city of Rio de Janeiro the arrival of the royal family was a momentous break with the past, the beginning of "the joyous epoch, that made [the city's residents] leave behind the misery that surrounded [them], and enter the history of policed Nations."[99] To be "policed," in this sense, was both to transcend a past of European colonialism as well as, somewhat paradoxically, to embrace European origins. Making the city into the court, in other words, meant bringing to fruition an original imperial project that, as we saw in the last chapter, the new empire also embraced: civilizing the New World.

Within Rio's transformation into a civilized, metropolitan court, subtractions kept pace with additions to the cityscape and public life. While new palaces, public buildings, the theater, academies, courtly fashions, and cleaner and illuminated streets produced what Luccock described as the "resemblance of European magnificence," the intendant, in turn, applied his resources toward ridding the city of its colonial attributes, including the use of lattices on residential buildings, features variously described by residents and visitors as gothic, deformed, and unhealthy. The removal of the lattice works, the intendant explained in the edict, would contribute to "the court's decorum and perfection" and constitute "unequivocal proof" of the residents' happiness that the royal family was among them, sweeping away "testimonies of [Rio's] old condition of conquest and colony" thereby "ennobl[ing] the court and distinguish[ing] it before the eyes of foreign nations." Indeed, as the edict more generally stated, "having elevated this city to the highest hierarchy of court of Brazil," it was no longer possible to maintain "old customs that could be tolerated only when [Brazil] was reputed to be a colony," customs that "populations of refinement and perfect civilization had not endured in a long time."[100] Thus, such intolerable old customs at cemeteries, hospitals, and pharmacies and lingering colonial "indecencies" were similarly targeted for reforms that complied with a "European standard," and at the theater, as Luccock recalled, "the manners, vices, dialect and other peculiarities of the colony, were ridiculed; and the public taste, in consequence, amended."[101] As a whole, these explicitly Europeanizing, or metropolitanizing, measures allowed royal officials and resident memorialists to articulate the meaning of the transfer of the court: while the presence of the prince regent and the royal family undermined the established political and cultural hierarchies of empire, reproducing European appearances and practices in the new royal court then affirmed both the power and the virtue that had motivated European expansion in the first place.

Yet, for royal officials to "civilize" Rio de Janeiro, to make it metropolitan, was also to confront a more formidable colonial attribute than lattices, poorly administered hospitals, and provincial habits. Indeed, the most striking difference between the old court and the new one was not architecture or manners, but rather the fact that half of the population of the new court was enslaved. In the early nineteenth-century Portuguese world, after all, slavery was an exclusively colonial practice, since decrees in 1761 and 1773 guaranteed the freedom of slaves in Portugal.[102] It was also a practice increasingly associated with not only immorality and cruelty, but also laziness and economic backwardness. If making Rio de Janeiro into a metropolitan court meant breaking with a colonial past, it thus appeared that the use of slave labor, like the lattices, would be foregone.

Indeed, there were memorialists and officials who argued that slavery presented obstacles to the new empire's and its capital's prosperity. In his treatise on how to improve Rio de Janeiro's climate, Manuel Vieira da Silva argued that slaves undermined the city's decorum. Many people, he explained, "come to possess one slave, or two" and so "living only from the work of these miserable men," cast aside "industry" for "a life of idleness . . . affectionate mother of vice. . . ." If "blacks were more expensive," he advised, "there would not be so many wretched people in Brazil." Yet Vieira da Silva's critique of slavery was also highly affected. The real challenge to courtliness, he clarified, was the presence of Africans. Therefore, it was "in the prince regent's interest," he wrote, "to increase the number of whites, be they Brazilian, or European, rather than propagate [the population] of blacks."[103] Although Viana urged the crown to benefit from "vassals of all colors," he shared this view and actively promoted "white" immigration through subsidies financed by the intendancy and endorsed the generally pessimistic view of color differences advanced, as we shall see in Chapter 6, by the political economist Silva Lisboa as well. As Viana explained to one of the city's judges, "white or brown men found gambling" and "white, or freed people of mixed racial ancestry, not too dark" (*pardos forros, não muito escuros*) could make good soldiers, yet free "blacks" were to be discouraged from royal service.[104] Calling for boys to work in manufacturing, the intendant also specified that they "should be mulattos or whites."[105]

These attempts at segregation not only reflected the white elite's persistent and, considering their dependence on slave labor, glaringly unfounded belief in Africans' limited potential to acquire skills, but also responded to their fears of disruptive and unproductive divisions within the labor force and society as a whole. While slave owners, explained royal minister Vila Nova Portugal, were "always in a state of domestic war,"[106] Viana further speculated that these conflicts outlasted changes in legal status. "Freed men," he wrote of a militia regiment of men of color, "are better friends of other blacks, their partners, and from whom they come, and of mulattos with whom they live, than of whites."[107] Such ostensibly irreconcilable divisions and conflicts undermined the prospects for unity in a new American empire and royal court. Accordingly, it was not only a social, economic critique of slavery, but also an official racism that appeared to spell the end of forced African labor in Brazil.

Yet, elite reasoning against both slavery and the African and African-Brazilian population was overwhelmed by anxieties about the imagined impact of the immediate abolition of slavery on Brazilian society and the economy: the end of export agriculture and widespread vagrancy.[108] Consequently, even as they lamented slavery's evils, royal officials allowed the use of slave labor to expand. While most of the growing number of Africans forcibly brought to Rio's port were sent south or to nearby plantations, many were retained in the city. In 1818 the intendant reported that to meet the demands of the "downpour" of 30,000 "whites" who arrived with the prince regent and the royal family, the city's and its hinterland's "black" population had increased between 60,000 and 80,000. Luccock, in turn, estimated that between 1808 and 1822 Rio's slave population increased 200 percent. As a consequence, remaking Rio de Janeiro into the court meant reconciling the larger quest to metropolitanize the city with slavery and with the African and African-

Brazilian residents who made up a majority of its population. While Europeanizing the city, in other words, officials had to account for the fact that the city was indeed more African and more enslaved.[109]

As a matter of "public security" and "tranquility," the task of defining the place of slavery and slaves in the new court was of primary concern to the intendant. A tax on newly arrived slaves funded the intendancy's efforts to provide this police and to supervise people whose daily tasks within the city often took them away from their owners' domain.[110] Following the same racist logic that informed the promotion of white immigration, Viana often emphasized the need for order among what he described as a hostile, or at least potentially disloyal, population. Brazil's "population is black," he explained in 1816, with "as many as ten times as many slaves as whites, and because of this [its population has] more propensity to be led astray, and [therefore] requires more police."[111] Within Rio de Janeiro, this supervision of slaves with public duties fell to the intendancy's guard. Prison records reveal the extent to which slaves living in the city had to contend with its patrols. An average of 80 percent of those arrested by the guard and other members of the intendant's staff, as Leila Mezan Algranti's research shows, were slaves. All but one percent of the remaining arrests, in turn, were of free people of color. Reasons given for these detentions varied from theft, disturbing the peace, possession of a weapon, assault and homicide, and flight. Many of the detentions also involved attempts to repress the practice of *capoeira*, an African-Brazilian martial art that owners and officials intimately associated with violent disobedience. As one magistrate reported, "as the crimes perpetrated by individuals of this city, some freed and others enslaved, known as capoeiras, are frequent, the vigilant police has sought to capture them, and judges have sought to try them, and the *casa de suplicação* has sought to sentence them with exemplary zeal."[112] Arrests, however, did not fully account for the guard's activity. As the intendant himself recognized, many confrontations between the guard's members and people of color were both unwarranted and unreported. Indeed, in 1811, chastising the guard's commander for the gratuitous beatings of black women selling sweets in the street, Viana found himself reminding his subordinate that the guard "was supposed to curtail disorder rather than create it."[113]

When the guard did formally arrest a slave in most cases the consequences were summary punishment with a sentence of lashes, service in a chain gang, or both, while the sentences of free people were primarily limited to labor and, in some cases, banishment. As Viana explained in a report justifying the arrest and forced labor of a free French "black" named João Baptista, those accused of what he called "minor incidents" (*pequenas desordems*) lacking in evidence necessary to pursue the matter further were put to work on the construction of nearby roads. According to Algranti, after 1814 the intendancy also began to incarcerate slaves. Indeed, although the *cal-*

abouço, a jail located in the area known as *Castelo,* held free and freed vagrants and deserters, it came to be associated almost exclusively with "the corrective punishments so necessary for slaves."[114] Incarceration, however, did not preclude labor at public works. Indeed, after the transfer of the court, as the intendancy embarked on a number of large projects to improve the city's infrastructure, the prison population of slaves and free persons, became, in effect, its primary source of labor and the length of "corrections" was adjusted in order to meet the intendant's needs.[115]

While in some cases sentencing a slave to work for the intendancy for an infraction committed while in public put the intendant at odds with the slave's owner, who counted on exclusive access to his or her labor, the intendancy also assumed a major role in controlling the slave population by administering punishments upon the request of owners. In these cases, slaves were deposited at the calabouço and then assigned to a chain gang or whipped, for which owners compensated the intendancy

FIGURE 6: Jean Baptiste Debret, "Marchand du Tabac," from Debret, *Voyage Pittoresque et Historique au Brésil, sejour d'un Artiste Français au Brésil* v. 2 (Paris: Firmin Didot Fréres, 1835). Copy and permission obtained from the Print Collection, Miriam and Ira D. Wallach Division of Arts, Prints and Photographs, The New York Public Library, Astor, Lenox and Tilden Foundations. Describing a chain gang of water carriers as they pause to buy tobacco, Debret explained that "the policemen who accompanies them always has a rod in his hand, with which he prods and separates them from the path of loquacious friends."

at 160 *réis* per one hundred lashes. As Algranti has argued, this intervention into the quasi-private realm of relations between slaves and slave owners distinguished the experience of slaves in the city from those in rural settings, where punishments were typically administered on behalf of the owner by a *feitor* (plantation foreman).[116]

Even as it reaffirmed the crown's support of slave owners, the practice of officially administering punishment on their behalf also allowed the crown and the intendancy more opportunities to define the features of slavery in the city. What Viana described as the need to confirm "the certainty that owners have that the state will always ensure the punishment of slaves" was circumscribed by the crown's will to maintain order. Consequently, as Viana commented on the case of slaves in nearby Irajá who, with their owner's knowledge, had insulted a royal official and therefore, according to Viana, attacked royal authority itself, he was not about to tolerate the insolence of owners when it translated into the insolence of their slaves.[117] At the same time, although sentences of corporal punishment appear to have become more severe, with slaves being sentenced to up to three hundred lashes after 1815, Viana also discouraged excessive punishment and in some cases refused to administer the number of lashes requested by the owner when he judged that it would generate further disturbances.

Indeed, although he left the threat of extreme and deadly punishment in tact, Viana questioned the expediency of the public punishment in general. He had "always been afraid to punish [blacks and common people] outside [the jail]," he claimed in 1818, "because whipping them in the streets and in the places of their infractions provokes uprisings."[118] In fact, although there was apparently no strict standard established for the punishment of slaves, by 1817, as one judge reported, "it was not practice to whip slaves at the pelourinho, the praça do rocio" or other public squares. Whereas freed people, he further noted, were whipped publicly, slaves were whipped in jail. In this particular case, however, the judge asked for an exception, hoping to make a "terrifying" example of two slave capoeira practitioners. The request was probably denied. For only one year later, when another judge proceeded to punish a slave with a public whipping at the pelourinho, the punishment was suspended and the officials administering the lashes were detained. Although the judge requested clarification on the proper manner to proceed, he himself recognized the pelourinho as the place "where whites are taken to be whipped on their backs."[119]

Viana regarded this curtailment of the public punishment of slaves as a move that attenuated the "shocking" corruption that, as many contended, the presence of a large slave population promoted.[120] It was "truly indecent within a court," he insisted, "to have whippings in public squares in the way that in Brazil the slaves are punished."[121] Punishment, however, was not the only shocking or troublesome feature of slavery in the city. Indeed, for many royal officials its most insalubrious consequences were associated with the arrival of Africans at Brazil and their subsequent sale. "Blacks disembark, and they are immediately put up for sale," the physician Vieira da Silva complained in 1808, "they enter different homes, and free exchange among them and the persons of the house is permitted, especially with children, as there are no other persons who care for them."[122] To ameliorate these conditions, new standards of hygiene were established for the slave market at Valongo. Although slave merchants complained of the fees charged, after 1810 the owners of intermediary warehouses near the market apparently were given the task of preparing slaves for sale, including a quarantine and clothing; in addition, Viana established standards for more orderly and sanitary burials at the "new slaves'" cemetery nearby.[123]

Such efforts to mitigate what officials construed to be the indecency of slavery also included ultimately futile attempts by owners to curtail the appearance of slave labor, even as they proceeded to rely on slaves in both commerce and at home. Visitors commented on the trend toward replacing African and African-Brazilian labor with Europeans in certain occupations. While the "mechanics were formerly all mulattoes," reported the British Ellis in 1816, "the residence of the court . . . encouraged not only Portuguese, but other Europeans, to establish themselves as artificers."[124] Luccock noted the preference for European labor as well, particularly as a means to reflect one's status. For formal processions, he explained, carriages were "drawn by horses instead of mules, and attended by white servants instead of slaves." Other owners, recognizing that the use of slave labor could not be hidden, reportedly gave more consideration to the appearance of the slaves themselves. As Luccock further explained, while following the arrival of the court "white servants were more generally seen, . . . slaves for domestic occupations, though less numerous, were more carefully selected, furnished with better clothing and food."[125] This limited concern with the clothing and appearance of slaves anteceded the arrival of the court, however, as Silvia Lara has explained, in expressions of seignorial ostentation predicated on the notion that, as one eighteenth-century critic of slavery observed, "the body of a slave or domestic servant is like part of the master's body."[126] Following the transfer of the court then, the dimensions of such ostentation grew as the city's elites used slaves and slave retinues, along with their carriages and attire, to project their now more courtly appearance.

While royal intervention in the punishment and the sale of slaves and elite pretense to refinement sought to obscure from view and to sanitize the brutality of slavery and therefore create the appearance of a metropolitan court, such measures were also seen as providing the basis for a more effective control of the slave population. They followed from the notion that order had moral as well as physical dimensions, or, as Viana argued, that "moral force is always more powerful than physical force." Indeed, in this sense, their initial treatment at Valongo market ideally marked the beginning of the slaves' immersion into European society under the aegis of their owners' paternal authority, a passage from what Viana and other elite residents regarded to be the slaves' savage ways of life characterized by nakedness and violence. Measured, rather than excessive punishment, in turn, ostensibly introduced slaves to European justice.

Yet the intendant also raised concerns that such paternal ideals had been forgotten in Rio de Janeiro in the 1810s. Those owners who set decorous standards and cared for their slaves' appearance, Viana lamented, were outnumbered by those who left them "barefoot and barely clothed" as well as ignorant of the "immortality of the soul and of eternal life." As a result, Viana explained in one report, slaves were resentful, full of hate, and disobedient. Under these circumstances, punishment led only to further conflict and disorder. Although this critique recalled earlier denunciations of slave owners made before the transfer of the court, Viana indeed attributed the lack of attention to the slaves' well-being to the expanded use of slavery in the city after 1808. "With the arrival of the court to this city," he wrote, "we enjoyed the good effects of a larger population" and many of these newcomers to the city, in turn, "took possession of slaves in the manner of this country because of the difficulty in securing whites, as in Portugal, to serve them." These new owners, the intendant continued, "wanting to earn a living, and capitalize on their wealth, took advantage of the practice of buying slaves to then bring them to work on public works, at the customs houses, and in services to the city." Although this practice of renting out slaves for wages was theoretically sound, Viana noted, in practice the "desire to immediately profit" from the newly arrived slaves meant that these new owners both failed to provide religious instruction and further mistreated their slaves. As a result, Viana lamented, "the old equilibrium was lost."[127]

Thus, the transformation of Rio de Janeiro into the New World court had resulted in profoundly contradictory approaches to slavery. On the one hand, the city's residents, royal exiles, and officials together sought either to hide the practice of slavery or make it decorous. On the other hand, the intendant observed, as the quest for prosperity in the New World resulted in the growth of the city's slave population, the process of metropolitanization was undermined. Just as Viana had encountered in the policing of public space and public life, in the culture of slavery the ideal of civilization embodied in morality, education, and manners, which, Viana nostalgically claimed, had been nurtured before Dom João's arrival, was jeopardized. As "a son of this country," Viana explained, he could recall "owners who called to their houses whites and blacks who earned a living teaching [religious] doctrine to their slaves."[128] Unfortunately, he then charged, newcomers to the city failed to appreciate this paternal dimension of ownership.

As a short-term solution to this problem Viana proposed that the intendancy,

FIGURE 7: Jean Baptiste Debret, "Negresses libres, vivant de leur travail," from Debret, *Voyage Pittoresque et Historique au Brésil, sejour d'un Artiste Français au Brésil*
v. 2 (Paris: Firmin Didot Fréres, 1835). Copy and permission obtained from the
Print Collection, Miriam and Ira D. Wallach Division of Arts, Prints and Photographs, The New York Public Library, Astor, Lenox and Tilden Foundations.
Signs of empire and of the colony of Brazil—African cloth and a basket of bananas
and pineapples—are juxtaposed to new standards of opulence, *Modas Francez*
(French fashion). As Debret explained, free women of color worked as seamstresses
for French tailors, acquiring profitable skills, exhibited in the "elegance and decency" of their own dress.

the church, and tribunals should assume a more direct role in ensuring that owners
provided their slaves with a "moral education." Just as the courtiers taught the city's
elites to be metropolitan, the city's residents and officials would teach the courtiers
to be, in effect, colonial; to recognize the means of preserving order and civility amid
the brutal practice of slavery, and to be, as Viana described the local disposition, "less
startled by these matters."[129] Making the new, metropolitan city of Rio, in other
words, required the tolerance of old, unmetropolitan practices.

Indeed, while royal officials reserved the right to persecute African and African-
Brazilians on Rio's streets, they also acknowledged that as long as Brazil had the institution of slavery, the very public presence of slaves, their gatherings, and their
ways of life were social and political, as well as economic, facts. As royal minister the
Marquês de Aguiar conceded to the Conde dos Arcos, not only was it "impossible"

to prohibit gatherings of slaves, "who . . . serve all of the families of Brazil, bring their owners to church, to the theater, and fetch water at the fountains," but indeed the nature of these activities meant that slaves gathering together should be accepted as "inevitable even if such a [circumstance] could lead to some disturbance. . . ."[130] Thus, the new city and New World court of Rio de Janeiro was a place where, as long as slaves did not participate in large-scale disorderly conduct, African and African-Brazilian brotherhoods gathered at the Campo de Santa Anna on Sundays and other feast days, securing, in the process, monetary contributions for their activities; and where, having secured the appropriate license from the intendant, African communities within the city and nearby region chose and celebrated their local leadership.[131] These features of life in Rio distinguished the new court from the old one, where the African population was a smaller and less prominent feature of public life. Yet, social gatherings of Africans and African-Brazilians also could be construed as ensuring continuity between a colonial past and an imperial future. After all, as one royal order noted, "in all the policed cities of the world public entertainment is permitted to even the most inferior classes of the nation."[132] Policing slaves, in this sense, approximated policing the free lower classes. In both cases, Viana repeatedly insisted, the affirmation of hierarchy and royal authority was at stake.

These contemporary perceptions of an urgent need to police and control slaves with both physical repression and social discipline were also shaped by an awareness of a changing political landscape that now explicitly included slaves themselves. The choice facing the residents of Brazil, one official explained, was between "the ancient respect" that men of color "gave to the class of whites" and the "dangerous maxim of equality with which frenetic philosophes had sought to totally annihilate civilized societies."[133] Of course, whether or not slaves expressed their political aspirations in terms of the liberal agendas advanced elsewhere in the Atlantic, the brutality, inhumanity, and the absence of civilization in slavery always demanded insurrection. The struggles between and within European powers afforded opportunities. And one insurrection in particular provided a spectacular example of the potential of colonial protest within European crisis for both slaves and owners to behold. Brazilian slaves, their owners frantically reported to royal officials in 1814, "spoke and knew of the fatal events of the Island of São Domingos."[134]

We have seen royal officials' wariness of the inspiration that the Haitian Revolution provided slaves and people of color in Brazil before the transfer of the court. In the 1810s responding to the question, as Silvestre Pinheiro Ferreira put it, of how to prevent "the danger of a reaction of races" that had and continued to devastate "the unfortunate Antilles" acquired a new urgency.[135] On the one hand, what Silva Lisboa described as "the horrid spectacle of the tremendous catastrophe of the *Queen of the Antilles* transformed into *Madagascar*" was a cautionary tale that supported arguments in favor of the need to displace people of color and the ostensibly unproductive and hostile slave population with European immigrants in the new American empire.[136] The intendant, on the other hand, perceived the example of Haiti, and its possible influence on slaves in Brazil, as a more immediate matter of security. Rebellion was, of course, intolerable anytime and anywhere in Brazil. Yet, the war in Europe, Viana argued, made it particularly dangerous. The slave population formed a weak point in the political and cultural defense against Napoleon that Brazil was supposed to represent. A rebellion of slaves in the prince regent's new court, he wrote in 1808, would surely encourage the Portuguese monarchy's "well-known enemies."[137] Even after the end of the war, Viana insisted in 1816, having been informed "with certain exaggeration, that there has been a spirit of insubordination among Bahian slaves, they [Napoleon's supporters] believe that there they will be well received."[138]

For both Viana and royal minister Souza Coutinho, the solution to the problem of potential insurrection was the scrutiny and detainment of anyone, white or black, reported to have connections in the Caribbean as well as, not surprisingly, those who expressed abolitionist agendas.[139] Thus, in 1816, "a black man" "of the French nation" named Carlos Romão found himself in the city's jail so that the intendant could determine whether he was "from the Island of São Domingos, or from there had come," whether there were "others, or mulattos, if he had been in Bahia, or if he knew of anyone who was there and had come from São Domingos, and their names and the marks by which they could be identified."[140] These actions, however, also carried a risk. As Viana commented to Souza Coutinho following his detainment of three "blacks from Martinique" so that he could verify their past and present occupations, "with these men I have always sought to avoid entering into judicial inquiries or investigations involving witnesses which always give body to formless things, and raise ideas unknown to the great part of the people."[141] Royal officials' perceptions of the politics of slavery, slaves, and people of color thus rested, like those of the politics of the popular classes in general, on contradiction and ambivalence. Slaves and people of color were, at once, suspected of promoting insurrection and regarded as unaware of the politics of contestation. Owner's claims that slaves were so "barbarous" that they were "not afraid to die" suggested limits to ideologically motivated organization and reassured them and royal officials that certain revolutionary agendas would remain, as Viana claimed, "unknown." Yet, ideas of liberty and equality were also perceived to be "contagious" and the potential consequences seemed so inevitable precisely because owners and officials recognized the potential appeal of these ideas to people who had no stake in preserving the inequalities, the lack of liberty, and the hierarchies that served only to oppress them. The crown's choice to maintain the institution of slavery in Brazil and its new American court meant, therefore, that the experiences of policing, governing, and living in Rio de Janeiro, and making the city a metropolis would be shaped by a colonial sense of vulnerability and the politics of elite fear.

The project to make Rio de Janeiro into the capital of the empire was a quest to make the city not only "splendorous" but also ordered, decorous, moral, and allegiant. Becoming the royal court, in this sense, the city became "policed." Policing, in turn, meant not only guaranteeing "public security," but also making Rio metropolitan, recognizing the difference between the metropolis and the colony so that those differences could be diminished. Such a project was sustained by eighteenth-century Europe's enlightened embrace of "civilization" and its mission. Yet, even as officials sought to eradicate colonial "indecencies," they also maintained a preeminent colonial institution: African slavery. Accordingly, while "perfecting" Rio entailed beautifying the city, improving its infrastructure, and disciplining vassals—making them "useful"—the city's elevation "to the highest hierarchy of court of Brazil" also meant the production of what Stoler and Cooper have associated with "the most basic tension of empire": the inevitable quest to define the status of difference amid a contingent and unstable "otherness."[142] Slavery, the intendant and other royal officials thus imagined, would be courtly and metropolitan if slaves were morally educated and their presence in the city was carefully controlled. The end of the "old colonial system" not withstanding, it would be an intensification of colonialism that made the "new city" of Rio de Janeiro imperial. This transformation of Rio de Janeiro into a royal court would, however, also require further negotiation of metropolitan imperatives and colonial realities; exchanges, as we shall see in the next chapter, with which the sovereign and his vassals, both free and slave, embarked on the task of reconstructing the practice of royal authority in the New World.

NOTES

1. The news, brought by the ship "Voador," arrived at Rio de Janeiro on January 14, 1808. See Luiz Gonçalves dos Santos, *Memórias para servir à História do Reino do Brasil* t. 1 (1825) (Belo Horizonte/São Paulo: Itatiaia/EDUSP, 1981), 167.

2. *Relação das festas que se fizerão no Rio de Janeiro quando o Principe Regente Nosso Senhor e toda a sua Real Família chegarão pela primeira vez d'quella Capital . . .* (Lisbon: Impressão Régia, 1810), 4–5, 6.

3. "Preparativos no Rio de Janeiro para receber a família real portuguesa," January 16, 1808, BNRJ Ms. II-35,4,1.

4. [Report on reception], March 1808, BNRJ Ms. II-35,4,1, f5; *Relação*, 11–12; Gonçalves dos Santos, *Memórias* t. 1, 167–187; and Anonymous, [ca. 1807–08], in Ângelo

Pereira, *Os filhos de el-rei D. João VI* (Lisbon: Empresa Nacional de Publicidade, 1946), 127–129.

5. Gonçalves dos Santos, *Memórias* t. 1, 335.

6. António Filipe Pimentel, "Absolutismo, Corte e Palácio Real—En torno dos palácios de D. João V," in *Arqueologia do Estado, Jornadas sobre Formas de Organização e Exercício dos Poderes na Europa do Sul, S.XVII–XVIII*, special issue of *História e Crítica* (Lisbon) (1988), 685–686.

7. A.J.R. Russell-Wood, "Portugal and the World in the Age of Dom João V," and Angela Delaforce, "Lisbon, 'This New Rome': Dom João V of Portugal and Relations Between Rome and Lisbon," in *The Age of the Baroque in Portugal*, ed. Jay Levenson (Washington, DC/New Haven: National Gallery of Art/Yale University Press, 1993); and Pimentel, "Absolutismo," 688–690, 706.

8. José Augusto França, *Lisboa Pombalina e o Iluminismo* (Lisbon: Livraria Bertrand, 1977); and idem, "Lisbon, the Enlightened City of the Marquês de Pombal," in *The Age of the Baroque*, ed. Levenson, 133–137.

9. Here the police intendant claimed that the town council's manner of conducting its affairs promoted the opposite. See Paulo Fernandes Viana [intendant] to the Marquês de Aguiar [Fernando José de Portugal e Castro, Ministro dos Negócios do Reino], September 6, 1811, ANRJ Ministério dos Negócios do Brasil (hereafter MNB) Caixa 6J 78.

10. John Luccock, *Notes on Rio de Janeiro and the southern parts of Brazil; taken during a residence of ten years in that country, from 1808–1818* (London: Samuel Leigh, 1820), 245–246, 254, 548. For a discussion of the street and urban form in Joanine Rio de Janeiro see James Holston, *The Modernist City: An Anthropological Critique of Brasília* (Chicago: University of Chicago Press, 1989), 109–119.

11. Marrócos both boasted of his aversion to the French and noted with interest the availability of new French wares in the city after the war. See Luiz Joaquim dos Santos Marrócos to his sister, April 10, 1815, and another undated letter, in *Cartas de Luiz Joaquim dos Santos Marrocos* (Rio de Janeiro: Biblioteca Nacional/Ministério de Educação e Saude, 1939), 223, 444. On imports see also the announcement in the *Gazeta do Rio de Janeiro*, March 2, 1816, in Delso Renault, *O Rio antigo nos anúncios de jornais, 1808–1850* (Rio de Janeiro: Francisco Alves, 1984), 56–57. As signs of a new openness to foreign fashion and culture in Rio, Renault also notes a growing number of announcements for instruction in French as well as the suspension of an earlier prohibition (in 1802) against wearing clothes made from cloth that was not manufactured in Portugal at viceregal audiences. See Renault, *Rio antigo*, 39, 40–41, 44, 48, 52. On the "Europeanization" of manners and other social practices in the Rio court, see also Jurandir Malerba, "A corte no exílio. Interpretação do Brasil joanino" (Ph.D. dissertation, University of São Paulo, 1997), 121–122, 127.

12. The decree is cited in Afonso de E. Taunay, *A Missão Artística de 1816* ([Rio de Janeiro]: Diretoria do Patrimônio Histórico e Artístico Nacional, 1956), 18. For examples of neoclassical design in Rio de Janeiro see Jean Baptiste Debret, *Viagem Pitoresca e Histórica ao Brasil* (1834) t. 3 (Belo Horizonte/São Paulo: Itatiaia/EDUSP, 1989), plate 41; and Clarival do Prado Valladares, *Rio, análise iconográfica do barroco e neoclássico remanentes no Rio de Janeiro* v. 2 (Rio de Janeiro: Bloch, 1978), especially "Ato inaugural da praça do comércio . . . 1820," plates 638–639, and "Primitiva câmara do comércio," plates 640–641. On the mis-

sion and its members see also Mario Barata, "Manuscrito inédito de Lebreton," *Revista do Patrimônio Histórico e Artístico Nacional* (Rio de Janeiro) 14 (1959), 283–307; Gean Maria Bittencourt, *A missão artística francesa de 1816* (Petrópolis: Museo de Armas Ferreira da Cunha, 1967); Pontifícia Universidade Católica do Rio de Janeiro, *Uma cidade em questão I: Grandjean de Montigny e o Rio de Janeiro* (Rio de Janeiro: PUC, 1978); J.F. de Almeida Prado, *D. João e o início da classe dirigente do Brasil (depoimento de um pintor austríaco no Rio de Janeiro)* (São Paulo: Companhia Editora Nacional, 1968), 189–213, 285–316; Carmen Sylvia Sicoli Seoane, "Aquarelas do Brasil: estudo iconográfico e textual da natureza do índio em Debret e Rugendas (1816–1831)" (M.A. thesis, Fluminense Federal University, 1990); and an outstanding essay by Rodrigo Naves in his *A forma difícil: ensaios sobre a arte brasileira* (São Paulo: Editora Ática, 1996). For recent analysis of the legacy of the French Mission and the Portuguese and Brazilian monarchies see Caren Ann Meghreblian, "Art, Politics and Historical Perception in Imperial Brazil, 1854–1884" (Ph.D. dissertation, University of California, Los Angeles, 1990) and Iara Lis Carvalho Souza, *Pátria Coroada: O Brasil como Corpo Político Autônomo, 1780–1831* (São Paulo: Editora UNESP, 1998), Chapter 6.

13. See Alvará, June 15, 1808, in *Código Brasiliense, Ou Collecção das Leis, Alvarás, Decretos, Cartas Régias, &c. Promulgadas no Brasil desde a feliz chegada de El Rey Nosso Senhor a Este Reino* (Rio de Janeiro: [Impressão Régia, 1811–1822]). On the royal chapel see Alcingstone de Oliveira Cunha, "The Portuguese Royal Court and the Patronage of Sacred Music in Rio de Janeiro, 1808–1821" (Ph.D. dissertation, Southwestern Baptist Theological Seminary, Fort Worth, Texas, 1998).

14. The 1810 decree is transcribed in J. Galante de Souza, *O Teatro no Brasil* v. 1 (Rio de Janeiro: Ministério da Educação e Cultura/INL, 1960), 138–140. Before the royal theater, Rio de Janeiro had smaller *salas* or *casas de espectáculos*, the most notable being Padre Ventura's *Casa da Ópera,* which opened in 1767 and burned in 1769, according to Galante. By 1776, Ventura's theater had been replaced by the *Ópera Nova,* built by Manuel Luiz de Almeida. On eighteenth-century theater see Galante de Souza, *Teatro,* 110–112; Adolfo Morales de Los Rios Filho, "História do teatro do Rio de Janeiro durante o século XVIII," *Anais do congresso comemorativo do bicentenario da transferencia da sede do governo* v. 4 (1967), 319–354; Almeida Prado, *D. João,* 162–188; and Ariadna Gonçalves Moreira, "The Influence of the Portuguese Royal Court on the Development of Opera, The Opera Nova, and the Real Teatro São João in Rio de Janeiro from 1808–1824" (Doctoral Essay, Doctor of Musical Arts, University of Miami, 1998). *O Juramento dos Numes* was published by Rio's Royal Press in 1813. The editor of the periodical *O Patriota,* Manuel Ferreira de Araújo Guimarães, attacked Coutinho's work. Coutinho in turn issued *Resposta Defensiva, e Analytica á Censura,* also published in 1813. For the popular presence at the theater see Luccock, *Notes on Rio de Janeiro;* Viana, "Registro do Ofício expedido ao Juiz do Crime de São José," May 15, 1809 and June 7, 1809 (including a reference to "spies" in the audience who could determine who was being disruptive), and Viana, "Registro do Ofício expedido ao Juiz do Crime do Bairro da Candelária," May 15, June 7 and June 11, 1809, ANRJ Códice 323 v. 1, f53v, f81, f86; Viana, "Registro do Ofício expedido ao Inspector do Teatro," August 4, 1814, ANRJ Códice 329 v. 2, f206v; Viana, "Registro do Ofício expedido ao Juiz do Crime do Bairro de Santa Rita," April 18, 1818, ANRJ Códice 329 v. 4, f89v-90. The presence of "blacks" in the audience is analyzed in Malerba, "A corte no exílo," 103–104.

15. "Alvará, porque Vossa Alteza Real he Servido Crear no Estado do Brasil hum Intendente Geral da Polícia, na forma acima declarada. . . ," May 10, 1808 ([Rio de Janeiro]: Impressão Régia, [1808]).

16. The alvará of June 25, 1760 that created the intendancy in Portugal is transcribed in Mello Barreto Filho and Hermeto Lima, *História da polícia do Rio de Janeiro, aspectos da cidade e da vida carioca, 1565–1831* v. 1 (Rio de Janeiro: S.A.A. Noite, n.d. [1939]), 165–176. For contemporary commentary on the intendancy and its responsibilities, see Viana to Marquês de Aguiar, August 22, 1815, ANRJ MNB Caixa 6J 79; Viana, "Abreviada demonstração dos trabalhos da polícia" (ca. 1821), *RIHGB* 55, pt. 1 (1892), 373–380; Viana to Sua Alteza Real, August 27, 1810, in *Dom João VI e o Império no Brasil, a Independência e a Missão Rio Maior*, ed. Marcos Carneiro de Mendonça (Rio de Janeiro: Biblioteca Reprográfica Xerox, 1984), 188; and Rodrigo de Souza Coutinho, "Representação a Sua Alteza Real o Príncipe Regente sobre uma reforma da câmara do Rio de Janeiro" [no date, ca. 1808], in Rodrigo de Souza Coutinho, *Textos políticos, económicos e financeiros (1783–1811)* v. 2 (Lisbon: Banco de Portugal, 1993), 347–348. For broader discussions of policing in Portugal and Brazil see José Subtil, "Os poderes do centro: governo e administração," in *História de Portugal: O Antigo Regime* v. 4, ed. António Manuel Hespanha (Lisbon: Estampa, n.d.), 174–176; Thomas H. Holloway, *Policing Rio de Janeiro: Repression and Resistance in a Nineteenth-Century City* (Stanford: Stanford University Press, 1993), 28–33; José Luiz Werneck da Silva, "A polícia na corte e no distrito federal, 1831–1930," *Estudos PUC/RJ* 3 (1981), 23; and Maria Beatriz Nizza da Silva, "A Intendência-Geral da Polícia: 1808–1821," *Acervo* 1, n. 2, (July–December 1986), 187–204.

17. Viana's grandmother was from the well-established Nascentes Pinto family and he married the daughter of Brás Carneiro Leão, a wealthy merchant and landowner who died the year the prince regent arrived. His niece married the son of Rodrigo de Souza Coutinho. See Rui Vieira da Cunha, "A vida do Rio de Janeiro através dos testamentos: 1815–1822," *RIHGB* 282 (January–March 1969), 53.

18. See Viana, "Registro do Ofício expedido ao Ministro e Secretário da Repartição de Guerra," May 23, 1808, ANRJ Códice 318 f16v; and Viana to Aguiar, June 9, 1812, ANRJ MNB Caixa 6J 79.

19. See Viana, "Abreviada demonstração"; and Viana to Aguiar, August 22, 1815, ANRJ MNB Caixa 6J 79. The intendancy recruited street lighters and sweepers with announcements in the *Gazeta*. See citation from December 1, 1810, in Renault, *Rio antigo*, 42.

20. *Relação*, 7.

21. In Brazil, as in Portugal, the intendancy had numerous jurisdictional conflicts with the town council, especially regarding public works. See Viana, [parecer], September 1, 1810, f5v–f6, ANRJ MNB Caixa 6J 78. Although Souza Coutinho argued that these conflicts could be avoided by making the intendant a member of the council, the advice apparently went unheeded.

22. See Joaquim José de Queirós [ouvidor], "Mappa da população da côrte e província do Rio de Janeiro em 1821," *RIHGB* 33, pt. 1 (1870), 135–142.

23. *Correio Braziliense ou Armazem Literário* 1 (October 1808), 420.

24. Marquês de Borba to the Condessa do Redondo [his daughter-in-law], Rio de Janeiro, February 20, 1809; and Borba to the Conde de Redondo [his son], May 10, 1810, in Pereira, *Os filhos*, 140, 143. John Mawe also noted that rents were as high as in London. See his *Trav-*

els in the Interior of Brazil . . . (London: M. Carey/Boston: Wells and Lilly, 1816), 106.

25. José Joaquim de Santa Anna, *Memória sobre o Enxugo Geral Desta Cidade do Rio de Janeiro . . .* (Rio de Janeiro: Impressão Régia, 1815), 17.

26. Luccock, *Notes on Rio de Janeiro*, 100–101. For attempts to evade the imposition of aposentadoria see Vieira da Cunha, "A vida do Rio de Janeiro." António Nascentes Pinto, for example, whose family had settled in Rio at the end of the seventeenth century, attempted to retain control of his property on the Rua Belas Noites by renting it to a royal official in need of accommodations before the crown could indiscriminately, and more permanently, assign it to someone else. In Pinto's case, however, the scheme backfired when the official then asked the crown to confirm his right to reside in the house through aposentadoria. Numerous examples of the conflicts arising from aposentadoria can be found in the *pareceres* of D. Francisco de Almeida de Melo e Castro, Conde de Galveias, *aposentador-mor da Corte e Reino no Rio de Janeiro*, Arquivo Nacional Torre do Tombo, Arquivo da Casa dos Condes de Galveias, Maço 10. Colorful stories of tribulations related to aposentadoria are particularly popular in folkloric accounts of Joanine Rio de Janeiro. Several describe how the letters "P.R." used to designate that property had been requisitioned in the name of the prince regent were also understood to signify "ponha-se na rua" (get out on the street) or "predio roubado" (stolen building). See, for example, Edmundo Luiz, *A côrte de D. João no Rio de Janeiro* 3 v. (Rio de Janeiro: Imprensa Nacional, 1939).

27. See Viana, [parecer, ca. 1808], BNRJ Ms. I-34,32,31; Viana, "Registro do Edital," June 11, 1808, ANRJ Códice 318, f26; Viana, "Registro da Representação. . . ," August 1, 1808, ANRJ Códice 318, f47-47v; and Viana, "Registro do Ofício expedido ao Ministro de Estado dos Negócios do Brasil [José de Portugal e Castro]," November 17, 1808, ANRJ Códice 318, f112.

28. Viana, [parecer], March 20, 1811, ANRJ MNB Caixa 6J 78.

29. "Alvará [Imposição da Décima aos Prédios Urbanos], June 27, 1808" ([Rio de Janeiro]: Impressão Régia, [1808]); Gonçalves dos Santos, *Memórias* t. 1, 209, 277–278.

30. Gilberto Ferrez, *O Paço da Cidade do Rio de Janeiro* (Rio de Janeiro: Fundação Nacional Pró-Memória, 1985), 33. As Viana explained in a report, an alvará of February 6, 1818 granted *aposentadoria passiva* to all residents of Rio. See Viana, "Registro de uma informação dada ao Ministro de Estado dos Negócios do Reino," October 23, 1818, ANRJ Códice 323 v. 5, f63; and Viana, "Registro da Informação expedida ao Ministro de Estado dos Negócios do Reino," November 1[8], 1818, ANRJ Códice 323 v. 5, f75.

31. See Alvará, June 27, 1808 (creation of *juizes do crime*) and Alvará, June 25, 1760, transcribed in Barreto Filho and Lima, *História da polícia* v. 1, 165–176. The intendant's jurisdiction extended to all crimes pertaining to the *corregedores* and *juizes do crime dos bairros* and allowed the intendant to deal summarily with cases or send them to the *casa da suplicação* when necessary. Before 1808, within Brazilian cities the duty to keep and restore the peace was entrusted to a variety of *ad hoc* functionaries: civilian guards contracted by the *senado da câmara* (town council), *quadrilheiros* (neighborhood inspectors) appointed by local judges and the town council, and, in cases of large scale disturbances, *ordenanças* (reserve militia units). The limited authority of these posts (guards and inspectors had no more powers of arrest than other residents) stood in contrast to the concerted powers of the intendant. See Holloway, *Policing*, 28–31.

32. Viana requested that the local judges furnish him with lists of residents in each of the city's neighborhoods. See Viana, "Registro do Ofício expedido ao Juiz do Crime do Bairro da Se," October 25, 1808, ANRJ Códice 318, f96-96v; Viana, "Registro do Ofício expedido ao Juiz do Crime do Bairro de São José," March 15, 1809, ANRJ Códice 323 v.1; Viana, "Registro do Ofício expedido ao Juiz do Crime do Bairro da Se," June 3, 1809, ANRJ Códice 323 v. 1, f78v.

33. "Decreto," May 13, 1809 ([Rio de Janeiro]: Impressão Régia [1809]). For Viana's request for the creation of the guard see "Registro do Ofício expedido ao Ministro de Estado dos Negócios Estrangeiros e de Guerra," March 1, 1808, ANRJ Códice 318, f187. The guard's commander, the newcomer José Maria Rebelo, answered to both the city's governor of arms and the intendant. Its rank and file were to be chosen from the best soldiers and would wear the same uniform as the guards in Lisbon.

34. Souza Coutinho, "Composição, e Regulação da Divizão Militar da Guarda Real da Polícia do Rio de Janeiro," May 13, 1809 ([Rio de Janeiro]: Impressão Régia, [1809]), 7. On the guard see also Viana, "Registro do Ofício expedido ao Ministro de Estado dos Negócios Estrangeiros e de Guerra," April 25, 1809, ANRJ Códice 323 v. 1, f 43v-50v.

35. Gonçalves dos Santos, *Memórias* t. 1, 203–204; Viana, "Registro do Ofício expedido ao Juiz do Crime do Bairro de Santa Rita," April 18, 1818, ANRJ Códice 329 v. 4, f89v-90.

36. Viana, "Registro do Ofício expedido ao Juiz de Fora desta Cidade," August 5, 1808 ANRJ Códice 318, f52v; Viana to Aguiar, August 22, 1814, and Viana to Aguiar, September 15, 1814, ANRJ MNB Caixa 6J 79.

37. Viana to Tomás António Vila Nova Portugal [Ministro dos Negócios do Reino], July 19, 1818, ANRJ MNB Caixa 5B 243. Among numerous reports of public disorder see Viana, "Registro do Ofício expedido ao Juiz do Crime do Bairro de Santa Rita," February 11, 1809, ANRJ Códice 318, f148; Viana to Aguiar [Ministro dos Negócios do Reino], August 22, 1814, ANRJ MNB Caixa 6J 79; Viana, "Registro do Ofício expedido ao Juiz do Crime do Bairro da Se," March 31, 1818, ANRJ Códice 329 v. 4, f82; and Souza Coutinho to João Baptista de Azeredo Coutinho [General das Tropas], n.d., BNRJ Ms. II-34,27,7 n. 5.

38. Viana, "Registro do Ofício ao General das Tropas" [João Baptista de Azeredo Coutinho], July 20, 1808, ANRJ Códice 318, f46v-47. On policing the theater and public entertainment see also Viana, "Registro do Ofício expedido ao Commandante da Guarda Real," December 29, 1810, ANRJ Códice 323 v. 2, f47v; "Registro do Ofício expedido ao Juiz do Crime do Bairro de São José," July 11, 1812, ANRJ Códice 329 v. 1, f181; "Registro do Ofício expedido ao Desembagador Duque Estrada," February 10, 1814, ANRJ Códice 329 v. 2, f153v; and an unsigned report, in Viana's handwriting [ca. 1812], BNRJ Ms. I-33,30,43.

39. Viana, "Registro do Ofício expedido ao Juiz de Fora desta Cidade," April 3, 1809, and "Registro do Ofício expedido ao Juiz do Crime do Bairro de Santa Rita," April 5 and 11, 1809, in ANRJ Códice 323 v. 1; Viana, "Registro do Ofício expedido [aos Juizes do Crime dos Bairros]," July 28, 1813, ANRJ Códice 329 v. 2, f103v-104; Viana, "Registro do Ofício expedido ao [Ministro de Estado Vila Nova Portugal]," August 11, 1819, ANRJ Códice 323 v. 5, f133.

40. Viana, "Registro[s] do[s] Ofício[s] expedido[s] ao[s] Juiz[es] do Crime do Bairro da Se e da Candelária," May 1, 1809, and Viana, "Registro do Ofício expedido ao Juiz do Crime do

Bairro da Candelária," April 25, 1809, ANRJ Códice 323 v. 1; Viana, "Registro do Ofício expedido ao Juiz do Crime do Bairro de S. José," September 15, 1818, ANRJ Códice 329 v. 4, f125 (on Teresa dos Moleques); and Viana, "Registro do Ofício dirigido a Secretaria de Estado dos Negócios Estrangeiros e de Guerra," June 7, 1815, ANRJ Códice 323 v. 4 (on Mathildes de Jesus). *Moleque* may refer to a young boy, especially a young boy of color, as well as someone of ill-repute. See António de Moraes e Silva, *Grande Dicionário da Língua Portuguesa* (1789) (Lisbon: Confluencia, 1949).

41. See Viana, [parecer], September 1, 1810, and Viana to Aguiar, June 9, 1811, ANRJ MNB Caixa 6J 78; Holloway, *Policing*, 34.

42. Viana to Vila Nova Portugal, February 7, 1820, ANRJ MNB Caixa 6J 86.

43. José Subtil, "Os Poderes do centro," 176; Kenneth Maxwell, *Pombal: Paradox of the Enlightenment* (New York: Cambridge University Press, 1995), 88; Gonçalves dos Santos, *Memórias* t. 1, 273; Viana, [representação], November 24, 1816, f11, ANRJ MNB Caixa 6J 83.

44. Viana, "Registro do Ofício expedido ao Juiz do Crime de São José," June 19, 1811, ANRJ Códice 329 v. 1, f61.

45. Viana, "Registro do Ofício expedido ao Comandante do Districto de Macacú," May 9, 1809, ANRJ Códice 323 v. 1, f42v-43v; Viana, [informe], November 17, 1810, ANRJ MNB Caixa 6J 78; Viana to Vila Nova Portugal, September 3, 1820, ANRJ Códice 323 v. 6, f20v. In 1809 Viana identified a series of categories to be targeted for "correction": (1) single men who are not farmers and who are not the only son of a widow; (2) single men with the reputation of *valentão* and *briguento* even if they were only sons; (3) married men who had abandoned their wives and children to live with other women; (4) sons of farmers with many sons. In these cases, he added, "whites and mulattos will serve." As Viana also reported, however, there were not enough *vadios* in the city to meet the demands for recruits. See Viana, "Registro do Ofício expedido ao Ministro de Estado dos Negócios Estrangeiros e de Guerra," July 3, 1811, ANRJ Códice 323 v. 3, f57.

46. Viana to Vila Nova Portugal, May 27, 1818, ANRJ MNB Caixa 6J 81; Viana to Aguiar, February 7, 1813, ANRJ MNB Caixa 6J 79.

47. António Manuel Hespanha, "A punição e a graça," in *História de Portugal: O Antigo Regime* v. 4, ed. António Manuel Hespanha (Lisbon: Editorial Estampa, n.d.); Francisco António de Novaes Campos, *Príncipe Perfeito, Emblemas de D. João de Solórzano* (1790) (Lisbon: Instituto de Cultura e Lingua Portuguesa, 1985), f153.

48. "Almanaque da cidade do Rio de Janeiro para o ano de 1817," *RIHGB* 270 (January–March 1966), 217.

49. Vila Nova Portugal, "Sobre a questão da escravatura," n.d. [ca. 1814], BNRJ Ms. I-32,14,22.

50. Geine de Cailhé, "Projet" and "Memoire et notes explicatives sur le projet," Rio de Janeiro, December 15, 1820, BNRJ Ms. I-33,29,8 and I-33,29,16; R.R. Palmer, *The Age of Democratic Revolution: A Political History of Europe and America* 2 v. (Princeton: Princeton University Press, 1959–64). Palmer's understanding of the late eighteenth century as a critical moment in the history of "Atlantic Civilization" was shared by officials in the Rio court, although they despaired at signs of what Palmer called "a new feeling for a kind of equality."

51. Viana to Aguiar, June 9, 1812, ANRJ MNB Caixa 6J 79. These responsibilities were

delineated upon the creation of the intendancy in Lisbon. See "Instrucções conforme o alvará de 25 de Junho de 1760—A jurisdição do intendente geral da polícia da corte no reino," in Barreto Filho and Lima, *História da polícia*, v. 1, 169–172. On strategies for alta polícia see also Viana, "Registro do Ofício expedido ao [Ouvidor do Crime de Bahia]," June 28, 1808, ANRJ Códice 318, f35v; Viana, "Abreviada demonstração," 379; and Viana to Sua Alteza Real, [parecer], September 1, 1810, f2, f5, ANRJ MNB Caixa 6J 78. Viana also claimed that the intendancy needed money "for an extraordinary case, or for a hidden expenditure which the sovereign orders. . . ." Alta polícia indeed was listed as the fourth largest expenditure (14:820$704 out of a total budget of 108:061$079) after infrastructure (roads, landfills, bridges), lighting and loan payments. See "Conta corrente da receita e dispeza que te[m] a Intendência Geral da Polícia da Corte, e Reino do Brasil," (1820) ANRJ MNB Caixa 6J 86.

52. Viana to Aguiar, July 24, 1815, ANRJ MNB Caixa 6J 79; Viana, "Registro do Ofício expedido ao Ministro do Estado dos Negócios Estrangeiros," March 20, 1817, ANRJ Códice 323 v. 4. As Viana described in one report, the acquisition of a passport required an *abono* (guarantee) from the diplomatic representative of the applicant's country of origin that affirmed his or her name and destination. The intendancy would then ratify this document with an inquiry into the person's conduct in Rio and issue the passport. For the intendant's understanding of policing foreigners and other new arrivals to Rio see also Viana, "Registro do Ofício expedido ao Intendente do Ouro," April 5, 1811, ANRJ Códice 329 v. 1, f29; "Registro do Ofício expedido ao Intendente do Ouro," August 31, 1815, ANRJ Códice 329 v. 3, f44v; Viana, "Registro do Ofício expedido ao Juiz do Bairro de São José," September 22, 1815, ANRJ Códice 329 v. 3, f58v.

53. Viana to Vila Nova Portugal, November 24, 1816, f5, f11, ANRJ MNB Caixa 6J 83; Viana to Aguiar, July 24, 1815, f2, ANRJ MNB Caixa 6J 79. At the end of the decade Viana worked with Geine de Cailhé, who reportedly had served in the French army and, once in Rio, sought to open a casino. On another informant Tremeau, who Viana identified as a former secretary of a justice of the peace in Paris, see Arnold B. Clayton, "The Life of Tomás Antônio Vilanova Portugal: A Study in the Government of Portugal and Brazil" (Ph.D. dissertation, Columbia University, 1977), 235. Tremeau's activities included reporting to Vila Nova Portugal on the activities of Spanish Americans residing in Rio and their alleged allegiances to the freemasonry. In 1818 Tremeau provided the crown with a report on the English Alien Act and the policing of foreigners in Brazil. See ANRJ MNB Caixa 6J 80.

54. Domingos António de Souza Coutinho to Sua Alteza Real, London, June 30, 1808 and Ângelo Pereira, *D. João VI, príncipe e rei* v. 3 (Lisbon: Empresa Nacional de Publicidade, 1956), 52–53; Viana, "Registro do Ofício expedido ao Juiz do Crime do Bairro de Santa Rita," March 4, 1811, ANRJ Códice 329 v. 1, f17v; Rodrigo de Souza Coutinho to Vossa Alteza Real, September 21, 1811, BNRJ Ms. I-33,29,32; Viana, "Registro do Ofício expedido ao Juiz do Crime da Candelária," September 9, 1811, October 10, 1811, ANRJ Códice 329 v. 1, f89, f96v. For investigations into emissaries and their Portuguese contacts see Viana, "Registro do Ofício expedido ao Ministro de Estado dos Negócios do Brasil," March 14, 1811, ANRJ Códice 323 v. 3, f28; Viana to Aguiar, May 22, 1810 and November 23, 1810, ANRJ MNB Caixa 6J 78 (on the royal official Francisco de Melo Manuel da Camara); and "Correspondência sobre João Pereira de Souza Caldas . . . e outros suspeitos de terem vindo de França como emissarios de Napoleão I," BNRJ Ms. II-34,18,39. Spanish officials were also

tracking this group, which included a Spanish vassal. See António Portalan to Marquês de Casa Irujo, March 2, 1811, AHI Lata 171 Maço 6 Pasta 10; Viana to Linhares, August 7, 1811, and "perguntas feitas," in BNRJ Ms. I-3,17,10 and [Sousa Coutinho], "Prisão e inter-rogatório feito por ordem do Conde de Linhares a João Pereira de Sousa Caldas," transcribed in Pereira, *D. João VI* v. 3, 276-277. On the question of emissaries see also Donatello Grieco, *Napoleão e o Brasil* (Rio de Janeiro: Civilização Brasileira, 1939).

55. Viana, "Registro do Ofício expedido ao Ministro de Estado dos Negócios Estrangeiros e de Guerra,"April 24, 1811, ANRJ Códice 323 v. 3, f42v. On mistaken identities see also "Sumário [Vitoriano José de Almeida Troam]," [1810–1811], ANRJ MNB Caixa 6J 78.

56. Viana, "Registro do Ofício expedido ao Ministro de Estado dos Negócios Estrangeiros e de Guerra," July 30, 1811, ANRJ Códice 323 v. 3, f60.

57. Arcos to Vila Nova Portugal, March 31, 1818, AHI Lata 179, Maço 3.

58. Viana, "Registro do Ofício dirigido ao Ministro de Estado dos Negócios Estrangeiros e de Guerra," June 7, 1808, ANRJ Códice 318, f21; Viana, "Registro do Ofício expedido ao Ministro de Estado dos Negócios Estrangeiros e de Guerra," January 6, 1811, ANRJ Códice 323 v. 2, f7v; Viana, "Registro do Ofício dirigido ao Ministro de Estado dos Negócios Es-trangeiros e de Guerra," June 17, 1811, August [13], 1811, December 14, 1811, ANRJ Códice 323 v. 3, f54, f63v, f91v; Viana to Aguiar, March 10, 1813, ANRJ MNB Caixa 6J 79; Viana, "Registro do Ofício expedido ao Ministro de Estado dos Negócios do Ultramar," June 4, 1813, ANRJ Códice 323 v. 3; Viana to Vila Nova Portugal, February 18, 1818, AHI Lata 180 Maço 5 Pasta 13; and correspondence between the Spanish crown's representative Mar-quês de Casa Irujo, Souza Coutinho, Vila Nova Portugal, and Viana, AHI Lata 176 Maço 2 Pasta 1, Lata 183 Maço 2 Pasta 3–4, and Lata 181 Maço 2.

59. Viana to Vila Nova Portugal, July 21, 1818, ANRJ MNB Caixa 5B 243.

60. [Carta Régia, "Constando com toda a certeza, a existencia de huma conjuração . . . "], May 31, 1817 ([Rio de Janeiro]: Impressão Régia, [1817]); Carvalho Souza, *Pátria Coroada*, 57–74.

61. Arcos cited in Carlos Guilherme Mota, "Presença francesa em Recife em 1817," *Ex-trait des Cahiers du Monde Hispanique et Luso-Brésilien* caravelle 15 (1970), 49. On the plan to recover Napoleon see Mota, and J.A. Costa, "Napoléon I au Brasil," *Revue de monde latin* (Paris) v. 8 (1883–89), 205–216. On relations between the provisional government in Per-nambuco and the United States see Moniz Bandeira, *Presença dos Estados Unidos no Brasil (Dois séculos de história)* (Rio de Janeiro: Civilização Brasileira, 1978), 32–37.

62. Gonçalves dos Santos, *Memórias* t. 2, 99–100.

63. On the freemasonry in Brazil and its role in the 1817 insurrections see Frei Amador da Santa Cruz to Sua Alteza Real, [Bahia], n.d. [ca. 1817] transcribed in Pereira, *Os filhos*, 251–253; Roderick Barman, *Brazil: The Forging of a Nation, 1798–1852* (Stanford: Stanford University Press, 1988), 57–63; Manuel Rodrigues Ferreira and Tito Lívio Ferreira, *A maçonaria na indepêndencia brasileira* v. 1 (São Paulo: Gráfica Biblos, 1962), 196–216; Célia Galvão Quirino dos Santos, "As sociedades secretas e a formação do pensamento liberal," *Anais do Museu Paulista* 19 (1965), 51–59; and Teixeira Pinto, *A maçonaria na independência do Brasil (1812–1823)* (Rio de Janeiro: Salogan, 1961). According to Barman, masonic activi-ties existed in Brazil before but intensified after the transfer of the court. On proscription see alvará of March 30, 1818, in *Código Brasiliense*. José Albano Fragoso, a magistrate assigned to

investigate the Pernambuco rebellion, was also given cases concerning masonic activities in Rio. Before the proscription Viana corresponded with cabinet members about information collected by his *moscas* in lodges in São Gonçalo and Praia Grande. See Viana to Vila Nova Portugal, December 2, 1817; Viana to [Fragoso?], December 9, 1817; Fragoso to [Vila Nova Portugal?], December 10 and 11, 1817; and Viana to [Vila Nova Portugal?], December 12, 1817, AHI Lata 183 Maço 2 Pasta 4; Viana, "Registro do Ofício expedido ao Ministro de Estado dos Negócios do Brasil," February 9, 1821, ANRJ Códice 323 v. 6, f63 (on Luiz Prates de Almeida e Albuquerque, banished to Asia). Viana also reportedly targeted the crown-sponsored French artists for surveillance. See Arcos to Sua Alteza Real, July 1, 1818, AHI Lata 170 Maço 5 Pasta 4.

64. Viana, "Registro do Ofício expedido ao Ministro de Estado dos Negócios do Brasil," March 14, 1811, ANRJ Códice 323 v. 3, f28; Viana, "Registro do Ofício expedido ao Juiz do Crime do Bairro de Santa Rita," November 14, 1812, ANRJ Códice 329 v. 2, f31; Viana to Vila Nova Portugal, December 16, 1817, ANRJ ASH Desembargo do Paço Caixa 842 Pacotilha 2.

65. Manuel Ribeiro da Sa, Capitão da Forteleza de Santa Cruz, [report given at the Quartel do Campo de Santa Anna], August 23, 1816, ANRJ MNB Caixa 6J 83.

66. "Sumário" [1815–1816], ANRJ MNB Caixa 6J 79.

67. Conde de Aguiar [to the Conde dos Arcos?], Rio de Janeiro, January 21, 1813, BNRJ Ms. II-34,5,107. Police records and correspondence from early nineteenth-century Rio de Janeiro often note the appearance of *pasquins* (pasquinades). The word is derived from the Italian *pasquinata*, after Pasquino, a name given to a statue in Rome where lampoons were posted. For additional examples see Marrócos to his father, February 29, 1812, *Cartas*, 64. On the earlier history of the use of placards and pasquinades see Christian Jouhaud, "Readability and Persuasion: Political Handbills," in *The Culture of Print: Power and the Uses of Print in Early Modern Europe*, ed. Roger Chartier (1987) (Princeton: Princeton University Press, 1989), 235–260.

68. Arlette Farge, *Subversive Words: Public Opinion in Eighteenth-Century France* (University Park: The Pennsylvania State University Press, 1995), 62–63.

69. "Sumário" [1815–1816], ANRJ MNB Caixa 6J 79.

70. Manuel Ribeiro da Sa, August 23, 1816, ANRJ MNB Caixa 6J 83.

71. Viana to Aguiar, September 26, 1816, ANRJ MNB Caixa 6J 83. The complete transcription of the pasquinade reads: "A cada canto um; A agua está no c. . . . em / A Polícia esta no. . . . tal parte / Providencia nenhuma / O Intendente em Andrahi / E El Rei em Santa Cruz / So tu, o Grande Bonaparte / Que para reinar nascente / E para providencias o primeiro / Estas em Santa Helena prisonado!!"

72. Viana to Aguiar, December 6, 1815 and October 12, 1816, "Sumário," ANRJ MNB Caixa 6J 79. A priest with whom Ferreira had the altercation that set off Viana's investigation was banished to Rio Grande for, as Ferreira had correctly denounced, the possession of forged documents. In 1819, at least four years following his initial sentence of banishment, Ferreira was still in Rio de Janeiro in jail, where he continued to attack royal officials, spread the word that "he was in jail because he was a freemason," and, exhibiting what Viana dismissed as "the cunning characteristic of men of color," petitioned the king to commute his sentence. See José da F. Ramos to Viana, Cadeia, September 18, 1816, "Sumário," ANRJ MNB Caixa 6J 79;

Viana, "Ofício expedido ao Ministro de Estado, Conde dos Arcos," March 23, 1819, ANRJ Códice 323 v. 5, f108.

73. Viana to Souza Coutinho, January 20, 1810, ANRJ MNB Caixa 6J 78.

74. Farge, *Subversive Words*, 3–4.

75. Viana, "Registro do Ofício expedido ao Ministro de Estado dos Negócios do Brasil," March 14, 1811, ANRJ Códice 323 v. 3, f28.

76. Viana, "Registro do Ofício expedido [aos Juizes do Crime dos Bairros]," July 22, 1817, ANRJ Códice 329 v.4, f32; [Carlos Manly], ANRJ Desembargo do Paço Caixa 169 Documento 5; and on the interdiction of the "antipolitical" pamphlet *O Preto e o Bugío Ambos no Mato, Discorrendo sobre a Arte de Ter Dinheiro Sem Ir ao Brazil, Dialogo em que o Bugio com Evidentes Razões Convence o Preto sobre a Verdade desta Proposição* (Lisbon: Impressão Régia, 1816) see Arcos to Barca, March 3, 1817, BNRJ Ms. I-28,31,34. On censorship see Lúcia Maria Bastos Pereira das Neves, "Comércio de livros e censura de ideias: A actividade dos livreiros franceses no Brasil e a vigilância da Mesa do Desembargo do Paço (1795–1822)," *Ler História* 23 (1992): 61–78. On the interdiction of pamphlets see also Viana, "Registro do ofício expedido ao Juiz da Alfandega," May 8, 1809 and June 5, 1809, ANRJ Códice 323 v. 1, f71, f76; Viana, "Registro do Edital," May 30, 1809, and "Registro do ofício expedido ao Ouvidor do Crime da Relação da Bahia," June 6, 1809, ANRJ Códice 323 v. 1, f85, f83v.

77. *Correio Braziliense*, February 1819, in *Antologia do Correio Braziliense*, ed. Barbosa Lima Sobrinho (Rio de Janeiro: Cátedra/Instituto Nacional do Livro, 1977), 238–242.

78. Aréas to D. de Souza Coutinho, March 17, 1821, *DHI*, 240; José Augusto dos Santos Alves, *Ideologia e Política na Imprensa do Exílio, "O Portuguez" (1814–1826)* (Lisbon: Imprensa Nacional/Casa da Moeda, 1992).

79. Viana to Luiz Pedreira do Couto Ferraz, October 26, 1819, ANRJ Códice 330 v. 1; Carvalho Souza, *Pátria Coroada*, 77. Royal officials in Portugal shared concerns about these periodicals, including the *Correio Braziliense*, and in 1817 banned their importation into Portugal.

80. *Correio Braziliense*, April 1813, in *Antologia*, ed., Lima Sobrinho, 90–96.

81. Lisa Jane Graham, "Crimes of Opinion: Policing the Public in Eighteenth-Century Paris," in *Visions and Revisions of Eighteenth-Century France*, eds. Christine Adams, Jack R. Censer, and Lisa Jane Graham (University Park: The Pennsylvania State University Press, 1997), 95.

82. Carvalho Souza, *Pátria Coroada*, 75–76; Viana to Sua Alteza Real, November 8, 1818, BNRJ Ms. I-33,27,10.

83. Heliodoro Jacinto de Araújo Carneiro to Sua Alteza Real, n.d., n.p. [Rio de Janeiro, ca. 1818?], AHI Lata 170 Maço 5 Pasta 6.

84. Keith Michael Baker, "Politics and Public Opinion Under the Old Regime: Some Reflections," in *Press and Politics in Pre-Revolutionary France*, eds. Jack R. Censer and Jeremy Popkin (Berkeley: University of California Press, 1987), 232–233.

85. José da Silva Lisboa, *Memoria dos beneficios politicos do governo de El-Rey Nosso Senhor D. João VI* (Rio de Janeiro: Impressão Régia, 1818), 130 (emphasis in original).

86. José da Silva Lisboa, October 30, 1820, ANRJ ASH Desembargo do Paço Caixa 170 Documento 5; Baker, "Politics and Public Opinion," 234.

87. *Correio Braziliense*, February 1819, in *Antologia*, 238–242.

88. Lúcia Maria Bastos P. Neves, "Leitura e leitores no Brasil, 1820–1822: o esboço frustrado de uma esfera pública do poder," *Acervo*, 8, n. 1/2 (December 1995), 123–138. There is no comprehensive study of literacy in early nineteenth-century Rio de Janeiro. On possible readerships see Neves, "Corcundas, constitucionais e pes-de-chumbo: a cultura política da Independência" (Ph.D. dissertation, University of São Paulo, 1992), v. 1., 104–106. Neves uses Barman's analysis of the "Fico" petition of 1822 and its 8,000 signatures to estimate literacy at 56 percent of free men, a level of literacy relatively similar (considering only Brazil's free population) to that of provincial cities in eighteenth-century France (See Barman, *Brazil*, 83, n. 81). Although, as Neves recognizes, in neither Brazil nor France does a signature verify literacy, she suggests that a growing number of readers is further attested to by the approximately twenty sellers of books and periodical publications by 1820. As Maria Lígia Prado has argued, in the 1810s a limited degree of literacy among women is also implied by a series of feminine *novelas* published through the Royal Press by the bookdealer Paulo Martin and by the appearance of their names on Royal Press subscription lists. See Maria Lígia Prado, "Lendo Novelas no Brasil Joanino," in Prado, *América Latina no Século XIX: Tramas, Telas e Textos* (São Paulo: EDUSC/EDUSP, 1999).

89. Baker, "Politics and Public Opinion," 212–213; and idem, "Public Opinion as political invention," in Baker, *Inventing the French Revolution: Essays in French Political Culture in the Eighteenth-Century* (New York: Cambridge University Press, 1990), 168. On the concept of public opinion see also Anthony La Vopa, "Conceiving a Public: Ideas and Society in Eighteenth-Century Europe," *Journal of Modern History* 64 (March 1992), 79–116; Joan Landes, *Women and the Public Sphere in the Age of the French Revolution* (Ithaca, New York: Cornell University Press, 1988); Roger Chartier, *The Cultural Origins of the French Revolution*, trans. Lydia G.Cochrane (Durham: Duke University Press, 1991); J.A.W. Gunn, "Public Spirit to Public Opinion," in Gunn, *Beyond Liberty and Property: The Process of Self Recognition in Eighteenth-Century Political Thought* (Kingston, Canada: McGill-Queens University Press, 1983), 260–315.

90. Junot, "O Governador de Paris, Primeiro Ajudante de Campo de sua Magestade o Imperador e Rei . . . " (February 1, 1808) ([Lisbon]: Impressão Régia, [1808]), 1.

91. See *Correio Braziliense, ou Armazem Literario* 1 (London: W. Lewis, 1808), (July and August 1808), 121–123, 203–205, for comments on Ralph Rylance's *A Sketch of the Causes and Consequences of the Late Emigration to the Brazils* (London: Longman, Hurst, Rees and Orme, 1808) and Edward James Lingham's *Vindiciæ Lusitanæ, or an answer to a pamphlet entitled The Causes and Consequences of the Late Emigration to the Brazils* (London: J. Budd, 1808).

92. See Viana to the Conde de Aguiar, [November] 27, 1809, ANRJ MNB Caixa 6J 78. An article in Rio de Janeiro's Royal Press *Gazeta* publicized the need for "writers to unmask the crimes and intrigues of the common enemy." See *Gazeta do Rio de Janeiro* (April 29, 1809), cited in José Antônio Sá, *Defeza dos Direitos Nacionaes e Reaes da Monarchia Portugueza* (Lisbon: Impressão Régia, 1816).

93. The archive of the Imprensa Nacional, which included that of its predecessor, the Impressão Régia, was destroyed in a fire in 1911. The most complete reconstruction of the press's publications is the two volume *Bibliografia da Impressão Régia* by Camargo and Moraes. An analysis of the *Bibliografia* reveals that in the first two years of operation, more than half of its annual publications concerned the French invasion and the Peninsular War. This was followed

by a gradual decline in publications on these subjects. From 1810 to 1812 the annual average was 20 percent, whereas from 1813 to 1815 the annual average was 9 percent.

94. *Manifesto, ou Exposição Fundada, e Justificativa do procedimento da Corte de Portugal a respeito da França* . . . (Rio de Janeiro: Impressão Régia, 1808), in Rodrigo de Souza Coutinho, *Textos políticos, económicos e financeiros (1783–1811)* t. 2 (Lisbon: Banco de Portugal, 1993), 335–343; José Acúrsio das Neves, *Manifesto da Razão Contra as Usurpações Francezas. Offerecida á Nação Portugueza, aos Soberanos, e aos Póvos* (Rio de Janeiro: Impressão Régia, 1809), 20–22. Neves sent his manuscript to Souza Coutinho in Rio de Janeiro where he had it published. See Neves to Souza Coutinho, October 28, 1808, AHI Lata 187 Maço 4 Pasta 4. For justifications of the crown's conduct see also *Ensaio Histórico, Político e Filosófico do Estado de Portugal, Desde o Mez de Novembro de 1807 até o Mez de Junho de 1808* (Rio de Janeiro: Impressão Régia, n.d.), 10.

95. On the genre of the anti-Napoleonic pamphlet see Nuno Daupias D'Alcochete, "Les Pamphlets Portugais Anti-Napoléoniens," *Arquivos do Centro Cultural Português* (Paris, Fundação Calouste Gulbenkian), 11 (1977). On prices see the *Bibliografia* and Nizza da Silva, *Cultura e sociedade*, 6–7, 14. Although pamphlets cost as little as 160 reis, a simple meal at a *casa de pasto* (public eating house) cost 800 reis in 1809; a pastry, 60–80 reis in 1812; a bottle of *aguardente*, 250 reis in 1815. Examples of pamphlets include: *Receita Especial para Fabricar Napoleões* . . . (Reprint) (Rio de Janeiro: Régia Officina Typografica, 1809); *A,B,C, Poetico, Doutrinal e Antifrancez, ou Veni Mecum. Para a utilidade e recreio dos Meninos Portuguezes* (Reprint) (Rio de Janeiro: Impressão Régia, 1810); [Luiz de Sequeira Oliva e Souza Cabral], *Verdadeira Vida de Bonaparte, ate a Feliz Restauração de Portugal* . . . (Reprint) (Rio de Janeiro: Impressão Régia, 1809); *Protecção à Franceza* (Reprint) (Rio de Janeiro: Impressão Régia, 1809); [Nuno Álvarez Pereira Pato Moniz], *A Queda do Despotismo: Drama Dedicado a Sua Alteza Real* . . . (Reprint) (Rio de Janeiro: Impressão Régia, 1810). Moniz, born in Cabo Verde in 1781, established himself in Portugal as a playwright, poet, and polemicist. See Jacinto Prado Coelho, *Dicionário de Literatura*, 3a. ed. (Porto: Figueirinhas, 1979), v. 2, 662.

96. On the crown's subsidies for the *Correio Braziliense* see Barman, *Brazil*, 53; Vicente Pedro Nolasco da Cunha to Domingos [de Sousa Coutinho?], London, October 24, 1809, AHI Lata 203 Maço 2 Pasta 5; Heliodoro de Araújo Carneiro to Viana, London, August 8, 1814, and Hipólito José da Costa to Viana, August 20, 1820, in *Dom João VI*, ed. Carneiro de Mendonca, 266, 398; Araújo Carneiro to the Marquês de Pombal, January 8, 1810, and March 9, 1810, BNRJ Ms. Arcaz; Guilherme Cypriano de Souza to the Conde de Linhares, London, March 7, 1810, and Viana to Sua Alteza Real, November 28, 1818, BNRJ Ms. II-31,1,3.

97. Farge, *Subversive Words*, 198.

98. Gonçalves dos Santos, *Memórias* t. 1, 187–189.

99. Manuel Vieira da Silva, *Reflexões sobre alguns dos Meios Propostos por Mais Conducentes para Melhorar o Clima da Cidade* (1808), transcribed in "Hygiene da cidade do Rio de Janeiro," *ABN* 1 (1876), 187–190.

100. Viana, "Registro do Edital. . . , " June 11, 1809, ANRJ Códice 323 v. 1, f88–88v; Gonçalves dos Santos, *Memórias* t. 1, 237.

101. Luccock, *Notes on Rio de Janeiro*, 245–246, 254.

102. In the second half of the eighteenth century, Pombal crafted a series of reforms in the legal status of residents of the Portuguese empire. In 1761 all Asian subjects of the Portuguese

crown who were baptized Christians were guaranteed the same legal status as European Portuguese. The same year a decree established that black slaves landing in Portugal would be freed-persons. In 1773 a royal decree emancipated slaves. As Russell-Wood notes, although the emancipation of indigenous persons was guaranteed legally in 1755 and 1758, Brazil remained devoid of legislation dealing exclusively with African slavery. See A.J.R. Russell-Wood, "Iberian Expansion and the Issue of Black Slavery: Changing Portuguese Attitudes, 1440–1770," *American Historical Review* 83, n. 1 (February 1978), 40–41.

103. Manuel Vieira da Silva, *Reflexões sobre alguns dos Meios Propostos por mais Conducentes para Melhorar o Clima da Cidade do Rio de Janeiro* (Rio de Janeiro: Impressão Régia, 1808), 20.

104. Viana to Agostinho Petra de Bittencourt [magistrate], June 19, 1811, ANRJ Códice 329 v. 1, f73. On the intendant's support for white immigration see also Viana, "Abreviada Demonstração," 378–379; Viana, "Registro do Ofício expedido ao Ajudante da Intendência Geral da Polícia de Portugal," December 29, 1810, ANRJ Códice 323 v. 2, f52; and Viana, "Registro do Ofício expedido ao Ministro de Estado dos Negócios do Ultramar," February 2[8], 1811, ANRJ Códice 323 v. 3, f24v.

105. Viana, "Registro do Ofício expedido ao Juiz do Crime do Bairro de S. José," December 10, 1810, ANRJ Códice 329 v.2, f16; and April 15, 1814, ANRJ Códice 329 v. 2, f173. See also Viana, "Registro do Ofício expedido ao Juiz do Bairro de Santa Rita," March 26, 1814, ANRJ Códice 329 v. 2, f176-176v; Viana, "Registro do Ofício expedido ao Juiz do Crime do Bairro da Se," November 12, 1816, ANRJ Códice 329 v. 3, f163v. In the process of recruitment, Viana struggled with neighborhood judges who failed to share his penchant for degrees of differentiation and instead filled quotas by having guards round up any member of the lower classes, including sailors and slaves. See Viana, "Registro do Ofício expedido ao Juiz do Crime do Bairro da Se," November 29, 1816, ANRJ Códice 329 v .3, f169; Viana, "Registro do Ofício expedido ao Juiz do Crime do Bairro da Se," November 13, 1816, ANRJ Códice 329 v. 3, f164; Viana, "Registro do Ofício expedido ao Juiz do Crime do Bairro da Se," November 22, 1816, ANRJ Códice 329 v. 3, f166v. See also Viana, "Registro do Ofício expedido ao Juiz do Crime do Bairro da Se," November 23, 1816, ANRJ Códice 329 v. 3, f166v-167; and "Registro do Ofício expedido ao Juiz do Crime do Bairro da Candelária," November 29, 1816, ANRJ Códice 329 v. 3, f169.

106. Vila Nova Portugal, "Sobre a questão da escravatura," f2.

107. Viana, "Registro do Ofício expedido ao Ministro e Secretário da Repartição de Guerra," May 23, 1808, ANRJ Códice 318, f16v. Here, Viana referred specifically to "os Henriques," members of a battalion named after Henrique Dias, a hero in the war against the Dutch occupation of Pernambuco in the seventeenth century. See João José Reis, *Slave Rebellion in Brazil: The Muslim Uprising of 1835 in Bahia* (Baltimore: The Johns Hopkins University Press, 1993), 30.

108. For a dissenting opinion in favor of increasing the slave trade and regulating African reproduction, see Vicente António Oliveira Tenente General [Rio, n.d. after 1815], transcribed in Pereira, *D. João VI* v. 3, 260–267.

109. Viana to Sua Alteza Real, August 10, 1818, ANRJ MNB Caixa 6J 81; John Luccock cited in Leila Mezan Algranti, *O feitor ausente: estudos sobre a escravidão urbana, 1808–1822* (Petrópolis, Rio de Janeiro: Vozes, 1988), 32–33. According to Algranti, after 1809, annual arrivals to the city jumped from 6,000–10,000 to 34,000 ca. 1820. The results of another

study of Rio's slave population reveal that although in 1799 slaves comprised 35 percent of the total population by 1821 this figure had risen to 46 percent. See Mary C. Karasch, *Slave Life in Rio de Janeiro, 1808–1850* (Princeton: Princeton University Press, 1987), 61–62. On African arrivals to the port of Rio de Janeiro see Manolo Garcia Florentino, *Em Costas Negras: Uma História do Tráfico Atlântico de Escravos entre a África e o Rio de Janeiro (Séculos XVIII e XIX)* (Rio de Janeiro: Arquivo Nacional, 1995), 59.

110. Viana to Aguiar, July 1, 1809, ANRJ MNB Caixa 6J 78. The tax was 800 reis for each "new slave" and 4$800 reis for those who were sent to the southern regions. Viana complained about problems with the collection of the tax and in 1810 he petitioned to extend it to slaves arriving at the port of Rio who were then sent north. See Viana [parecer], September 1, 1810, ANRJ MNB Caixa 6J 78. Along with local town councils and militia commanders, Viana also supervised the activities of *capitães do mato*, bounty hunters paid by owners to hunt runaway slaves and attack communities of runaways (*quilombos*) in rural areas nearby. See "Portaria," May 2, 1809, ANRJ Códice 323 v. 1, f34; and Viana, "Registro do Ofício expedido ao Ouvidor da Comarca," July 27, 1809, ANRJ Códice 323 v. 1, f109v. In 1818, an exasperated Viana wrote a report calling for more clearly defined duties and procedures for these capitães and other authorities involved. See Viana "Ofício expedido ao Ministro de Estado dos Negócios do Reino," November 11, 1818, Códice 323 v. 5, f68v.

111. Viana, [representação], November 24, 1816, ANRJ MNB Caixa 6J 83.

112. António Felipe Soares de Andrada de Brederode, Corregedor da Corte e Casa, February 27, 1817, ANRJ ASH Casa da Suplicação Caixa 1707 Antiga Caixa 774 Pacotilha 3. Algranti found that the majority of detentions involved accusations of flight and *capoeira*. See *O feitor*, 189, 209. On capoeira see Carlos Eugênio Líbano Soares, *A negreada instituição: os capoeiras no Rio de Janeiro* (Rio de Janeiro: Prefeitura do Rio de Janeiro, 1994), 25–27. Free people of color were often accused of the same kinds of transgressions as slaves. See for example "Registro do Ofício expedido ao Juiz do Crime do Bairro da Candelária," December 20, 1816, ANRJ Códice 329 v. 3, on the arrest of Manuel de Oliveira, "crioulo forro, chefe dos capoeiras." Following the end of both Viana's tenure as intendant and Dom João's reign in Brazil, methods for repressing capoeira were reevaluated. In 1821 the new intendant confronted attempts on the part of the commisão militar to give the guard's commander license to publicly whip capoeiras who were arrested, whereas, in the absence of evidence, Viana had released them. For the new intendant, writing in a decidedly "constitutional" moment, such a blatant contradiction of due process was unthinkable. He questioned both the efficacy of whipping capoeiras, suggesting that "education" and "morality" would provide a better solution, and called attention to the possibility of arresting free people who, he noted, could not be whipped. See "Registro do Ofício dirigido a Secretaria de Estado dos Negócios de Guerra," December 8, 1821, ANRJ Códice 323, v. 6. Algranti notes an earlier portaria of October 31, 1821 that provided for the public punishment of capoeiras. See *O feitor*, 21, note 12. A few months later, Prince Regent Dom Pedro also complained of capoeiras, called for punishment of one hundred lashes for enslaved capoeiras, and stipulated that "any soldier who caught a capoeira would receive four days of leave." Cited in Almeida Prado, *D. João*, 254.

113. Viana to Tenente Colonel José Maria Rebelo, Comandante da Guard Real da Polícia, January 17, 1811, ANRJ ASH Caixa 1227 Pacotilha 1. See also Viana, "Registro do Ofício expedido ao General das Tropas," April 1, 1809, ANRJ Códice 323 v. 1, in which he admon-

ishes the guard for failing to follow procedure in the arrest of two *pardos*.

114. Algranti, *Feitor*, 194; Viana, "Registro do Ofício expedido ao Ministro de Estado dos Negócios Estrangeiros," January 24, 1817, ANRJ Códice 323 v. 4; and Viana to Aguiar, February 25, 1813, ANRJ MNB Caixa 6J 79. Writing on the calabouço, Viana explained, "it is of the crown, and in it besides the corrective punishments so necessary for slaves . . . prisoners sentenced to *gales* and public works are deposited, and all others who independent of any [legal] process for whom it is necessary for the police to give some correction so that they serve in those services. . . ." In the same year, Viana reported that the calabouço prisoners usually numbered above 120, in addition to slaves sent by their owners to be punished and others sentenced to *gales* and "corrections" at public works. See Viana, "Registro do Ofício expedido ao Ministro de Estado dos Negócios do Brasil," May 6, 1813, ANRJ Códice 323 v. 3, f162v.

115. The use of prison labor on public works was a practice that intensified in late eighteenth-century Brazil to provide for the expansion of urban services. See Patricia Ann Aufderheide, "Order and Violence: Social Deviance and Social Control in Brazil, 1780–1840" (Ph.D. dissertation, University of Minnesota, 1976), 302–303. Karasch clarifies the different forms of prison labor. *Limbambos* referred to chain gangs of slaves in correction at the request of their owners or by the intendant and justices of the peace for misdemeanors, whereas *gales* consisted of "convicts sentenced by the courts for serious crimes." See Karasch, *Slave Life*, 118–121. Filling prisons in order to have a labor supply was criticized in 1822 by Viana's successor. See Algranti, *Feitor*, 81. On Viana's supervision of the calabouço and his attempts to extend detentions to meet labor needs see also Viana, "Registro do Ofício expedido ao Ministro e Secretário da Repartição de Guerra" [Souza Coutinho], May 23, 1808, ANRJ Códice 318, f16v; Viana to General das Tropas, João Baptista de Azeredo Coutinho de Montaury, December 9, 1808, ANRJ Códice 318, f130-130v; Viana, "Registro do Ofício expedido ao Juiz do Crime do Bairro da Candelária," May 5, 1809, ANRJ Códice 323 v. 1, f37v-38; Viana, "Registros dos Ofícios expedidos aos Juizes do Crime do Bairro de São José e Santa Rita," December 9, 1810, ANRJ Códice 323 v. 2, f14-16; Viana, "Registro do Ofício expedido ao Ministro e Secretário do Estado dos Negócios Estrangeiros," January 24, 1817, ANRJ Códice 323 v. 4; Viana, "Registro do Ofício expedido ao Ministro de Estado dos Negócios do Brasil," August 6, 1817, ANRJ Códice 323 v. 4; Viana, "Registro do Ofício expedido ao Ministro de Estado dos Negócios do Reino," April 27, 1820, ANRJ Códice 323 v. 5 f173v; Viana to Vila Nova Portugal, September 9, 1820, ANRJ MNB Caixa 6J 86. Members of black militias accused of possession of weapon or capoeira posed a dilemma for Viana because they were deemed unfit for public works. Rather than letting them "rest" in prison, however, Viana advised that they could recover their utility by being sent to serve as black regiments in the army in Montevideo. See Viana to Vila Nova Portugal, May 16, 1820, ANRJ Códice 323 v. 6, f3.

116. Algranti, *Feitor*, 51, 198; Karasch, *Slave Life*, 122–124. The practice, in effect, anticipated the more complete incorporation of slave punishment into the public sphere in the late 1820s and 1830s. See Aufderheide, "Order and Violence," 293. Attempts to control the slave population in Rio thus stood in contrast to efforts deployed in the countryside and small towns and villages, where the recapture of escaped slaves was entrusted to the *capitão do mato*.

117. Viana to the Conde de Linhares [Rodrigo de Souza Coutinho], December 10, 1811, BNRJ Ms. I 33,27,19; Viana, "Registro do Ofício expedido ao Ministro de Estado dos Negócios Estrangeiros e de Guerra," August 28, 1811, ANRJ Códice 323 v. 3, f65.

118. Viana to Sua Alteza Real, August 10, 1818, ANRJ MNB Caixa 6J 91; Algranti, *Feitor*, 193, 197.

119 António Felipe Soares de Andrada de Brederode, Corregedor da Corte e Casa, February 27, 1817, ANRJ ASH Casa da Suplicação Caixa 1707, Antiga Caixa 774, Pacotilha 3; José Albano Fragoso, Corregedor do Crime da Corte e Casa, April 4, 1818, ANRJ ASH Casa da Suplicação Caixa 1707, Antiga Caixa 774, Pacotilha 4. Not all magistrates were as resolute as Viana on the issue of public punishment and debates about the punishment of slaves continued. According to Debret, who provided both visual and textual descriptions of the public whipping of slaves, the practice was "reestablished with all rigor" in 1821 and then curtailed once again in 1829, although some slave criminals and capoeiras were still punished so publicly. See his *Viagem* t. 2, 175–177, and plate 45; and Karasch, *Slave Life*, 122–125. Legally, whipping was a *pena vil* (low punishment) and a range of exceptions related to office and status were stipulated that did not apply in the case of certain crimes such as *lesa majestade*, sodomy, witchcraft, bearing false witness, and counterfeiting. In the independent Empire of Brazil, the practice of whipping was discontinued except in the Army and the Navy and in the case of slaves. See *Ordenações Filipinas* (1603), Livro V, Titulo 138. Efforts to restrain excessive slave punishment also continued in the nineteenth century, even as, in certain cases, courts dispensed severe sentences that seemed to contradict these conventions. See Alexandra Kelly Brown, "'On the Vanguard of Civilization': Slavery, the Police and Conflicts between Public and Private Power in Salvador da Bahia, Brazil, 1835–1888" (Ph.D. dissertation, University of Texas at Austin, 1998).

120. Marquês de Borba to the Condessa do Redondo [his daughter-in-law], Rio de Janeiro, February 20, 1809, in Pereira, *Os filhos*, 140.

121. Viana to Sua Alteza Real, August 10, 1818, ANRJ MNB Caixa 6J 81.

122. *Reflexões*, 18–19.

123. Noronha Santos, "Anotações de Noronha Santos," in Gonçalves dos Santos, *Memórias* t. 1, 104; "Representação de Negociantes d'esta Corte Abaixo Assignados, Proprietarios, Consignatarios, e Armadores de Resgate de Escravos," n.d. [post 1810–16], BNRJ Ms. II-34,26,19, f1; Viana to Juizes do Crime do Bairro de São José, Santa Rita, Candelária e Se, Feburary 15, 1811, ANRJ Códice 329, v. 1, f10.

124. Henry Ellis, *Journal of the Proceedings of the Late Embassy to China . . .* (1817) (Wilmington: Scholarly Resources, 1973), 11.

125. Luccock, *Notes on Rio de Janeiro*, 245, 548.

126. Manuel Ribeiro Rocha, *Etíope Resgatado* (1758), cited in Silvia Hunold Lara, "Signs of Color: Women's Dress and Racial Relations in Salvador and Rio de Janeiro, ca. 1750–1815," *Colonial Latin American Review* 6, n. 2 (1997), 214.

127. Viana to Sua Alteza Real, August 10, 1818, ANRJ MNB Caixa 6J 81. For an earlier discussion of slave owners' failures, see [Padre] André João Antonil [João Antônio Andreoni], *Cultura e opulência do Brasil* (1711) (Belo Horizonte/São Paulo: Itatiaia/EDUSP, 1982); Ronaldo Vainfas, *Ideologia e escravidão: os letrados e a sociedade escravista no Brasil colonial* (Petrópolis, Rio de Janeiro: Vozes, 1986). On the practice of using slaves as wage laborers, peddlers, and as purveyors of other paid services see Reis, *Slave Rebellion*, Chapter 9; and Karasch, *Slave Life*, Chapter 7.

128. Viana to Sua Alteza Real, August, 10, 1818, ANRJ MNB Caixa 6J 81.

129. Viana, "Registro do Ofício expedido ao Ministro dos Negócios Estrangeiros e de Guerra," March 5, 1811, ANRJ Códice 323 v. 3, f25.

130. Aguiar to Conde dos Arcos, June 6, 1814, BNRJ Ms. 33,34,29. João José Reis describes these allowances, which Arcos adamantly defended, as "enlightened slave control." They aimed both to "attenuate seignorial excess," he explains, and to divide and conquer the African population by giving "free expression to African traditions" and therefore, Arcos claimed, exacerbating ethnic differences. The actual effects were not so evident. As correspondence between Aguiar and Arcos noted, slaves in Bahia continued to rebel whereas Rio's owners and officials were spared. See Reis, *Slave Rebellion*, 44–53.

131. Viana to Aguiar, April 20, 1813, ANRJ MNB Caixa 6J 79; Viana "Registro do Ofício expedido ao Juiz do Crime do Bairro de São José," October 15, 1813, ANRJ Códice 329 v. 2, f122v. After 1817, when the practice of soliciting alms was prohibited, the intendancy agreed to supplement the deficit. See also Viana's report on a dispute that arose during a leadership succession in 1813 within the community of Cassange, in ANRJ Códice 323 v. 3, transcribed in Leila Mezan Algranti, "Costumes afro-brasileiros na corte do Rio de Janeiro: um documento curioso," *Boletim do Centro de Memória UNICAMP* 1, n. 1 (January/June 1989), 17–21. The "kings of the Congo people" were also among the local African and African-Brazilian leaders in Rio de Janeiro and other Brazilian cities. They not only enjoyed status within their respective communities, but also had participated historically in ritual glorifications of Portuguese sovereignty in Brazil and Portugal prior to the transfer of the court. See for example, *Epanafora festiva, ou relação summaria das festas, com que na cidade do Rio de Janeiro, capital do Brasil se celebrou o feliz nascimento do Serenissimo Principe da Beira . . .* (Lisbon: Miguel Rodrigues, 1763), 27; Luiz Edmundo, *O Rio de Janeiro no tempo dos vice-reis* (Rio de Janeiro: Editôra Aurora, 1951), 554; Luiz da Câmara Cascudo, *Made in Africa (pesquisas e notas)* (Rio de Janeiro: Civilização Brasileira, 1965), 17–33; Melo Morais Filho, *Festas e tradições populares do Brasil* (Rio de Janeiro: F. Briguiet, 1946), 381–386; and Silvia Hunold Lara, "Significados Cruzados: As Embaixadas de Congos no Brasil Colonial," Paper delivered at the meeting of the Latin American Studies Association, April 1997.

132. "[Cópia do Ordem do Dia]," April 10, 1814, BNRJ Ms. II 34,6,57. This order prohibited certain forms of dancing and drumming but provided for other African and African-Brazilian gatherings and was rigorously opposed by Bahian owners.

133. Vicente António de Oliveira, "Reflexões sobre a instituição das forças armadas da capitania do Rio de Janeiro," February 15, 1816, BNRJ Ms. I-33,50,35.

134. "Representação do corpo do comércio e mais cidadões da praça da Bahia," [1814], BNRJ Ms. II-34,6,57.

135. On the specter of Haiti see Cailhé, "Projet" and "Memoire et notes explicatives sur le projet," Rio de Janeiro, December 15, 1820, BNRJ Ms. I-33,29,8 and I-33,29,16; Silvestre Pinheiro Ferreira, "Memórias Políticas sobre os Abusos Gerais e Modo de os Reformar e Prevenir a Revolução Popular Redigidas por Ordem do Principe Regente no Rio de Janeiro em 1814 e 1815," in Pinheiro Ferreira, *Idéias Políticas* (Rio de Janeiro: Editora Documentário, 1976), 31; and João Severiano Maciel da Costa, *Memória sobre a necessidade de abolir a introdução dos escravos africanos no Brasil . . .* (Coimbra: 1821), in ed. Graça Salgado, *Memórias sobre a escravidão* (Rio de Janeiro: Arquivo Nacional, 1988).

136. Silva Lisboa, *Memoria*, 160.

137. Viana, "Registro do Ofício expedido ao Ministro e Secretário da repartição de Guerra," May 23, 1808, ANRJ Códice 318, f16-16v.

138. Viana, [representação to Dom João], November 24, 1816, ANRJ MNB Caixa 6J 83.

139. On the case of Padre Joaquim de Sousa Ribeiro who claimed to have served as a bishop in Saint Domingue and reportedly spread news of the revolution to slaves in Brazil's northeast, see João Severiano Maciel da Costa to Aguiar, Cayena, November 21, 1814; Viana to the Juiz do Crime do Bairro da Candelária and "Auto das Perguntas," April 13, 1815; Viana to Aguiar, May 1, 1815; as well as Ribeiro's "Diário de Lisboa até Londres e Barbados," in ANRJ MNB Caixa 6J 79; and on a case of an abolitionist from nearby Irajá, see Viana, "Registro do Ofício expedido ao Ministro de Estado [Vila Nova Portugal]," November 12, 1818, ANRJ Códice 323 v. 5, f71v.

140. Viana, "Registro do Ofício expedido ao Juiz do Crime do Bairro de Santa Rita," April 11, 1816, ANRJ Códice 329 v.3.

141. Viana, "Registro do Ofício expedido ao Ministro de Estado dos Negócios de Guerra," July 8, 1808, ANRJ Códice 318, f38.

142. Ann Laura Stoler and Frederick Cooper, "Between Metropole and Colony: Rethinking a Research Agenda," in *Tensions of Empire: Colonial Cultures in a Bourgeois World*, eds. Ann Laura Stoler and Frederick Cooper (Berkeley: University of California Press, 1997), 7.

FIVE

"Tropical Versailles":

THE POLITICS OF MONARCHY IN THE NEW WORLD

"*ERA NO TEMPO DO REI*" (IT WAS IN THE TIME OF THE KING). SO MANUEL ANTÔNIO de Almeida begins his classic mid-nineteenth-century novel of life in Dom João's New World court and of the trials and tribulations of Leonardo, the quintessential *malandro* (trickster), yet soon to be *sargento de milícias.*[1] The story of Leonardo's brushes with his notoriously ruthless nemesis, the intendancy's Major Vidigal, evokes a political culture in which, as Brazilian literary critic Antônio Cândido has argued, "order and disorder are solidly articulated" and "the apparently hierarchical world reveals itself to be essentially subverted when the extremes come into contact."[2] Almeida's fictional vision of early nineteenth-century Rio de Janeiro also recalls the historical archive where, as we have seen, the city's residents are revealed as agents of political and social allegiance, repression, and resistance, and where courtiers, officials, petty functionaries, soldiers, merchants, and artisans emerge in a web of relationships that suggests links between the elite and popular experiences of constructing the New World empire and New World court. As Almeida exposes the shifting terms for encounters between the ostensibly powerless and the powerful, he then raises the possibility of another instance of contact between extremes: the encounter between the city's residents and the king. Although Dom João is absent from the novel, his presence, as Almeida initially claims, defines the era.

What, indeed, did this unprecedented and, as contemporaries described it, "immediate" presence of the monarch mean for Rio de Janeiro's residents? What forms did their encounters with the prince regent take? What, in turn, were the consequences of such exchanges? This chapter examines these questions, taking as a point of departure the practice of petitioning the crown. As we saw in Chapter 3, the establishment of a New World court was predicated upon the ideal of reciprocity. As one exiled courtier rendered the court's arrival, when the prince regent disembarked "the people of Brazil" expressed their allegiance and unequivocal joy, "an effusion of heartfelt sentiment," offering him all that was theirs, and the prince regent responded by prodigiously bestowing both honorific and pecuniary rewards. With these symbolic and material exchanges of patronage, the sovereign and his vassals to-gether reproduced bonds of loyalty that formed the ancient basis of royal power. As memorialists also noted, however, the quest for royal grace was not limited to the city's propertied and exiled courtiers. In the new court, as in the old, the practice of petitioning the crown extended to all vassals, regardless of social status. Intervening on behalf of soldiers, petty functionaries, and shopkeepers in disputes and during hardships, circumventing judicial process, and undercutting other authorities lesser than his own, the prince regent protected "the good order of things." He made man-ifest his absolute authority and conveyed a sense of his liberality, magnanimity, and justice. Such exemplary acts of intervention were balanced, in turn, with a more gen-eral defense of the law and of social and political hierarchies. In this sense, the econ-omy of royal grace in the New World resembled that of the Old. Yet, in what Brazilian historian Oliveira Lima described as a "tropical Versailles," the crown also had to account for New World petitioners and their demands. Although formally denied the status of vassals, the city's slaves also joined other residents in seeking jus-tice at the throne. Consequently, remaking Rio de Janeiro into the court and re-defining the monarchy in America meant reconciling the ideals of vassalage and royal justice with a widespread use of slavery and with the African and African-Brazilian residents who made up the majority of the city's population. As "all of the people without exception of either status or color" claimed their "rights" as vassals, the authority of the king confronted the authority of the master.[3]

"At the Royal Feet of His Royal Highness": Royal Authority and the Practice of Vassalage

In 1811, on the road to nearby Andrahi, a prostitute named Teresa de Jesus encoun-tered the prince regent's sister. For Teresa the meeting was particularly opportune. She had recently been evicted from her house on orders of the police intendant so that it could be used to accommodate a servant of the papal nuncio now residing in the city. Hoping for a royal intervention on her behalf, she made her plight known to the princess. Perhaps she surmised that regardless of whether the princess decided to help her, the encounter alone would put pressure on the intendant and "in the meantime" she resolved to confront him herself. Indeed, in his report on her peti-tion, the intendant explained that after their meeting he had reconsidered the cir-cumstances and presented the case to the monarch. The prince regent, however, determined that the eviction order would stand.[4]

Although Teresa's attempt to secure her residence was unsuccessful, she did af-firm her right to present herself, and to make her appeal, before the crown. Such a prerogative, as contemporaries noted, was well established. "The Sovereigns of Portugal," wrote the Portuguese political theorist José António Sá, "have always facilitated public and private audiences and even listened to their vassals during strolls or while hunting."[5] Indeed, images of the monarch amid his people, as Ana Maria Alves explains, figured prominently within medieval and early modern Portuguese political discourse. "The Princes went out / on Holy Days they rode their horses," the fifteenth-century chronicler Resende wrote, "all of their peoples saw them and they [the princes] saw and heard / all that they told them."[6] More recently, in 1790, two years before Dom João assumed his regency in place of his ailing mother Maria I, the Coimbra-educated Francisco António de Novaes Campos had presented him with a text that in drawing on the collection of emblems of the seventeenth-century Spanish jurist Solórzano Pereira (1575–1654) also unequivocally reasserted the precept that "a good King listens to the grievances of his Vassals." "The King permits the People to enter freely," one emblem revealed, for, as Novaes Campos explained, "to listen to them provides him with more than a Treasure."[7] The prostitute's encounter with the princess near the city of Rio thus was one of many enactments of this at once idealized and historic encounter between sovereign and vassal.

Yet, for Teresa petitioning the royal family was also a novelty. Even as the custom of holding popular audiences gained renewed vigor when Dom João assumed his regency,[8] for most residents of Brazil the opportunities to request royal grace were almost nonexistent. The quest for the prince regent's "paternal diligence" required an expensive journey to Portugal or dependence on the costly and often inefficient proceedings of imperial bureaucracy. After the transfer of the court, however, what one contemporary described as the "Immediate Presence of the Sovereign and all of the Royal Persons" in the city provided opportunities to directly plead one's case, both at audiences and, as Teresa's story suggests, during informal encounters. Thus, for residents of the new royal court what Gonçalves dos Santos described as the "rights" of vassalage previously denied by geographic distance could finally be exercised. Or, as the allegory of Brazil boasted in one commemorative royal press publication, with Dom João's arrival at Rio a political equality had been established: "My time arrived . . . I too am Portuguese, . . . Equal in honor, and equal in vassalage."[9]

This celebration of New World vassalage was framed as an indictment of the "old colonial system" (*antigo sistema colonial*), which not only had kept Brazil closed to a potentially prosperous trade, but also unfairly separated its residents from their monarch.[10] Although the Portuguese monarchy always promoted the "happiness of its Vassals," an early publication of the royal press acknowledged, "the enormous distance between the Seat of the Portuguese Throne, and its Vassals in Brazil, until now made the execution of [the royal] will impossible."[11] Such a charge suggested that in establishing colonial rule in America, the Portuguese crown had failed to effectively establish the presence of the legal person, or *persona ficta*, of the king. Whereas within the Spanish monarchy, as Anthony Pagden explains, the institution of the viceroyalty served to sustain "the fiction of the king's simultaneous presence" in all of his kingdoms by, among other things, ritually displaying this legal person,[12] in Portuguese America governors were seen as administrators only. The governor-general of Brazil executed but did not embody royal authority. Accordingly, as we saw in Chapter 2, he had come to be called "viceroy" only in the eighteenth century and even then his authority over the other captains-general remained considerably more limited than his Spanish counterpart. He was, as one Brazilian historian has explained, a "viceroy without a viceroyalty."[13] Consequently, while the early modern Spanish theorist Solórzano had insisted that within an empire "Kingdoms must be ruled and governed as if the King who held them together was only the King of each one of them,"[14] early nineteenth-century memorialists in Rio concluded that until 1808 Brazil had been governed in a manner that clearly reflected its secondary status among the Portuguese crown's dominions. Before 1815, after all, Brazil was not, as were the Spanish Indies, a "kingdom," but rather was regarded as a "conquest" and a "colony." And, as the resident preacher São Carlos explained, while "an estate required the presence of its Lordship to prosper," royal government in Brazil before 1808 was characterized by an absence of true seigniorial care. "No matter how attentive [its] administrators were," he denounced, "the idea that they are also mercenaries diminishe[d] a great part of their concern." Brazil, as a consequence, had languished.[15] Such a critique did not impugn the monarch, however, for the errors of his representatives and, more specifically, their failure to execute his will, as the Marquês de Penalva wrote in 1804, did not reflect upon the king himself.[16]

Of course, as São Carlos and others argued, with the prince regent's arrival all of this had changed. For what Gonçalves dos Santos described as "the real presence" of the monarch implied not only a new status within the empire, but also real royal governance for the first time in Brazil's history, government that would deliver New World vassals from the "abjection and misery" that its absence had produced.[17] Accordingly, this "real" royal presence also dominated the city's public life. Royal officials and Rio's residents staged elaborate commemorations of the royal life cycle: birthdays, three royal births, three royal weddings, and three royal funerals, including that of Maria I. The crown also sponsored large-scale commemorations of extraordinary events such as Peninsular War victories, the creation of the Kingdom of Brazil, the arrival in 1817 of the bride of the heir to the Portuguese throne, the Archduchess Leopoldina of Austria, as well as the prince regent's Acclamation to the throne the following year. In these cases, for several days festively illuminated facades transformed the city into a stage for private and public ceremonies, processions through triumphal arches, and the dancing, fireworks, and in some cases free theatrical performances that followed, all of which aimed to spectacularly display the majesty of the House of Braganza.[18]

Such festivities served to fulfill the Portuguese monarch's duty to show himself. For as the chronicler Resende had written, "no one can be loved, by whom he is not known."[19] Before the transfer of the court, as we saw in Chapter 2, the monarchy and His Majesty had been revealed to American vassals in local celebrations and prayers for the distant "king and kingdom" that both conjured up the magnificence of royal authority and, as the intendant Viana recalled, promoted political allegiance. The presence of the figure of the monarch himself had been invoked by the reverent and ceremonious display of the royal portrait.[20] Following the transfer of the court, royal counselors argued, it then was imperative that the prince regent affirm the image of magnificence that had been proffered in his absence. He had to show, in other words, that the ideal image of His Majesty embodied in the royal portrait was true; or, as one resident who witnessed the royal disembarkation reassuringly reported by wisely placing the burden of proof on the portrait rather than the monarch, that in the presence of the monarch the portrait indeed was akin to a mirror, "so natural that it seemed to be [the prince] himself."[21]

With the larger scale of royal commemorations in Rio compared with those of viceregal times, the crown also sought to affirm that the residents' expectations of a once distant and now present spectacularly displayed grandeur were well founded. To ensure the required decorum of the prince regent's ceremonial appearances, a royal official was appointed to instruct and resolve questions concerning the residents' use of insignia and procedure in public processions.[22] In this case, the crown sought to defend the gradations of social and political hierarchies among courtiers and local elites. Yet, as the Marquês de Bellas explained, the goal of public ceremony was to project, above all, the simpler and more fundamental hierarchy of sovereign and vassal. A most "splendorous pageantry," he advised, "needed to be reserved for Your Royal Highness alone." Indeed, Bellas counseled, the prince regent should not "appear in public, principally in Brazil, without a certain distinction in show and pomp." For with such a singularly splendorous public appearance, Dom João would impress upon his American and, as Bellas implied, relatively uninstructed vassals "the decency and parsimony of members of various [social and political] estates, which is not the case with princes, whose magnificence is inseparable from their greatness so that they can be better served and obeyed."[23]

Yet, the goal of such a magnificent and ostensibly pedagogical display was not simply that the prince regent show himself to his American vassals and thus reassure them of his authority. The monarch's public presence, as Alves has observed, had "to make evident the qualities of the royal figure."[24] In other words, the prince regent had to display the nature of his authority. Accordingly, royal commemorations in

Rio both featured allegorical figures of the prince regent's virtue, piety, and justice and provided moments in which the residents could witness the act of royal virtue itself: the granting of titles, offices, and other rewards for faithful service. As we saw in Chapter 3, as a "true father of his vassals," Dom João's generous liberality was not limited to those who came from Lisbon "in his company." Rather, as Gonçalves dos Santos recalled the celebrations of the court's arrival, the prince regent's "paternal solicitude" was "profusely extended to the inhabitants of Brazil" as well. And while they too received bureaucratic posts and honors, the "unlimited liberality and magnanimity" of the sovereign, the memorialist suggested, was most effectively displayed in acts of extraordinary condescension. Thus, for the "national jubilation" upon the Restoration of Portugal from the French "even the small ones of [the prince regent's] people" received royal beneficence: "refreshments" for the city's regiments and "abundant alms for the indigent and the incarcerated."[25] To demonstrate both his beneficence and justice, the prince regent also pardoned the condemned. Like its European counterpart, the new court of Rio featured both social discipline and what Portuguese historian António Manuel Hespanha has described as a "dialectic of terror and clemency" that legitimated the power of the monarch and symbolically constituted justice.[26] As one magistrate explained, in bestowing a pardon, or commuting a death sentence, the prince regent "exercised the virtues of a Monarch . . . not only as Sovereign, but also as a Father of his Vassals."[27] Fittingly, the most extraordinary invocation of paternal mercy and the power to punish, the suspension of the investigations into the republican insurrection in Pernambuco of 1817, commemorated the most extraordinary moment in Dom João's reign in Brazil, his Acclamation.[28]

Such acts of royal justice, however, were not limited to singular occasions and commemorations. Both royal justice and the "real" royal presence were displayed more regularly at the royal audience, known as the *Beijamão* (handkissing). Royal audiences, as historian Diogo Curto explains, were ceremonial appearances that since the seventeenth century had been beheld as spectacles of royal power that provided evidence of "the possibility of direct access" both to "the king's person" and the "immediate practice of exemplary justice." Even the aristocratic João V (d. 1750) was observed dispensing gold coins to officials and "women in distress" as he chastised nobles for the abuses that those of lesser social standing had denounced.[29] Before his departure from Portugal, the prince regent Dom João had cultivated a still more expansive affair, distinguishing himself, as one visitor to his court observed, with his willingness to endure the great number of petitioners as well as the "coarseness of their manners, the familiarity of their address; the tautology of some, the prolixity of others," providing, in return, "hopes, promises, encouragement." Indeed, the visitor explained, in spite of certain formalities, the "awful majesty which surrounds the throne, [did] not increase the difficulty of approach to it."[30]

FIGURE 8: Henry L'Évêque, "The Audience of the Prince," from Henry L'Évêque, *Portuguese costumes* (1814) (Lisbon: INAPA, 1993). Permission obtained from the Biblioteca Nacional, Lisbon. Commenting on the audience in Portugal, L'Évêque described it as a familial encounter. "If he [the prince regent] is preceded by a few soldiers," L'Évêque explained, "it is not for the purpose of guarding his person. In the midst of his children what has he to fear?"

Following this tradition then, in Rio de Janeiro the prince regent held audiences regularly; daily, according to Rio's almanac, weekly, according to Luccock, as well as on special occasions.[31] Those who came to a royal audience presented themselves before the prince regent, kissed his hand, and then dropped to one or both knees to present their case in written or verbal form. New royal suppliants could draw on the experience of petitioning the viceroy, as well as on published manuals that both explicated proper conduct in the presence of royalty and provided model petitions.[32] For those without such resources, however, the spectacular royal audience itself was instructive. As Luccock observed, in Rio "on high days, the ceremony of kissing hands was exhibited almost in public . . . at a balcony, where [the prince] could be seen by the crowd of people assembled in front of the palace." The transition from spectator to petitioner then was simple and apparently did not require a prior encounter with royal officials. During royal audiences, as Luccock noted, "every subject decently dressed [was] admitted, and allowed to present, personally, his or her petition."[33]

Residents of the new royal court seized the opportunity to seek, as one petitioner described it, "refuge from the imminent evils that caused them distress."[34] Although there apparently is no record of the precise number of petitioners, one visitor observed that the prince regent was "thronged with petitioners of every description," calculating the average at each audience to be "no less than one hundred and fifty." And, as had been the case in Lisbon, along with exiled courtiers, wealthy residents, and visitors to the city, the presence of "the poor" became a regular feature of Rio de Janeiro's audiences. As the observer reported, Dom João was "worthy to be called the father of his people," for he admitted "into his presence the meanest of his subjects and listen[ed] to their supplications": pleas for the resolution of domestic and property disputes, requests for financial assistance, and pardon from military service and punishment.[35] Such capaciousness probably stood in great contrast to the restrictions of viceregal audiences. Whereas the Viceroy Lavradio, for example, did not allow *pardo* officers to approach him at his own beijamão, in the 1810s in Rio de Janeiro, the British Henderson reported with both surprise and disdain, generals found themselves waiting alongside "mulattos."[36]

As in Portugal, royal audiences in Rio also could be granted outside the palace, during visits to the royal chapel, when surrounding avenues and corridors reportedly would fill, and during more extended royal outings. In 1811, for example, "taking advantage" of the prince regent's first visit to Magé, Joaquim José da Silva approached the prince regent to request a pardon from punishment for having killed his own slave.[37] And in 1817 the Marquês de Loulé, seeking a pardon for having collaborated with the French during the Napoleonic invasion of Portugal, recorded a strategic encounter with royalty that recalled that of Teresa and the princess previously described. Privy to the monarch's itinerary, the Marquês explained, on a road near the city "I waited for My King and at a distance that appeared appropriate I knelt in the middle of the road. His Majesty arrived and," to the relief of Loule, "ordered [the carriers of] his palanquin to stop."[38] One year later, perhaps in the interest of avoiding such potentially exhausting stake outs, one of Rio's more entrepreneurial residents proposed that he could provide carriages for those who similarly wished to take advantage of the occasions of royal outings. The intendant wholeheartedly endorsed the proposal and considered the possibility of providing a subsidy and expanding the practice to include rides to the royal palace in São Cristovão. "The people," Viana explained, "would have comfortable transportation, [to use] to make their requisitions, and to have the honor of Kissing the Hand of His Majesty." It would allow them to enjoy "something necessarily new among us," he continued, and "it would give comfort to the class worthy of compassion" and "the State" would have "the pleasure of preventing the ruin of the measly fortunes of those who in order to subsist must petition."[39]

With such enthusiasm for opportunities for giving comfort and preventing

FIGURE 9: A.P.D.G., "Court Day at Rio," from A.P.D.G, *Sketches of Portuguese Life, manners, costume and character* (London: George B. Whittaker, 1826). Copy and permission obtained from the General Research Division, The New York Public Library, Astor, Lenox and Tilden Foundations. With this disparaging portrait of the audience the foreign observer argued that the prince regent's willingness to listen to the supplications of "the meanest of his subjects" was as misguided as it was remarkable.

ruin, Viana underscored that for the prince regent the practice of attending to the
needs of his subjects, regardless of their social status, was politically expedient. "A
liberal King comes to the aid of the poor," Dom João had been instructed by Novaes
Campos, because "the defense of the poor is the surest one."[40] Or, as the cleric
Manuel Joaquim da Mai dos Homens explained, the monarch "does not lose sight of
the small ones, who as contributing parts, form the harmonious union of the perfect
greatness of the Sovereign Empire."[41] Thus listening and responding to petitions of
all "good vassals," the prince regent conjured up the image of a political family in
which even "the poor and the destitute" were tied to their "Sovereign who is also
their Father."[42] Furthermore, strategically interceding on behalf of his vassals at the
expense of lesser authorities, the sovereign not only cultivated the "love" of his vassals, as the intendant claimed, but also reaffirmed that his royal authority was above
all others. The audience, in other words, both engendered the unity of vassals and asserted that this unity was founded on an unequivocal political center. It showed that
if, as São Carlos prayed, "the state was a living body," it was the king, as its "heart,"
who "brought the life-giving blood to Society's extremities."[43]

While in projecting such images of paternal authority and the relationship between sovereign and vassal as above and beyond all other social hierarchies, Rio's audiences and royal interventions approximated those of Lisbon, they also showed that
this relationship transcended the hierarchies of empire. They revealed the Portuguese
monarchy's understanding of its *regnum* as what Anthony Pagden has described,
writing of its Spanish counterpart, as corresponding to a "multicultural society, all of
whose members enjoyed the same notional legal status before the crown." In other
words, the crown both recognized "vassal" as a political, legal identity that, as Stuart
Schwartz has noted, no longer referred to "the specific relationship of the nobility to
the crown" and confirmed that, although originally associated with the specific geographic space of Portugal, the community of Portuguese vassals extended along with
Portugal's empire to include the residents of the crown's ultramarine possessions.[44]
As the transfer of the court itself had shown, and as Gonçalves dos Santos and other
residents celebrated, the one difference between "European" and "American" vassals—distance from the crown—was only circumstantial.

Furthermore, reaffirming that vassalage was both universal and imperial facilitated the crown's attempts to remake Rio de Janeiro in the image of the European
court it left behind. Calling attention to a political, legal identity shared by American and European residents of empire, the monarchy enunciated the transatlantic
unity and continuity that, as we shall see in Chapter 6, ideally marked the transition
from the ancient empire of Portugal to the new "prosperous empire" of Brazil. At a
time when monarchy had been successfully challenged on both sides of the Atlantic,
cultivating an active relationship between sovereign and vassal also allowed the Por-

tuguese crown to rehabilitate the image of a formerly ineffectual royal government in Brazil and to mitigate the potential damage to its own reputation that, as royal counselors cautiously noted, resulted from the French occupation of the Kingdom of Portugal. Indeed, such counsel suggests a "revalorization of the practice of the royal audience" similar to that which emerged in the context of another moment of crisis for the Portuguese monarchy: the mid-seventeenth-century struggle for independence from the crown of Castile and the restoration of Portuguese royal authority under the aegis of the prince regent's ancestor, the Duke of Braganza. While the political culture of the Restoration, Diogo Curto explains, featured an intensification of debates over the need for the monarch to directly attend to the needs of his vassals and "a preoccupation in representing the prince and his court as accessible to all" (an accessibility denied when they were ruled from Spain), in the 1810s royal officials called attention to the beneficent consequences of the sovereign's residence in the hopes of prevailing over revolutionary alternatives.[45]

This use of the royal audience to project an image of accessibility, as well as political unity, and to convey a sense of the prince regent's absolute authority, liberality, beneficence, and justice, then depended on a proper assessment of whether to reward or punish, whether the residents' requests for royal grace should be granted or denied, whether the prince regent should undercut or uphold lesser authorities, and whether he should reward the nobility's service or protect others from their demands. In other words, staging audiences and responding to petitions required a careful administration of what António Manuel Hespanha has called "the economy of grace."[46] To assess petitions and define the scope of this economy, Dom João turned to his counselors. And when considering the petitions of Rio's popular classes, he turned to one counselor in particular: the police intendant. Unlike most royal officials, Viana's daily activities took him beyond the palace to Rio's streets. The intendant's staff, his network of informants, and his former experiences as a colonial magistrate made his knowledge of the local and, in his case, native setting an invaluable resource for the newly arrived prince regent. Viana's role as broker, his ability to both facilitate and undermine a royal solution to a problem, was recognized by Rio's popular classes as well. They both appeared before the sovereign out of dissatisfaction with Viana—and with his approach to their conduct or their troubles—and sought out the intendant to request his assistance in obtaining a royal grace. Consequently, he played a central role in defining the scope of the relationship between the prince regent and his petitioners in Rio.

When assessing petitions Viana considered, in the most general sense, whether granting a request would promote the "good order of things."[47] More specifically, this meant ensuring that an extraordinary royal intervention did not suggest a repudiation of the law or *meios ordinários*, the established channels for seeking justice. After all, Viana asserted in one report on a petition, the "security of any state consisted chiefly in a precise observance of the law, and in the good administration of justice.[48] Thus, commenting on Sergeant Anacleto Elias Ferreira de Noronha's request for royal intervention in a conjugal conflict, the intendant Viana advised against it, explaining that if "the Prince Our Lord were to intervene in these matters," it would not only violate custom, but also dismantle an established legal process, in this case ecclesiastical divorce proceedings.[49]

Ensuring that royal interventions promoted the "good order of things" also meant ensuring that the crown did not grant requests that suggested disrespect for social and political hierarchies. The crown, in other words, had to guard against what one official characterized as "the confusion of classes and hierarchies" that, he claimed, was "the main cause of the unhappy state in which Europe finds itself."[50] For Viana this meant that the petition, and the request that it contained, had to be assessed in relation to the petitioner. As he explained in an initial report on Noronha's case, although when the prince regent "commands as Sovereign and with full knowledge of the case" intervention is always just, "the rule is that the Sovereign never interferes in these questions on behalf of just any vassal" and rather "only when it concerns a person who because of status and service . . . deserves these attentions." Although Noronha served the crown as a solider, and was an acquaintance of Viana himself, his dishonorable conduct, Viana explained, excluded him from this category.[51]

To balance recognition of status, service, and public virtue with a defense of the law and justice, Viana argued that although those who served the crown, including petty functionaries and soldiers, retained a privilege of royal intervention that other vassals did not have, requests for certain exemptions, such as *aposentadoria*, had to be denied. To avoid "scandal" and "great grumblings," he explained, royal interventions could not appear to favor the particular interests of royal servants over the public interest embodied in the law.[52] Indeed, Viana argued in 1820, officials who petitioned the crown for exceptions to the law under the "pretext of public benefits" undermined "the whole" in favor of "trivialities" and attacked government itself by inciting distrust among "the people."[53] This principled supremacy of public good over private interests was defended as well by royal minister Vila Nova Portugal, who urged the crown to suppress "feudal rights" that he judged to be both an infringement on royal authority and "injurious to the people."[54] In other words, although Dom João had a recognizable obligation to give—for "to give" was a particularly princely trait[55]— royal counselors also insisted that the scope of these transactions had to be narrowly defined. Petitioners had be to worthy, the request had to be virtuous—neither trivial, arrogant, nor in the interest of revenge—and the intervention both had to provide an exemplary defense of the larger principle of a public good and to display the monarch's unrivaled authority without promoting a general disregard for other lesser authorities.[56] In what cases, then, did Viana counsel the monarch to intervene?

Among numerous pleas for charity, employment, and pardon for crimes, one kind of petition that appeared to the intendant to fulfill these requirements for intervention was the request to resolve domestic conflict by upholding patriarchal rights.[57] Commenting, for example, on Francisco de Souza Oliveira's request that the crown send his "disobedient" son to serve in India, Viana justified his endorsement by claiming that "in this way young men could be made to respect the great authority of fathers," an authority that, according to Viana, provided the "nexus" that "strengthen[ed] and deepen[ed] the bonds of society."[58] As Viana affirmed in commenting on a similar request to send an insubordinate son to serve in the army in southern Brazil, royal intervention in these cases was justified because "public authority has always aided paternal power."[59] Such interventions were, however, approached with caution. They could not, as noted above, suggest a disregard for established channels and procedures for resolving disputes nor promote "intrigue and indisposition between the sovereign and his magistrates."[60] To warrant the prince regent's attentions domestic discord also had to have public consequences. The effects of the conflict had to transcend the boundaries of the household in question and intervention had to afford the crown the possibility of promoting public morality and virtue within the court. Thus, commenting on a magistrate's petition that the crown sentence his abusive son-in-law to military service outside the city, the intendant energetically urged the prince regent to approve the request because, as he explained, by sending him to India "the court will be free of a vagrant and the family of an object that disgraces it and all [will have] the certainty that the prince is the common father that responds to all these evils, [and] from which can follow the great good that others correct themselves, [thus] improving society."[61]

To protect patriarchal rights, and make manifest the alliance between "public authority" and the authority of "heads of family," Viana also advised interventions into disputes between husbands and wives.[62] As we have seen in the case of Anacleto Ferreira de Noronha noted above, these petitions were duly scrutinized for the morality and public status of those involved, and royal intervention was not advised when it interfered with ecclesiastical authority. The source of discord, often charges of adultery, had to be verified.[63] Yet, notwithstanding these standards for intervention, conjugal discord often produced situations that, for Viana, uniquely warranted circumvention of the legal proceedings he otherwise ardently defended. Thus, in 1812 when José Lopes de Saraiva, who worked as a royal librarian, petitioned the crown for permission to send his wife Brigida Teresa, who he claimed was notoriously adulterous, to a recolhimento outside the city in Taipú, the intendant advised that "in spite of legislation concerning the way in which husbands accuse their wives . . . it is always good to help them using extraordinary means, by way of the seclusion of the wife." The husband, he explained, would be spared the "more public affront" that a formal accusation and sentence would entail.[64] In 1818, commenting on another petition, Viana more carefully outlined the guidelines for royal action in such cases, plainly reflecting his concern with moral and social order that, as we saw in Chapter 4, guided his efforts at policing. When a member of a family "strays in conduct," he explained, "it has always been a consolation for the heads of families to seek in the wisdom of government a limit to their affront, requesting the confinement of this person, in the case of a woman in a recolhimento, and in the case of a man to the *praças das conquistas* (military service abroad), thus removing from them the object that offends them and giving a punishment that particular authority alone cannot."[65] Fathers and husbands, in other words, could count on the sovereign to "correct" insubordinate family members (*sem alguma sugeição*).[66] Even Anacleto Elias Ferreira de Noronha, whose own conduct was less than ideal, could benefit from a royal intervention, Viana conceded a few weeks after his original dismissal, because his wife had proceeded to live so scandalously with her own stepfather, contradicting the terms of her divorce. It was only "royal authority" and its use of "force," he judged, that would succeed in containing such "libertinage."[67]

This commitment to defend patriarchal rights and the intolerance of female independence also meant that Viana adopted a considerably more skeptical position when considering pleas from women for extraordinary intervention into similar domestic disputes.[68] In 1814, when Dona Anna Joaquina Miranda, in the midst of securing an ecclesiastical divorce from Captain José Joaquim de Rego, asked the prince regent to grant her formal custody of her children, Viana categorically dismissed the request. It was "arduous," he argued, "because it attacked paternal rights which the law of all nations always respected." Wives separated from their husbands, he further explained, enjoyed custody of their children only until the age of three, when care and the duties of raising the child (*criação*) were supplanted by the father's right to provide an upbringing and education (*educação*).[69]

Yet, as this same case revealed, occasionally the crown's commitment to defend public morality and order also could justify interventions that curtailed paternal authority. When Viana later received evidence that Rego both physically abused his children and left them unattended, he reversed his decision and advised the crown to take action against him. "If both the mother and the state are to lose these two children," he speculated, "without them being raised to someday become useful sons and vassals, it is better that His Royal Highness, now knowing the father's incapacity . . . should order that these boys be given to their mother who is capable of treating them well."[70] In 1820 Viana similarly cited the defense of a greater public good when he advised the crown to intervene against surrogate parental authority on behalf of José António Nogueira Ferrão, a captain in the Portuguese Army serving in Rio de Janeiro. Ferrão had petitioned the crown to overrule the decision of the Misericórdia's council to deny his request to marry Rosa de Jesus, an orphan currently in its care. Such a decision, the council claimed, simply upheld a restriction, established by Rosa's benefactor, that her marriage had to be approved by the benefactor himself in writing. For Viana, the council's claims were indefensible and royal intervention was warranted because "the Sovereign [could] supplant the lack of consent" in a case such as this in which "everyone" knew that the supplicant's "quality of person and position" represented an advantage for Rosa de Jesus. Furthermore, in obliging Rosa to secure his consent "regardless of her age," Viana argued, the benefactor had not only attacked the institution of marriage that it "suit[ed] the state to promote," but also acted in a manner that was both "arbitrary, cruel and intolerable" and contrary to "good customs."[71]

The royal defense of fathers and husbands thus was both affirmed and limited by the practice of considering petitions. Even as the affinity between "the great authority" of fathers and the authority of the "common father of all vassals" meant that the crown enhanced its own paternal authority by defending the paternal authority of others, Dom João could undercut the authority of individual fathers as well, especially when those fathers contradicted the larger principle of his own paternal power. In other words, if husbands and fathers had a natural ally in the prince regent, it was also the case that they could not act in a way that the sovereign did not. The crown could not tolerate a publicly abusive or "cruel" and "arbitrary" exercise of authority. In preserving social and political hierarchy and its own authority, the crown could not appear to defend tyranny.[72] This, after all, would undermine the basis for the royal audience and the ideal of absolute, yet just and liberal, royal power itself, which was so insistently and ceremoniously displayed in the new royal court of Rio and in which, as one petitioner explained, "all good vassals" expected to find refuge.

The Economy of Royal Grace in the New World:
Rio's Slaves Petition the Throne

As the prince regent and the police intendant considered Rio's residents' numerous petitions for royal intervention, they renegotiated long-standing, Old-World debates on the economy of royal grace. The New World, however, also presented new circumstances in which the relationship between "the people" and their sovereign had to be defined. In stark contrast to Lisbon, the majority of Rio's residents did not, after all, enjoy the same legal status before the crown. Instead, they served both residents and royal officials as slaves. Thus, as Oliveira Lima suggested, in Dom João's court "European contact" had to be reconciled with "the effect of the servile institution,"[73] an effect witnessed in the imperial capital of Lisbon but that, now more than ever before, the Portuguese sovereign was forced to contemplate in a city as African as it was Portuguese.

While Oliveira Lima argued that such a reconciliation resulted in a decadent "preference for luxuriousness and vice," slaves had an entirely different understanding of the meaning of their presence among courtiers. Although slaves were formally excluded from the community of vassals in Rio, following the transfer of the court they nevertheless claimed a particular relationship with the crown. "Everyone knows," the intendant lamented only weeks after Dom João's reception, "that the thousands of slaves who exist in Brazil are hopeful that with the arrival of His Royal Highness here they will be liberated from their captivity."[74] Such a conviction reportedly was announced in the chant of the porters who first carried the prince regent's sedan chair: "Our master has arrived, Slavery is over."[75] The claim revealed the slaves' own understanding of the logic of the crown's quest to remake Rio de Janeiro as a European court. If, after all, slavery had been deemed inappropriate for the old court, it followed that it would be abolished in the new one. Indeed, as we have seen, a number of royal officials and memorialists reached similar conclusions and condemned the institution of slavery on civilizing, humanitarian, and racist grounds.

In Rio de Janeiro, along with their speculative hopes for abolition by way of royal intervention, slaves also came to behold an appeal to the prince regent as a way to secure an individual *carta de alforria* (letter of liberty).[76] They recognized, in other words, that the monarch was the source of justice to which all were subject and to which all could appeal when faced with hardship and, as one group of slave petitioners explained, the "tyranny" of their owners. Indeed, with extraordinary "acts of grace," eighteenth-century Portuguese monarchs had demonstrated the possibility of royal intervention on behalf of people of color and slaves in disputes over their legal status and their rights to manumission. While in these cases slaves and people of color in Brazil had depended on substantial resources for the expense of written statements and intermediaries in Lisbon, following the transfer of the court, like free vassals in the city, they seized on the end of these obstacles and the less costly process of petitioning the crown that the immediate presence of Dom João afforded.[77] In the new royal court to express their need for royal intervention slaves secured messengers, family members, or representatives from religious brotherhoods who petitioned the sovereign on their behalf. In 1812, for example, Gabriel Garces Gralha, the "elected king of the Congo people" in Rio, petitioned the crown to grant liberty to António Monjolo, explaining that "his Brotherhood was chartered to take care of manumissions."[78] Other slaves, however, directly petitioned for a royal intervention. Availing themselves of unsupervised moments in their day, they reportedly visited the royal palace personally. Thus, by 1817, when a "black man" named Boaventura presented himself "before the King Our Lord in the Royal Quinta da Boa Vista," to request that the crown grant his freedom, royal officials treated the occurrence as routine.[79]

As was the case with petitions from Rio's free popular classes, the crown called on the police intendant to comment on slaves' requests for royal intervention. Slave petitioners threatened Viana's narrow understanding of the relationship between the scope of royal grace and social hierarchies, and the image of the prince regent surrounded by a "crowd of [slave] petitioners" disrupted the ideals of metropolitan decorum and social and political order that the new court was supposed to embody. "The idea," the intendant warned, "that His Majesty protects their cause will make them withdraw from service to their owners in order to petition for their liberty, and when they discover that it will not be obtained, they will not return to their owners' houses and rather will become fugitives, highway robbers, and dangerous enemies." Accordingly, in commenting on their petitions, Viana sought to establish that the slaves' claims to a relationship with the crown were misguided.[80]

More specifically, Viana often responded to petitions by attempting to discredit the individual slave petitioner. Such was the case in 1814 when a *crioulo* (a Brazilian-born person of African descent) named Matheus petitioned the throne for his freedom on the grounds that three years earlier, when he became ill, his owner, João de Campo da Silveira, had abandoned him. A letter to Silveira from Friar José de São Francisco de Sales confirmed both that Matheus had "appeared at the door of the Convent of Santo António" and that Silveira had refused to pay for his subsequent treatment at the Misericórdia's hospital and instead had left him to beg. In spite of this evidence against Silveira, however, in his report Viana described Matheus's tale as "a ruse" used by many other "blacks in Brazil in order to make their owners give them their freedom without any basis in the law." Rather than "abandoning" Matheus, Viana claimed his investigation had revealed that the owner had taken him to see some "black *curandeiros*" (folk healers) in Irajá as Matheus himself had requested. Matheus, he explained, then took advantage of the situation and secretly returned to the city.

The intendant's commentary on slave petitions also referred to a larger politics of slavery and revealed elite anxieties about the potential of manumission. In the case of Matheus, for example, having first indicted him for a particular deceit, the intendant then proceeded to both acknowledge and dismiss the larger social context of his plea. The illegitimate nature of intervention in this case, Viana counseled, stemmed equally from the fact that it would establish a dangerous precedent. The throne would be overwhelmed with so many "representations of this nature," he wrote, "that there would not be any space for others."[81] In 1819 when Clara Maria de Jesus "implored [the crown] to have the grace to grant" her son Jorge his liberty, Viana offered a similarly pointed assessment. Clara's request had been precipitated by Jorge's sale to a priest from Bahia. To avoid permanent separation from her son, she hoped to purchase his freedom for the price established in the transaction (200$000 réis). Her request was further justified, she explained, because although Jorge was born when she was still a slave, his father was José Joaquim Marques da Graça Correa, a Lieutenant Coronel, currently serving His Majesty in Angola. Manumission in similar circumstances, her petition noted, had been upheld by royal legislation and decree. In his report on her petition, however, Viana dismissed the possibility of precedent and instead called attention to the crown's need to defend property rights. Outside the context of mistreatment, he explained, "no one can be forced to sell a slave." "Knowing from experience that in a country where slavery is permitted, a good slave is a . . . precious commodity," he then concluded, "the particular politics" of the crown should be that "the Sovereign never gets involved in these matters."[82]

These attempts to exclude questions of slave ownership from the realm of royal intervention were endorsed as well by Vila Nova Portugal, a member of the royal cabinet who, along with other ministers, supervised Viana's execution of his duties. Commenting on allegations of cruelty to slaves in Bahia, Vila Nova Portugal counseled that under no circumstances should the crown intervene in the relationship between slave and slave owner, nor could anyone take or hold a slave against the will of his or her owner unless a debt was owed and no other movable goods existed. For "in Brazil," he explained, "to rob a farmer of his slave is to do injury not only to that man but to the whole public."[83] Thus, although the sovereign's grace ideally responded to the needs of his vassals, the overwhelming dimensions of slaves' necessity disqualified them from royal intervention because such an intervention appeared to undercut established economic and social hierarchies entirely. It was not, in other words, that slaves did not have the need for royal grace, but rather that their need was unfathomable and, therefore, always disruptive. As Viana, writing to Vila Nova Portugal concerning the request of one slave who "desired to benefit from liberty," rhetorically posed the problem: "And what slave will not so desire?"[84]

Such resolute disqualification of royal intervention as a means to secure a letter of liberty was founded as well on explicitly racist perceptions of the people involved. In Clara's case, for example, Viana bolstered his dismissal of her request by conjuring up images of the "anarchy," "laziness," and "evil" of freed people of color, and by calling attention to Clara's own color, social condition, and gender as reasons for why the crown could not intercede on her and her son's behalf. If it had been the Portuguese father who submitted the petition for Jorge's freedom, the intendant admitted, rather than Clara, a *cabra* of "low status" and, Viana further and perversely speculated, without the means to provide for her son as his owner had, the prince regent could have intervened. As this statement also revealed, the logic of racism could at once reinforce and undermine the logic of the conflict between the concession of liberty and larger social and economic interests and "powerful political reasons," as the intendant described them: manumission produced anarchy; white fathers could free their enslaved sons. Such an exception signaled that even as Viana discouraged slaves and people of color from petitioning the crown the question of royal intervention on their behalf and the larger relationship among slavery, slaves, people of color, and the crown was largely unresolved.

Indeed, his categorical denial of slaves' right to petition the sovereign notwithstanding, the intendant often undermined his own discriminatory discourse by endorsing slaves' established prerogative to resolve disputes and seek a legal manumission using royal courts. In 1813, for example, when "António *Pardo*" "appeared with a petition" requesting that the crown require the merchant Pascoal Cosme dos Reis, his former owner, to return to him a horse, a saddle, the furniture of his *senzala* (slave quarters), and a slave named Joaquim, Viana responded, typically, with an investigation. While António claimed to have left behind these possessions when Reis sent him and his wife to the Misericórdia in Bahia "to serve the ill," Viana substantiated that António was offended because he expected to be manumitted upon his former owners' death, but instead was retained as a slave of the owner's wife and Reis, her second husband. In retaliation António allegedly had led uprisings at Reis' sugar mill where he worked as a foreman. In spite of the fact that Reis then had sent him to Bahia with the stipulation that he never again return to the city, António and his wife had come back to Rio and proceeded to live secretly at Reis' estate. Viana concluded his summary of the case by characteristically denying the request for compensation, arguing that in this case the absence of proof of a legal manumission meant that António was still a slave. Consequently Reis' right to banish him from the city once again was also upheld. However, the intendant added that although "extraordinary" intervention was out of the question, António had grounds to pursue "his right" to seek legal manumission in court.[85]

In 1815 when Estevão de Jesus, a stonemason, requested that the crown oblige his former owner João Coelho Marinho to pay him "the value of a slave named Manuel" whom he "possessed" during "the time of his own captivity," Viana arrived at a similar conclusion. Although Viana upheld Marinho's right to keep and then sell Manuel because "not having given his consent for the purchase of the slave" the "well-known rule that nothing that a slave has does not also belong to his owner" prevailed, he added that his decision did not mean that Estevão could not use "established channels" to resolve his dispute.[86] Writing in 1820, on a petition for liberty submitted by Paschoa and Antónia, Viana even more pointedly advised that although the crown could not intervene on their behalf they should be instructed "to continue to use their right by way of ordinary means," in this case the *juizo de fora*, where they originally presented their grievance.[87] An even more dramatic defense of slaves' recourse to courts then was made on behalf of Romaria da Silva, who sought to secure her own liberty, as well as that of her children and grandchildren, on the grounds that she had indigenous ancestry on her mother's side. In this case, Viana not only endorsed her right to do so, but also secured her a royal grant of funds to continue her litigation, to be provided by the intendancy's own coffers.[88] And, as the intendant also recognized, if royal courts were to provide the recourse that, as he insisted, Dom João could not, their cases would have to be protected against intervention on behalf of slave owners who sought to avoid the social and material costs, including the placement of the slave in neutral custody during review and adjudication, that these proceedings implied.[89] Thus, commenting on the petition of Dona da Cunha that her slave Magdalena be returned to her domain while she settled charges of abuse in court, Viana counseled that although he found Magdalena's case against her owner to be unsound, based on a public petition signed by "clerks and people of little account," legal proceedings had to run their course and therefore the crown "could not give extraordinary aid to the owner."[90]

Thus directing slaves to use royal courts to pursue their grievances Viana both defended judicial process and the authority of magistrates and recognized the integrity of slaves' grievances and, as he wrote in the case of Magdalena, "their sad condition" in Brazil. In doing so he also, and perhaps unwittingly, constructed a unique political identity for slaves. Like other vassals, slaves had "rights" and, as the intendant often noted in reports on the petitions of the city's residents free and slave, ensuring recourse to these rights was a crucial part of maintaining order, unity, and loyalty and mitigating potentially violent consequences of discontent. Yet for slaves alone rights were uniquely limited; they stopped, according to Viana, before they reached the throne. In other words, if as one nineteenth-century jurist later argued, the position of slaves and freed people made them subject to a "peculiar legislation,"[91] in Dom João's Rio de Janeiro, this same position appeared to make them peculiar vassals. In a poignant contradiction of the principle of absolute monarchy— that all power was resolved in the figure of the monarch alone—the requests of slaves and former slaves could be considered by a royal magistrate, but not by the monarch that the magistrate represented.

Yet what Viana perceived to be a limited vassalage did not mean that slaves did not have access to the prince regent or that they stopped seeking his attention and requesting intervention. As the intendant was forced to recognize, his exclusionary efforts notwithstanding, the Quinta da Boa Vista had been identified by slaves as a place of "refuge." When Jacinta Rosa went there to avoid being sold and separated from her children, she reported to Viana, two servants living on the estate even helped her draft a petition.[92] Earlier, in 1809, the slave owner Dona Aguida Francisca de Queiros Malheiros also reported that the prince regent's residence had become a symbol of resistance to owners' abuse. Late one night, she recalled, some of her slaves had come to her house making noise, claiming that their disorderly conduct would go unpunished because "they came from the palace where they served His Royal Highness." "They are all persuaded," she lamented, "that Your Royal Highness is going to free them." What Dona Aguida failed to mention, and of which Viana was aware, was that her slaves also "went to the palace to complain" of mistreatment.[93] They, like many others, made appealing to the monarch a form of self-defense against their owner's violence and an additional dimension of resistence to slavery that also included rebellion, flight, and pleas to colonial tribunals and officials.[94]

The strategy was based both on principle and a limited degree of success. As Viana also noted in his report on Dona Aguida, the appearance of slaves on the grounds of the palace or in the presence of Dom João often led to their placement in protective custody, temporary removal from their owner's property, while their accusations were investigated. Although they "complain of any insignificant punishment," Viana explained, it was "customary" to do so "when they go there [the palace]" "in order to not provoke the insubordination of slaves in this country."[95] In other words, although royal intervention on behalf of slaves seeking freedom was disqualified, for both royal officials and slaves, the palace and the prince regent nevertheless had become part of the process of maintaining what Viana described as the "equilibrium" between owners and slaves.

Often slave petitioners justified this search for royal justice at the palace by citing their repeatedly unsuccessful attempts to secure redress elsewhere. Challenging Viana's recommendations that they take their cases to the courts, they argued that their "low status" qualified them for royal intervention because such a status also, in effect, disqualified their use of established judicial processes that favored the "rich and powerful."[96] Manumissions indeed rarely were attained through the courts,[97] a fact that was evident to a group of brothers and sisters who jointly petitioned the crown for their liberty in 1812. "At the Royal Feet of Your Royal Highness," their carefully worded petition began, they came to rectify a problem that began when their mother, Paula Rodrigues da Costa Reis "of the Angola Nation," having come to Brazil as a free woman, was "falsely sold as a slave." In 1803, they explained, they had been declared free persons "as descendants of a free womb," a decision that was confirmed three years later, but then "rich and powerful persons" had secured the revocation of their freedom. As their subsequent appeals had resulted only in their sale to new owners, they now sought "permission to appear and seek" justice from the prince regent himself. They came, as their petition stated, as "most humble vassals" without "lawyers or agents who assumed responsibility for their defense." While indicting a judicial process that favored the rich, their plea, they also stressed, was founded on respect for the law, which they argued was in their favor. On the contrary, their owners both disregarded the law and mistreated them, leading several of them to seek refuge in the countryside and forsake their honorable service to His Majesty as members of a militia of people of color. Thus, they discredited the possibility of an alliance between their owners and the crown by claiming that their rich owners had corrupted the courts and, consequently, threatened the sovereign's authority itself. Such a tactic was partially successful. Rather than upholding their status as slaves, the crown ordered an inquiry. Two years later, however, the petitioners had secured only the guarantee of further judicial review.[98]

The social limits of seeking a remedy through litigation were also evident to a "black" slave named Magdalena who challenged the intendant directly and persistently petitioned Dom João. Her owner, José António Rodrigues Chaves, she explained in her first petition, had agreed to grant her freedom with the stipulation that she serve him until his death. Later, however, he had begun to mistreat her and, although he had signed a *termo* (agreement) in which he pledged that the abuse would stop,[99] it had continued. A subsequent investigation by the intendant revealed that although Chaves indeed had agreed to grant Magdalena her freedom, on another occasion, he had revoked it and had proceeded to sell her to his son. Viana then determined that both the original grant of liberty and its revocation were invalid, the first one due to Magdalena's "ungratefulness" and the second, because it had not been properly recorded. The dispute and the question of Magdalena's status, he concluded, would have to be solved in the courts. "In the meantime," however, unhappy with Viana's decision, Magdalena "went to the throne" to insist on a more favorable solution. Her appearance must have put pressure on the intendant because he reapproached the case with a new perspective. In fact, he now noted in a subsequent report, because Chaves had not begun the proper procedure to revoke her freedom, Magdelena was a free person with an obligation to work for Chaves, an obligation that she did not fulfill because of his abuse. Furthermore, Viana reported, she resented Chaves because he had forced her to live with him as his concubine, a fact that if it were to be legally substantiated, he wrote, "would be [sufficient grounds] for her to obtain pure liberty." To eliminate opportunities for "revenge" and further "sin," Viana decided that Chaves should be forced to grant Magdalena "pure and complete liberty," provided that she compensate him the service provided for in the original grant of freedom. To avoid any further confusion the transaction would be duly registered in the intendancy.[100]

Viana had allowed for a similar concession in the case of António Monjolo and his representative, Gabriel Garces Gralha, noted above. Gralha petitioned the crown on behalf of António Monjolo because, as he reported, when his owner Padre José

Garcia promised that he would grant him his freedom if he were provided with another slave trained, as António Monjolo was, to sell groceries, the Brotherhood provided him with the necessary funds. Garcia, however, then reneged on his offer, claiming that the "new black" was not properly conducting business and was not even familiar with local currency. When Gralha then appealed to the crown to uphold Garcia's original obligation, Garcia claimed, in turn, that the money António Monjolo used to buy the slave had not been lent by the Brotherhood, but rather was stolen from him and, therefore, both António and the new slave were his. Viana, initially demonstrating a characteristic sympathy for the slave owner, nevertheless decided that after three months António should be granted his freedom, and the new slave, who by that time would be properly trained to serve Garcia, should take his place. Even more remarkable in this case, however, was Viana's commentary on the established process for resolving similar conflicts. While Viana demanded that slaves, and all vassals, respect the decisions of royal courts, here he conceded that although António Monjolo could have pursued his freedom through established judicial channels, these channels placed him, and all slaves, at a disadvantage. Their owners, he observed, "trick them, and take advantage of their miserable condition." In other words, even as Viana insisted that the slaves did not belong in line to petition the prince regent, he came to acknowledge that the supposed alternative was a failure, and that, worst of all, this very failure of judicial process then increased the number of slave petitioners.[101]

To restore the possibility of recourse to royal courts and thus diminish the need for slaves' petitions, Viana considered modifying the process of formal adjudication with what he described in 1821 as "legislation that mitigates the sad condition of slaves without . . . destroying the right of owners."[102] More specifically, Viana proposed in both 1812 and 1818 the creation of a royal office exclusively entrusted with the adjudication of disputes between slaves and owners. This *juiz das liberdades*, he argued, would streamline normal procedures with hearings, a "simple procedure" (*simples processo*) based on a petition or the slave's appearance and oral testimony, and thus eliminate "the delays of meios ordinários."[103] Although the advice went unheeded, Viana himself occasionally acted out the role he had imagined.[104] In 1817, for example, a "black" named José dos Passos petitioned the crown for a letter of liberty because, as he recounted, "as a slave in Bahia" his owner sent him to the Mina coast, where he was taken prisoner by an English corsair and later left in Sierra Leone. After spending two years there and another year in São Tomé, "he came to this court in an English schooner" where he proceeded to earn a living as a sailor and then as a blacksmith in His Majesty's Royal Stables. Although his owner had lost all rights to his service, both as a result of his capture and because the King of England had compensated the Bahians' losses on the Mina coast, he never legally obtained his freedom. After Viana contacted his former owner, who confirmed the story, the petition was approved and Passos was spared the expense and the delays of royal courts.[105]

Such an intercession was not the product of Viana's passion for judicial economy, or at least not only. Rather, he linked the imperative of establishing new forms of adjudication and redress to very specific political and social contexts. In 1818 commenting on an investigation into Dona Anna Joaquina Mesquita's abuse of a slave named Policena, who he first had placed into protective custody and then recommended be freed, Viana explained that mistreatment such as that exhibited by Mesquita, which, as both witnesses and a doctor attested, included the mutilation of a number of her slaves and subsequent defiance of the intendant's order to curtail Policena's punishment, contributed to the "reduction of the black population," which, in turn, represented a loss for both owners and the "public wealth of the state." And it was prudent, he reminded the crown, to take note of the new politics of commerce in slaves. If before it was easy to buy a new slave, now it was no longer the case, and it would be "much less so in the future," he contended, considering the "prohibitions, taxes, and restrictions" on the slave trade.

As Viana also recognized, an effective solution to this larger economic and imperial dilemma was linked to the question of the authority of masters. The frequency with which slaves both petitioned the intendancy and "the Sovereign and All Royal Persons" who in turn then sent the abused slaves to the intendancy, Viana explained, called for "a legal measure" that would not only curtail mistreatment per se, but also end the generally "unlimited freedom" that owners had assumed in relation to their slaves. Although he advised against the creation of a *Código dos Negros*, the "lack of adequate legislation on the present state of affairs," Viana insisted, made any attempts to regulate slavery seem unfounded and therefore easier for slave owners to ignore. New legislation, in turn, would prepare the owners for further necessary restrictions on their "misunderstood and arbitrary authority," actions that, in some cases, led to unpunished murders and provoked the disappearance of slaves, the creation of *quilombos* (runaway slave communities), and other types of disorder. Providing a more efficient recourse to justice would, in this sense, preserve social order and slavery in Brazil, and also mitigate a larger, future confrontation. For as Viana ambivalently observed, "the great edifice of liberty, and of the vengeance of a persecuted humanity will grow."[106]

Yet, even as Viana suggested that responding to slaves' denunciations of abuse by way of adjudication would prevent other forms of resistance and therefore indirectly work in their owners' favor, he also recognized, as Rio's slave petitioners themselves asserted, that in their owners' "arbitrary authority" and "unlimited freedom" they and the prince regent had a common enemy. Not only did the rights of owners not exist in cases of inhumanity, but, as he explained, "His Majesty's laws cannot allow that an inhumane owner has more freedom [to continue to abuse slaves], than public authority." In other words, the monarchy's authority itself, theoretically recognized as absolute, was undermined when slave owners acted in ways that their sovereign could not. The solution, the intendant counseled, was to make clear that the slave owner's authority was clearly circumscribed by the law and the crown it represented. And, as Dom João himself had made evident on one occasion when he personally intervened in a public whipping he encountered during a royal outing, this included the possibility of extraordinary royal intervention on slaves' behalf.[107] In a report written three years later, Viana reinforced this uncodified principle in practice. Although in this case, citing the defense of property rights, the intendant found against Florencio Alves' petition for liberty for having performed service in the army after he fled his owner's domain, when he interviewed his owner and discovered his plans for revenge—incarcerating Florencio "for all his life"—he added qualifications to this decision. As incarceration was a "right that his owner did not have," Viana counseled, Alves could be returned only "with the stipulation that he should not be punished" or, alternately, he would be sold in a transaction supervised by the intendancy.[108]

Following the court's arrival at Rio slaves thus confronted a monarchy that was, as Algranti has argued, committed to a defense of the interests of their owners. Consequently, the effects of their petitions and of their defiance of official discrimination were varied and depended on their resources, especially money and assistance from free people.[109] As in the case of Rio's free petitioners, the fortunate few secured a royal intervention that perhaps only momentarily alleviated dire circumstances or, at best, permanently changed their status. Yet, as a whole, Rio's slave petitioners succeeded in making royal officials reaffirm what had led them to the royal palace in the first place: even in the context of their captivity, their owners' authority, like everyone else's, was limited by the power of the monarch. As Viana conceded in one report, the "benefit" of a royal concession of liberty could be granted in cases of abuse and "good service." Indeed, while the intendant claimed a "natural instinct" drove the slaves to seek "the clemency of His Majesty," it was the slaves' recognition of the logic of the Portuguese old regime that motivated their petitions.[110] As vassals, they looked to the king for protection, rewards for their loyalty, and, as Florencio Alves had claimed, service "to the state in favor of the public cause." This recognition of monarchical authority may have been reconciled, as João José Reis has argued, with African conceptions of leadership re-created in Brazil.[111] Rio's slaves, however, also exploited the contradictions in the royal project to transform the city into "the court," a project that sought to reassert the monarchy's power and legitimacy by celebrating New World vassalage even as the majority of the city's residents were disqualified from being vassals.[112]

"The time of the king" was indeed, as Manuel Antônio de Almeida's novel suggests, a moment when the extremes of Rio de Janeiro's social hierarchy came into contact. If, however, in Almeida's fictional account Dom João remains removed from the scene, in historical Rio de Janeiro his "immediate" presence reshaped the local practice of politics. For Rio's residents both the city's streets and the royal palace became venues where they could encounter the sovereign and seek redress. For the crown, in turn, listening to petitions and granting extraordinary interventions were gestures that were politically prudent. In undermining the injustices and tyrannies of other lesser authorities, interventions revealed that absolute royal power was virtuous. Thus, in becoming a royal court Rio de Janeiro had become a site in which the sovereign confronted his New World vassals and where these vassals also defined the terms for this encounter. Although royal officials attempted to limit royal grace to "persons of status and service," petitioners also included those who Almeida entirely excluded from his vision of early nineteenth-century Rio and who officials formally excluded from Rio's community of vassals: the city's slaves.[113] Exploiting the tensions between principle and practice, slave petitioners presented at times successful challenges to the limited scope of royal intervention as envisioned by royal officials and in so doing momentarily subverted the hierarchies of slavery. In challenging the hierarchy of owners and slaves, slave petitioners, like others who sought royal grace, also reaffirmed the hierarchy of sovereign and vassal. Dom João's new royal residence thus became a "tropical Versailles" not, as Oliveira Lima argued, because "the effect of the servile institution" together with "European contact" produced decadence, but rather because in the process of both constructing a new court and forging a politics of monarchy in the New World the imperatives of colonial society and the imperatives of a royal court were reconfigured together.

Notes

1. Manuel Antônio de Almeida, *Memórias de um sargento de milícias* (1855) (Rio de Janeiro: Ediouro, n.d.).

2. Antônio Cândido de Mello e Souza, "Dialética da malandragem (caracterização das *Memórias de um sargento de milícias*)," *Revista do Instituto de Estudos Brasileiros* 8 (1970), 81.

3. Anonymous, "Jornada do Sr. D. João 6° ao Brazil em 1807," in Ângelo Pereira, *Os filhos de el-rei D. João VI* (Lisbon: Empresa Nacional de Publicidade, 1946), 114; *Relação das festas que se fizerão no Rio de Janeiro quando o Principe Regent Nosso Senhor e toda a Sua Real Familia chegarão pela primeira vez d'quella Capital . . .* (Lisbon: Impressão Régia, 1810), 15.

4. Paulo Fernandes Viana [police intendant] to José de Portugal e Castro, the Marquês de Aguiar [Ministro dos Negócios do Brasil], August 3, 1811, ANRJ Códice 323 v. 3, f61v.

5. José Antônio Sá, *Defeza dos Direitos Nacionaes e Reaes da Monarquia Portugueza* (Lisbon: Impressão Régia, 1816), 205.

6. Garcia de Resende, *Crónica de D. João II e Miselânea*, cited in Ana Maria Alves, *Iconologia do poder real no período manuelino, à procura de uma linguagem perdida* (Lousã: Imprensa Nacional, 1985), 89.

7. Francisco António de Novaes Campos, *Príncipe Perfeito, Emblemas de D. João de Solórzano* (1790) (Lisbon: Instituto de Cultura e Lingua Portuguesa, 1985), f113, f123. This facsimile edition is edited by Maria Helena Teves Costa Ureña Prieto who notes in her introduction that in 1790 other sixteenth- and seventeenth-century works on the education of the prince were reedited as well. To Solórzano's emblems, published in Valencia in 1658, Novaes Campos added Portuguese sonnets. As part of the royal library the original text was taken to Rio de Janeiro where it remains. For a discussion of the *Príncipe Perfeito* and its political theory see Iara Lis Carvalho Souza, *Pátria Coroada: O Brasil como Corpo Político Autônomo, 1780–1831* (São Paulo: Editora UNESP, 1998), 21–38. As Carvalho Souza and Ureña Prieto note, the education of Dom João acquired a certain urgency after the death of his brother, the original heir to the throne, and in the context of Maria I's failing health. Solórzano's counsel notwithstanding, the Portuguese monarch's historic interest in "showing himself" stands in contrast to his Spanish counterpart, for seventeenth-century representations of the Spanish monarch reflected a curtailed visibility and accessibility. See Antonio Feros, "'Vicedioses', pero humanos': el drama del Rey," *Cuadernos de Historia Moderna* (Madrid) 14, 111–113.

8. Pereira, *Os filhos*, 55.

9. Luiz António da Silva Souza, *A Discordia Ajustada, Elogio Dramatico para Manifestação do Real Busto do Senhor D. João VI . . .* (Rio de Janeiro: Impressão Régia, 1819), 5–6.

10. Luiz Gonçalves dos Santos, *Memórias para servir para à História do Reino do Brasil* t. 1 (1825) (Belo Horizonte/São Paulo: Itatiaia/EDUSP, 1981), 187–189, 194.

11. Manuel Vieira da Silva, *Reflexões sobre alguns dos Meios Propostos por mais Conducentes para Melhorar o Clima da Cidade . . .* (Rio de Janeiro: Impressão Régia, 1808), in "Hygiene da cidade do Rio de Janeiro," *ABN* 1 (1876), 187–190.

12. Anthony Pagden, *Lords of All the World: Ideologies of Empire in Spain, Britain and France c. 1500–c. 1800* (New Haven: Yale University Press, 1995), 139; Alejandro Cañeque, "The King's Living Image: The Culture and Politics of Viceregal Power in Seventeenth-Century New Spain" (Ph.D. dissertation, New York University, 1999), 300–327.

13. Heloísa Liberalli Bellotto, "O Estado Português no Brasil: Sistema Administrativo e Fiscal," in *Nova História da Expansão Portuguesa. O Império Luso-Brasileiro* v. 8, ed. Maria Beatriz Nizza da Silva (Lisbon: Estampa, 1986), 276.

14. Juan de Solórzano Pereira, *Política Indiana*, cited in Pagden, 140. According to Pagden, Solórzano was referring to America. A somewhat different reading of Solórzano is provided by J.H. Elliott who notes that Solórzano distinguished between "accessory unions," such as that of the Spanish Indies and the Crown of Castile, and the union of *aeque principaliter*, "constituent kingdoms," that explicitly preserved laws and privileges. According to Elliott it was these kingdoms to which Solórzano referred. See J.H. Elliott, "A Europe of Composite Monarchies," *Past and Present* 137 (November 1992), 52–53. In any case, however, it should be noted that, as both Pagden and Elliott concur, Spanish political theorists, including Suárez, Soto, and Juan de Palafox, Bishop of Puebla, were concerned with the degree to which Spanish sovereignty accounted for local privileges and custom in different parts of the monarchy and in so doing ensured that the monarch's domain over these parts remained

intact. In contrast, such a debate was not pursued to the same extent by the Portuguese. Furthermore, what Pagden wishes to stress in the Spanish case—the reaffirmation of "the distinction between the king's real and legal person" for all of the monarchy's dominions—is absent in Portuguese discourse. Consequently, as Rio's residents charged in the 1810s, the absence of the real person of the king had not been filled with an effective legal presence.

15. Frei Francisco de São Carlos, *Oração Sagrada que na Solemne Acção de Graças pelo muito Feliz e Augusto Nascimento da Serenissima Senhora D. Maria da Gloria, Princeza da Beira* . . . (Rio de Janeiro: Impressão Régia, 1819), 21; see also São Carlos, *Oração de Acção de Graças* . . . (Rio de Janeiro: Impressão Régia, 1809), 11. A similar critique of colonial government was made in the *Correio Braziliense,* June and November 1808, in *Antologia do Correio Braziliense,* ed. Barbosa Lima Sobrinho (Rio de Janeiro: Cátedra/Instituto Nacional do Livro, 1977), 19, 49–52. For a discussion of the political expediency of geographic closeness to the king, see António Manuel Hespanha, *La gracia del derecho: economia de la cultura en la edad moderna* (Madrid: Centro de Estudios Constitucionales, 1993), 188.

16. Fernando Teles da Silva Caminha e Meneses, Marquês de Penalva, *Dissertação sôbre as obrigações do vassalo* (Lisbon: Régia Officina Tipographica, 1804), 78.

17. Gonçalves dos Santos, *Memórias* t. 1, 229.

18. Gonçalves dos Santos' *Memórias* includes detailed accounts of all of the royal commemorations in Dom João's Rio de Janeiro. Although Marrócos disparaged the celebrations for the creation of the Kingdom of Brazil, he recognized their intention to imitate "Royal Festivities of Lisbon." See *Cartas de Luiz Joaquim dos Santos Marrocos* (Rio de Janeiro: Biblioteca Nacional/Ministério de Educação e Saude, 1939), 262–263, 311. For recent analysis of these festivities see Ligia Pinheiro, "Portuguese Court Festivities and Dance in Early Nineteenth-Century Monarchical Brazil" (M.A. thesis, Ohio State University, 1998); Carvalho Souza, *Pátria Coroada,* 207–237; Maria Eurydice de Barros Ribeiro, *Os símbolos do poder. Cerimônias e imagens do Estado monárquico no Brasil* (Brasília: Editora UnB, 1995); and Jurandir Malerba, "A corte no exílio. Interpretação do Brasil joanino" (Ph.D. dissertation, University of São Paulo, 1997).

19. Alves and Resende, cited in Alves, *Iconologia,* 89.

20. Viana to Aguiar, May 24, 1810, ANRJ Ministério dos Negócios do Brasil (hereafter MNB) Caixa 6J 78.

21. [Report on reception], March 1808, BNRJ Ms. II-35,4,1, f4.

22. Arnold B. Clayton, "The Life of Tomás Antônio Vilanova Portugal: A Study in the Government of Portugal and Brazil" (Ph.D. dissertation, Columbia University, 1977), 84. On the difficulties of maintaining courtly etiquette see also Malerba, "A corte no exílio," 57.

23. [José Vasconcellos e Souza], Marquês de Bellas, [parecer (plan for reforms)] n.d. [ca. 1808], in Ângelo Pereira, *D. João VI, principe e rei* v. 3 (Lisbon: Empresa Nacional de Publicidade, 1956), 39, 42.

24. Alves, *Iconologia,* 89.

25. Gonçalves dos Santos, *Memórias* t. 1, 185, 228–229.

26. António Manuel Hespanha, "A punição e a graça," in *História de Portugal: O Antigo Regime* v. 4, ed. António Manuel Hespanha (Lisbon: Editorial Estampa, n.d.), 248. As we saw in the last chapter, in early nineteenth-century Rio symbolically enacted justice was joined by attempts to police and to achieve social discipline on an increasingly broader scale.

27. António Felipe Soares de Andrada Brederode, Corregedor do Crime da Corte e Casa, to Sua Alteza Real, November 6, 1812, ANRJ Antiga Seção Histórica (hereafter ASH) Casa da Suplicação Caixa 1707, Antiga Caixa 774, Pacotilha 3. See also "Discurso recitado em Presença de Sua Alteza Real, na Meza do Desembargo do Paço, pelo Desembargador António Rodrigues Velloso de Olveira, Communicado por hum amigo do Autor," *O Patriota* 5 (May 1813); and Decreto, October 22, 1810, for the pardons bestowed on occasion of the wedding of Dom João's daughter, Dona Maria Teresa, with the Spanish prince Dom Pedro Carlos.

28. See "Decreto," February 6, 1818, in *Código Brasiliense, Ou Collecção das Leis, Alvarás, Decretos, Cartas Régias, &c. Promulgadas no Brasil desde a feliz chegada de El Rey Nosso Senhor A Este Reino* (Rio de Janeiro: [Impressão Régia, 1811–1822]). The decree that ended the investigations of the Pernambuco rebellion also ordered sentencing based on what had been substantiated to date and stipulated that, with the exception of the rebellion's alleged leadership, no further arrests would be made.

29. Diogo Ramada Curto, "Ritos e cerimónias da monarquia em Portugal (séculos XVI a XVIII)," in *A Memória da nação*, eds. Francisco Bethencourt and Diogo Ramada Curto (Lisbon: Livraria Sá da Costa, 1991), 232–234, 237. As Curto notes, one seventeenth-century ceremonial protocol explicitly accounted for the appearance of "the poor, the miserable and women" before the monarch. On João V Curto cites Merveilleux's account of 1738.

30. Henry L'Évêque, *Portuguese Costumes* (London: 1814) (Lisbon: INAPA, 1993).

31. "Almanaque da cidade do Rio de Janeiro para o ano de 1811," *RIHGB* 282 (January–March 1969), 108; John Luccock, *Notes on Rio de Janeiro and the southern parts of Brazil; taken during a residence of ten years in that country, from 1808–1818* (London: Samuel Leigh, 1820), 245–246, 558 and L'Évêque, *Portuguese Costumes*. L'Evêque described the routine for the prince regent's audiences: "Every day, at appointed hours, the prince receives, at the palace where he is residing, such of his subjects as necessity obliges to have recourse to him. Besides these special audiences, he once a week grants a general one. The day for this is fixed at the commencement of the year, and announced in the almanack." Along these lines, the almanac of 1811 announced daily audiences and thirteen days of *grande gala* and twenty-five days of *simples gala*, which would probably include the beijamão. Although the almanacs for 1816 and 1817 did not list daily audiences, the numbers for galas are similar.

32. João de Nossa Senhora da Porta Sequeira, *Escola de política ou tratado prático da civilidade portuguesa, com as regras e exemplos do estylo epistolar em todo o genero de cartas* (Rio de Janeiro: Impressão Régia, 1812). Sequeira based his work on a similar French manual by Blanchard. Although the Royal Press edition was the first Brazilian edition of the manual, it was published earlier in Portugal. The second Portuguese edition was published in 1761 in Porto. On the royal audience see pages 67–68 of the 1833 Portuguese edition published in Lisbon by Typografia Rollandia.

33. Luccock, *Notes on Rio de Janeiro*, 558. Luccock recorded that a "poor woman" entered the audience chamber, "lifted her hand," and chastised the prince regent for pardoning the murderer of her husband. It was a scene that, according to Luccock, could "seldom be paralleled in the history of Courts." The intendancy records also include many references to the apparent ease in attending audiences. One Spanish resident of Rio, for example, arrested and then sentenced to be banished from the city for having praised the revolutionaries of Buenos Aires, was able to use a furlough granted so that he could sell his pharmacy "to present himself

to His Royal Highness at the Quinta da Boa Vista with a petition" to defer the date of his departure. See Viana, "Registro do Ofício expedido ao Ministro de Estado dos Negócios Estrangeiros e de Guerra." June 17, 1811, August 11, 1811, October 19, 1811, ANRJ Códice 323 v. 3, f54-54v, f63v-64, f85; Viana, "Registro do Ofício expedido ao Juiz do Crime de São José," October 21, 1811, ANRJ Códice 329 v. 1, f103.

34. [Representação a Sua Alteza Real], [1818], ANRJ MNB Caixa 6J 80.

35. A.P.D.G. *Sketches of Portuguese Life, manners, costume and character* (London: George B. Whittaker, 1826), 174, 179. The author identified himself as a foreign member of Portuguese civil service from 1793 to 1804 who returned to Portugal in the British army during the war. His account, critical and at times sarcastic, also refers to his experiences in Rio de Janeiro. For descriptions of petitions for financial assistance and conflict resolution, see, for example, Viana, "Registro expedido ao Ministro de Estado dos Negócios do Reino," March 2, 1818, and Viana to Vila Nova Portugal, April 16, 1818, ANRJ Códice 323 v. 5, f16, f27v.

36. James Henderson, *A history of the Brazils, comprising its geography, commerce, colonization, aboriginal inhabitants* (London: 1821), cited in Joaquim de Souza Leão Filho, "O Rio de Janeiro de Dom João (1808–1821)," *RIHGB* 276 (July–September 1967), 77. On the viceroy, see Dauril Alden, *Royal Government in Colonial Brazil, with Special Reference to the Administration of the Marquis of Lavradio, Viceroy, 1769–1779* (Berkeley: University of California Press, 1968), 479, 484.

37. On petitioners at the royal chapel see A.P.D.G., *Sketches*, 178–179. On the incident at Magé see Viana, "Registro do Ofício expedido ao Ministro dos Negócios do Brasil," September 4, 1811, ANRJ Códice 323 v. 3, f68v.

38. "Diario do Marquês de Loule," Biblioteca da Ajuda (Lisbon), 54-X-13-(118).

39. According to Viana, an earlier request for permission to establish "coches e seges de posta para Santa Cruz e a Quinta da Boavista" was referred to the Ministro dos Negócios Estrangeiros and granted, but the plan did not come to fruition. See Viana, "Registro da Representação feita a Sua Magestade," January 29, 1817, ANRJ Códice 323 v. 5, f49. On the second proposal see Viana to Tomás António Vila Nova Portugal, June 14, 1818, ANRJ MNB Caixa 6J 81. This plan also included the creation of an *hospedaria* in Santa Cruz. See also Viana to Vila Nova Portugal, February 2, 1819, ANRJ MNB Caixa 6J 81, and February 11, 1819, Códice 323 v. 5, f100, in which Viana suggests that the intendancy could subsidize the carriages. Although another resident also requested permission to provide service to Santa Cruz in 1818, in 1819, when the king stopped going to his retreat in Santa Cruz, the viability of the concession was called into question. See Viana, "Ofício Expedido ao Ministro de Estado dos Negócios do Reino," September 24, 1818, and Viana to Sua Alteza Real, August 26, 1820, ANRJ Códice 323 v. 5, f60 and v. 6, f17.

40. Novaes Campos, *Príncipe Perfeito*, f133, f185.

41. Manuel Joaquim da Mai dos Homens, [requerimento, ca. 1813], ANRJ ASH Desembargo do Paço Caixa 171 Documento 3.

42. Viana, [informe], November 17, 1810, f2v-f3, ANRJ MNB Caixa 6J 78. For contemporary reflections on the king as a "common Father" see also Francisco Ferreira de Azevedo, *Oração de Acção de Graça que no Dia 7 de Março de 1816 Anniversario da Chegada de El Rey Nosso Senhor ao Rio de Janeiro Recitou na Capella Real . . .* (Rio de Janeiro: Impressão Régia, 1816); and Marquês de Penalva, *Dissertação*, 68.

43. São Carlos, *Oração Sagrada . . . pelo muito Feliz e Augusto Nascimento*, 15–16.

44. Pagden, *Lords*, 140; Stuart B. Schwartz, "The Voyage of the Vassals: Royal Power, Noble Obligations, and Merchant Capital before the Portuguese Restoration of Independence, 1624–1640," *American Historical Review* 96, n. 3 (June 1991), 744–745; Ana Cristina Nogueira da Silva and António Manuel Hespanha, "A identidade portuguesa," in *História de Portugal: O Antigo Regime* v. 4, ed. António Manuel Hespanha (Lisbon: Estampa, n.d.), 29–31.

45. Curto, "Ritos e cerimónias," 209–210, 235.

46. As Novaes Campos instructed Dom João, "The King should reward, and give punishment." See *Príncipe Perfeito*, f155; and Hespanha, "La economia de la gracia," in Hespanha, *La gracia del derecho*.

47. Viana to Aguiar, November 29, 1808, ANRJ Códice 318, f123v.

48. Viana, "Registro do Ofício expedido ao Ministro de Estado dos Negócios Estrangeiros e de Guerra," December 6, 1810, ANRJ Códice 323 v. 2, f10. Viana's reports on petitions often cited a defense of *meios ordinários*. Commenting on a request for intervention in a case of eviction, Viana wrote: "it is to not confide in the law, and to be always overburdening the throne with unnecessary measures, because everything is provided for in the law. . . ." See Viana to Vila Nova Portugal, February, 11, 1819, ANRJ MNB Caixa 6J 81; Viana, "Registros do Ofícios expedidos ao Ministro de Estado dos Negócios Estrangeiros e de Guerra," January 15, 1811, and March 29, 1811, ANRJ Códice 323 v.2, f68v and v.3, f35v; and Viana to Vila Nova Portugal, January 5, 1820, ANRJ MNB Caixa 6J 86.

49. Viana to Aguiar, July 2, 1810, ANRJ MNB Caixa 6J 78. See also the *requerimento* of Anacleto Elias Ferreira de Noronha, identified as "alferes." In the early nineteenth century *divórcio* (divorce) was the term used to indicate that an ecclesiastical judge had given permission for husband and wife to live separately and to divide their patrimony. It signified, as Nizza da Silva points out, what would come to be known later as "separation" and did not allow the parties involved to remarry. This was allowed only after attaining an annulment. The supplicants, who were mostly women, typically justified their requests by citing instances of abuse. While the ecclesiastical judge was reviewing the case the wife would be placed in an "honest house." According to Nizza da Silva, requests for divorce rose in the early nineteenth century. Indeed, the new Royal Press published models for petitions for divorce. See Maria Beatriz Nizza da Silva, *Sistema de casamento no Brasil colonial* (São Paulo: Queiroz/EDUSP, 1984), 210–213.

50. John David Parker, "The Tridentine Order and Governance in Late Colonial Brazil, 1792–1821" (Ph.D. dissertation, University of Washington, 1982), 187.

51. Viana to Aguiar, July 2, 1810, ANRJ MNB Caixa 6J 78. Viana was often incensed at the requests of "unworthy" petitioners. In 1820, he angrily counseled the crown to dismiss one man's request for pardon from his banishment to Brazil from Portugal, the "plea with which he surprised the King Our Lord," because of his criminal past and his failure to disclose this past to Dom João. See Viana, "Registro do Ofício expedido ao Ministro de Estado dos Negócios do Reino," February 6, 1820, ANRJ Códice 323 v. 5, f164v.

52. Viana to Vila Nova Portugal, May 1, 1820, ANRJ MNB Caixa 6J 86. See also Viana, "Registro de uma Informação dada ao Ministro de Estado dos Negócios do Reino," October 23, 1818, ANRJ Códice 323 v. 5, f63.

53. Viana, "Registro do Ofício expedido ao Ministro de Estado dos Negócios do Reino [Vila Nova Portugal], November 25, 1820, ANRJ Códice 323 v. 6, f42v-43v. Commenting on one petitioner's request to avoid imprisonment, Viana defended both his case against him and "public" interest by noting that a contrary decision might suggest that he had been bribed. See Viana, "Registro do Ofício expedido ao Ministro de Estado dos Negócios do Reino," March 2, 1818, ANRJ Códice 323 v. 5, f16.

54. Vila Nova Portugal cited in Clayton, "The Life of Tomás Antônio Vilanova Portugal," 93.

55. Hespanha, *La Gracia*, 165.

56. See Viana to Aguiar, March 10, 1813, ANRJ MNB Caixa 6J 79. Viana dismissed a Spanish cleric's efforts to avoid expatriation by noting that "he had the nerve to go to the Quinta da Boa Vista and appear before His Royal Highness," and he judged a case of destruction of property to be "so trivial that it excludes the recourse to extraordinary measures" because the law "had marked a civil action for such a cause." See Viana, "Registro do Ofício expedido ao Ministro de Estado dos Negócios do Brasil [Vila Nova Portugal]," November 14, 1820, ANRJ Códice 323 v. 6, f37. For a case judged to be vengeful see Viana, "Registro do Ofício expedido ao Ministro de Estado dos Negócios de Ultramar," December 1, 1814, ANRJ Códice 323 v. 2.

57. This defense had precedent. In the 1770s, the Portuguese crown had taken major steps to protect patriarchal authority, ruling that sons could not marry without their father's permission. See Muriel Nazzari, *Disappearance of the Dowry: Women, Families and Social Change in São Paulo, Brazil, 1600–1900* (Stanford: Stanford University Press, 1991), 130–134.

58. Viana to Aguiar, December 8, 1810, ANRJ MNB Caixa 6J 78. In a number of cases, Viana also recommended the "correction" of disobedient sons on behalf of their widowed mothers, emphasizing the need for public order rather than the protection of paternal authority per se. See Viana, "Registros dos Ofícios expedidos ao Ministro de Negócios Estangeiros e de Guerra," July 11, 1814, and August 7, 1814, ANRJ Códice 323 v. 4.

59. Viana, "Registro do Ofício expedido ao Ministro de Estado dos Negócios Estrangeiros e de Guerra," February 14, 1809, ANRJ Códice 318, f171v. For additional cases see Viana, "Registro do Ofício expedido ao Ministro e Secretário de Estado dos Negócios do Reino," October 3, 1809, ANRJ Códice 323 v. 1, f142v; December 8, 1810, Códice 323 v. 2, f22; March 17, 1814 and March 30, 1814, ANRJ Códice 323 v. 4; Viana to Aguiar, July 11, 1814, ANRJ MNB Caixa 6J 79; and Viana, "Registro do Ofício expedido ao Ministro de Estado dos Negócios Ultramarinos," April 15, 1815, ANRJ Códice 323 v. 4.

60. See Viana, "Registro do Ofício expedido ao Ministro de Estado dos Negócios do Brasil," August 1, 1812, ANRJ Códice 323 v. 3, f112; Viana, "Registro do Ofício expedido ao [Ministro Vila Nova Portugal]," April 2, 1819 and July 10, 1819, ANRJ Códice 323 v. 5, f114v and f122v. In the first case, initiated with a husband's request for the recolhimento of his wife, the crown intervened when ecclesiastical procedures had been exhausted. In the second case, regarding a father and his daughter, Viana argued that the matter was to be solved with "mere and indispensable police" rather than by the sovereign; in the third, concerning the marriage of a person in jail, Viana insisted on the poor reputation of the supplicants. In another case, Viana dismissed a husband's plea to have his wife cloistered due to her drinking by simply instructing him to more "carefully supervise his household." See Viana, "Registro

do Ofício expedido ao Ministro do Estado dos Negócios do Brasil," November 18, 1813, ANRJ Códice 323 v. 3.

61. Viana to Aguiar, April 15, 1815, ANRJ MNB Caixa 6J 79. For other cases of father-son conflict and military service as a correction, see Viana, "Registros dos Ofícios expedidos ao Ministro de Estado dos Negócios do Brasil," December 17, 1815, December 19, 1815, January 16, 1816 in ANRJ Códice 323 v. 4.

62. Viana, "Registro do Ofício expedido ao Ministro de Estado dos Negócios do Reino," October 21, 1809, ANRJ Códice 323 v. 1, f161; Viana, "Registro do Ofício expedido ao Ministro de Estado dos Negócios do Reino," November 18, 1813, ANRJ Códice 323 v. 4.

63. See Viana, "Registro do ofício expedido ao Ministro de Estado dos Negócios do Brasil," October 17, 1815 and January 3, 1816, Códice 323 v. 4. Viana dismissed husbands' pleas to intern their wives in recolhimentos when the husband had exhibited "poor conduct." He also deemed certain women unworthy of recolhimentos, although the one at Taipú was regarded as more appropriate for women of the popular classes than the patrician Misericórdia and the Ajuda convent. Viana also recognized that the recolhimento was intended to preserve and restore family honor, rather than to provide punishment per se. Consequently, he often noted, Rio needed a women's jail. See also Viana "Ofício expedido ao Ministro de Estado dos Negócios do Brasil," April 15, 1814, and November 18, 1814, ANRJ Códice 323 v. 4; Viana, "Ofício expedido ao Ministro de Estado dos Negócios do Reino," January 29, 1820, ANRJ Códice 323 v. 5, f163.

64. Viana to Aguiar, November 16, 1812, ANRJ MNB Caixa 6J 79. Viana made similar claims about sparing a husband from the public disclosure of his wife's adultery in legal proceedings in the case of João da Silva Guimarães by advising the crown to send his wife's alleged lover to serve in the army in Rio Grande do Sul. See Viana, "Ofício expedido ao Ministro de Estado dos Negócios do Reino," January 25, 1819, ANRJ Códice 323 v. 5, f92.

65. See Viana, "Registro do Ofício expedido ao Ministro e Secretario de Estado dos Negócios do Reino," March 13, 1818, ANRJ Códice 323 v. 5, f21. Here Viana wrote to counsel the crown to grant the request of José António de Mattos that his nephew, to whom he was "at times a father," be banished to India rather than sentenced to death for attempting to poison him.

66. See the case of Maria Clara de Jesus in Viana, "Registro do Ofício expedido ao Ministro e Secretário de Estado dos Negócios do Reino," May 28, 1811, ANRJ Códice 323 v. 3, f49; and Viana, "Registro do Ofício expedido ao Ministro de Estado dos Negócios do Reino," October 6, 1816, ANRJ Códice 323 v. 4.

67. Viana, "Registro do Ofício expedido ao Ministro e Secretário de Estado dos Negócios do Brasil," August 3, 1811, ANRJ Códice 323 v. 3, f61v. By 1814 Anacleto was in trouble again for not providing the required financial support for his wife's confinement in the Misericórdia. See Viana, "Registro do Ofício expedido ao Ministro e Secretário de Estado dos Negócios Estrangeiros e de Guerra," July 30, 1814, ANRJ Códice 323 v. 4.

68. In one case, for example, involving conflict among a grandmother and her grandsons and an apparent abduction of her daughters, Viana counseled the crown to dismiss the petition because it was "all business within the family." Viana, "Registro da Representação feita a Sua Magestade" January 29, 1817, ANRJ Códice 323 v. 5, f49.

69. Viana to Aguiar, October 26, 1814, ANRJ MNB Caixa 6J 79. Children, Viana ex-

plained, "are given to the mother until the age of three, because only in her is entrusted *criação* (raising the child); after that the matter concerns *educação* (upbringing), and this is always supervised by fathers." The *Novo Dicionário Aurélio da Língua Portuguesa* defines *criação* as both "the period of childhood" (*meninice*) and of "breast-feeding, lactation."

70. Viana to Aguiar, December 24, 1814, ANRJ MNB Caixa 6J 79.

71. Viana to Vila Nova Portugal, April, 27, 1820, ANRJ MNB Caixa 6J 86.

72. Viana made his case against one petitioner by noting that his family's "pride" had reached the point of contempt for public authority, exhibiting "such vanity that it was necessary to refute it." See Viana, "Registro expedido ao Ministro de Estado dos Negócios do Reino," March 2, 1818, ANRJ Códice 323 v. 5, f16.

73. Manuel de Oliveira Lima, *Dom João VI no Brasil (1808–1821)* (1908) (Rio de Janeiro: José Olympio, 1945), v. 1, 129. On the petitions of slaves and people of color in Lisbon see A.J.R. Russell-Wood, "'Acts of Grace': Portuguese Monarchs and Their Subjects of African Descent in Eighteenth-Century Brazil," *Journal of Latin American Studies* 32 (2000): 307–332.

74. Viana, "Registro do Ofício expedido ao Ministro e Secretário da Repartição da Guerra," May 23, 1808, ANRJ Códice 318, f16v.

75. Cited in Mary C. Karasch, *Slave Life in Rio de Janeiro, 1808–1850* (Princeton: Princeton University Press, 1987), 239: "Nosso Sinhô chegô, Cativêiro já acabô."

76. On the process of manumission and the *carta de alforria*, the legal document that recognized manumission, see Karasch, *Slave Life*, Chapter 11; Leila Mezan Algranti, *O feitor ausente: Estudos sobre a escravidão urbana no Rio de Janeiro, 1808–1822* (Petrópolis, Rio de Janeiro: Vozes, 1988), 94, 113, 116–117; and Katia M. de Queirós Mattoso, *To Be a Slave in Brazil, 1550–1888* (1979) (New Brunswick: Rutgers University Press, 1986), 145–149; 155–176.

77. Russell-Wood, "'Acts of Grace.'"

78. Viana to Aguiar, June 4, 1812, ANRJ MNB Caixa 6J 79.

79. Viana to Vila Nova Portugal, September 21, 1817, ANRJ MNB Caixa 6J 83. Boaventura justified his request by citing his heroic action against some Frenchmen who attempted to capture a slave ship sailing from Mozambique. According to Viana, Boaventura had made his plea earlier before the arrival of the court to Viana himself, when he served as *ouvidor geral do crime* (circuit judge). "After time passed," Viana wrote, "he had means to present himself to the King Our Lord at the Royal Quinta da Boa Vista, and he deigned to send him to me."

80. Viana to Vila Nova Portugal, December 17, 1818, ANRJ MNB Caixa 6J 80. Commenting on the petition of Damasio Dias, Viana wrote, "Because of a natural instinct all seek recourse in the Clemency of His Majesty. . . ." Viana made clear his denial of slaves' legal and political personhood in the case of an owner who had killed his slave and then requested a pardon, cited above. "These are cases in which a royal pardon may apply," he wrote, "because there is no offended party besides justice." See Viana, "Registro do Ofício expedido ao Ministro dos Negócios do Brasil," September 4, 1811, ANRJ Códice 323 v. 3, f68v. In the eighteenth century, royal officials in the colony of Brazil similarly sought to discredit slave petitioners and the process of petitioning the crown to secure manumission. See Russell-Wood, "'Acts of Grace,'" 321–322.

81. Viana to Aguiar, March 5, 1814, ANRJ MNB Caixa 6J 79. See also the supporting

document from Frei José de São Francisco de Sales, Procurador do Convento de Santo António, to João de Campos da Silveira, June 29, 1813.

82. Viana to Vila Nova Portugal, July 11, 1819, ANRJ MNB Caixa 6J 81. On this case see also Algranti, *O feitor*, 107.

83. Vila Nova Portugal cited in Clayton, "The Life of Tomás Antônio Vilanova Portugal," 95.

84. Viana to Vila Nova Portugal, December 17, 1818, ANRJ MNB Caixa 6J 80.

85. Viana to Aguiar, January 25, 1813, ANRJ MNB Caixa 6J 79.

86. Viana to Aguiar, May 6, 1815, ANRJ MNB Caixa 6J 79. When Estevão renewed his quest for royal intervention in 1817, now appealing to his military service in Montevideo, Viana affirmed his own initial claims that he could use the courts but insisted that he had no new rights for royal intervention. See Viana, "Registro do Ofício expedido ao Ministro de Estado dos Negócios do Reino, July 29, 1817 and August 29, 1817, ANRJ Códice 323 v. 4. See also the cases of Boaventura and Damasio Dias, cited above, and Viana's report on the petition of Pedro Congo, in which he also sided against their requests but advised that this did not preclude a quest for a *carta de liberdade* "by way of ordinary channels . . . for which the law provides." See Viana to Vila Nova Portugal, September 21, 1817, ANRJ MNB Caixa 6J 83; Viana, "Ofício expedido ao Ministro [Vila Nova Portugal]," December 5, 1818, ANRJ Códice 323 v. 5, f83v; Viana, [Ofício expedido a Vila Nova Portugal], August 19, 1819, ANRJ Códice 323 v. 5, f134v. In response to Dias' second petition that contradicted the facts of the first, Viana responded with harsher criticism of Dias' claims in general. See Viana to Vila Nova Portugal, December 17, 1818, ANRJ MNB Caixa 6J 80. On slaves as property owners see Manuela Carneiro da Cunha, "Silences of the Law: Customary Law and Positive Law on the Manumission of Slaves in 19th-Century Brazil," *History and Anthropology* v. 1 (1995), 430, published in Portuguese as idem, "Sobre os silêncios da lei: lei costumeira e positiva nas alforrias de escravos no Brasil do século XIX," in Carneiro da Cunha, *Antropologia do Brasil: mito, história, e etnicidade* (São Paulo: Brasiliense, [1988]). As Carneiro da Cunha notes, slaves had a "peculium"; they had no *de jure* property rights, but *de facto* their ownerships were recognized, including in particular ways of branding their cattle.

87. Viana to Vila Nova Portugal, December 5, 1820, ANRJ Códice 323 v. 6, f51v. The juiz de fora was a circuit judge. A year earlier, commenting on a particularly convoluted case involving a disputed grant of freedom for two youths he described as *mulatinhos*, Viana counseled the crown to jail the owner who had challenged a court decision in their favor with a petition filled with lies and suggested as well that the owner owed the youths compensation for the work they performed for him following their *de jure* grant of liberty. See Viana, "[Ofício expedido a Vila Nova Portugal]," July 14, 1819, ANRJ Códice 323 v. 5, f124.

88. See summary of the case in António Luiz Pereira da Cunha, "Ofício expedido ao Ministro de Estado [Conde dos Arcos]," May 24, 1821, ANRJ Códice 323 v. 6, 71v.

89. The term used by Viana to refer to this temporary custodial arrangement was *depósito* and could apply to movable property in general. See also Viana to Desembargador Luiz Pedreira Couto Ferraz, January 15, 1819, ANRJ Códice 330 v. 1. On depósito see Keila Grinberg, *Liberata, a lei da ambigüidade: as ações de liberdade da corte de apelação do Rio de Janeiro no século XIX* (Rio de Janeiro: Dumará, 1994), 22, where she explains "the contract of de-

pósito" as "one in which someone is obligated to guard and then restitute, when it is demanded, whatever movable object which from another he should receive." Depósito was also used by ecclesiastical authorities during "divorce" proceedings.

90. Viana, "Ofício expedido ao Ministro de Estado dos Negócios do Reino," January 25, 1821 and February 9, 1821, ANRJ Códice 323 v. 6, f53v, f63v.

91. Augusto Teixeira de Freitas, *Consolidação das leis civis*, cited in Robert Edgar Conrad, *Children of God's Fire: A Documentary History of Black Slavery in Brazil* (University Park: The Pennsylvania State University Press, 1984), 235.

92. Viana to Vila Nova Portugal, October 11, 1820, ANRJ Códice 323 v. 6, f36-36v. The possibility of hiding out at the Quinta is also suggested in the case of Alexandre António Teixeira, a free person, who reportedly avoided arrest by going there "to the kitchens and an adjacent house" on the estate. See Viana, "Registro expedido [a Vila Nova Portugal]," ANRJ Códice 323 v. 5, f18v.

93. Dona Aguida Francisca de Queiros Malheiros, [petition, ca. 1809], ANRJ MNB Caixa 6J 78, f1v.

94. On slaves' relations with courts in Brazil see Grinberg, *Liberata*, and Lenine Nequete, *O Escravo na jurisprudência brasileira: magistratura e ideologia no segundo reinado* (Porto Alegre: n.p., 1988). Although both deal with the later nineteenth century they also address colonial legislation and precedents.

95. Viana [parecer], April 19, 1809, ANRJ MNB Caixa 6J 78.

96. See the case of Estevão de Jesus described in Viana to Aguiar, May 6, 1815, ANRJ MNB Caixa 6J 79. Estevão argued that he could not pursue his dispute through meios ordinários because Marinho was "rich and powerful." Karasch cites a later case in which the supplicant's "miserable condition" was put forth as a reason to circumvent established judicial process. See Karasch, *Slave Life*, 339.

97. Algranti, *O feitor*, 113.

98. [Petition, ca. 1812], ANRJ ASH Desembargo do Paço Caixa 680 Documento 8: "At the Royal Feet of Your Royal Highness, the miserable Francisco Rodrigues, Rodrigo, Inacio, Feliciano appeal . . . all persons of black color, and descendants of one Paula Rodrigues da Costa Reis of the Angola Nation. . . ."

99. The intendancy brokered conflicts among family members, neighbors, and, in some cases, between owners and slaves by requiring the interested parties to sign a *termo do bem viver* (an agreement to live in peace). See Leila Mezan Algranti, *Honradas e devotas: mulheres da Colônia: Condição feminina nos conventos e recolhimentos do Sudeste do Brasil, 1750–1822* (Rio de Janeiro/Brasília: José Olympio/EDUNB, 1993), 126–127; and Marcos de Freitas Reis, "A intendência geral da polícia da corte e do estado do Brasil: os termos de bem viver e a ação de Paulo Fernandes Viana," *Anais da II Reunião da Sociedade Brasileira de Pesquisa Histórica (SBPH)* (São Paulo: SBPH, 1993), 95–100.

100. Viana to Vila Nova Portugal, January 4, 1820, ANRJ MNB Caixa 6J 86.

101. Viana to Aguiar, June 4, 1812, ANRJ MNB Caixa 6J 79. Algranti also comments on the case. My reading of the document differs somewhat. See *O feitor*, 111. Compare this case with the intendant's report on Tiburcio Gomes de Sa's petition for intervention against a series of judicial decisions against his quest for liberty. See Viana, "[Ofício expedido ao] Secretário de Estado dos Negócios do Reino," May 22, 1819, ANRJ Códice 323 v. 5, f119.

102. Viana, "Ofício expedido ao Ministro de Estado dos Negócios do Reino" ANRJ Códice 323 v. 6, f53v.

103. Viana to Aguiar, June 4, 1812, ANRJ MNB Caixa 6J 79.

104. Throughout the nineteenth century Brazilian law remained "silent" on the question of slaves' rights to manumission. See Carneiro da Cunha, "Silences of the Law," 438. Carneiro da Cunha argues that these legal silences served to keep manumission under private control (as a function of the owner's "generosity"), which, in turn, bolstered relations of dependency among owners, slaves, and former slaves. She also concludes that "the State" did not mediate the relations between owners and slaves as earlier observers and scholars had claimed. Whereas the intendant's correspondence suggests that in the 1810s this question was actively debated, the lack of legalized mediation also reinforced the image of a powerful royal authority. In other words, the king both defended the law and possessed the power to fill its silences and contradict or affirm customary practices.

105. José dos Passos, [petition, 1817], ANRJ MNB Caixa 6J 83. When a "black man" named Alexandre petitioned to have his manumission confirmed Viana similarly reviewed the circumstances, endorsed the manumission, and declared the case closed. See Viana, "Registro do Ofício dirigido ao Ministro e Secretário de Estado dos Negócios do Brasil," March 15, 1815, ANRJ Códice 323 v. 4.

106. Viana argued that Policena, who was also ill, should be appraised and, with her owner compensated accordingly, given a letter of liberty. See "Bairro da Se . . . Sumário . . . acerca das sevícias feitas por Dona Anna Joaquina Mesquita a sua escrava Policena, parda [feito por] Desembargador Manuel Pedro Gomes," ANRJ MNB Caixa 6J 81, including witness testimony and Viana to Sua Alteza Real, November 16, 1818.

107. Jacques Etienne Victor Arago, *Promenade Autour du Monde. . .* , cited in Karasch, *Slave Life*, 339.

108. Viana, "Ofício expedido ao Ministro de Estado dos Negócios do Reino" February 13, 1821, ANRJ Códice 323 v. 6, f66v. A following opinion was offered by João Ignacio da Cunha [intendant], "Ofício expedido ao Ministro de Estado dos Negócios do Reino," October 19, 1821, ANRJ Códice 323 v. 6, f93v.

109. Algranti, *O feitor*, 113.

110. Viana to Vila Nova Portugal, December 17, 1818, ANRJ MNB Caixa 6J 80. For a comparative view of slavery and the political culture of monarchy see Robert Olwell, *Masters, Slaves and Subjects: The Culture of Power in the South Carolina Low Country, 1740–1790* (Ithaca: Cornell University Press, 1998).

111. João José Reis, "Quilombos e revoltas escravas no Brasil," *Revista USP* (Universidade de São Paulo) 28 (January–February 1995–96), 32–33. The encounter between African and European conceptions of kingship was rendered performatively in the election of kings of the Congo, noted in Chapter 4, as well as in African embassies. One such embassy from the Kingdom of Dahomey attempted to present itself to the court in Rio, but made it only as far as Bahia. See Pierre Verger, "Uma rainha africana mãe de santo em São Luiz," *Revista USP* (Junho–Agosto 1990): 154–157.

112. The potential contradictions between colonialism and absolutism were evident to royal minister Vila Nova Portugal. In commentary on a conflict over housing, he counseled that "expressions of disregard due to difference of color" were "not permissible in documents

issued by Public Authority" because they privileged hierarchies other than that of monarch and vassal. See Vila Nova Portugal cited in Clayton, "The Life of Tomás Antônio Vilanova Portugal," 94.

113. Mello e Souza, "Dialética da malandragem," 71, 74, 82.

SIX

"Império Florescente":
REMAKING THE PORTUGUESE EMPIRE

"YOUR MAJESTY'S RESIDENCE IN BRAZIL," PROCLAIMED THE PORTUGUESE DIPLOMAT
José Anselmo Correa Henriques in 1816, "having made from this vast continent a
flourishing empire (*império florescente*), is the work of the most perfect politics that
human understanding has created."[1] Thus invoking the image of American power
and prosperity, Correa Henriques in effect recapitulated the expectations for renewal
shared by exiles and Rio de Janeiro's residents alike. As we have seen, they argued
that in the wake of the transfer of the court, the political and moral integrity of the
Portuguese nation could be restored and the Portuguese monarchy could be more
formidable than ever. In constructing the new, virtuous, and allegiant city and royal
court of Rio de Janeiro, royal officials, newcomers, and residents then made manifest
this renewal and prosperity, and affirmed that the American future rested on the vin-
dication of their rights as vassals as much as a defense of the sovereign's authority.

Yet Correa Henriques was most concerned about the conditions for prosperity
beyond Rio de Janeiro, in the empire as a whole, and with the political power that
both local and imperial prosperity would provide the Portuguese crown. How were
the imperial dimensions of renewal and the promise of wealth and well-being, invoked by the Marquês de Bellas even before the exiles' arrival at Brazilian shores, to be
achieved? How could an empire divided by war and an extraordinary and controversial relocation of the royal court "flourish"? How could the empire overcome the end
of the "old colonial system" that the transfer of the court produced? This chapter examines these questions as they were asked and answered in Rio de Janeiro in the 1810s.

As Correa Henriques own *memorial* attests, the politics of empire encompassed
a range of ideas and, consequently, inspired debate. On the one hand, these politics
sought to reconcile a counterrevolutionary politics with the undeniably "new order
of things" that recent events had produced. Such a reconciliation was achieved, I argue, with a redefinition of boundaries within the empire in which tradition and history provided both rhetorical means and ends. In creating a "United Kingdom" royal
officials offered a vision of a new status quo in which the elimination of political

hierarchies among the different parts of the empire was presented as the culmination of the Portuguese monarchy's history. Change, in other words, was defined as having strengthened rather than diminished the monarch's authority. The opening of Brazil's ports and the "new science" of political economy, in turn, were hailed for having dismantled the hierarchical colonial economy, thus allowing for a truly empire-wide prosperity. As the statesman and political economist José Silva Lisboa argued, this new openness, like the United Kingdom, provided for stronger ties among the empire's constituent parts as well. It restored the original meaning of empire, and the spirit of the glorious empire in Asia, that had been thwarted by recent politics.

On the other hand, the ideal of "restoration" notwithstanding, the imperial politics of the 1810s also produced and then embraced circumstances for which tradition and history could not entirely account. For, as Correa Henriques lamented, constructing the *império florescente* meant contending with another imperial imperative, as compelling as it was contestable: British merchants and their quest to remake "the Brazils" into what the British statesman Canning described as "an emporium for British manufactures destined for the consumption of the whole of South America."[2] Consequently, even as royal officials and memorialists sought to establish the most solid basis for unity in the empire's history, in Rio de Janeiro the British presence and the new practices of empire that this presence signaled appeared to undermine both unity and the promise of prosperity.

THE "UNITED KINGDOM": THE QUEST FOR IMPERIAL UNITY AND THE TRIUMPH OF MONARCHY IN THE NEW WORLD

In 1815 the Portuguese crown bestowed upon Brazil the title of *reino* (kingdom).[3] With the corresponding change in the royal title—the first in 300 years—Dom João became the first, and ultimately the last, sovereign of the "United Kingdom of Portugal, Brazil and the Algarve." The new title, as the royal charter noted, was already in use at the Congress of Vienna, where Portuguese representatives thus evaded awkward references to the prince regent's "colonial" residence. As the statesmen José da Silva Lisboa explained, it was "absurd to consider as a Colony the *Sovereign's Land of Residence*." Indeed, with the transfer of the court, one Portuguese expatriate wrote to minister Vila Nova Portugal, "the politics of Europe and perhaps of the universe changed" because the prince regent had given a certain "*tom*" (character) to the New World, making "the name colony disappear." In other words, the new title simply affirmed what to many was already evident: the prince regent's presence in Rio alone ended Brazil's former subordinate position within the Portuguese empire.[4]

Yet, as Silva Lisboa and others argued as well, both the transfer of the court and the subsequent designation of Brazil as a kingdom needed to be considered as resulting from, rather than leading to, a change in Brazil's status. If the sovereign's residence could not be regarded as a colony, it was also "absurd," Silva Lisboa wrote, to regard Brazil as a "simple Commercial Factory" or an "uncultivated Tropical *Sesmaria*" (royal land grant). As we saw in Chapter 1, even before the prince regent's arrival at Rio eighteenth-century reformers, such as Silva Lisboa's patron, the Minister of Foreign Affairs Rodrigo de Souza Coutinho, had argued that Brazil's size and natural resources made it the "most essential" part of the monarchy. Whereas geography, or what Silva Lisboa described as "the geological system," had relegated Brazil to the category of "appendix of the territory, albeit venerable, of the *Estado-Pai*" (Father-State), with the outbreak of the Peninsular War it had become apparent that Brazil itself contained the means to safeguard the Estado-Pai. Within the American continent, he asserted, the Portuguese monarchy could "build a towering front so as to gain respect from friendly Nations, and expel the envy and malignance of any Instigators of Public Disorder." In granting the title of kingdom, the prince regent formally acknowledged this truth.[5]

As memorialists and officials weighed these various motives behind the royal charter, all agreed that for the Portuguese monarchy the end of its American "colonies" did not mean the end of its empire. The redenomination was conceived as a measure that indeed strengthened, rather than weakened, the ties between Portugal and Brazil. While the terms "conquest," "possession," and, in the eighteenth century, "colony," were part of what Silva Lisboa described as a "vulgar nomenclature, that impolitically separated into distinct classes and castes, Vassals of the same Sovereign," the charter designating Brazil as a "kingdom" was, on the contrary, superior "in motive and effect" to even the English Magna Carta. For, as Silva Lisboa explained, it reflected a "new conciliatory System" that nurtured a "Spirit of Nationality" and invigorated the "homogeneous Political Body of the Monarchy."[6] Evoking an earlier reformism that had sought to ensure the unification of what Souza Coutinho referred to in 1787 as "all the parts that constituted the whole," Dom João "consolidated" the empire, one preacher proclaimed, by bringing "the principles of social life" to "the most distant parts of [this] political Body."[7] Thus, to further convey this understanding of the empire as what Correa Henriques described as "a single moral and political dominion,"[8] the royal charter not only established that Brazil itself was a kingdom, but also reasserted the empire's inherent unity by simultaneously defining Brazil as one part of the "one and only Kingdom" (*um só e único Reino*), the "United Kingdom" (*Reino Unido*), of the Portuguese monarch.

This fundamental preeminence of the United Kingdom cohered with the ad hoc nature of administrative change in the 1810s. Although powerful institutions of imperial scope, such as the *Desembargo do Paço* (Tribunal of the High Court), the

Casa de Suplicação do Brasil (Court of Appeals), and the *Erário Real* (Royal Treasury), were re-created in Rio de Janeiro, in chartering the Kingdom of Brazil the crown did not seek to create an autonomous administrative unit. Judicial and bureaucratic jurisdictions in the north and northeastern provinces of Brazil remained as divided between Rio de Janeiro and Lisbon as they were before the transfer of the court. While this may have amounted to, as one historian has recently argued, a "failure to consolidate the new kingdom,"[9] it also reflected the crown's vision of and primary commitment to the "homogeneous" whole. "One political body," embodied in the layers of bureaucracy that stretched to and from Portugal and Brazil and beyond, remained more important than any one of its parts. As a new imperial discourse and practice the United Kingdom thus affirmed the change in Brazil's status produced by the transfer of the court by giving it a legal dimension, and defined that change as having served a fundamentally conservative goal: the triumph of a unified, historic empire.

In delineating the new imperial status quo, royal officials and memorialists also responded to a question asked throughout the contemporary Atlantic world: How to represent unprecedented events?[10] In this case, how to represent the end of the European-American hierarchy within the Portuguese world in a way that reconstituted rather than undermined the historic empire? One answer came a year after the prince regent issued the charter when the United Kingdom was given a simple, yet ultimately enduring, visual expression in a new coat of arms (Figure 10). The Portuguese monarchy's ancient heraldry, the *quinas*—five small coats of arms forming one large coat of arms inaugurated in the reign of Afonso III (1245–1279)—filled the center of a blue and gold sphere, "the arms of [Rio's] City Council." Above both the heraldry and the sphere stood a crown.[11] This iconographic fusion, as the royal charter sanctioning the new seal explained, was a reflection of the "perfect union and identity"of the residents of Portugal, the Algarve, and Brazil. As the seal also made manifest, this union was guaranteed by the crown, a truly imperial force above all, and therefore greater than any one of its territories.[12] Or, as Correa Henriques asserted in his memorial written that same year, in the Portuguese empire "the integrity of dominion" belonged only to the "permanent moral force" of the sovereign.

Here, however, Correa Henriques was not writing to defend the United Kingdom alone. The death of Maria I in 1816 and the prince regent's imminent succession had given the questions of sovereignty and of the sovereign's "land" and "place" a particular urgency. For Correa Henriques, the unprecedented ascension to the throne of a European sovereign in the New World was justified precisely because of his empire's "wholeness." As long as the prince regent lived within his "land or dominion" (*terreno ou dominação*), Correa Henriques explained, recalling Luiz da Cunha's justifications for a transfer of the court, his residence would be "the seat of the general union, from which emanated a primary force that gives him power as a

ESCUDO REAL DO REINO UNIDO DE PORTUGAL, BRASIL E ALGARVES

FIGURE 10: Jean Baptiste Debret, "Escudo Real do Reino Unido de Portugal, Brasil e Algarves," from Ângelo Pereira, *D. João VI, principe e rei* v. 3 (Lisbon: Empresa Nacional de Publicidade, 1956). Even as the coat of arms was a symbol of the "perfect union and identity" of the residents of Portugal, the Algarve, and Brazil, guaranteed by the powerful Portuguese monarch, it could be read, as Ana Cristina Araújo has explained, as the consecration of the monarchy's American destiny.

political body to govern." In other words, because the kingdom was "united" and because Portuguese law did not recognize a "certain place" for succession within the "whole of the dominion," the place where the ceremony took place, as well as the monarch's residence, had no particular political-legal consequence.[13] Two years later, commemorating the tenth anniversary of Dom João's arrival at Rio, the royal preacher Januário de Cunha Barbosa offered a similarly reassuring explanation of imperial integrity in the wake of the transfer of the court: "the nature of bodies does not change with a change of center."[14]

In 1818, then, the Acclamation, as the rite of royal succession was called, was celebrated in Rio de Janeiro as the triumph of both royal authority and the indivisible and historic unity of the three kingdoms. The novelty of the commemorations within the city, the "magnificence and beauty never before seen in Rio de Janeiro," was circumscribed by that which was old: a ritual of monarchical power that originated with Afonso Henriques (1128–1185), the first king of Portugal. On a large veranda, "according to ancient custom," Dom João both took and received oaths of loyalty.[15] In Dom João's procession to the royal chapel and in the festivities that followed, sumptuously decorated chambers and facades, triumphal arches, fireworks, music and allegorical tributes evoked the empire's history and, as the official chronicler suggested, the "ecstacy" that both the United Kingdom and the Acclamation produced in all of its vassals.[16]

Yet, even as the United Kingdom and the Acclamation presented a conservative discursive framework in which the historical monarchy ensured the unity of the empire, this framework was also sufficiently broad as to allow for competing under-

FIGURE 11: Jean Baptiste Debret, "Vue de l'exterieur de la galerie de l'acclamation," from Debret, *Voyage Pittoresque et Historique au Brésil, sejour d'un Artiste Français au Brésil* v. 3 (Paris: Firmin Didot Fréres, 1839). Copy and permission obtained from the Print Collection, Miriam and Ira D. Wallach Division of Arts, Prints and Photographs, The New York Public Library, Astor, Lenox and Tilden Foundations. Following the ritual of acclamation and oath taking, and before departing for the royal chapel, Debret explained, the new king stood at the balcony "to show himself to the people and to receive his first tributes."

standings of the consequences of recent events. Recourse to history in defining royal authority and empire in the New World, in particular, produced its own crisis of representation. For while history revealed that Brazil was, as Silva Lisboa wrote as a royal censor in 1818, "the amplification of the Mother Country (*Mai Pátria*) for the Lusitanian Monarchy [obtained] through just titles of discovery, occupation and conquest in accordance with the laws of nations,"[17] with the transfer of the court this historical amplification of Portugal appeared to have reached an ultimate conclusion. The result was, as one playwright suggested the same year, bewildering. "Are you not my conquest?" asks the allegory of Portugal, heroic conqueror, of Brazil, "an Indian richly dressed in feathers" and "reanimated" in the "August Presence" of the king, in a drama presented to commemorate the Acclamation. Although the past could not be "denied," Brazil responds, the status of conquest nevertheless "was ended" by the Portuguese monarch and his grace of making Brazil a kingdom. The reconciliation of these differences and "discord," both the allegories and the audience then learn, depended on Portugal's and Brazil's recognition of the need to "bury once and for all ancient quarrels."[18] Rather than an indisputable lesson of history, the consequences of the transfer of the court—the end of Brazil as a conquest—would have to be negotiated.

This challenge of reconciling the past and the future, as well as the potential for equivocation, was also summarized in the title of one report on the "Empire of Brazil, *or* New Lusitanian Empire" (emphasis is mine).[19] On the one hand, the "Empire of Brazil" and the "New Lusitanian Empire" were synonymous expressions of both the historic Portuguese ideal of political renewal and the European project to civilize the New World. Thus, as Silva Lisboa argued, "the Union of [the crown's] States, with equitable political Rights" was "the most expedient and decisive Consolidation of the Greatness and Stability of the Lusitanian Monarchy, and of the place that it deserves in the Order of the Powers who most influence the progress of civilization in both Hemispheres."[20] As Gonçalves dos Santos allegorized the culmination of this progress and the moment of union, Brazil, represented by an Indian, shed his past, "the ribbons and feathers with which he was adorned until December 16, 1815," in order to receive the monarchy. America's "former nakedness" was finally covered by the "brilliant crown" and "the royal cloak" offered by the prince regent. America, in other words was once again redeemed from savagery and paganism by the beneficent tutelage of Europe.[21]

On the other hand, however, the "Empire of Brazil" and the "New Lusitanian Empire" could be read as alternatives: America or Europe. The new coat of arms itself, as Ana Cristina Araújo has noted, embodied this tension. As "a symbolic recapitulation of the history of the Portuguese colonial empire," she explains, the sphere suggested not only the expansive Portuguese dominions, but also the emerging

power of Brazil. While the *quinas*, in turn, recalled Portugal's glorious past, their location within the sphere consecrated the empire's American destiny (*ponto de
chegada*).[22] Even Gonçalves dos Santos' well-established iconographic configuration
suggested the possibility of this fundamental departure from the centuries-old trajectory of European expansion and colonization. Europe's conquests notwithstanding,
it was, after all, America who now wore the crown and to whom "powerful European
monarchs" gave homage, a fact, as Gonçalves dos Santos' himself recognized, that
was dramatized for Rio's residents in 1817 when the Austrian princess Leopoldina,
"the daughter of a caesar," arrived to assume her position as spouse of the heir to the
Portuguese throne, Dom Pedro.[23]

Fueling this tension between Europe and America, between imperial integrity
and an Americanization of the monarchy, was what the statesman and memorialist
Silvestre Pinheiro Ferreira characterized as the decade's great "question of state": the
future, and permanent, location of the sovereign himself. At stake, wrote Pinheiro

FIGURE 12: Jean Baptiste Debret, "Débarquement de la Princess Leopoldine," from
Debret, *Voyage Pittoresque et Historique au Brésil, sejour d'un Artiste Français au
Brésil* v. 3 (Paris: Firmin Didot Fréres, 1839). Copy and permission obtained from
the Print Collection, Miriam and Ira D. Wallach Division of Arts, Prints and Photographs, The New York Public Library, Astor, Lenox and Tilden Foundations. As
Debret explained, the triumphal arch through which Leopoldina entered the city
featured the coat of arms of the "new United Kingdom."

Ferreira, was "nothing less than the end of the torrential evil with which the century's revolutionary vertigo . . . devastated Europe, and threatened the [prince regent's] states with dissolution and total ruin," for both a continued absence of royalty in Portugal and the royal family's departure from Brazil left the monarchy vulnerable to revolution. The salvation of both the monarchy and the empire, Pinheiro Ferreira surmised, therefore would require an entirely new organization of royal power. In 1814 he responded to this question by recommending that royal authority be divided within the empire, with Dom João assuming the title of "Emperor of Brazil, sovereign of Portugal," while his son Pedro would go to Portugal as "king, heir to the throne of Brazil." Decentering royal power and multiplying the source of political authority so as to provide for a forceful representation of that authority over a larger area, Pinheiro Ferreira sought to diminish the sense of marginality as well as the physical margins that had previously defined Brazil's relation to Portugal and that now appeared to define Portugal's relation to Brazil.[24]

In creating the United Kingdom, however, the crown left both the structure of royal governance unchanged and the future residence undefined. Instead, potential contradictions within the United Kingdom were resolved by recalling the events that had precipitated the empire's reconfiguration. Conflicts within the monarchy and empire, in other words, were suppressed in favor of conflicts that transcended the Portuguese world. The creation of the United Kingdom and the Acclamation thus became celebrations of the defeat of the French Revolution. As one commemorative ode rendered recent events: "The Lusitanians were ruled by a light and gentle Scepter / Within the stormy Universe / Of a perverse system / the Pious Prince offered Benign shelter. . . . "[25] The Kingdom of Brazil also emerged as a victorious bulwark against the spread of republican insurgencies from neighboring Spanish America and a check against the influence of the United States, which, according to Silva Lisboa, "showed all the symptoms of supporting the presumptuous system of the Autocrat of France." For a besieged old regime and empire, the path of restoration and the victory had led to Brazil. Or, as Silva Lisboa allegorized the creation of a new court, history was rendered meaningful by mythology. Rio de Janeiro was, he proclaimed, "the Promontory Peak from which were issued the rays of an active and holy war" used by "the Heavens to defeat the Titans who dared to attack Olympus."[26]

THE "LIBERATION OF COMMERCE": EMPIRE AND THE "NEW SCIENCE" OF POLITICAL ECONOMY

While following the transfer of the court, the empire was defined by the triumph of the monarchy and its United Kingdom over the French Revolution and Napoleon, it was also, memorialists argued, built upon the ruins of mercantilism. Dom João both "delivered the herculean blow to the Hydra of Jacobinism" and, as Silva Lisboa wrote, slew the "Dragon of Monopoly" that together "had attacked the vital organs of the Social Body." Indeed, in Silva Lisboa's new imperial geography, the most prominent feature of Rio de Janeiro's landscape, the mountain of rock known as the Sugar Loaf, became the second Cape of Good Hope, the site from which the prince regent, in the spirit of his fifteenth-century ancestors, secured both "the salvation of Civil Order" and "the opening of Global Commerce."[27]

The act to which Silva Lisboa referred with such grandiose imagery was the opening of Brazil's ports, an act that consistently has been cited by historians as the defining moment of Dom João's reign. In Bahia in 1808, even before his arrival at Rio de Janeiro, the prince regent issued a royal charter that dismantled Portugal's three-hundred-year-old commercial monopoly. For the first time in the history of the empire, merchants of all powers "in peace and harmony" with the Portuguese crown were allowed to both import and export from Brazilian ports. It was an act, as well, in which Silva Lisboa himself, the future Visconde de Cairú, played a central role, for it was reportedly he who succeeded in convincing the prince regent and his counselors that the French occupation of the Iberian Peninsula made it impossible to continue to limit trade exclusively to Portugal. Opening Brazil's ports, he explained, would allow American commerce to continue during the war. Consequently, the crown would collect required duties, revenue needed to fund its continental armies.[28]

The charter inspired by this line of argument thus was an "interim and provisional" wartime measure that made important exceptions for the royal monopolies of brazil-wood and diamonds as well as for wine, oil, and *aguardente*. In the months that followed, further restrictions limited the scope of "free trade" and the new, increased duties on direct commerce, originally applied without regard to the origin of the manufactures or the ships that brought them, were reduced in favor of Portuguese goods.[29] Yet these exceptions not withstanding, supporters of the charter defined it as the first step toward creating a new "general system" for commercial exchange based on liberal principles. It was, they repeatedly insisted, an unequivocal point of no return and the harbinger of a new greater era. For after 1808, wrote a characteristically enthusiastic Gonçalves dos Santos, "Brazil [was] no longer an enclosed garden, forbidden to other mortals." Or, as one slogan revealed at the Acclamation proclaimed, Dom João had "liberated commerce."[30]

Beginning in 1808, the task for royal officials and memorialists thus became how to define the meaning of this liberation within the empire's future: to articulate the end of imperial monopoly and the discourse of imperial unity. For some, a connection was established in the creation of the Kingdom of Brazil itself, recognized as the end of a process that open ports had initiated: the demise of what Gonçalves dos

Santos called "the old colonial system."[31] Indeed, throughout the decade that followed the transfer of the court, the end of monopoly was cited together with the creation of political equity as an act that established the first solid basis for unity in the empire's history. Opening the commerce "of this most rich portion of the New World to all civilized people," claimed the newly arrived Portuguese military official and memorialist Francisco de Borja Garção Stoeckler, "made available to its inhabitants the most abundant source of wealth, and prosperity." "Justice," he explained, had "ma[de] all equal," "elevat[ed] Brazil to the dignified status of Kingdom and ended the disastrous rivalry that existed between American and European Portuguese."[32] The Minister of Foreign Affairs, Rodrigo de Souza Coutinho, similarly asserted that open ports created a new basis for imperial integrity. "Liberal principles," he wrote, created a "vast System of Commerce" stretching from the Atlantic to Asia, in which Europe, if no longer at the center, certainly remained a beneficiary. "Portugal will always be a natural storehouse for the products of Brazil," he wrote in 1809, and now "the size of that production will be much larger."[33] One year later, he made the same point more dramatically. "[N]otwithstanding all the anxieties of the visionaries who follow the principles of mercantilism," he asserted, "the emancipation of Brazil will be very useful [to Portugal]."[34] Under the aegis of "liberal legislation" the potential of Brazil's "copious and various precious resources," noted in justifying the royal charter of 1815, would finally be fulfilled. Breaking "the chains that imprisoned commerce" would unleash ostensibly natural processes of expansion. Utility would join paradisiacal fertility to create a universal prosperity into which any divisions within the empire would be subsumed.[35]

Such a reconciliation of open ports and imperial unity, however, was based on the idea that the liberation of commerce produced quantitative rather than qualitative change and that the benefits of this liberation would be measured primarily within the empire itself. Indeed, Souza Coutinho's vision of a new "System of Commerce" recalled earlier mercantilist reforms that sought to reduce particular colonial monopolies in order to invigorate Portuguese-Brazilian commercial exchange as a whole. In contrast to earlier reforms, however, Brazil's ports were now open not only to Portuguese in Portugal, Brazil, Africa, and Asia, but to merchants of all friendly nations as well. Open ports allowed foreigners direct and legal access to resources and markets that the Portuguese crown had previously guarded for the benefit of metropolitan interests. Consequently, to redefine the new empire also required accounting for the apparent elimination of its historic boundaries.

One way to explain these changes was to redefine the empire's center. Although Souza Coutinho earlier had claimed that following imperial reform Portugal would retain the role of entrepot, he gradually acknowledged that this position was truly occupied by Brazil. Thus, the opening of Brazilian ports could be understood as the transference to Brazil of the access to ports in Portugal that foreign merchants had enjoyed historically. In 1811 in legislation supported by Souza Coutinho that ratified the rights of merchants in Brazil to trade directly with the eastern Portuguese dominions, the crown indeed named Brazil as the "commercial emporium" between Europe and Asia.[36] The problem with this redefinition, however, was that it simply inverted the hierarchies and inequalities between Portugal and Brazil that the opening of Brazil's ports was said to have destroyed. Distinct interests within the empire continued to appear as necessarily either superior or subordinate to one another. The "old colonial system" was simply replaced by a new colonial system in which, as critics in Portugal denounced, Portugal was the colony.[37]

Another way of integrating open ports and the future of the empire was offered by José da Silva Lisboa. Silva Lisboa also saw this "new empire" as American, yet his imperial vision did not depend on a redefinition of center and periphery, or a new hierarchy of interests. On the contrary, recognizing the true nature of commerce, he argued, rendered these categories unnecessary. For Silva Lisboa, the opening of Brazil's ports and subsequent debates represented the high point in a long career in royal service that was well underway when the prince regent arrived in Brazil. Born in Bahia in 1756, the son of a Portuguese architect and his Bahian wife, Silva Lisboa was sent to study at Coimbra, where he earned degrees in Greek, Hebrew, canon law, and philosophy. After leaving Coimbra he entered royal service as a professor of philosophy in Salvador, Bahia. In 1797 he was appointed Deputy and Secretary to the *Mesa de Inspecção da Agricultura e Comércio* (Board of Agriculture and Commerce) at the Bahian capital, a position compatible with his growing interest in commercial law and the principles of the "new science" of political economy. It was during these years leading up to the transfer of the court that Silva Lisboa established himself as the Portuguese-speaking world's most committed disciple of Adam Smith (1723–1790), whose defense of "an independent and voluntary world market" he passionately endorsed.[38] Indeed, within a historiography that has broadly defined the Brazilian reception of liberalism as incomplete, misunderstood, or misplaced,[39] Silva Lisboa has the ironic honor of being criticized for having embraced the Invisible Hand too completely. Comparing Silva Lisboa and the North American Hamilton, Celso Furtado both noted that "the Brazilian more clearly reflected ideas which were to prevail in England years later" and dismissed the grounds for his conviction. Silva Lisboa "superstitiously believed in the 'invisible hand,'" Furtado claimed, and merely "repeated: *laissez faire, laissez passer, laissez vendre.*"[40]

Silva Lisboa's enthusiasm for political economy, however, was in fact not superstitious, but rather based on the reading and dissemination of political economy's texts. His own reading of Adam Smith, whom he identified as the "second Father of Civilized People," led him to write *Princípios de Economia Política*, published in Lisbon in 1804,[41] and undoubtedly inspired his son's translation of a three-volume compendium edition of Smith's *Wealth of Nations*, published by the Royal Press in Rio de Janeiro in 1811–1812. The "most substantial principles of Political Economy," Bento da Silva Lisboa wrote in his introduction to the first volume, should be of interest not only to statesmen, but also to "the middle classes, who have contributed so much to the good order of national wealth." Indeed, he asserted, it "is of interest to all uninstructed citizens that the just rules of civil life, upon which industry and prosperity depends, do not remain, as they have up until now, merely arcane."[42] As this passage also reveals, for Silva Lisboa and his son political economy was conceived of not only as the administration of public revenue, but also as what J.G.A. Pocock has defined as "a more complex, and more ideological, enterprise aimed at establishing the moral, political, cultural, and economic conditions of life in advancing commercial societies."[43] In other words, the scope of Silva Lisboa's inquiry was not contained by the "quantifiable material entities" of economy, although they were also very much a concern. Rather, as John Stuart Mill would assert some years later, his study of economic conditions belonged to a "moral and social science . . . the object of what is called Political Economy."[44]

This "commercial humanism"—to use Pocock's term—represented a break with both "enlightened mercantilism" and Souza Coutinho's most recent reformism, in which commerce was held to be a simple exchange of commodities that generated wealth. For Silva Lisboa, in contrast, commerce produced not only quantitative, but also qualitative results. "Where Commerce is free," he wrote, paraphrasing Montesquieu, "this openness brings with it the correction of transitory anomalies,"[45] a fact that was evident, Silva Lisboa argued, in the redress of afflictions it afforded the United States following its war of independence.[46] From this principle it followed that the end of European monopolies could not be regarded as either the cause or symptom of Portugal's decadence. For "free trade, regulated by morality, righteousness and common good," Silva Lisboa wrote in his *Observações sobre o Comércio Franco no Brasil*, published in 1808, was "the life-giving principle of social order and the most natural and sure means to the prosperity of nations." Nor could the end of barriers to foreign trade with Brazil be regarded as the end of the monarchy's imperial boundaries. Rather, open ports signified the infinite expansion of these boundaries; they formed "the Cornerstone of the edifice of civilization" and the basis for a "New Empire."[47]

This defense of commerce as a "civilizing agency," as Anthony Pagden has recently shown, was debated widely throughout Europe in the late eighteenth and early nineteenth centuries and summarized in a passage from *The Spirit of the Laws*, which Silva Lisboa himself cited: "where there is commerce, there is gentleness of customs, and where there is gentleness of customs there is commerce."[48] In the case of Silva Lisboa, this firm link between trade and civilization also meant that even as the principles of political economy dismantled "the old colonial system," they retained the European colonial project intact. In other words, in Silva Lisboa's ideally liberal nineteenth-century empire, free trade would supplant conquest as the vehicle through which the European "social order" would be spread. Evincing what Pagden has described as political economy's commitment to the idea that "contemporary commercial society was the highest condition to which man could aspire and that such a society was a possible outcome—possible for peoples everywhere—of a determinate, intelligible, and, to some degree, controllable, historical process," Silva Lisboa's work stood, as we shall see below, as an attempt to discern and foster that process within the Portuguese empire.[49]

Silva Lisboa's persistent references to "social order" also make clear his assessment of revolutionary politics. He was, as Sérgio Buarque de Holanda categorized him, a "traditionalist," committed to defending the Portuguese monarchy, religion, and aristocracy. "The Coryphaei of impiety, libertinage and religious and civil heterodoxies," Silva Lisboa insisted, could not be tolerated within the new empire, for these had inspired the French to usurp "established government" and, consequently, "annihilate the fundamental principles of civil order" manifest in nobility.[50] Accordingly, as a member of the *Junta da Impressão Régia* (Royal Press Board) in Rio, he presented a formidable although, as he himself recognized, only partially successful defense against the "opiates" of the French Revolution by censoring both imported works and manuscripts, ensuring that they were duly expurgated "of that which was most offensive to Christianity and the current establishments of civil order."[51] This commitment to a traditional order also meant that in using the principles of the "new science" of political economy to define the new empire, Silva Lisboa had both to reconcile the opening of Brazil's ports with historic imperial unity and to explain why dismantling economic privileges did not mean the end of other (political) privileges as well. In other words, Silva Lisboa had to explain how the Portuguese empire could withstand a transformation without undermining the pillars of its historical edifice: the monarchy, tradition, and religion.

To do so, Silva Lisboa turned not to Smith, but to another critic from the British Isles, Edmund Burke (1729–1797), whose work he translated and published in Rio de Janeiro in 1812 with a dedication to the British representative to Dom João's court, Lord Strangford.[52] Burke's claim that liberty could not exist outside the established "social order" was a principle that, as José Honório Rodrigues noted, guided Silva Lisboa's career.[53] Burke's analysis of the French Revolution appealed to Silva Lisboa because, among other things, it rescued liberality from revolutionary liberty by reasserting its basis in "ancient chivalry" and manners.[54] As Silva Lisboa explained in the preface to his translation, Burke made plain the difference between "the liberal ideas of a Paternal Regency" and "the crude theories of metaphysical speculators, or Machiavellists, who had perturbed, or perverted, the immutable Social Order."[55] Burke then further elucidated the fundamental relationship between a conservative "social order" and commerce in his claim that in the "spirit of gentlemen" and the "spirit of religion" were the principles upon which "all good things which are connected with manners and with civilization" had been based. "[C]ommerce and trade and manufacture," Burke explained, were consequently "but effects [of manners and civilization] which, as first causes, we choose to worship." From this claim it followed, as Pocock has explained, that to "overthrow religion and nobility" was "to destroy the possibility of commerce itself."[56] Accordingly, with Burke Silva Lisboa could firmly place the defense of monarchy, religion, and an aristocratic "intelligentsia" at the base of the new empire, making a reassuringly clear connection between the monarch's traditional "liberality" and the "liberal" gesture of opening Brazil's ports. His traditionalism, in this sense, represented neither a departure from, nor, as Buarque de Holanda argued, a misreading of Smith,[57] but rather a reading of Smith, and of political economy in general, through Burke. As Silva Lisboa thus learned, if commerce were to achieve its civilizing mission, its own civilized origins had to be secure.

And yet there is, as may be clear, an important tension in the work of Smith and Burke, and in Silva Lisboa's readings of their works. While Burke's assertion, as Pocock notes, "that commerce is dependent upon manners" was shared by some political economists, Smith and others had identified the growth of exchange, along with production and the diversification of labor, as "the motor force which created the growth of manners."[58] Perhaps in engaging in these two visions of the origins of commercial civilization Silva Lisboa, like Montesquieu, wanted it both ways: "everywhere there are gentle mores, there is commerce" and "everywhere there is commerce, there are gentle mores."[59] There is, however, also a feature of Burke's thought that allowed Silva Lisboa to elide the tension between causes and effects of commerce in his own understanding of the empire in which he lived. Burke, as Pocock explains, "anchored commerce in history, rather than presenting it as the triumph over history."[60] The same could be said of Silva Lisboa and, as Silva Lisboa would assert, of the Portuguese nation itself. The Portuguese were not, as were the French revolutionaries and the British functionaries in India who, as Uday Singh Mehta notes, Burke derided as rootless, "commercial mercenaries unmarked by the burdens and privileges" of society.[61] Portuguese commerce was, on the contrary, both historic and noble. Since the fifteenth century, the King of Portugal ruled over not only his "conquests," but also the "navigation and commerce of Ethiopia, Arabia, Persia, and India." The monarch himself had become a merchant, or "the grocer king," as one French monarch disparagingly referred to Dom Manuel I (1495–1521).[62] Consequently, for the Portuguese it made no sense to distinguish the causes and effects of commerce and aristocratic civilization because their national character, their Montesquiean "spirit of the laws," an ideal to which both Burke and Silva Lisboa referred to with critical regard, was mercantile and chivalrous at once.[63] In the nineteenth century, therefore, a privileged elite and Dom João's "paternal Regency" could sustain the open, commercial empire and also, as Burke had insisted, build on "old foundations."[64]

Portuguese chroniclers of empire, however, had not been so eager to perceive such a harmonious integration of profit and glory in narrating what Richard Helgerson describes as "the voyages of a nation." In the 1810s, it was thus left to Silva Lisboa to realize this imperative in his *Memoria dos Benefícios Políticos do Governo . . . de Dom João VI*, a recapitulation of the history of the Portuguese empire in which Dom João's achievements are enumerated in dialogue with an earlier theorist of empire, João de Barros (1496–1570). In his *Décadas* (1552–1563), Barros had presented a history of Portuguese expansion up to 1505, including Vasco da Gama's voyage to India and Cabral's voyage to Brazil. For Silva Lisboa, the work of "the eminent Historian of the Portuguese Discoveries" provided emblematic links between the Portuguese empire in Asia and the Portuguese empire in America. Read in tandem with the story of Vasco da Gama, the Acclamation, the event that the *Memoria* commemorated, appeared as the fruition of the monarch's American destiny inaugurated in India. The arrival of the prince regent to Rio and the Acclamation, Silva Lisboa claimed, recalled the "ecstatic" greeting that the inhabitants of India offered to "our first Discoverer of the East," an encounter poetically rendered in a passage from Luiz de Camões' *The Lusiads* (1572), which Silva Lisboa transcribed: "It is not without reason, no, hidden and dark, / That you come from the far away Tagus: / God certainly brings you, / because He intends / that You perform his Service. . . ."[65] As the use of Camões also signaled, both encounters were achievements of epic proportions.[66]

Silva Lisboa's history of the empire thus recalled the providentialist explanations of the transfer of the court that saw the year 1808 as a divinely inspired turning point for the monarchy. In Silva Lisboa's case, however, the aim was not to glimpse a sublime postapocalyptic future, but rather to reclaim the past and the empire's original ethos, to return to the principles that guided the original voyages. According to Silva Lisboa, Dom João embodied these principles. His willingness to justify his actions before "the Public and all the Orders of the State" recalled "the Great Albuquerque, founder of our Empire in Asia," whose government, as Barros had written, was one of transparent justice. The prince regent's attempts to maintain Portuguese neutrality, Silva Lisboa also argued, reflected not only his "Character" but also the "Example of his most glorious Predecessors," Dom Henrique and Dom Manuel, who, as Barros established, together with Portuguese colonial governors, excelled at "the ways and arts of establishing peace."[67]

This exaltation of empire as the framework for quiescent material exchange, as Helgerson has observed, can be found as well in one contemporary English reading of Camões, where the historic Portuguese empire served as a symbol of the dawn of commerce itself. Dom Henrique, wrote William Julius Mickle in the introduction to his 1776 translation of *The Lusiads*, was "born to set mankind free from the feudal system and to give the whole world every advantage, every light that may possibly be diffused by the intercourse of unlimited commerce."[68] Such a rendering of early European expansion served to suppress the violence of the British empire, a violence directed at Britain's colonial subjects, as well as, to a certain extent, at the Portuguese themselves, who, as we shall see below, although "allies" of the crown of England also judged that Britain sought to replace Portugal's "peaceful" pursuit of "unlimited commerce" with their own. Yet, what Helgerson describes as Mickle's "massively overdetermined" reading, reflective of both "two centuries of discourse prompted by trade" and the force of England's eighteenth-century commercial enterprise, would have appealed to Silva Lisboa. Like Mickle, he effaced the violence of empire, argued that the Portuguese monarchy had given trade its limitless dimensions, and appreciated the way in which the Portuguese and British empires converged in commerce. Indeed, bringing Portuguese and British imperial rhetoric to yet another point of intersection, Silva Lisboa cited the early eighteenth-century British poet Thomson's tribute to Dom Henrique. The fifteenth-century navigator had envisioned that "in unlimited Commerce the World embraces." Three centuries later, Silva Lisboa concluded with satisfaction, it was Dom João who made that vision a reality. If, however, as Helgerson explains, Mickle's "misreading" of Camões' epic of conquest as an "epic of commerce" was intended to celebrate the triumph of a mercantilism that Camões himself sought to suppress in favor of the nobility of empire, Silva Lisboa's "retrospective renaming" of empire entailed bringing both its aristocratic and commercial dimensions to the fore. If Camões wrote for the king and the nobility and Mickle wrote for merchants, Silva Lisboa perceived a need to write for both."[69]

To persuade both royalty and merchants of the virtues of free trade, Silva Lisboa then linked the history of Portuguese commerce to an idealized origin. The Portuguese monarchs created an empire that made commerce "limitless," he explained, because they recognized the practice to be "natural." Once again, Silva Lisboa based his assertions on Barros, referring in one passage to his praise for the dynasty of "Ahmed, the Moorish Tartar" who, Barros had claimed, both discerned the natural principle that "men and wealth are what make kingdoms and republics most prosperous" and, accordingly, with "justice and liberality," opened his territory's markets to both foreign goods and currencies.[70] With such a claim Silva Lisboa completed his own massively overdetermined reading of the history of the Portuguese empire. An empire that had been circumscribed by monopoly and justified by *mare clausum* and the right of navigation defined in positive rather than in natural law became, in Silva Lisboa's *Memoria*, the champion of the natural practice of free trade.[71]

Such a rewriting of imperial history was, of course, strategic. Establishing that free trade was part of a "natural Politics," historically encountered "when the Economy of Nations was not corrupted by the guile of Monopolists," and that Portuguese expansion itself inaugurated free trade, allowed him to articulate a critique of the old colonial system and monopoly without attacking, as the French Revolutionaries had, "old foundations." He could, as he contended of Dom João, ensure that religion remained "unscathed" and maintain "a secure Civil Order, respect for the Dignity of the Crown, a firm National Independence, solid Systems of Public Good, progressive Improvements of Society." From this claim it followed that open ports did not undermine either the old regime or the empire, but rather restored the original and "natural" framework of Portuguese expansion in the place of what the empire had become only subsequently: a closed "colonial system." "Good reason," Silva Lisboa wrote, revealed that "the Economy of the State should not disturb the Order of the Ruler of Society, and the natural course of things," an order that he defined, in turn, by citing Barros: "each one reaps from the earth that which he has sown." "The Colonial System," he went on to explain, "had this intrinsic defect," whereby one group of people were, through "an indirect or direct System of force," prevented from "working" and "developing their territorial and mental resources for the progress of industry and wealth." Such a system, in other words, prevented the pursuit of Smithian self-interest. That the Portuguese courtiers arriving at Rio did not encounter opulence, Silva Lisboa concluded, implicitly comparing the wealthy sixteenth-century empire and the decadence that followed, proved that Adam Smith was right when he argued that for both the metropoles and their colonies free trade was better than monopoly.[72]

In bringing imperial history to the nineteenth century, Silva Lisboa also completed his final move in writing monopoly out of the old regime: displacing it to the old regime's enemy. France, he wrote in an earlier pamphlet, where the "first luminaries of orthodox Political Economy, Fenelon and Montesquieu, wrote of the advantages of free trade," had been betrayed by the "Monsters" of Revolution, who attacked civilization and debased commerce with their "barbaric physiocratic system." Napoleon's attempt to blockade British commerce as well revealed a hatred of "legitimate commerce" and of those who defended it: the Portuguese and the English, "followers of the Tyrians and Phoenicians."[73] However, the transfer of the court, he argued, evoking both the Bible and *The Wealth of Nations*, rectified these errors. It accelerated "the development of a Plan" in which "with an Invisible Hand, Providence prepared the reestablishment of an order that was at once Civil and Cosmological." Brazil's open ports thus were absorbed into a discourse of imperial unity in which the Portuguese political old regime was hegemonic. The "Liberation of Commerce" became synonymous with the "Restoration of Monarchy" and sixteenth-century imperial glory.[74]

"O Jardim Aberto": The New Empire Practiced

Both the discourse of a United Kingdom and the discourse of political economy promised a restoration of former glory and prosperity based on a redefinition of imperial space as homogeneous, unified, and equitably denominated. The achievement of such a redefinition of empire, however, also required translating these discourses into practices across the empire and at the local level. How, then, were the United Kingdom and the "liberal principles" that it was said to embody practiced in the new court and open port of Rio de Janeiro? How were the ideals of unity and prosperity disseminated within the city? And, how did Rio's residents respond to the consequences of the policies that these ideals informed?

In Rio de Janeiro, the transfer of the court and the opening of its port consolidated trends that began in the eighteenth century: the growth of the city's population, of its merchant community, and of the volume of goods exchanged in its port and market. Between 1808 and 1821 the city's population doubled to at least 80,000 persons. The number of retail business increased over 100%. And, in 1808 alone, four times as many ships entered the city's port as in the previous year.[75] This increase in the city's population, together with economic growth, appeared to fulfill the promise of imperial renewal in the New World. As Silva Lisboa sustained, *"the dignity of the King is found in the multitude of his people, and population makes the power of States"* (emphasis in original).[76]

Yet, as contemporary statesmen and theorists also agreed, the status and wealth of nations depended not only on the size, but also on the nature of their population. In this case, rather than fulfilling promises, both the new court and Brazil as whole, many argued, presented problems. In the eighteenth century, as we saw in Chapter 2, viceregal officials in Rio had linked social and economic problems to the city's African and African-Brazilian population, blaming the institution of slavery and their labor force for what they perceived to be a lack of productivity and the idleness of the population in general. In the new court of Rio de Janeiro, we saw in Chapter 4, this critique of slavery was further advanced. Although royal cabinet Minister Vila Nova Portugal argued that slavery provided much needed labor for plantations and mines, he also recognized that slavery made Brazil "intrinsically weak" because, as he explained, "half of the energy that should be applied in service to the sovereign" was spent in maintaining order among what he perceived to be a hostile population.[77] Silva Lisboa, in turn, characterized slave labor as both costly and inefficient. Slavery was an institution, he asserted, that had resulted in the "inertia" of Brazilian plantations and their reliance on primitive methods. And, there were, he stressed, no extraeconomic factors that justified the maintenance of such an institution. The claim that "the heat of the torrid Zone was inhospitable to the European constitution, and that without Africans, Brazil could not flourish" was, he denounced, the "vulgar" pretense of those who "try to escape the *Law of Work*, wanting to live off the sweat of others." Likewise, the mission of Christianizing Africans was, as he characterized it, nothing more than an unsubstantiated "pretext."[78]

The indictment of slavery, however, was based on more than the inadequacies of the structure of labor. The ideal of the new empire was, as we have seen, a "homogeneous political body." At the local level in Rio, this ideal was understood to mean a uniformity not only of political identities (a unity of the monarch's "vassals"), but also of culture and color. Brazil, Silva Lisboa explained, needed "a natural, prudent and legitimate population," rather than one that was "foreign, barbarous and abusive, as was [its population] of Africans."[79] Royal minister Tomás António Vila Nova Portugal clarified this imperative: because Brazil did not have a large population of poor whites, it did not have a "*povo*" (people). What Brazil did have, slaves and free and freed persons of color, did not constitute a people because, as Vila Nova Portugal further argued, they were incapable of sharing the Portuguese "National Spirit."[80] Indeed, in Brazil, Silva Lisboa similarly asserted, slavery had subverted the social and cultural basis for political viability. It "made difficult marriages between people of European extraction," he explained, and "prevented the formation of a homogeneous and compact nation."[81]

We have seen how officials in the new court contended with what Silva Lisboa characterized as a "foreign" and "barbarous" population, as those of the colony of Brazil had, with repression and social discipline, as well as the consequences of this pessimistic vision of cultural and color differences for the free people of color and the African and African-Brazilian slaves who found themselves in confrontations with the police. In the 1810s such a pessimism also inspired royal officials to search for an alternative source of peoplehood. Displacing African "foreigners" with European ones by way of voluntary, "white" immigration, they imagined, an even more complete exclusion of people of color from civil society in both the present and the future would be achieved.[82] The success of this immigration, according to Silva Lisboa, depended on the end of the slave trade, which he vigorously defended, as well as on the eventual and "gradual" end of slavery itself, to which, he more cautiously predicted, the reduction in trade would lead. It was "impossible," he explained, "that a

considerable number of Europeans expatriate themselves to Brazil, as was imperative, if they [could] hope for no better fortune than to be mixed-up with Kaffirs."
The temporary economic disruption that would follow the end of the slave trade, he
further pledged, would be exceeded by the results of immigration. "Experience has
shown," Silva Lisboa claimed, "that, where the importation of Africans has ended,
the race does not decline . . . but rather [is] elevated, improves, and lightens."[83]

In 1810 and 1814 the crown did agree to curtail the slave trade, but only by
limiting it to its own possessions and then to below the equator; and the move, as we
shall see below, was not identified with any compelling vision of reform of the population or of labor in Brazil.[84] In contrast, the question of immigration appears to
have inspired a more concerted response from royal officials. In the 1810s the settlement of Azorean and later Swiss immigrants as farmers was subsidized by the crown,
while otherwise "useless" Portuguese arrivals were similarly settled in areas both far
from and near to the city. "Improving" the nature, or "race," of the population thus
was linked to an ideal of productivity as embodied in small-scale rural enterprise.
Such projects, Rio's police intendant reported, produced "advantages" in the present
and promised to yield further "good."[85] As Rodrigo de Souza Coutinho similarly
promised, creating incentives for immigration such as land grants was "not in favor
of Foreigners . . . but rather in favor of the Greatness, Population and Culture of
Brazil." For proof of "these principles," he argued, one need look no further than the
"most convincing" example, or "identical and analogous" case, as Silva Lisboa described it, of the United States, where "greatness" had been achieved in spite of an
African and African-American population.[86]

As royal officials took inspiration from the fact that the experiences of slavery
and color hierarchies were shared, as well as from the United States' ostensible ability
to surmount the consequences of these experiences, they also faced crucial dispari-
ties, and one in particular had significant consequences for the meaning of immigration in each context: the status of religious difference. Whereas in the United States
various religious sects were officially tolerated, Brazil was within the sphere of a historically militant and exclusive Tridentine Catholicism. Accordingly, in recruiting
European immigrants the Portuguese crown had specified that they be Catholic. In
fact, however, many of those who came to Brazil were Protestant. The crown, in
turn, as John Parker has observed, responded to their presence by expanding its understanding of religion as "a source of order" to include Protestantism and, in spite
of criticism from the papal nuncio, paid the salary of the Swiss settlement's minister.
Although in the 1810s the scope of this new religious difference, and of European
immigration in general, remained relatively limited, the symbolic implications of
"officially acknowledged religious toleration" were significant.[87] It meant that in the
new prosperous empire, at least in official visions of the political-economic future,

whiteness and the ideal of utility as embodied in the small farmer could challenge successfully the ideal of linguistic, historic, and cultural unity and religious homogeneity of a heroic Portuguese nationhood that both exiles and residents evoked in explaining the transfer of the court.

Although most foreign settlements were in the hinterland some distance from Rio de Janerio, within the city the new dimensions of cultural and religious differences were also manifest. After 1808, foreign merchants began to assume a prominent role within Rio's growing economy, "invited by the Spirit of the Sovereign," boasted the preacher Januário da Cunha Barbosa, "who gave them a much greater commerce."[88] This foreign population was diverse and with the end of the Napoleonic Wars came to include a sizable number of French.[89] The city's largest foreign community, however, was British. The British, after all, had the advantage of well-established trading relations with the Portuguese, some of which, following the court, were transferred to Rio. Even before 1808, by way of isolated royal authorizations and contraband, some British merchants had gained experience in Brazil. Consequently, by 1809, the year that an association of merchants with interests in Brazil was formed in London, there were over one hundred British firms in Rio. After an initial wave of speculation based more on what the British could supply than on what the Brazilian market demanded, many of those who the North American merchant Henry Hill referred to as "adventurers" returned to England. A stable community of British mercantile interests nevertheless remained: importers of linen and cotton cloth, hardware, and earthenware, and exporters of sugar, cotton, and coffee.[90]

This British presence in Brazil was guaranteed in a series of treaties signed by the Portuguese and British crowns in 1810. Along with establishing the specific terms for "Commerce and Navigation" between the British and the Portuguese, discussed below, the treaties also provided for a number of political arrangements. The British received indemnification for losses incurred in Portugal during the war in an allowance for cutting wood from Brazilian forests to build war vessels. It was also here that the Portuguese crown agreed to curtail the slave trade by limiting it to its own possessions. The British then further gained a reaffirmation of their right to a judge conservator as they had in Portugal, one who, as John Mawe, a British resident of Rio, noted, was "to attend solely to the concerns of the English, and to see justice done them."[91] Finally, the Portuguese crown conceded that the Inquisition would never be established in Brazil and pledged to guarantee both a "perfect freedom of Conscience" and the right to Protestant worship in homes or in churches, as long as these churches "externally resembled residential housing" and as long as no attempts were made to proselytize or "declaim against" Catholicism.[92]

In the early 1810s the local reception of the British in Rio de Janeiro, and of their new and more formidable presence in Brazil that the treaties authorized, was, to a large extent, shaped by the experience of the Peninsular War. The British had escorted Dom João to Brazil and a British General and British troops were at the forefront of joint efforts to expel the French from Iberia. In Portugal, as Valentim Alexandre observes, with victory appearing more imminent, the alliance between the crowns of Portugal and Great Britain was regarded as a guarantee for both Portugal's salvation and an enhanced stature for the crown in Europe. The Portuguese periodical press, some of which was read in Rio, engaged in an "Anglomanic" celebration of the achievements of Wellington and Beresford as well as English history and literature.[93] In Rio a certain Anglophilia was also evident. *O Patriota* reported on British politics and on the joy elicited by the visit of "Visconde Mylord Strangford" to Minas Gerais, and, as we have seen, the Royal Press published translations of Pope, Burke, and Smith along with pamphlets celebrating the wartime alliance. As one poetic satire of the French pretension to "protect" Portugal affirmed: "The British Ally / of the Sovereign Regent / forms a decisive plan / In favor of the Portuguese people."[94]

Such enthusiasm for the alliance, however, could not entirely alleviate concern about the unprecedented presence of foreigners in the city of Rio de Janeiro or contain debate over the treaties' guarantee of Protestant worship. While the advocates of European immigration insisted that religious toleration was indispensable,[95] for others the presence of Protestants challenged the political viability of the Portuguese crown's kingdoms. During the negotiations with the British, the Conde de Galveas had argued that the toleration of Protestantism "was all that was wanting to render Brazil an English colony."[96] In 1814 Vila Nova Portugal similarly attacked what he argued were British attempts to subvert the integrity of the new empire. "If the British did not have a hidden agenda for our souls," he asked, "why did they raise the subject of religion in a commercial treaty?" After all, he continued, religion had proved to be the most effective obstacle to the seventeenth-century Dutch invasion of the Brazilian northeast. "The true politics" and "interest of the monarchy," Vila Nova Portugal asserted in what amounted to an indictment of non-Portuguese immigration in general, consisted in "neither los[ing] one's own vassals, nor acquir[ing] those of [other monarchs]." To nurture "the national spirit" that "made Portuguese proud to be called Portuguese," he concluded, it was necessary to keep that spirit "separate, and different from others." Perhaps, he suggested in another policy report, "invalid" Portuguese soldiers could be recruited in place of "dangerous" foreigners.[97] By the end of the decade the magistrate Maciel da Costa, while continuing to endorse the need for European immigration, nevertheless offered a similarly defensive view of demographic transformation, acknowledging the obstacles that even the United States faced. As the United States had been opened to all with "human physiognomy," including revolutionary refugees from Europe, he reported, it now contended with the problems of "an immense" population that was "heterogeneous,

cosmopolitan and debauched in customs." Brazil, therefore, needed to be more circumspect in recruiting immigrants. Citing one French traveler to the Caribbean,
Maciel da Costa concluded "one does not, in one day, in one year, in ten years, transform a population of slaves into a population of vassals and citizens."[98]

Such skepticism about immigration and the religious and cultural diversity that
it implied was also manifest at the local level. In the countryside, according to Swiss
Protestant reports, there were efforts to convert the newcomers to Catholicism. In
the city of Rio de Janeiro, in turn, the negotiation of both new religious and cultural
differences was also tense. A most public showdown was staged by the U.S. consul,
who, as an expression of his republicanism, refused to kneel before the queen on en-
countering her in the city. Although at this first incident, the royal attendants forced
the consul to kneel, at his next encounter with the queen the consul defended his
position by brandishing a pair of pistols. The ongoing impasse was resolved only by
Dom João himself, who responded not with force, but by dispensing foreigners from
exhibiting the degree of servility before His Majesty that was required of Portuguese
vassals.[99] The question of foreigners' due deference also publicly surfaced in 1810,
when what the police intendant described as a "religious riot" ensued after an Englishman reportedly insulted the Catholic faith during a procession on Good Friday.
In this case, however, the common status of the offender and the uniquely sacred status of the offended meant that no exceptions would be made and, subsequently, the
Englishman was permanently expelled from Brazil.[100]

For the British merchant John Luccock, such incidents of conflict in Rio de
Janeiro were to be attributed to the "military, who act as the inferior officers of Police" and, as he claimed, were both infused with a "rancorous spirit" and "much disposed to abuse their authority, and to molest our countrymen."[101] The police
intendant similarly characterized relations with the British as particulary contentious
although, not surprisingly, he discerned other causes of conflict. Although local
magistrates were instructed to "treat well the vassals of His British Majesty," he reported to Souza Coutinho, the British failure to reciprocate often precipitated "unpleasant confrontations," especially at the opera and the bull ring where the British
were known to "enter [private] boxes as if they were common verandas."[102] This tension and animosity between the British and Rio's residents were noted as well by
Strangford himself, who in spite of intervening on behalf of British involved in police matters, nevertheless acknowledged that "the insults . . . offered to [the] Prejudices, Customs, and Religion [of the 'Brazilians'], by the English Settlers of this
country" occurred daily.[103]

For both the intendant and Rio's residents at stake in these confrontations was,
as John Parker has argued, "the whole deferential order" that characterized Portuguese society and politics.[104] Local regimes of adjudication and punishment were

jeopardized, Viana noted in his dispatches to the royal cabinet, by British refusal to abide by Portuguese laws, such as restrictions on incursions into the Brazilian countryside, by their "bad humor and excessive sensitivity" when confronted with their errors, and by the arrogance with which they extended these corruptive tendencies beyond their own community.[105] As Viana reported in 1812, following the arrest of a slave for throwing rocks, his English owners sought his release by claiming spuriously (considering, Viana noted, that the British were not supposed to either own or traffic in slaves) that the slave should be "handed over to their judge conservator because he held the privilege given to all members of [a British] family."[106] This pretense of privilege and impunity also extended to Portuguese vassals associated with the British, especially "the Portuguese clerks of English firms" who, Viana fumed, possessed "a conceit deserving of much correction." One clerk, after assaulting a black woman who was, the intendant noted, a slave of "another poor black," smugly failed to pay for her doctor and then, faced with what the intendant characterized as much deserved jail time, "allege[d] privileges of the English house" and solicited the interventions of his employer. "For the general credit of our nation," Viana concluded in a report to the Minister of Foreign Affairs, "these clerks should be severely punished" because of the "deceit and bad faith with which they treat even the English who with the most good faith and liberality find themselves compelled" to hire these clerks "because of the need of having someone who better understands the language of their customers."[107] The British presence, in other words, created a cycle of disorder. British arrogance produced Portuguese insolence from which, in turn, British and local residents suffered alike.

As the above report also indicated, however, the residents of Rio de Janeiro contended with what they construed to be British threats to their religious, political, and cultural integrity because of a shared interest in what John Luccock described as "the prospects of commerce." It was, after all, commerce with foreigners, rather than their ostensibly disruptive presence in the city, that the opening of ports had sought to promote. In the 1810s in the interest of advancing this commerce, cultivating "utility," "national wealth," and "the expansion of the market" the crown had ended prohibitions on local manufacturing and restrictions on wholesaling and retailing, created a Board of Commerce and a Bank of Brazil, extended the privilege of royal land grants to foreigners, pledged incentives for the climatization of new commercial crops, issued a number of regulations for the city's busy port,[108] sponsored *Aulas de Comércio* (courses on commerce), and created a course in "Economic Science," supervised, not surprisingly, by Silva Lisboa, so that its principles could be "put in practice" and so that the prince regent's vassals, "better instructed in them," could "serve [him] to greater advantage."[109] Anglo-Luso commercial relations, in particular, were guaranteed in 1809–1810, when along with the treaty of alliance the

Portuguese crown negotiated a "reciprocal liberty in Commerce and Navigation" with the British. British access to Brazilian markets was affirmed and Brazilian products were granted access to British markets, a particularly crucial concession, as Valentim Alexandre has noted, considering that the admission of Brazilian goods to major continental markets had been disrupted by the Napoleonic Wars.[110]

Yet, in spite of these reciprocities, the treaties also provided for what Alan Manchester described as a "British preeminence" in Brazil, a preferential status in the Portuguese empire's ports that had been staked out in London before the transfer of the court, but then temporarily undercut, as Lyra observes, by the 1808 charter that opened Brazil's ports to all nations.[111] More specifically, the Treaty of Commerce and Navigation provided for import duties of 15 percent on British goods, a figure lower than that applied to both other foreign and Portuguese merchandise. Although the Portuguese crown gained the status of "most favored nation" within the British empire, Brazilian sugar and coffee, "articles similar to the products of the British colonies," were denied direct entrance to British markets. Within Brazil, the British also gained the unreciprocated privilege of selling retail.[112] Such preferences were not lost on contemporaries. As the British set out to demonstrate that, as Luccock proclaimed, in "the amelioration of Brazil" one "contemplates the benefit of mankind, and more especially of the British dominions,"[113] throughout the territories of the Portuguese crown many came to doubt the commercial order that the treaties guaranteed.

Although, as Valentim Alexandre explains, in Portugal the treaties of 1810 were at first accepted as a temporary feature of the period of war and alliance, when it became clear that the new postwar regime would not feature changes that favored merchants in Portugal, who had been undercut by British access to Brazil that previously only they enjoyed, the Portuguese were beset by a profound sense of "disenchantment."[114] At the royal court in Rio de Janeiro, in turn, confidence about both the treaties and the British reportedly died with Rodrigo de Souza Coutinho in early 1811. Subsequently, the British representative Strangford found himself in conflict with the Portuguese crown over what the British believed were the violations of the treaties presented by the Oporto Wine Company monopoly and Portuguese failures to sufficiently curtail the slave trade. As Manchester explained, the British, hoping to recapture their influence, then began to encourage, and in 1814 spectacularly pressure in the form of a British naval escort in Rio's harbor, Dom João's return to Portugal. What even the reputedly pro-British Conde de Palmela characterized as the need to ensure "that our independence is respected by [Great Britain], just as that of the United States" prevailed, however. The crown rejected the escort, renewed the Oporto charter for fifteen years, and prohibited the transport of British goods between Brazilian ports.[115] Nor did the British succeed in ending the slave trade.

Although the abolition of traffic north of the equator was negotiated at the Congress of Vienna and the British later obtained agreements concerning searches and seizures of vessels in violation of these and later accords, the numbers of African slaves arriving at Brazil did not decrease.[116]

What did increase were expressions of opposition to what Maciel da Costa described as the British "plan for universal domination of the sea," rather thinly veiled in the case of the slave trade, he noted, considering their own actions in Ireland and India, by "philanthropy."[117] The Portuguese, after all, had witnessed British imperial ambition at the beginning of the decade, during the chaotic days of the transfer of the court, in the British occupation of Madeira and Portuguese outposts in Asia; a subsequent proposal that the Azores could serve as payment for a debt owed to Great Britain was met with angry response in the Portuguese press.[118] In Rio de Janeiro, the police intendant sensed that similar ambitions were at work in British attempts to circumvent a municipal concession to slaughter, butcher, and distribute beef within the city. Although, as Viana reported to the royal cabinet, attempts had been made to treat the "allies" well and, in accordance with "sound principles of political economy," accommodate their demands for their own butcher, British attempts to undercut the concessioner and sell to local residents as well, he judged, amounted to an unwarranted extension of "the objects" of the treaties at the expense of municipal sovereignty.[119]

For one courtier the potential of British designs corresponded to nothing less than Portuguese impotence. In 1809, he recalled, a Portuguese threatened two Englishmen after, as the intendant Viana discovered, they attempted to seduce "a girl that the Portuguese maintained." The Englishmen complained to Rodrigo de Souza Coutinho who ordered the police intendant to arrest the alleged assailant. Viana responded that, in his opinion, such an incident "did not appear to warrant the state's attentions," suggesting as well that the Portuguese's position as a well-regarded slave merchant disqualified the minister's recommendation that as a punishment for his aggression he should be drafted into the army. Souza Coutinho persisted, however, calling the Portuguese before him and warning him not to "interfere with the English." As the courtier noted, it was an order that implied that the girl should be "ceded" to the Englishmen. Recorded in 1810, the anecdote also made reference to Souza Coutinho's analogous complicity in the surrender of other Portuguese interests. After all, the courtier concluded sarcastically, "what would the Court of London say if the Minister of Foreign Affairs did not prefer an English over a Portuguese" in such a dispute.[120]

Beyond the circle of courtiers and royal officials similar criticism of British ambition was made in both the pulpit and the press. In Rio de Janeiro in 1812, in a funeral prayer for Spanish Prince Pedro Carlos, Friar João da Costa Faria gave residents a lesson on English "despotism" and Great Britain's "political preponderance over all nations."[121] A far courser, and more threatening, critique was made the following year. While the sidewalk in front of the British Consulate on the Rua dos Ourives was being paved, the royal servant Ignacio Mello e Serra went to the middle of the street, ordered his slave to fill a pipe with rocks, and "then in front of all the neighbors began insulting the vice-consul with the most injurious names, saying that the same that he had done to the pipe, he would do to those who lived there."[122] Such an attack may have come in response to what Strangford described as the consul's "haughty language and proceedings" that "offended" the city's residents. Yet, the attack may also have been directed more generally at the British commercial interests that the consul and the consulate represented, for as Strangford also reported, Rio's residents had come to view the British "as usurpers of their commerce."[123] Indeed, even works intended to celebrate the alliance with the British noted that while Portugal received "Force that help[ed] it sustain its glory," "From Lusitanian possessions Britannia extract[ed] / Riches which [gave] it an Oceanic empire."[124] In 1815 over one hundred merchants and retailers expressed a similar sense that British prosperity came at the expense of the interests of Portuguese vassals, denouncing, in a petition presented to the crown, that the British were unscrupulous, "using . . . all sorts of exchange rates, and algorithms" and even itinerant peddlers "to take over" (*apoderar*). To restore the integrity of the laws that "sustained the independent sovereignty of the state and the nation" and to rid the city of the "usurious intrigues and swindles more common to women," they claimed, than beneficial to "the public good," the petitioners then requested that the crown prohibit English vendors.[125]

There were, however, defenders of the treaties and the British presence in the city. Although during the negotiations Silva Lisboa criticized the degree to which tariffs on British goods were reduced, after the treaties' ratification he became their advocate and, as John Mawe noted, "greatly distinguished himself by his zeal for the English nation."[126] As a censor and a pamphleteer, Silva Lisboa sought at once to suppress criticism of the treaties and to disseminate what he regarded to be a proper understanding of political economy, which would, he surmised, reveal the local benefits of both open ports and trade with the British. While, as he explained in one censorship report, "after the decree that opened Brazil's ports to all nations it was not appropriate to propagate contrary ideas," it was nevertheless "in the state's interest," he asserted in another, "that the information about public economy be exposed to a public discussion."[127] Thus, following lines of argument staked out in *Observações sobre o Comércio Franco no Brasil*, in 1810 Silva Lisboa published *Refutações das Reclamações contra o Commercio Inglez* in which he hailed the benefits that British commerce brought to Brazil through an attack on French claims that continental manufacturing suffered due to the presence of British products in those markets.[128]

A rebuttal to similar criticisms of the 1810 treaties was also included in his *Memoria*. There he attacked lament for the so-called destruction of national interests as a disguise of private interests and monopolies. In the absence of open ports and commercial treaties, he further asserted, the crown would continue to lose potential revenue to contraband, which, given the size of Brazil's coast, was practically impossible to prevent. To these specific observations, he then added a more principled and theoretical justification for trade with the British and its apparent inequalities. The opening of ports and the negotiation of commercial treaties, he claimed, were steps toward creating the conditions for the "exact equilibrium" of supply and demand that Smith himself had envisioned. Equilibrium, however, did not mean that the dividends of commerce were equal; rather, they varied according to investments. "As English Capital is larger," he explained, "it is not a mystery that they have an advantage." This overall advantage, however, did not preclude advantages for Portuguese commercial interests. British capital served to introduce Brazilian products into more European markets and in greater volume. If, as Silva Lisboa conceded, the initial price to be paid for having followed the "lesson of mercantile tyranny" was high, in the long run, he argued, "the truth of experience" showed that trade with the British and their "superior capital" would also enrich the "Nation with fewer funds." Across the empire, he proclaimed, in both Portugal and Brazil, the "expansive, natural force" of "public opulence" would distribute, "like rays of sunlight," the profits of the rich to the "still parasitic, industrious poor."[129]

While affirming the civilizing dimensions of free and open commerce, Silva Lisboa's conflation of criticism of the British with a lack of understanding of political economy and a more general resistence to open ports also revealed his misunderstanding of the specific nature of this criticism in Rio. For local criticism of the British was not fueled by a defense of monopoly or by a rejection of liberal principles per se, but rather by what residents charged was the British refusal to abide them. Accordingly, the principles of political economy that Silva Lisboa disseminated as part of a defense of British commerce also served to bolster arguments to the contrary. Whereas Silva Lisboa asserted that in "the Court, and its suburbs, where there are many English, there are also shining examples of public prosperity,"[130] the petitioners of 1815, for example, argued that just the opposite was true. Using terms that Silva Lisboa himself would have recognized, they asserted that British merchants, vagrants without "fixed address" and "proof of their good standing," undermined rather than served the interests of commerce and "civilization."[131] An earlier petition, in turn, similarly criticized the effects of unregulated supply and demand by arguing that British practices distorted a voluntary economy. Protesting against rent increases, almost one hundred residents argued that the problem originated not only in the arrival of courtiers and the subsequent housing shortage, but also in that "the English were disposed to pay any price." The resulting "criminal usury" was, they claimed, detrimental to both English and Portuguese renters and did an injustice to the principle of "openness."[132] Earlier, in 1808, when over one hundred retailers petitioned the crown complaining that the recently established English merchants were running them out of business, they too justified their plea by claiming that liberal openness was at stake. "All of the commerce of this court is in the hands of the English," they asserted, because they retailed goods "at the same time that they were the principal wholesale merchants." In this way they "establish[ed] monopolies" that could be dismantled only if "the English were not permitted to establish retail stores or to sell in small quantities."[133]

The politics of commerce and empire and the claim that it was the British who forged unliberal monopolies also surfaced in an investigation of reports of a curious plan to stage an insurrection. In 1810 Francisco Xavier de Noronha Torresão, an official in the Ministry of Overseas Affairs, reported that a merchant named Manuel Luiz da Veiga had told him that Rio's merchants had lost confidence in "the state of government" and were planning a "revolution" in secret assemblies. Veiga, a newcomer to Brazil, may have traveled to Rio from his new home in Pernambuco, as customs and censorship records suggest, to secure the release of one hundred copies of a pamphlet he wrote and then had published in England entitled *Analyse dos factos practicados pelos Inglezes com as propriedades Portuguezas*. In this endeavor he did not succeed, for the pamphlet was banned in 1809 due the "calumny against the English nation and government" and the "absurdities about political economy" that it contained. Nor did Veiga succeed in obtaining a license to print a short work he had written in which he criticized the editor of the London-based periodical *Correio Braziliense* and, as Silva Lisboa noted in his censorship report, raised inflammatory and "unpleasant questions concerning the seizure of our ships, for which His British Majesty later ordered restitution." Veiga then appealed, claiming that he was being unduly denied the license because Silva Lisboa was his enemy.[134] Indeed, prior to the transfer of the court Veiga had published a number of works on the Portuguese economy including *Reflexões críticas sobre a obra de José da Silva Lisboa* (Lisbon, 1803) and *Escola mercantil sobre o commércio, assim antigo como moderno entre as nações mercantis dos velhos continentes* (Lisbon, 1803) in which, as José Luiz Cardoso explains, Veiga posed an older understanding of commerce as the host of activities through which human needs were satisfied in contrast to the innovative visions of economy offered by Silva Lisboa and other Portuguese engaged in political economy.[135]

Yet, in spite of Veiga's unquestionably dissident voice on questions of commerce and the British, as the investigation proceeded it was Torresão who ultimately emerged as the rebel. Torresão, Veiga succeeded in convincing the police intendant, had appealed to him to supply him with information about the disposition of the people of Pernambuco, predicting that they would be willing to revolt once they learned of new taxes. Torresão had also criticized the negotiations with the British, Veiga testified, arguing that they violated the principle of free trade and that they threatened Brazil's "independence." When Veiga countered by arguing that as a "young nation," Brazil could not afford to dismiss the benefits of relations with England, Torresão, he recalled, had remained unpersuaded.[136] In defending himself, Torresão acknowledged that the conversations took place, but claimed that it was Veiga, rather than he, who had spoken of the commercial treaty and argued that it would leave Brazil "dependent on England." Indeed, Torresão insisted, Veiga had explained that the treaties were bad because they went "against the doctrines of José da Silva Lisboa."[137]

Whether Torresão or the police intendant were aware of Veiga's critique of Silva Lisboa's work, and whether it was Torresão or Veiga who told the truth, or some approximate version of it, their accounts of such an exchange suggest that both the new American empire and the "new science" of political economy entered conversations and debates within Rio de Janeiro. If, however, Silva Lisboa succeeded in disseminating the principle of commercial openness as the basis for the United Kingdom's integrity and prosperity, he also failed to associate that openness with British commerce. The city's residents, instead, used the discourse of political economy to express a critique of what were perceived as British violations of both its larger principles and local interests and sovereignties. For them, a restoration of the empire's integrity and prosperity required, as Correa Henriques asserted, a further inversion of imperial discourse and practice. By 1814 it was no longer the French Revolution or mercantilism that threatened the United Kingdom of the Portuguese monarch; after all, they had been defeated. Rather, the enemy of the "liberty of Commerce and Navigation" was the "English usurpation of the seas."[138]

At the end of the decade the perception of besieged economic and political sovereignties and a more general dissatisfaction with the local politics of the new political economy of empire came to a head within what Valentim Alexandre calls the "internal contradictions" of the Luso-Brazilian empire and laid bare the political limits of imperial reconfiguration. The center of the crisis, however, formed not in Rio de Janeiro but across the Atlantic in Portugal, where the crown had failed to convince its vassals of the promise of a new American future and instead left both the British postwar occupation and the opening of Brazil's ports to be read as signs of the former metropolis's new "colonial" status. There a growing movement to reverse the trend toward "national decadence" focused on the structure of the empire represented in the United Kingdom and, above all, on the nature of sovereignty itself.[139] The spread to, and the impact of this movement on, the new royal court of Rio de Janeiro, as we shall see in Chapter 7, would shape the end of Dom João's reign in Brazil.

NOTES

1. José Anselmo Correa Henriques, "Memorial sobre a residencia d'El Rey no Brasil," BNRJ Ms. I-33,28,11, f1. In a letter to Rio's police intendant, Henriques also wrote of the bases for an "Império Permanente" in Brazil. See Henriques to Paulo Fernandes Viana, Lisbon, December 16, 1814, transcribed in *Dom João VI e o Império no Brasil, a Independência e a Missão Rio Maior*, ed. Marcos Carneiro de Mendonça (Rio de Janeiro: Biblioteca Repográfica Xerox, 1984), 273–276. Henriques, who was born in Madeira in 1778 and died in Paris in 1831, was assigned to a diplomatic post in Hamburg from 1806 to 1821. Other sources indicate that during this time Henriques also spent time in London, where he had disputes with the ambassador Domingos de Souza Coutinho and the newspaper editor Hipólito José da Costa, as well as Lisbon and Rio de Janeiro, where he apparently drafted this memo. From Europe he corresponded with the police intendant in Rio and royal minister Vila Nova Portugal, often attacking the British and extolling counterrevolutionary politics. On Henriques see Ângelo Pereira, *D. João VI, principe e rei* v. 3 (Lisbon: Empresa Nacional de Publicidade, 1956), 296; and Arnold B. Clayton, "The Life of Tomás Antônio Vilanova Portugal: A Study in the Government of Portugal and Brazil" (Ph.D. dissertation, Columbia University, 1977), 233–234.

2. George Canning cited in Alan K. Manchester, *British Preëminence in Brazil, Its Rise and Decline: A Study in European Expansion* (1933) (New York: Octagon, 1964), 78.

3. "Carta de Lei," December 16, 1815 ([Rio de Janeiro]: Impressão Régia, [1815]).

4. "Carta de Lei," 1815; Heliódoro Jacinto de Araújo Carneiro to Vila Nova Portugal, [London], March 3, 1818, AHI Lata 180 Maço 1; José da Silva Lisboa, *Memoria dos Benefícios Politicos do Governo de El-Rey Nosso Senhor D. João VI* (Rio de Janeiro: Impressão Régia, 1818), 68, 114 (emphasis in original). On the history of the royal title see Janet Ladner, "John VI of Portugal: Contemporary of Napoleon and Wellington," in Consortium on Revolutionary Europe, *Proceedings* 20 (1990), 869–892. The sovereign's new title also necessitated a change in the title of his heir. See Alvará, January 9, 1817, in *Código Brasiliense, Ou Collecção das Leis, Alvarás, Decretos, Cartas Régias, &c. Promulgadas no Brasil desde a feliz chegada de El Rey Nosso Senhor a este Reino* (Rio de Janeiro: [Impressão Régia, 1811–1822]), which established that Dom Pedro would be "Principe Real do Reino Unido de Portugal, e do Brasil e Algarves, Duque de Braganza," rather than "Principe do Brasil," a title held since 1645.

5. Silva Lisboa, *Memoria*, 115.

6. Silva Lisboa, *Memoria*, 69, 116.

7. Romualdo António de Seixas, *Sermão de Acção de Graças que no Dia 13 de Maio Celebrou o Senado da Camara desta Capital do Pará pela Feliz Acclamação do Muito Alto, e Poderoso Senhor D. João VI . . .* (Rio de Janeiro: Impressão Régia, 1818), 14. Seixas' first appearance in the new royal court was in 1809, when he was sent by the bishop of Pará to congratulate the prince regent for his arrival at Rio de Janeiro. Seixas reportedly was a talented orator and enjoyed praise from royal officials such as the Conde dos Arcos, a fact that may have facilitated the publication of three of his sermons by the Royal Press in Rio de Janeiro. See John David Parker, "The Tridentine Order and Governance in Late Colonial Brazil, 1792–1821" (Ph.D. dissertation, University of Washington, 1982), 170.

8. Correa Henriques to Viana, Lisbon, December 16, 1814, in *Dom João VI*, ed. Carneiro de Mendonça, 276.

9. Roderick Barman, *Brazil: The Forging of a Nation (1798–1852)* (Stanford: Stanford University Press, 1988), 44–45, 53–54.

10. On the late eighteenth-century crisis of representation see Antoine de Baecque, "The Allegorical Image of France, 1750–1800: A Political Crisis of Representation," *Representations* 47 (Summer 1994), 111–116; and Ronald Paulson, *Representations of Revolution (1789–1820)* (New Haven: Yale University Press, 1983).

11. "Carta de Lei," May 13, 1816 ([Rio de Janeiro]: Impressão Régia, 1816). Images of a sphere or spheres juxtaposed to the *quinas* had appeared in Portuguese royal heraldry since the sixteenth century. See Ana Maria Alves, *Iconologia do poder real no período manuelino, à procura de uma linguagem perdida* (Lisbon: Imprensa Nacional, 1985), figures 25–67. The language of the charter and other commentary, however, suggests that by the nineteenth century the royal heraldry was conceived as separate from the sphere, now identified with both Brazil and the city of Rio. See Januário da Cunha Barbosa, *Oração de Acção de Graças que Celebrando-se na Real Capella do Rio de Janeiro, no dia 7 de Março de 1818 o Decimo Anniversario da Chegada de Sua Magestade . . .* (Rio de Janeiro: Impressão Régia, 1818), 20. The "Sacred Quinas," he wrote, "will be no less formidable appearing above the Sphere of Brazil, than encircled by the Castles of the Algarves." An earlier description of a similar emblem suggests that the new coat of arms was prefigured in the celebration of the prince regent's arrival. See *Relação das festas que se fizerão no Rio de Janeiro, quando o Principe Regente Nosso Senhor e toda a Sua Real Familia chegarão pela primeira vez a'quella Capital . . .* (Lisbon: Impressão Régia, 1810), 10: "above the Sphere the Royal Arms within, because the Arms of the City Council are a Sphere." The sphere adorned atop with a crown was at the center of the flag of the nineteenth-century Brazilian empire, while the sphere alone appears in today's republican flag. See José Murilo de Carvalho, *A formação das almas: o imaginário da República no Brasil* (São Paulo: Companhia das Letras, 1990), 104–105, 109–121.

12. Commenting on the new coat of arms, Luccock wrote: "In that which was adopted, the Government has been thought, by persons ignorant of Heraldic mysteries, to have displayed a little of its vanity, if not of its designs, and to have given to the people a lesson which they are not slow to comprehend, nor reserved enough to conceal." See John Luccock, *Notes on Rio de Janeiro and the southern parts of Brazil; taken during a residence of ten years in that country, from 1808–1818* (London: Samuel Leigh, 1820), 570.

13. Henriques, "Memorial," ff3-3v (emphasis in original).

14. Barbosa, *Oração*, 8.

15. Luiz Gonçalves dos Santos, *Memórias para servir à História do Reino do Brasil* (1825) t. 2 (Belo Horizonte/São Paulo: Itatiaia/EDUSP, 1981), 153–156, 165. On the Portuguese tradition of the Acclamation see Maria Eugénia Reis Gomes, *Contribuição para o estudo da festa no antigo regime* (Lisbon: Instituto Português de Ensino a Distancia, 1985), 37. On ceremonies of the monarchy in nineteenth-century Brazil see Iara Lis Carvalho Souza, *Pátria Coroada: O Brasil como Corpo Político Autônomo, 1780–1831* (São Paulo: UNESP, 1998), 35; and Maria Eurydice de Barros Ribeiro, *Os símbolos do poder. Cerimônias e imagens do Estado monárquico no Brasil* (Brasília: Editora UnB, 1995), 74–88. The affinities between the Acclamation of João VI and the foundation of the Portuguese monarchy were suggested by the 1818 publication of António José de Pina Leitão's *Alfonsíada. Poema heroico da fundação da monarquia portugueza . . .* (Bahia: Manuel António da Silva Serva, 1818).

16. See Bernardo Avellino Ferreira [Souza], *Relação dos Festejos, que a Feliz Acclamação do Muito Alto, Muito Poderoso, e Fidelissimo Senhor D. João VI* . . . (Rio de Janeiro: Typografia Real, 1818), 5, 14; Gonçalves dos Santos, *Memórias* t. 2, 176–177, 216. See also Jean Baptiste Debret, *Viagem Pitoresca e Histórica ao Brasil* t. 3 (Belo Horizonte/São Paulo: Itatiaia/EDUSP, 1989), 70–71 and plates 37–39.

17. See José da Silva Lisboa's comments on Diogo Duarte Silva, "Elogio a Sua Magestade e á nação, que por ocasião de celebrar-se a pacificação de Pernambuco recitou no dia 2 de Julho de 1817," February 25, 1818, ANRJ Antiga Seção Histórica (hereafter ASH) Desembargo do Paço Caixa 169 Documento 19. Reviewing manuscripts by José Eugenio Aragão, Silva Lisboa also struck references to the rivalry of interests and what he considered to be "the less decorous" reference to Portugal as "a secondary or tertiary power before the transfer of the court to Brazil." See José da Silva Lisboa to Sua Alteza Real, April 23, 1818 and February 21, 1820, ANRJ MNB Caixa 5F 205.

18. Luiz António da Silva Souza, *A Discordia Ajustada, Elogio Dramatico para Manifestação do Real Busto do Senhor D. João VI* . . . (Rio de Janeiro: Impressão Régia, 1819). The play was performed in Goiás in 1818 and published in Rio de Janeiro the following year.

19. António Luiz de Brito Aragão Vasconcellos, "Memórias sobre o estabelecimento do Império do Brazil, ou novo Império Lusitano," *ABN*, 43–44 (1920–21).

20. Silva Lisboa, *Memoria*, 113.

21. Gonçalves dos Santos, *Memórias*, t. 2, 151.

22. Ana Cristina Bartolomeu Araújo, "O 'Reino Unido de Portugal, Brasil e Algarves' 1815–1822," *RHI* 14 (1992), 250.

23. Gonçalves dos Santos, *Memórias* t. 2, 151. Gonçalves dos Santos defined the period between the elevation of Brazil to the status of kingdom and the Acclamation as the "second epoch," the epoch of the "Honor of Brazil." The Acclamation, in turn, marked the beginning of a third epoch, that of the "Glory of Brazil." On Leopoldina in Brazil see J.F. de Almeida Prado, *D. João e o início da classe dirigente do Brasil (depoimento de um pintor austríaco no Rio de Janeiro)* (São Paulo: Companhia Editora Nacional, 1968).

24. Silvestre Pinheiro Ferreira, "Memórias Políticas sobre os Abusos Gerais e Modo de os Reformar e Prevenir a Revolução Popular Redigidas por Ordem do Príncipe Regente no Rio de Janeiro em 1814 e 1815," in Pinheiro Ferreira, *Idéias Políticas* (Rio de Janeiro: Editora Documentário, 1976), 20.

25. Ferreira [Souza], *Relação*, 20.

26. Silva Lisboa, *Memoria*, 82–83.

27. Silva Lisboa, *Memoria*, 83.

28. Marquês de Bellas [José Vasconcellos e Souza], [parecer], transcribed in Pereira, *D. João VI*, 40; Manchester, *British Preëminence*, 70–71; Wanderley Pinho, "A Abertura dos Portos—Cairú," *RIHGB* 243 (April–June 1959), 102–108; "Memória escripta por seu filho o conselheiro Bento da Silva Lisboa," in José da Silva Lisboa, *Cairú: excertos da obra inédita "O Espirito de Cairú"* (Rio de Janeiro: Arquivo Nacional, 1958).

29. "Carta Régia," January 28, 1808. The complete text of the royal charter is transcribed in Gonçalves dos Santos, *Memórias* t. 1, 171. As Manchester explains, direct commerce with Brazil initially was "subject to importation duties of twenty-four percent *ad valorem* on dry-goods and double the current duty on certain provisions (*generos molhados*)." Duties on ex-

ports remained the same. Only months later, however, duties on Portuguese goods were reduced, imported raw materials were granted exemptions, and, in order to favor Portuguese shipping, "coast-wise trade was closed to foreign vessels, and foreign commerce was restricted to the ports of Rio, Bahia, Pernambuco, Maranhão and Pará." See Manchester, *British Preëminence*, 70–74; and Valentim Alexandre, *Os sentidos do império: questão nacional e questão colonial na crise do antigo regime português* (Porto: Afrontamento, 1993), 212.

    30. Gonçalves dos Santos, *Memórias* t. 1, 347–349; Ferreira [Souza], *Relação*, 4.

    31. Gonçalves dos Santos, *Memórias* t. 2, 25.

    32. Francisco de Borja Garção Stoeckler, transcribed in Gonçalves dos Santos, *Memórias* t. 2, 196–197.

    33. Rodrigo de Souza Coutinho to Prince Regent Dom João, August, 16, 1809, cited in Maria de Lourdes Viana Lyra, *A Utopia do Poderoso Império, Portugal e Brasil: Bastidores da Política, 1798–1822* (Rio de Janeiro: Sette Letras, 1994), 133.

    34. Souza Coutinho to José Bonifácio de Andrada e Silva, April 26, 1810, cited in Lyra, *Utopia*, 142–143; and "Carta de Lei," 1815.

    35. Seixas, *Sermão de Acção de Graças*, 14; Gonçalves dos Santos, *Memórias* t. 2, 25. Images of Brazilian fertility and paradise abound in writings from the 1810s. See Silva Lisboa, *Memoria*, 113; Tomás António dos Santos Silva, *Braziliada, ou Portugal Immune, e Salvo, Poema Epico em Doze Cantos* (Lisbon: Impressão Régia, 1815); and Henrique José Bernardes, in Pereira, *D. João VI* v. 3, 44–46.

    36. In the 1790s Souza Coutinho referred to Portugal as an "entrepot"; in 1809, Portugal was a "natural storehouse"; in 1811, it was Brazil that played the role of "Commercial Emporium and Entrepot between Europe and Asia (*Empório do Comércio de Entreposto entre a Europa e a Ásia*)." See Alvará, February 4, 1811, cited in Alexandre, *Os sentidos*, 243.

    37. The Marquês de Fronteira e Alorna referred to Portuguese dissatisfaction with the state of being "a colony of a colony." See his *Memórias*, cited in Alexandre, *Os sentidos*, 452. Writing from exile in London the Franco-Portuguese merchant Jacome Ratton also articulated a sense of Portugal's new colonial status and countered that although the potential of the Brazilian economy should be developed, Portugal, and more specifically Lisbon, should remain the center of the imperial economy. See Ratton's article entitled "Pensamentos Patrióticos Império Luzo" (1816), published in the *Investigador Portuguez*, reprinted in "Lettres de Jacques Ratton a António de Araújo de Azevedo, Comte da Barca (1812–1817)," *Bulletin des Etudes Portugaises* (nouvelle série) 25 (1964), 219–228. In contrast, Vasconcellos, writing in Brazil, claimed that Brazil "will no longer be a maritime Colony excluded from the commerce of Nations, as until now, but indeed a great Empire, that will come to be the adjudicator of Europe, the arbiter of Asia and the master of Africa." See Vasconcellos, "Memórias," 7.

    38. Silva Lisboa, *Memoria*, 119. For biographies of Silva Lisboa see the "Memória escripta por seu filho"; Alfredo do Valle Cabral, "Vida e Escriptos de José da Silva Lisboa, Visconde de Cayru," in Silva Lisboa, *Cairú*, 15–54; and António Paim, *Cairu e o liberalismo económico* (Rio de Janeiro: Tempo Brasileiro, 1968). While, as José Luiz Cardoso explains, between 1792 and 1802 Portuguese, including Souza Coutinho and Vila Nova Portugal, first read and "assimilated" Smith's work, Silva Lisboa was most engaged and most interested in apprehending and endorsing it "as a self-contained doctrinaire vision that accepted no correction or adaptation." See José Luiz Cardoso, "Economic thought in late eighteenth-century Portugal: physio-

cratic and Smithian influences," *History of Political Economy* 22, n. 2 (1990), 433–441; and idem, *O Pensamento económico em Portugal nos finais do século XVIII, 1780–1808* (Lisbon: Estampa, 1989), 289–300.

39. Historians have generally argued that in Brazil liberal ideas were either not well disseminated or not meaningfully integrated into Brazilian political culture. The evidence for this failure is slavery and authoritarianism. See Sérgio Buarque de Holanda, *Raízes do Brasil* (21st edition) (Rio de Janeiro: José Olympio, 1989), 119; Roberto Schwarz, "As idéias fora do lugar," in idem, *Ao vencedor as batatas: forma literaria e processo social nos inícios do romance brasileiro* (São Paulo: Livraria Duas Cidades, 1977). Although Schwarz recognized that Brazilian "misplacements" of liberalism could be original, he argued that in Brazil liberal ideas not only did not correspond to unliberal practices (i.e., slavery), but they also failed to hide, or falsely describe, those practices and so made them more abject. Emilia Viotti da Costa has similarly argued that in Brazil "everywhere economic and social structures set the limits of liberalism and the conditions for its critique." See her *The Brazilian Empire: Myths and Histories* (Chicago: Chicago University Press, 1985), 55.

40. Celso Furtado, *The Economic Growth of Brazil, A Survey from Colonial to Modern Times*, trans. Ricardo W. de Aguiar and Eric Charles Drysdale (Berkeley: University of California Press, 1965), 101, 109 (emphasis in original). Furtado may have paraphrased Silva Lisboa's *Princípios de Economia Política* (1804) (Rio de Janeiro: Pongetti, [1956]), 173: "Depois de segura a arrecadação dos necessários impostos para a despesa pública, o único Código racionável de comércio será: *Deixai fazer, deixai passar, deixai comprar, deixai vender*" (emphasis in original).

41. Silva Lisboa, *Memoria*, 68. Silva Lisboa wrote *Princípios de Economia Política* to promote the ideas of Adam Smith in the Portuguese-speaking world and, as Cardoso notes, to respond to the critique of Smith advanced by J.J. Rodrigues Brito in his *Memórias políticas sobre as verdadeiras bases da grandeza das nações* 3 v. (Lisbon: 1803–05). Although Brito did not reject Smith's thought outright, Silva Lisboa charged that he was too influenced by the ideas of the physiocrats which, he argued, had been nullified by Smith. See Cardoso, "Economic Thought," 436; and idem, *Pensamento*, 281–300. Also in 1804, to further disseminate his understanding of commerce, Silva Lisboa published *Princípios de Direito Mercantil e Leis de Marinha para uso da mocidade portuguesa, destinada ao commercio. . .* , republished in Lisbon in 1815 by the Royal Press. Here he declared that his audience was not men of letters who would consult the original texts that also contained these principles but rather, as he indicated in the title, "young Portuguese" engaged in commerce.

42. *Compendio da Obra da Riqueza das Nações de Adam Smith Traduzida do Original Inglez, por Bento da Silva Lisboa* (Rio de Janeiro: Impressão Régia, 1811), x. Two additional volumes were published in 1812. While the Portuguese edition appeared later than most translations (German, 1776; French and Italian, 1779; Spanish 1794), its appearance was timely for reasons I will address below and to the extent that, as Palyi noted, Smith supplied arguments against the Napoleonic system of continental blockade appreciated throughout Europe. See Melchior Palyi, "The Introduction of Adam Smith on the Continent," Separata, *Lectures commemorating the sesquicentennial of the publication of The Wealth of Nations* (n.p., n.d.), 181.

43. J.G.A. Pocock, "The political economy of Burke's analysis of the French Revolution,"

in idem, *Virtue, Commerce, and History: Essays on Political Thought and History, Chiefly in the Eighteenth Century* (New York: Cambridge University Press, 1985), 194.

44. John Stuart Mill, *Principles of Political Economy* (1848), cited in Christopher Herbert, *Culture and Anomie: Ethnographic Imagination in the Nineteenth Century* (Chicago: University of Chicago Press, 1991), 77. An alternative reading of Silva Lisboa's "economic liberalism" as materialistically instrumental, via Furtado, can be found in Alfredo Bosi, *Dialética da colonização* (São Paulo: Companhia das Letras, 1992), 206–207.

45. Silva Lisboa, *Memoria*, 145. Silva Lisboa may have been inspired by this aphoristic passage from Montesquieu: "Commerce cures destructive prejudices . . . Commerce has spread knowledge of the mores of all nations everywhere; they have been compared to each other and good things have resulted from this." See Charles de Secondat, Baron de Montesquieu, *The Spirit of the Laws* (1748) (New York: Cambridge University Press, 1989), 338 (Book 20, Chapter 1).

46. Silva Lisboa, cited in Cabral, "Vida e Escriptos," in Silva Lisboa, *Cairú*, 3.

47. José da Silva Lisboa, *Observações sobre o comércio franco no Brasil* (Rio de Janeiro: Impressão Régia, 1808) cited in Cabral, "Vida e Escriptos," in *Cairú*, 20. It was, of course, not only in Portuguese America where visions of a new, and improved, nineteenth-century empire were formed. Before U.S. independence, Anglo elites on both sides of the Atlantic considered ways of enhancing equality and reciprocity in the British imperial economy. In the United States, however, elites would come to embrace a "republicanized version of the imperial in projecting the prosperity and freedom of their expanding union of states." See Peter S. Onuf, *Jefferson's Empire: The Language of American Nationhood* (Charlottesville: University Press of Virginia, 2000), 58. On reform in late eighteenth-century Spain and Britain see also Anthony Pagden, *Lords of All the World: Ideologies of Empire in Spain, Britain and France, c.1500–c.1800* (New Haven: Yale University Press, 1995).

48. Pagden, *Lords*, Chapter 7; José da Silva Lisboa, *Refutações das Reclamações contra o Commércio Inglez Extrahida de Escriptores Eminentes* (Rio de Janeiro: Impressão Régia, 1810), iv: "Montesquieu observou no *Espirito das Leis, que onde ha commércio, ha doçura de costumes, e onde ha doçura de costumes, ha commércio*" (emphasis in original). Here, Silva Lisboa seems to have reversed the second sentence of Book 20, Chapter 1 of *The Spirit of the Laws*: "it is an almost general rule that everywhere there are gentle mores, there is commerce and that everywhere there is commerce, there are gentle mores."

49. Anthony Pagden, "The 'defense of civilization' in eighteenth-century social theory," in Pagden, *The Uncertainties of Empire* (Norfolk, G. B.: Variorum, 1994), 34. Cardoso, in contrast, reads Silva Lisboa's work as promoting the "autonomous economic development of Brazil" rather than the empire above all. See *Pensamento*, 295.

50. Buarque de Holanda, *Raízes*, 53–54; Silva Lisboa, *Memoria*, 85; and idem, [censorship report on a translation of "Oberon"], November 16, 1818, in ANRJ ASH Desembargo do Paço Caixa 170 Documento 47. Coryphaei are the leaders of a Greek chorus.

51. Silva Lisboa, [censorship report on "Pensées de J.J. Rousseau"], November 19, 1817, ANRJ ASH Desembargo do Paço Caixa 169 Documento 101.

52. *Extractos das Obras Políticas e Econômicas de Edmund Burke por José da Silva Lisboa* 2 v. (Rio de Janeiro: Impressão Régia, 1812). The translation was supported initially by Rodrigo de Souza Coutinho, Minister of Foreign Affairs, who died before it was published. Silva

Lisboa and Strangford then commiserated on the loss of an important ally for both. See Silva Lisboa to Strangford, n.d. ANRJ Arquivo Particular Caixa 1 Pasta 1 Documento 6.

53. José Honório Rodrigues, *Independência: revolução e contra-revolução* v. 4 (Rio de Janeiro: Francisco Alves, [1975–76]), 4.

54. Civil liberty, in other words, could not be confused with what both Burke and Silva Lisboa viewed as libertinage or with rights conjured up by abstract reason instead of inherited through positive law. See Edmund Burke, *Reflections on the Revolution in France* (1790) (Indianapolis: Bobbs-Merrill, 1955), 90. On the French Assembly he wrote, "Their liberty is not liberal. Their science is presumptuous ignorance. Their humanity is savage and brutal." On Burke's understanding of social order, and the threats to order posed by the French Revolution, see also Pocock, "Burke and the Ancient Constitution: A Problem in the History of Ideas," in Pocock, *Politics, Language and Time: Essays in Political Thought and History* (New York: Atheneum, 1971); and Uday Singh Mehta, *Liberalism and Empire: A Study in Nineteenth-Century British Liberal Thought* (Chicago: University of Chicago Press, 1999), 159–161. As Mehta explains, in Burke's work "political society does not turn exclusively on such individual capacities as reason, will, and the ability to choose, but also on the presence of a certain shared order on the ground."

55. Burke, *Extractos*, xv.

56. Burke, *Reflections*, 89–90; Pocock, "Burke's analysis," 199.

57. Buarque de Holanda, *Raízes*, 51–53.

58. Pocock, "Burke's analysis," 199.

59. Montesquieu, *The Spirit of the Laws*, Book 20, Chapter 1.

60. Pocock, "Burke's analysis," 210.

61. Mehta, 138, 172–173. As Mehta argues, the British empire was incompatible with social order as Burke understood it. Like the Jacobins, Mehta explains, the East India Company "disorders the spacial complex that represents the accretion and effects of a long history and the feelings that are attendant on it."

62. Richard Helgerson, *Forms of Nationhood: The Elizabethan Writing of England* (Chicago: University of Chicago Press, 1992), 160; and Sanjay Subrahmanyam, *The Portuguese Empire in Asia, 1500–1700, A Political and Economic History* (London: Longman, 1993), 47–51. As Subrahmanyam explains, the late fifteenth- and early sixteenth-century empire was shaped by both "royal mercantilism" and messianism; "those who were so religiously motivated could often be equally the persons in whose breasts the mostly fervent mercantilist spirit resided."

63. Pocock, "Burke and the Ancient Constitution," 225.

64. Burke, *Reflections*, 39.

65. Silva Lisboa, *Memoria*, vi–vii, 56n. The citation is from Camões's *Lusiadas*, VI, 30 and 31. Elsewhere Silva Lisboa similarly bases his claim that Brazil was a "Promised Land" by citing Dom Henrique via Barros, *Décadas* I, Book 1, Chapter 2. This same passage was also cited by Gonçalves dos Santos. See Chapter 2.

66. Helgerson, *Forms of Nationhood*, 155–156.

67. Silva Lisboa, *Memoria*, 27n, 90–91n. Here he cites Barros, *Décadas* I, Book 1, Chapter 8, and *Décadas* IV, Book 8, Chapter 15, respectively.

68. William Julius Mickle, *The Lusiad* (1776), cited in Helgerson, *Forms of Nationhood*,

190. Mickle's translation, advertised as "the poem of every trading nation . . . the epic poem of the birth of commerce," was the second English-language translation of *Os Lusíadas* and would become the best known. See George Monteiro, *The Presence of Camões: Influences on the Literature of England, America and Southern Africa* (Lexington: University of Kentucky Press, 1996).

69. Helgerson, *Forms of Nationhood*,189–190; James Thomson (1700–1748), "The Seasons," cited in Silva Lisboa, *Memoria*, 58–59. As Monteiro notes, Mickle was an employee of the East India Company and he presented the translation to "the Gentlemen of the East India Company" as an "Epic Poem, particularly their own."

70. Barros, *Décadas* IV, Book 5, Chapter 3, cited in Silva Lisboa, *Memoria*, 99–100n.

71. See Chapter 1 here. The classic seventeenth-century defense of the Portuguese empire and *mare clausum* is Frei Serafim de Freitas, *Do justo império asiático dos portugueses* (1625) 2 v (Lisbon: Instituto Nacional de Investigação Cientítica, 1983).

72. Silva Lisboa, *Memoria*, 8, 99, 104, 117, 117n, 118. Here he cites Barros, *Décadas* III, Book 3, Chapter 7; and Smith, *The Wealth of Nations*, Book 4.

73. Silva Lisboa, *Refutações*, iii–iv; idem, *Memoria*, 43.

74. Silva Lisboa, *Memoria*, 2, 38. Silva Lisboa's articulation of free trade and empire as historically continuous can be contrasted with discussions in Spain, where the need to remake the empire as commercial, Anthony Pagden argues, was seen as a break with a past of conquest, a "shift in the nation's identity." See Anthony Pagden, "Liberty, Honour, and *Comercio Libre.*"

75. See Joaquim José de Queirós, "Mappa da população da côrte e provincia do Rio de Janeiro em 1821," *RIHGB* 33, pt. 1 (1870), where the population is recorded as 43,439 free persons and 36,182 slaves for a total of 79,321. On the growth of population and local economy see also "Almanaque da cidade do Rio de Janeiro para o ano de 1799," *RIHGB* 267 (April–June 1965), 93–214; "Almanaque da cidade do Rio de Janeiro para o ano de 1811," *RIHGB* 282 (January–March 1969), 97–236; "Almanaque da cidade do Rio de Janeiro para o ano de 1816," *RIHGB* 268 (July–September 1965), 179–330; "Almanaque da cidade do Rio de Janeiro para o ano de 1817," *RIHGB* 270 (January–March 1966), 211–370; Larissa Brown, "Internal Commerce in a Colonial Economy: Rio de Janeiro and its Hinterland, 1790–1822" (Ph.D. dissertation, University of Virginia, 1986), 61, 67; and Riva Gorenstein, "Comércio e Política: o enraizamento de interesses mercantis portugueses no Rio de Janeiro (1808–1830)," in Lenira Menezes Martinho and Riva Gorenstein, *Negociantes e Caixeiros na Sociedade da Independência* (Rio de Janeiro: Secretaria Muncipal de Cultura, 1992), 135. Between 1789 and 1822, the number of business establishments, warehouses, eating houses, taverns, and inns all increased by no less than 100 percent.

76. Silva Lisboa, *Memoria*, 163. Here he cites *Proverbs*. See also Vasconcellos, "Memórias," 11, 16.

77. Tomás António Vila Nova Portugal, "Sobre a questão da escravatura," n.d. [1814], BNRJ Ms. I-32,14,22, f2.

78. Silva Lisboa, *Memoria*, 163, 165–169 (emphasis in original). See also *Correio Braziliense*, 1814, 1815, in *Antologia do Correio Braziliense*, ed. Barbosa Lima Sobrinho (Rio de Janeiro: Cátedra/Instituto Nacional do Livro, 1977), 102–108, 131–136.

79. Silva Lisboa, *Memoria*, 163–164.

80. Vila Nova Portugal, "Sobre a questão da escravatura," f2. A remarkably similar argument was made by João Severiano Maciel da Costa in the late 1810s and early 1820s. See his *Memória sobre a necessidade de abolir a introdução dos escravos africanos no Brasil* . . . (1821), in *Memórias sobre a escravidão*, ed. Graça Salgado (Rio de Janeiro: Arquivo Nacional, 1988), 21. Maciel da Costa was a magistrate and governor of Portuguese occupied French Guiana (1809–1817).

81. Silva Lisboa, *Observações sobre a franqueza da industria.* . . , transcribed in *Cairú*, 104.

82. See Vasconcellos, "Memórias," 19, 24, 31; Maciel da Costa, *Memória*, 44; Luiz Mott, "A escravatura: o propósito de uma representação a El-Rei sobre a escravatura no Brasil," *Revista do Instituto de Estudos Brasileiros* 14 (1993), 127–136; and, on Vila Nova Portugal, Clayton, "Life," 111. Both Maciel da Costa and Vasconcellos advocated promoting immigration in European gazettes.

83. Silva Lisboa, *Memoria*, 157, 164. Writing in London, Hipólito José da Costa, the editor of the *Correio Braziliense,* also advocated European immigration. See *Correio*, December 1810, May 1811, March 1813, 1816, 1818, 1820, in *Antologia*, 54–55, 69–71, 89–90, 142–153, 200–202, 257–262.

84. Manchester, *British Preëminence,* 91, 170–171.

85. Viana, "Abreviada demonstração," *RIHGB* 55, pt. 1 (1892), 378–379; Viana to Sua Alteza Real, November 17, 1810, ANRJ MNB Caixa 6J 78; Clayton, "Life," 40, 176–187. Azorean immigrants were given an exception from military service. See Viana, "Registro do Ofício ao Ministro de Estado dos Negócios do Ultramar," February 10, 1813, Códice 323 v. 3 f139v. On Swiss immigration see Martin Nicoulin, *A Gênese de Nova Friburgo. Emigração e colonização suíça no Brasil (1817–1827)* (Rio de Janeiro/Nova Friburgo: Biblioteca Nacional/Prefeitura Municipal de Nova Friburgo, 1996).

86. Souza Coutinho to Fernando José de Portugal, [ca. November 23, 1808], ANRJ MNB Caixa 5B 530 (commenting on the English Consul's attempt to purchase a house that belonged to the Benedictines); Silva Lisboa, *Observações sobre a franqueza,* in *Cairú*, 102–108. Here Silva Lisboa saw "analogies" in what he regarded to be a sound and gradual promotion of industry that avoided the hazards of competing with Europe. He also endorsed immigration out of fear that otherwise Brazil would become a "Negroland." See *Memoria*, 175. In a review of Silva Lisboa's work the editor of the *Correio Braziliense* defended Silva Lisboa's perception of the United States as a model (claiming that slavery was abolished there), and extended this argument to advocate an embrace of political and civil liberties. See *Correio*, July 1809, in *Antologia*, 32–41.

87. Parker, "Tridentine Order," 185. On Vila Nova Portugal's enthusiasm for Catholic immigrants see Clayton, "Life," 177–180.

88. Barbosa, *Oração*, 18.

89. A decade after the prince regent's arrival, Brazil was home to Dutch, Russians, Germans, Italians, and Chinese, as well as the almost 2,000 crown-sponsored Swiss immigrants who settled in the province of Rio. See "Mappa dos estrangeiros . . . nos livros da matricula feita pela intendência geral da polícia da côrte, e Reino do Brasil" [1817], BNRJ Ms. I 3,13,15; "Mappa dos estrangeiros . . . " [1819], BNRJ Ms. II 34,32,28; "Mappa dos estrangeiros . . . " [1820], BNRJ Ms. I 31,30,95; "Mappa dos estrangeiros que consta a polícia terem estabelecimentos no Reino do Brasil" [1818], BNRJ Ms. II 34,32,28; *Os Franceses resi-*

dentes no Rio de Janeiro, 1808–1820 (Rio de Janeiro: Arquivo Nacional, 1960). The figures provided by the summaries are as follows:

1817: French, 183; English, 352; Spanish, 220
1819: French, 412; English, 490; Spanish, 319
1820: French, 301; English, 443; Spanish, 310; Swiss, 1,749

Members of a small group of Chinese residents reportedly worked as peddlers, cooks, and, especially, in the cultivation of tea, which many were recruited to promote. See Carlos Francisco Moura, *Os Chineses do Rio de Janeiro Requerem a D. João VI um consul e intérprete* (Macau: Imprensa Nacional, 1974); idem., "Colonos Chineses no Brasil no Reinado de D. João VI," *Boletim do Instituto "Luiz de Camões"* (Macau) 7, n. 2 (Summer 1973). Writing anonymously, one courtier characterized Souza Coutinho's interest in Chinese immigration as absurd. See Pereira, *D. João VI* v. 3, 48–49. For a discussion of the cultural politics of Asian immigration in Brazil see Jeffrey Lesser, *Negotiating National Identity: Immigrants, Minorities, and the Struggle for Ethnicity in Brazil* (Durham: Duke University Press, 1999), 14–39.

90. Gorenstein, "Comércio e Política," 137; Henry Hill, *Uma visão do comércio do Brasil em 1808/ A [v]iew of the commerce of Brazil* ([Salvador]: Banco da Bahia, s.d.), 55; Leslie Bethell, "The Independence of Brazil" in Bethell, ed. *The Independence of Latin America* (New York: Cambridge University Press, 1987), 171; Jean Franco, "Un Viaje Poco Romántico: Viajeros británicos hacia Sudamérica: 1818–28," *Escritura* 4, n. 7 (1979), 129–142. On the "sanguine speculations to which [the British] were incited," see also John Mawe, *Travels in the Interior of Brazil* . . . (London: M. Carey/Boston: Wells and Lilly, 1816), 110, 334–335. As Mawe noted, an example of the most senseless speculation was the importation of skates "for the use of people," he imagined, "who are totally uninformed that water can become ice."

91. Mawe, *Travels*, 110; Alvará, May 4, 1808.

92. The text of the treaty is in Manuel Pinto Aguiar, *A abertura dos portos, Cairú e os inglêses* (Salvador: Progresso, 1960) and is summarized in Manchester, *British Preëminence*, 88–89.

93. Valentim Alexandre, "O nacionalismo vintista e a questão brasileira: esboço de análise política," in *O Liberalismo na Península Ibérica na primeira metade do século XIX* v. 1, ed. Miriam Halpern Pereira (Lisbon: Sa da Costa, 1982), 288.

94. *O Patriota* 4 (October 1813), 73; Joaquim José Lisboa, *A Protecção dos Inglezes: Versos* (Rio de Janeiro: Impressão Régia, 1809), 4. See also António José de Lima Leitão, *Ode ao Illustrissimo, e Excellentissimo Senhor Duque de Wellington* . . . (Rio de Janeiro: Impressão Régia, 1816); Francisco Mãi dos Homens, *Oração que na Real Capella desta Corte Celebrando-se as Acções de Graças pelas noticias do Armisticio Geral* . . . (Rio de Janeiro: Impressão Régia, 1814), 22–23; 29, 37; *Profecia Politica Realizada no Excellentissimo Arthur Lord Wellington* . . . (Rio de Janeiro: Impressão Régia, 1811); José da Silva Lisboa, *Memoria da Vida Publica do Lord Wellington* 2 v., and *Appendice á Memoria da Vida de Lord Wellington* (Rio de Janeiro: Impressão Régia, 1815). Faced with accusations of Brazilian antipathy for the English published in Andrew Grant, *History of Brazil* . . . (London: 1809), the editor of *O Patriota* criticized Grant for errors of fact and asserted that the British were well received and that the alliance was celebrated, and pledged his own admiration for Adam Smith. See "Exame de algumas passagens de hum moderno Viajante ao Brazil, e refutação de seus erros mais grosseiros, por hum

Brazileiro" and "Continuação," *O Patriota* 3 and 5 (September and November 1813).

95. See Vasconcellos, "Memórias," 20, 23; "Lettres de Jacques Ratton," May 15, 1813, December 6, 1814, January 3, 1816, and May 6, 1816. Although Ratton suggested recruiting Irish Catholic immigrants, he was against establishing the Inquisition in Brazil. The editor of the *Correio Braziliense* also linked the success of immigration to religious tolerance.

96. Galveas cited in Manchester, *British Preëminence*, 86.

97. Vila Nova Portugal, "Sobre a ratificação dos tratados" [n.d. ca. 1814], BNRJ Ms. I-32,14,22, f.1; idem, "Sobre o recrutamento" [n.d. ca. 1814], BNRJ Ms. I-3,17,21.

98. Maciel da Costa, *Memória*, 14, 44–47, 52. He cites J.J. Dauxion-Lavaysse, *Voyage aux iles de Trinidad, de Tabago, de la Marguerite, et dans diverse parties de Vénézuéla . . .* (Paris, 1813).

99. Parker, "Tridentine Order," 180; Nicoulin, *Gênese*, 181–183. As Nicoulin explains, there were also conflicts within the Swiss community between Catholics and Calvinists.

100. See Viana to Aguiar, May 22, 1811, ANRJ MNB Caixa 6J 78.

101. Luccock, *Notes on Rio de Janeiro*, 249. For an analysis of the British experience in Brazil from the perspective of British accounts see Louise Helena Guenther, "The British Community of Bahia, Brazil, 1808–1850" (Ph.D. dissertation, University of Minnesota 1998).

102. Viana, "Registro do Ofício expedido ao Ministro dos Negócios Estrangeiros e de Guerra," March 8, 1811, ANRJ Códice 323 v. 3, f26.

103. Strangford cited in Manchester, *British Preëminence*, 99.

104. Parker, "Tridentine Order," 180.

105. Viana, "Registro do Ofício expedido ao Ministro de Estado dos Negócios Estrangeiros e de Guerra," December 14 and 22, 1810, ANRJ Códice 323 v. 2, f31, f41v. See also Viana, "Registro do Ofício expedido ao Ministro de Estado dos Negócios Estrangeiros," July 25, 1809, ANRJ Códice 323 v. 1.

106. Viana, "Registro do Ofício expedido ao Ministro de Estado dos Negócios Estrangeiros e de Guerra," February 22, 1812, ANRJ Códice 323 v. 3, f98v.

107. Viana, "Registro do Ofício expedido ao Ministro de Estado dos Negócios Estrangeiros e de Guerra," June 18, 1811, ANRJ Códice 323 v. 3 f54v.

108. See *Código Brasiliense*; Manchester, *British Preëminence*, 74–76.

109. "Decreto," February 23, 1808, transcribed in Aguiar, *A abertura*, 173. According to Lenira Martinho, after 1808 there was a proliferation of *aulas* on commerce in the city. Those sponsored by the crown were modeled after a course in Portugal created by the Marquês de Pombal and followed a curriculum that included algebra, geometry, geology, geography, mining, agriculture, commerce, and accounting, using, among other texts, the works of Silva Lisboa. A royal decree granted José da Silva Lisboa the *cadeira da aula pública* in Rio de Janeiro. See Decreto, Bahia, February 23, 1808, BNRJ Ms. I-31,28,40; José António Lisboa, "Aula de Comércio," *RIHGB* 28 (July–September 1950), anexo IV, 172–173; and Lenira Menezes Martinho, "Caixeiros e Pés-Descalços: Conflitos e Tensões em um Meio Urbano em Desenvolvimento," in *Negociantes e Caixeiros*, 53–56.

110. Alexandre, *Os sentidos*, 210–221.

111. Lyra, *Utopia*, 132. The British *chargé* in Strangford's absence commented that although the opening of Brazil's ports did not "fail to produce a good effect in England . . . had

it authorized the admittance of British vessels, and of British manufactures upon terms more advantageous than those granted to the Ships and Merchandise of other Foreign Nations, it would necessarily have afforded greater satisfaction." See citation in Manchester, *British Preëminence*, 71.

112. Manchester, *British Preëminence*, 87–89; Alexandre, *Os sentidos*, 217–225.

113. Luccock, *Notes on Rio de Janeiro*, iv.

114. Alexandre, "O nacionalismo," 290–291. As Alexandre reminds us, news of the treaties arrived as the French were launching their third invasion of Portugal, when the alliance seemed as crucial as ever. See David Gates, *The Spanish Ulcer: A History of the Peninsular War* (New York: Norton, 1986). The *Correio Braziliense* also published criticisms of the treaties and the British. See *Correio*, January 1811, in *Antologia*, 57–61.

115. Conde de Palmela to João Paulo Bezerra, London, November 8, 1817, in *Dom João*, ed. Carneiro de Mendonça, 345–353; Manchester, *British Preëminence*, 99–105.

116. Manchester, *British Preëminence*, 165–185; Manolo Garcia Florentino, *Em Costas Negras: Uma História do Tráfico Atlântico de Escravos entre África e o Rio de Janeiro (Séculos XVIII e XIX)* (Rio de Janeiro: Arquivo Nacional, 1993).

117. Maciel da Costa, *Memória*, 17–19. For a similar critique see Anselmo Correa Henriques to Viana, Lisbon, August 6, 1814, in *Dom João VI*, ed. Carneiro de Mendonça, 267–269.

118. Alexandre, *Os sentidos*, 171–172; *Representations of the Brazilian Merchants against the Insults Offered to the Portuguese Flag, and against the Violent and Oppressive Capture of Several of Their Vessels . . . to which is added, a short analysis of a work entitled, The History of the Azores, or Western Islands, etc. in which is shown the injustice of that author towards the Portuguese Nation, and the Impudence with which he proposes to the English government to seize upon those islands, as an indemnity for the debt which is owning from Portugal to Great Britain . . . translated from the original Portuguese Investigator* (London: J. Darling, Minerva Press, 1813).

119. Viana to Souza Coutinho, February 10 and 15, 1810, ANRJ MNB Caixa 6J 78; Viana, "Registro do Ofício expedido ao Ministro de Estado dos Negócios Estrangeiros e de Guerra [Souza Coutinho]," December 13, 1810, ANRJ Códice 323 v. 2, f21v; Viana to Aguiar, November 23, 1816, ANRJ MNB Caixa 6J 83; Viana to Vila Nova Portugal, December 1 and 18, 1818, ANRJ MNB Caixa 6J 80; Luiz José Viana Gurgel de Amaral Rocha, "Memoria," December 18, 1819, ANRJ Códice 807 Livro 22, f48–49.

120. [Anonymous], Pereira, *D. João VI* v. 3, 49–50. See also Viana, "Registro do Ofício expedido ao Ministro de Estado dos Negócios Estrangeiros e de Guerra," July 10, 1809, ANRJ Códice 323 v. 1, f97v. According to Viana, no witnesses would attest to the merchant's aggression.

121. Frei João da Costa Faria, "Oração funebre recitada em 13 de Outubro de 1812 na parochial igreja de São José, celebrando-se as exéquias do . . . Dom Pedro Carlos . . . ," ms., ANRJ ASH Desembargo do Paço Caixa 169 Documento 95, f7v. Faria's submission of the prayer for publication by the royal press led to a private debate with Silva Lisboa, his censor. In "Memória em sustentação da censura official á oração funebre . . . em resposta do reverendo pregador com protestação contra a inovação de se introduzir política no pulpito," Silva Lisboa objected to the author's description of England as "almost queen of both worlds" and references to its "political preponderance over all nations." See Documento 95, f19-20v.

122. British vice consul to Viana, July 23, 1813, ANRJ MNB Caixa 6J 79.

123. Strangford cited in Manchester, *British Preëminence*, 99.

124. [Nuno Álvarez Pereira Pato Moniz], *A Gloria do Oceano, Drama que se Representou no Theatro Nacional da Rua dos Condes, em Obsequio do Fausto Dia Natalicio de S.M. Britanica El Rei Jorge III . . .* (Reprint) (Rio de Janeiro: Impressão Régia, 1810), Scene I. For a similar slippage see Leitão, *Ode ao Illustrissimo, e Excellentissimo Senhor Duque de Wellington*, 9.

125. "Representação dos comerciantes desta corte contra os mascates," April 25, 1815, BNRJ Ms. II-34,27,24 (108 signatures).

126. Alexandre, *Os sentidos*, 219; Mawe, *Travels*, 111.

127. See, for example, Silva Lisboa's comments on Manuel Joaquim da Mai dos Homens, "Ensaio Político Histórico," February 20, 1815, ANRJ ASH Desembargo do Paço Caixa 171, Documento 3. Silva Lisboa objected to characterizations of the English such as "with the pretense of friendship they take [our] money" and references to English "despotism" and encroachment on Portuguese Asia, such as "it is not known whether they [the Asian colonies] are Portuguese or English." In 1815, Mai dos Homens responded by claiming that Silva Lisboa was "a man of foreign partisanship." See also Silva Lisboa's report on Luiz Prates de Almeida e Albuquerque's translation of Herreschwand's *Discurso Fundamental sobre a População*, May 10, 1813, ANRJ ASH Desembargo do Paço Caixa 169 Documento 77. In this case, Silva Lisboa did not stop the edition but rather insisted on the need for footnotes that placed criticisms of Adam Smith and praise of "offensive" authors in context. The translation was published by the Royal Press in 1814.

128. José da Silva Lisboa, *Refutações*. In 1809, reviewing *Observações*, the editor of the *Correio Braziliense* endorsed Silva Lisboa's defense of the benefits of trade with the British, although he urged him to establish a fuller reciprocity in Portuguese-British trade. See *Correio*, July 1809, in *Antologia*, 32–41.

129. Silva Lisboa, *Memoria*, 97–98, 139, 142, 146–149, 152.

130. Silva Lisboa, *Memoria*, 150.

131. "Representação . . . contra os mascates."

132. "Representação dos moradores do Rio de Janeiro contra a subida de algueis," n.d. [ca. 1808–09], BNRJ Ms. II-34,25,24.

133. [Petition], n.d. [ca. 1808], BNRJ Ms. II-34,27,10.

134. See ANRJ ASH Desembargo do Paço Caixa 171 Documento 13 [1809–10].

135. Cardoso, *Pensamento*, 215–216. Here Cardoso contrasts Veiga's work with that of Rodrigues de Brito with whom, as noted above, Silva Lisboa debated. See also Augusto Victorino Sacramento Blake, *Diccionario bibliographico brazileiro* v. 6 (1900) (Nendeln, Liechtenstein: Krause Reprint, 1969), 151; Innocencio Francisco da Silva, *Diccionario bibliographico portuguez* (Lisbon: Imprensa Nacional, 1858–1923), v. 6, 41–42; v. 16, 256–257. Both list the complete pamphlet title as *Analyse dos factos practicados em Inglaterra, relativamente ás propriedades portuguezas de negociantes residentes em Portugal e Brasil* (London: W. Glendinning, 1808).

136. "Auto de Perguntas feitas a Manuel Luiz da Veiga preso na Fortaleza da Ilha das Cobras," October 23, 1810, ANRJ Devassas Caixa 2754.

137. "Auto das Terceiras Perguntas [feitas a Torresão]," October 25, 1810, ff2-2v, ANRJ

Devassas Caixa 2754. A similar critique was made in the *Correio Braziliense* with which Torresão claimed to be familiar.

138. Correa Henriques to Viana, Lisbon, April 26 and December 16, 1814, in *Dom João,* ed. Carneiro de Mendonça, 264–265, 273–276; and idem, "Memorial," f1v. Henriques' concern for the effects of English ambition are also expressed in "Reflexões sucintas sobre a política inglesa, relativas aos imediatos interesses de Portugal, e do modo de ganhar a influência sobre a sua existência política," Rio de Janeiro, September 25, 1815, transcribed in *Dom João VI,* ed. Carneiro de Mendonça, 305–310.

139. Alexandre, "O nacionalismo vintista," 290–293.

SEVEN

Legacies and Liberties:

CONSTITUTIONALISM IN RIO DE JANEIRO

IN 1821 THE DEVOTED ROYAL CHRONICLER LUIZ GONÇALVES DOS SANTOS RESOLVED to suspend the writing of his monumental *Memórias* of Dom João's reign in Brazil. It had become too difficult, he explained, to "commemorate events that happened in the midst of such a restlessness of spirit and interests difficult to reconcile."[1] The most "extraordinary" of these events to which Gonçalves dos Santos referred was Dom João's pledge of allegiance to a new constitution in February of that year. The concerted and ultimately successful demand for a written constitution had emerged only a few months earlier in August 1820. At that time, a diverse group of property owners, merchants, low ranking military officers, magistrates, clergy, and some members of the nobility in Porto, Portugal called on the king to return to Lisbon and proclaimed the "regeneration" of the Portuguese nation by convoking the Cortes, a formerly consultative institution representative of the kingdom as manifest in the reunion of the three estates (clergy, nobility, and the people), for the deliberative task of writing a new constitution.[2] "Long Live our Good Father," read one proclamation from 1820, "Long Live the Cortes, and with them the Constitution."[3] The slogan made clear both the movement's loyalty to the monarchy and the fact that this loyalty depended on the king's own allegiance to the Cortes and a new constitution that, in turn, would circumscribe royal power and restrict it to the role of executor. The nation rather than the crown would be sovereign. The crown then recognized the legitimacy of the movement and the Cortes after constitutionalists in Rio de Janeiro staged a rebellion in February demanding Dom João's allegiance to the new "constitutional system."

This chapter examines the process of establishing this "system" in the New World court. In Rio de Janeiro news of the Porto rebellion provoked debate and speculation among royal officials and residents about what this event would mean for the future of the monarchy, the new empire of open ports, and the Kingdom of Brazil. Having witnessed, and in some cases supported, the initial triumph of constitutionalism secured by the local February rebellion noted above, the city's residents

proceeded to forge their own critique of absolutist government and their own experience of the politics of constitutionalism in an assembly convened the following
April. Although the crown sought to suppress these politics, characterizing them as
"anarchy" and "seditious machinations," when Dom João returned to Portugal, he
nevertheless left his pledge to a new constitutional government in Brazil intact. In
the weeks and months that followed, constitutionalism became a transatlantic discourse founded on appeals to universal principles of liberty, equality, and popular
sovereignty, forged in sermons, prayers, and speeches made locally, and in pamphlets
and newspapers published in both Portugal and Brazil. It was a "creed," as Raymundo Faoro has argued, that offered the possibility of "an ideological embrace that
would homogenize the whole empire."[4] Yet constitutionalism also had a particular
resonance within Rio de Janeiro. The promise of a political "regeneration" embedded
within tradition and history recalled the vision of political renewal that defined the
New World empire and the New World court after 1808. In offering a more just and
direct relationship between the people and the king, constitutionalism also reinforced claims to the exercise of rights made by Rio's residents following Dom João's
arrival. Consequently, whereas in Portugal constitutionalism featured a reaction
against the "new order of things" created by the transfer of the court, motivated by
the fear of what in Portugal was construed to be the state of being "a colony of a
colony,"[5] in Rio de Janeiro constitutionalism was another step toward achieving this
new order. The end of absolute royal power, in other words, followed from the end
of "the old colonial system." As these divergent interpretations of the meaning of
constitutionalism took shape, they then challenged the transatlantic political community that constitutionalists in both Portugal and Brazil, each in their own ways,
had sought to "regenerate."

"GREAT AND EXTRAORDINARY EVENTS": THE TRIUMPH OF CONSTITUTIONALISM IN THE NEW WORLD COURT

On the morning of February 26, 1821 Rio's residents awoke to the sound of ringing
bells and shots fired from nearby forts to find troops stationed at the Largo do Rocio
and artillery, "well stocked with powder and shot," placed at the intersections of
many of the city's streets. The previous night Portuguese troops stationed in Brazil
after the Peninsular War, together with a group of supporters described by witnesses
as "citizens of all classes," had convened to stage a revolt. As the rebel leadership then
made known, they wanted the king's pledge to accept the constitution being written
in Lisbon, whose norms would apply equally in Portugal and Brazil. Around five
o'clock in the morning, Dom João's heir, Prince Dom Pedro, appeared before the

troops and the now large group of people gathered in the square and presented a new royal decree in which the crown basically accepted the rebels' demands. At the insistence of those gathered, "some words that did not please the people were scratched out and others were substituted by the prince, *such as approve the Constitution in the version that arrives from Portugal . . .*" (emphasis in original). A list of names was given to the prince to present to Dom João, from which he was to choose a new government. When the prince then returned to the Rocio from the palace in São Cristovão he proceeded "among thousands of *vivas* from the People and the Troops" to the theater's veranda where he read the decree along with the names of those chosen to comprise the new royal cabinet. These ministers, as one witness reported, along with "a great number of persons of all classes who were gathered there," were called on to solemnly swear to defend the new constitution. At the insistence of those assembled, the prince then returned to the royal palace so that he could escort Dom João to the city's center where an official royal audience was held, followed by a "great gala" at the theater and a festive illumination of the city for nine days.[6] The "happy events" of "the memorable, marvelous day of February 26" were hailed as having guaranteed Rio's place in the new constitutional order. As one resident poet proclaimed, it signaled the "dawn of liberty" in Brazil.[7]

Both the rebellion and the crown's response represented the culmination of intense speculation and expectation that had consumed royal officials and the city's residents since October 1820, when news of the constitutionalist rebellion in Porto reached the court of Rio. As a steady stream of rumor and news had followed, including one accurate report that the rebellion had spread to Lisbon, the crown remained publicly impassive.[8] Within the palace royal counselors divided over how the crown should respond to the constitutionalists' agenda, which included a call for the return of the king to Lisbon. Royal Minister Tomás António Vila Nova Portugal led the faction opposed to concessions to the Portuguese constitutionalists. Insisting on the fundamental illegality of the Cortes and arguing that another member of the royal family should be sent in Dom João's place, he made his case through policy statements (*pareceres*) and a pamphlet published anonymously in French by the Royal Press entitled "Le Roi et la Famille Royale de Bragance doivent-ils dans les circonstances présentes, retourner en Portugal, ou bien rester au Brésil?" (Should the King and the Royal Family in the present Circumstances Return to Portugal or Instead Stay in Brazil). Probably written by Geine de Cailhé, a French resident who worked as an adviser and informant for the police intendancy, the pamphlet asserted that the departure of the king would lead to Brazil's independence from Portugal and generally reinforced Vila Nova Portugal's contention that in offering a solution to the crisis the crown, above all, needed to show the constitutionalists in Portugal that "Brazil was not to be a colony" and to "assure the Brazilians that nothing will be resolved without consideration for their interests." The new court of Rio de Janeiro, Vila Nova Portugal hoped, would serve, as it had in 1807–1808 and during the republican insurgency of 1817 in the Brazilian northeast, as absolute monarchy's haven, providing a base from which the crown could reestablish its undivided authority in Portugal.[9] An opposing strategy for responding to constitutionalist demands was championed by the Conde de Palmela, a recently arrived diplomat, who argued that the Porto rebellion was not an isolated instance of revolutionary sympathies, but rather part of a general trend toward representative government that the monarchy could no longer resist. According to Palmela, the crown therefore needed to take the lead in crafting the new political order: a constitutional monarchy with a royal residence alternating between America and Europe.[10]

As the impasse among royal counsel continued, rumor of constitutionalist advances and of the crown's possible response spread through Rio's streets. A more imposing escort exhibited during Dom João's visit to one neighborhood was interpreted as a sign of insecurity, Cailhé informed the police intendant. Rumors that the king had signed a constitution also circulated and caused "commotion." Cailhé's pamphlet itself reportedly provoked further discussion and, according to one British diplomat, led many to endorse action "in Unison with the Constitutionalists" rather than Vila Nova Portugal's conservative position. With frustration and trepidation Dom João's counselors exchanged reports of incendiary conversations on the *Passeio Público*, of the proliferation of pamphlets and handwritten pasquinades, and of the spread of support for the Porto rebellion among the city's residents. The king, in response, retreated from public view. Even the birth of his grandson, the future heir to the throne, was kept secret for fear that the announcement would be transformed into an occasion to declare constitutionalist allegiances.[11]

Amid this atmosphere of expectation, the rebellion of February 26 then was precipitated more directly by two events. First, on February 17, Rio's residents received news of a garrison revolt in Bahia and the subsequent establishment of a *junta de governo* in Salvador that recognized the Lisbon Cortes, a move that paradoxically sacrificed, the royal counselor Silvestre Pinheiro Ferreira surmised, the political integrity of Brazil in an attempt to preserve the political integrity of the empire as a whole under the aegis of a constitution.[12] This institutionalized advance of constitutionalism within American territory also challenged Rio's status as the political center of the empire and made the crown's irresolution seem all the more imprudent. Second, on February 22, having barely absorbed the news from Bahia, Rio's residents then learned of the crown's position in relation to the constitutionalists in Portugal. Hoping to end debate on constitutionalism and the Cortes' actions and to quell suspicions of its own incertitude, the crown acknowledged the call for political change. Yet it also denied the deliberative nature of the Cortes and instead affirmed its own authority to preside over the deliberations in Portugal, to "listen to the representations and complaints of the Peoples," and "establish the reforms and improvements and the Laws that can consolidate the Portuguese Constitution." The "just and appropriate measures to consolidate the Throne and ensure the happiness of the Portuguese Nation" further included the return of Prince Dom Pedro to Portugal, "provided with the Authority and necessary Instructions to immediately execute the measures and provisions that [His Highness] Judges convenient, with the purpose of reestablishing the general tranquility of that Kingdom."[13]

As Roderick Barman has observed, as the crown thus set out to reestablish its authority over Portugal and the unity of the empire, the decree also suggested an alternative to transatlantic constitutionalism and called into question the United Kingdom itself. For the constitution, the decree also asserted, could not be "equally adaptable and convenient in all its articles and essential points to the Population, locality and other circumstances so ponderous and in need of attention in this Kingdom of Brazil." Therefore, the crown called for a meeting of representatives from Brazil to convene in Rio de Janeiro "so that gathered here . . . they not only examine and consult which of these articles are adaptable to the Kingdom of Brazil, but also propose to Me the other reforms, improvements, establishments and other measures that they understand to be essential or useful. . . ."[14] Separating political reform in Portugal from reform in Brazil, the crown considered, would weaken the constitutionalist movement as a whole. If, on the contrary, the constitutionalists were to triumph in Portugal, Brazil, at least, as Vila Nova Portugal hoped, would remain within the absolute monarchy's domain.

Raising as many questions as it answered, however, the decree failed to meet the crown's goal of ending local debates on constitutionalism. Indeed, rather than curtail speculation on the future of the monarchy, the status of the new court within the empire, and the political rights of its residents, the observer José Aréas reported, the decree's publication provoked "a very great discussion in public" and galvanized both opposition and support for constitutionalism. As the Marquês de Alegrete reported to Dom João, now "nothing appear[ed] that [did] not make the excitement grow." As one opponent of constitutionalism surmised, "after the eighteenth [the date of the decree] nothing could be fixed." "Beware of the insolence—*Viva a Constituição* and death to all those who do not approve it—," he warned, for it was not "the golden pearl of our Beloved and Good Sovereign." This threatening defiance of which the resident warned was manifest, in another instance, in a slogan that defaced a copy of the decree posted outside the palace. "It is not an attribute of the king to give law to the people," its author proclaimed, "but rather from [the people] to receive it." A new round of pasquinades also "circulated," according to Cailhé, including a call to arms: "To arms citizens, take up arms / You shouldn't lose another moment / Because if kings don't understand reason / Arms will make the kings." To make matters worse for the crown, persistent division within the court was made public with the resignation of the Conde de Palmela, who then returned to the royal cabinet only after he made it known that he had not approved the decree and indeed judged it to be irresolute, a failure to squarely address the demand for legislative representation.[15] This new, tentative, and unsatisfactory state of affairs, however, also proved to be short lived, as the rebellion came just days later, undercutting the decree's evasive definition of the nature of constitutional reform entirely.

As Tobias Monteiro, Neill Macaulay, and Roderick Barman have noted, some residents suspected that Dom Pedro had fostered the rebellion in an attempt to "anticipate the revolution" and save the monarchy with himself at its head. As Aréas claimed, it was said that if the king had not consented to the rebels' demands, "the troops were resolved to acclaim his son Pedro IV."[16] Apologists for the rebellion, however, explained that any support exhibited by Dom Pedro was solicited strategically by the real leadership, men who, as Cecilia Helena de Salles Oliveira has argued, included landowners and merchants who perceived their own interests to be limited by the politics of absolutism and, more specifically, by an alliance of certain royal cabinet members and other landowners and merchants wealthier than they. The decree announcing that Dom Pedro would depart for Portugal and, implicitly, that Dom João would remain, together with a subsequent decree that enlisted absolutist courtiers, including Vila Nova Portugal, for a *Junta de Cortes* for Brazil, she explains, appeared to foreclose the possibility of reform that would allow them to promote their own political and economic power in Rio and, therefore, demanded a response.[17]

Yet the staging of the rebellion, as contemporary witnesses noted, also required and made manifest a broader, although divided, base of support and a complex alignment of both conservative and constitutionalist agendas with "European" and "American" "interests" related, as was the case following the court's arrival, to the perceived location of these interests rather than place of birth. On the one hand, a diverse group of residents of Rio who were unsatisfied with the conservative position that the crown had assumed, one that clearly bore the mark of Vila Nova Portugal's influence, saw the rebellion as a way to guarantee the deliberative authority of the Cortes and the inclusion of Brazil in the new constitutional order. On the other hand, the troops, and those Pinheiro Ferreira identified as "Europeans" objected, more specifically, to the creation of a second constitutional regime in Brazil. According to Aréas, this group also included "the *caixerada* of the city," primarily Portuguese-born commercial clerks. Having formed allegiances to the new regime in Portugal quickly, on February 26 they acted out of fear, Pinheiro Ferreira surmised, that Brazil would assume a position "different from that which the Cortes of the metropolis had decreed."[18] There were, however, also other "Europeans," including courtiers and royal servants who opposed the rebellion as a revolutionary attack on royal authority. This group included the absolutist Vila Nova Portugal, as well as the more moderate Pinheiro Ferreira himself, who nevertheless was obliged to assume a post in the new royal government. According to Pinheiro Ferreira, a more radical "Brazilian party" had emerged in support of the rebellion as well. Their support, Pinheiro Ferreira lamented, was strategic rather than principled, for they sought "to promote Brazil, without attending to the needs of Portugal" in the process of reform.[19]

Written in the days following the rebellion, the accounts of Aréas and Pinheiro Ferreira testify as much to the rebellion's effects as to its causes; to the perception of "factions," "parties," and "interests" that had been embodied publicly and, both men feared, permanently, with catastrophic consequences for the monarchy. Indeed, in spite of official claims that the rebellion and the crown's subsequent decree together resolved the question of the future of constitutionalism in the Portuguese world, in the city's streets questions about both supporters and opponents and their motivations persisted. In the first days of March fear of factions and opposition to a "Brazilian party," in particular, or what Aréas characterized as the "pretext of a Brazilian reaction in favor of independence," mounted and led the crown to arrest the magistrates Luiz José de Carvalho e Mello and João Severiano Maciel da Costa, the Visconde de São Lourenço, and the Almirante Rodrigo Pinto Guedes, placing them in

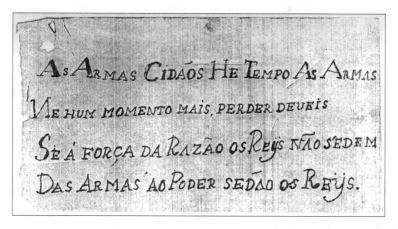

FIGURE 13: Anonymous, "To arms citizens, it is time to take up arms. You should not lose another moment. If to the force of reason kings do not cede, kings will give in to the power of arms" (AHI Lata 195 Maço 6 Pasta 13). Permission granted by the Arquivo Histórico do Itamaraty, Rio de Janeiro. The brevity and small format (15 cm x 8 cm) of the pasquinade may have lent itself to memorization and discreet circulation.

what was characterized officially, with references to threats to their personal security, as protective custody. Under uncertain circumstances they were released a few days later on March 16, "restored to the bosom of their [royal] offices," and the need for the arrests was attributed to "obscure machinations" that had whipped up "popular hatreds" and taken advantage of the "enthusiasm that in all classes of the residents of this Capital" had resulted from "the memorable day of February 26."[20]

By this time the crown also had made public the decision that in compliance with the demands of the constitutionalists in Portugal Dom João would return to Europe, leaving behind Dom Pedro "in charge of the Provisional Government of this Kingdom of Brazil, until the General Constitution of the Nation is established within it."[21] Subsequently, the public declarations of interests that Pinheiro Ferreira and Aréas found so troublesome intensified. By the end of March hundreds had registered their opposition to Dom João's departure by signing collective petitions. How could the king leave "the most interesting part of [the] monarchy" and "suffocate the giant in its crib," asked a group of merchants and property owners. The town council, in turn, submitted the largest petition, both arguing that an American court was in the general interest of "the monarchy and the nation" and announcing the fears of certain residents. "Imagine the hunger of the many families whose daily subsistence depends on employment in the Royal House," these petitioners demanded of Dom João. Others, signing the petition of the *corpo do comércio*, even more clearly stated what was at stake in the court's return to Lisbon: "It is not in the order of things," they asserted, "that Brazil so abandoned, remains united to Portugal much longer."[22]

Although Pinheiro Ferreira dismissed these petitions as either "an eternal monument of good spirit" or the opportunistic designs of the "revolutionary party" seeking to secure its own influence after the king's departure, he also conceded that they were the product of a continued sense of uncertainty about Brazil's political future. Failing to calm "the fury of ambition," the crown's response to constitutionalism had provoked further debate and speculation instead, "in the city's barracks, cafes, and stores along the Rua Direita and Quitanda," places that had become a "theater for the most uninhibited speech." The crown's allegiance to a new constitution notwithstanding, the city's residents lived "a restlessness" and an uncertainty about "the new order of things." "All foresee," Pinheiro Ferreira lamented, "that nothing that exists today can be preserved. But what will be the changes that are taking shape?" he imagined the city's residents asking both themselves and each other. "Who will be the victims of the reforms? And will [these reforms] be for the good or for the misfortune of the State?"[23] In other words, how would the crown and the constitution reconcile the royal family's return to Portugal with Brazil's new status as kingdom and the political and economic expectations and practices that had accompanied the construction of a new royal court in Rio de Janeiro? Would the crown continue to behold the prosperity and well-being of Rio de Janeiro and Brazil as its principal concern, or would "the old colonial system" be revived? Rather than providing answers, the rebellion and the crown's response had inspired questions. And while the rebellion may have been the work of certain groups and "interests," its effects, the "enthusiasm" decried by royal counselors, had transcended these groups, mobilized residents, and transformed politics in the city.

To respond to this enthusiasm and uncertainty, Pinheiro Ferreira counseled the crown to call for a meeting of electors, local elites already in the city for the purpose of selecting deputies to the Lisbon Cortes, during which a royal minister would present an "exposition of the text and spirit" of the instructions and powers that Dom João had given to the prince, as well as the names of those who would serve Dom Pedro as royal ministers. The electors, in turn, would be called on to advise the crown on these instructions. Thus, Pinheiro Ferreira hoped, the crown would firmly and resolutely establish the "new order of things," reassure the city's residents that the monarch recognized their rights, and eliminate the need for continued speculation and debate. The king then approved Pinheiro Ferreira's plan with certain modifications. Rio's *ouvidor* (circuit judge), rather than a royal minister, was ordered to preside over the meeting. And although Pinheiro Ferreira had recommended that the crown find a "decent and discreet room" in which to hold the meeting, the *praça do comércio* (the merchant's exchange), a large and "majestic" building in the city's center near the edge of Guanabara Bay, was chosen instead. This more spacious venue allowed for a more public meeting. Thus, the ouvidor also ordered the construction of bleachers within the building so that other residents could view the proceedings. Indeed, the *edital* of March 29 that officially convoked the electors stated that residents who wished to attend could do so as long as a certain decorum was maintained, noting as well that if during the meeting they wished to "make some reflections" they could submit a written note.[24]

According to one anonymous memorialist, the news that "the electoral junta was going to deliberate about the new government" spread quickly through the city. In response, he claimed, "the citizens gained confidence" and many resolved to attend "so that the selection of a government was not left in the hands of a small number [of people]." Many attendees, he also reported, "immediately wrote many memórias, in which each one explained one's sentiments, correlated them and displayed them publicly." Subsequently, on April 21, when the parish electors then convened, the "gathering of the people" was so great, one elector recalled, "that they took over the front door, the back door and the sides of the praça [building]." Many, as the memorialist noted, had "carried their reflections on paper to present them before the junta."[25]

The meeting then formally was begun as the ouvidor proceeded to read aloud the decree that contained the list of people who would form Dom Pedro's government after Dom João's departure. Almost immediately, however, there were signs that the meeting would not proceed as Pinheiro Ferreira had planned. A group of spectators demanded a rereading of the decree and, according to various accounts, soon after began to shout "loudly, over and over again," that they wanted the Spanish Constitution of 1812[26] "until the Constitution of the Lisbon Cortes arrive[d]." According to witnesses in a subsequent inquiry, the ouvidor then conceded that he had lost control of the gathering and proceeded to recruit José Clemente Pereira, *juiz de fora* of Praia Grande, along with others, to draft a document that stated the demand for the king's allegiance to the Spanish Constitution, which the electors then were called on to sign. A deputation was nominated to present the statement to Dom João. After the deputation departed, further demands were advanced. First, a group within the praça called for the nomination of "secretaries of state." Accordingly, the electors were asked to provide lists of nominees. Joaquim Gonçalves Ledo, Manuel José de Souza França, and the royal preacher Januário da Cunha Barbosa, themselves attending the meeting as electors, reportedly assumed responsibility for tabulating the results. Second, it was decided that another deputation would be sent to order the commander of the city's forts to stop "the departure of all and any ships."

As most witnesses testified, the meeting endured its most tense moments after these deputations had been dispatched, as those gathered waited for news of the king's response and grappled with rumors that troops were marching toward the praça. This tension dissipated, however, when the palace deputation returned and announced that Dom João had consented to their demands in a new royal decree. With shouts and waving handkerchiefs, the gathering commemorated its victory, "shouting Long Live the Spanish Constitution, the Royal Decree and the King." In spite of the late hour, the decree was printed and quickly distributed. As the author of an anonymous memoir explained, for those assembled the decree was "the most important artifact of all the events of this day." With it the king recognized "the legislative power that the junta had assumed," and "agreed to the votes of [his] subjects" (*subditos*). The crown became de facto "merely an executive power," for "not even after the decree had been signed was the junta ordered to disband."[27]

As was the case in the rebellion, witness accounts and testimony in a subsequent investigation of the assembly reveal a complex set of motivations and agendas at work in the praça. Pinheiro Ferreira, in an analysis that departed somewhat from the division of constitutionalist Europeans and revolutionary Brazilians of the February rebellion, contended that there were three "distinct factions" represented there, each "with great ramifications among the people and the troops." The first, composed of "Europeans and Brazilians," he explained, was concerned about the future government of Dom Pedro, a man who they saw as "endowed with great qualities, but without experience" and unfortunately surrounded by men who did not support "the cause of Brazil." For them the Spanish Constitution was a way of stopping "European despotism" from dominating the future royal government of Brazil and eroding gains made since 1808. As one witness similarly testified, this group included José de Souza França and Joaquim Gonçalves Ledo, an elector who, as we have seen, was enlisted to record the assembly's nominations and, as Salles Oliveira argues, had participated in the February rebellion. He played a "great role" in the assembly, the witness further explained, having "conceived of the best way to take power away from His Majesty to be swearing in the Spanish Constitution and nominating a Government of men chosen by the people."[28]

A second faction, which, as Pinheiro Ferreira noted, was ultimately victorious, was comprised of supporters of Dom Pedro and the royal minister the Conde dos Arcos. According to Pinheiro Ferreira, this group saw Dom Pedro's regency as the beginning of a new "golden age" for Brazil. More interested in establishing their influence than in defending a written constitution, they hoped that the king would leave the prince with "broad authority so that they could do . . . all that they understood to be for the good of this kingdom's interests." To guarantee this position, according to Salles Oliveira, Arcos had arranged for the meeting of electors to take place a day earlier than first scheduled so that Dom Pedro's regency could be consolidated in the absence of electors from the city's hinterland, due to arrive at Rio only the following day, who supported Ledo's opposition to the regency.[29] However, as Salles Oliveira further explains, a smooth implementation of this plan was foiled by Ledo who, together with the ouvidor, Joaquim José Queirós, had secured the larger venue of the praça and then mobilized the city's residents to attend. According to witnesses, "with hands joined" in "secret meetings," they also secured the support of "Doctor Macamboa," the Lisbon-born cleric Marcelino José Alves Macamboa, who had participated in the rebellion of February 26 and was known to oppose the Conde dos Arcos.[30] The more moderate Macamboa, in turn, was also joined in what Pinheiro Ferreira called a "European faction" by radical constitutionalists who wanted to form a local government loyal to the Cortes in Lisbon, men identified in the inquiry as João Pereira Ramos, a surgeon known as "Cavaquinho," and Luiz Duprad, a native of Lisbon who, in subsequent testimony, was characterized as the most passionate defender of a written constitution, having used "the most insidious and abusive words against royal authority."[31] The total attendance of the assembly, however, was not contained within these three groups. As witnesses testified, both electors and other residents of the city came to the praça with a range of expectations and emergent understandings of what the new "constitutional system" would mean.

While the assembly thus comprised both divergent political goals and provisional alliances and featured a confrontation between supporters of Arcos and Ledo, those gathered in the praça did share a desire to define the nature of sovereignty in Brazil. Rather than a simple bid to retain the king in Rio, as some historians have argued, the assembly represented an attempt to establish the future practice of politics in his absence. As the author of the anonymous memoir explained, the assembly's move to close the port was meant to stop "the departure of their sovereign *until the new state of things was consolidated*" (emphasis added).[32] As several witnesses also testified, the urgency to establish a de facto constitutional government was motivated by a sense that the accomplishments of the February rebellion were tentative, or, even worse, that the representative principles it defended had been betrayed. According to the anonymous memorialist, allegiance to an unwritten constitution and a new royal cabinet notwithstanding, royal government in Rio continued along "the same arbitrary course." For him, February 26 was "a farce," "a soporific medicine" with which the crown hoped to dupe Rio's residents, "binding them to a constitution that would be made two thousand leagues away, and in which the [royal] cabinet had hopes of securing influence by way of its agents." Duprad had expressed similar suspicions openly during the assembly, declaring that he came on behalf of "the people to protest that they did not confide in the government that the King Our Lord had left behind . . . the people having been deceived by the changes of February 26." And at another point in the meeting, when some of those gathered agreed to adjourn until the following day, others, "disillusioned by the twenty-sixth of February," insisted on completing the nomination of a government.[33] In this context of distrust and seemingly fleeting promises, Dom João's concessions and the new decree then represented the achievement of more durable rights in the future that the February rebellion had only promised.

The victory, however, proved to be short-lived. Although the king had pledged allegiance to the Spanish Constitution, the Conde dos Arcos and Dom Pedro, having lost control of the assembly and fearing for the future of the regency, later convinced him to disperse the gathering using force. In contrast to the February rebellion, those who championed the interim enforcement of the Spanish Constitution had not secured the support of Portuguese troops who, accordingly, remained at the disposal of the crown. The leaders of the deputation sent to close the city's ports were arrested and soldiers were sent marching toward the praça. When the troops reached the building, those who remained inside were trapped by a battalion reportedly twenty-five rows wide that proceeded to discharge fifty shots at the door before entering with bayonets drawn. The results, not surprisingly, were injuries and an undetermined number of fatalities. The magistrate José Clemente Pereira reportedly suffered bayonet wounds, and, as several witnesses testified, Miguel Feliciano Souza, a wine merchant on the Rua de São Pedro, was killed in a confrontation with a soldier. According to the author of the anonymous memoir, the number of casualties was even higher. "Other common people," he wrote, "were indiscriminately killed, and a larger number, having jumped into the sea to escape, met the death that they had tried to avoid amidst the waves." "The cadavers," he claimed, were then "clandestinely taken to the navy arsenal and there they were secretly buried."

In the days that followed the repression, arrests were made and Dom João refused to consider the list of nominated counselors. An investigation focused on Duprad, Macamboa, and Nogueira Soares, while Ledo and others who had assumed positions of leadership within the assembly were spared from punishment. In the meantime the king revoked his earlier pledge of allegiance to the Spanish Constitution and characterized those who comprised the deputations and the assembly as "men with evil intentions . . . who wanted anarchy." Subsequent decrees confirmed Dom Pedro's "broad powers" and warned the residents of Rio de Janeiro against the "passions and the fury of factions" and of the "seditious machinations" employed "to deceive you with the presumption of National Representation."[34] Then, three days later, Dom João, the royal family, and the courtiers called on to join them, boarded a convoy of ships anchored in Rio's harbor. In contrast to the very public disembarkation thirteen years earlier, the boarding was discreet, beginning only after dark. The next day the convoy then unceremoniously departed for Portugal.[35]

The violence and uncertainty of the preceding weeks formed a tragic counterpoint to Dom João's formerly celebrated public presence in the city and threatened to undermine the ideal of political renewal and prosperity that the New World court and empire had come to embody. Divergent understandings of what Vila Nova Portugal characterized as the "interests" of Brazil and those of Portugal had called into question the future of the United Kingdom. Yet, the ambivalent legacy of Dom João's Brazilian reign also included the crown's pledge to the yet-to-be-written constitution, secured by the February rebellion. Consequently, what Gonçalves dos Santos foresaw to be "a new epoch in the annals of Portuguese America" would be defined initially by the new constitutional order and its politics.[36]

"THE NEW ORDER OF THINGS": POLITICS AND PAMPHLETS IN RIO DE JANEIRO

The constitutionalism that transformed Rio de Janeiro's political landscape in the last months of Dom João's residence was the product of both transatlantic discourses and local practices, what Aréas disdainfully referred to as "the customary violence invented lately": open mobilization and public demands for change.[37] Above all, constitutionalism promised to ensure the exercise of popular sovereignty. For some residents of the city and its hinterland, according to Salles Oliveira, this defense of representative government was linked to demands for changes in the structure of internal markets. "Words and rhetoric," she writes of one constitutionalist newspaper, "simultaneously constituted instruments for mobilization, and enunciated the foundational knowledge and practices of bourgeois domination." Constitutionalism, in this sense, served to give a broader segment of the elite formal access to power.[38] Yet constitutionalism was not a simple instrument to defend certain interests; it also entailed a process of political representation. As the mobilization both before and during the April Assembly reveals, the proclamation of national sovereignty initiated a complex struggle to define what, precisely, this meant. Beginning in 1821, defenders of constitutionalism with diverse origins and agendas sought to reshape the perception of interests, both material and political, and enact what they regarded to be a new politics.[39]

While, as we have seen, the triumph of constitutionalism in Rio de Janeiro was guaranteed by the February rebellion, its meanings and its consequences for the monarchy were forged in a political culture of handwritten pasquinades and, increasingly since the transfer of the court, of print. Pamphlets, read clandestinely before and then openly after February, offered understandings of what was to be lost and what was to be gained with a new written constitution.[40] Many such pamphlets were published by the city's Royal Press, which became officially constitutionalist following the rebellion and the end of prior censorship, a transformation that then was consecrated when, along with its Lisbon counterpart, Rio's press was renamed as "National." Beginning in March 1821, when the publication of the two-page *Constituição Explicada* was announced, the National Press published reprints of constitutionalist works published first in Lisbon, as well as songsheets, works by local pamphleteers, and imprints of Rio's constitutional sermons and performances. Indeed, as was the case during the Peninsular War, political pamphlets formed the majority of Royal/National Press publications. After 1821, however, the overall volume of publication also increased, so that almost as many titles were published in 1821 and 1822 as in the twelve preceding years combined.[41] What thus amounted to an unprecedented proliferation of political pamphlets was further bolstered by an August 1821 decree that lifted any remaining restrictions on the press and by the establishment of additional presses within the city, such as the Nova Oficina Tipográfica, later renamed as Oficina de Moreira e Garcez, and the Tipografia do Diario, which published one of the many new newspapers that began to circulate as well. Book sellers also seized the opportunity to supply an increasing demand for pamphlets imported from Lisbon, Bahia, and Europe, including Rousseau's *The Social Contract*, a work that, as the announcement of the sale of one French edition noted, "formerly prohibited, in the present circumstances" had "become very interesting."[42] Like those published during the war, most pamphlets and newspapers were short—many only a few pages long—and, as Lúcia Neves has shown, inexpensive, more or less the price of a loaf of bread, a pound of flour, or a bar of soap.[43]

The purchase of pamphlets was limited, of course, to those who could read, a minority of the city's residents. Yet the larger impact of political pamphlets was not confined to readers. In eating houses, pharmacies, and other private and public places of gathering, the intendancy's informants reported, Rio's residents listened to recitations or heard conversations about the messages and meanings of constitutionalist works.[44] Indeed, while, as Raymundo Faoro has argued, the "political context of 1820 explains the content" of such pamphlets,[45] the pamphlets themselves also produced the political context of Rio de Janeiro in 1821. Pamphlets were, in other words, part of the city's political culture and they linked that political culture to the larger transformations in the Portuguese and Atlantic worlds. Works by local authors and reprints of texts first published in Portugal were recognized as important tools by both constitutionalists and their detractors, ones that revealed "the truth" or, as one "faithful friend of the friends of the king" denounced, served as dangerous weapons in the hands of "rogues" who threatened cherished hierarchies, "propagating their [constitutionalist] sentiments even to blacks who can read" (*patentiando os seus sentimentos até os negros que souberem ler*).[46]

The constitutionalist messages of these pamphlets and pasquinades began with a critique of absolutist government, "a science of deception" manifest in the self-interest and corruption of counselors who endangered both the monarch and the nation.[47] In Rio de Janeiro, as we saw in Chapter 2, expressions of this critique had been made by local artisans and men of letters in the 1790s; and in the 1810s they echoed in episodes of dissident commentary investigated by the police intendant. Following the arrival of news of the Porto rebellion, and in the midst of speculation about the crown's response to the declarations made there, local public criticism of absolutist government mounted and became more sharply defined. In the days leading up to the February rebellion, handwritten verses and other compositions that circulated among the city's residents denounced royal officials, many of whom were ousted on February 26, as "sycophants" and "thieves." The royal minister Tomás António Vila Nova Portugal, in particular, was often at the center of these attacks, figured as a "demonic" "enemy of the nation." His and other royal officials' "vain counsel" against the crown's recognition of the constitutionalist movement was identified as both an obstacle to Brazilian happiness and prosperity—the "spring from which all of your [Brazilians'] misfortunes have come"—and, as one satirical petition entitled "Tomás, you should present this to the king" claimed, the cause of the empire's demise. "If you still want to Reign," the petitioner explained to the king:

Look blessed João,
You should go to Portugal
And sign the constitution.

If you don't hurry
To your native country
Oh' João behold you'll lose
Brazil, and Portugal.

A sarcastic composition entitled "Commemoration of the ignorance of this Court" similarly indicted the royal cabinet and its corruption, declaring not only "Long Live the King Dom João, all of the Royal Family, and the new Constitution," but also "death to all thieves."[48] These "false friends" and "Perfidious Favorites and Counselors of Kings," as one pamphleteer further explained, had duped both the people and the king into thinking that royal power was limitless. Consequently, "bewildered by the resounding melody of applause," the absolute monarch could not "hear the clamor for justice."[49]

Constitutionalism, in turn, as pamphleteers proclaimed, promised to broaden the king's "horizon" and liberate Rio's residents from the abjection that absolutist government had created. To do so, it affirmed the power of the Cortes and thus limited royal power. As the chaplain Francisco da Mai dos Homens preached in a sermon published in 1821, a written constitution established the division of power that "Ministerial and Courtier preponderance" had "shackled."[50] As a consequence, proclaimed one poet during a commemoration in Rio's royal theater, the "people of Brazil" now "liberated from repression [could] breathe freely."[51] This liberation from absolutism was also defined as a more direct and open relationship between the king and the people. Indeed, the adoption of a written constitution, as the author of one pamphlet explained, was an act of political "union" between the king and the people.[52] Thus, along with ending the machinations of "corrupt favorites," constitutionalism also destroyed hierarchies that had inhibited this union. It tore down the "Walls, trenches, gates of bronze," as one pamphleteer defined them, that had "deprived the humble Citizen entrance into the Sanctuary of the Court."[53] As the magistrate Maciel da Costa explained, "national representation" therefore meant that "supplications will not be merely loose pieces of paper . . . subject to the despotism and ignorance of irresponsible ministers."[54] Indeed, this new and open politics had been manifest in the February rebellion itself when, as Pinheiro Ferreira lamented, hierarchies were "disorganized" and "the respect of the inferior classes of society" for their superiors, of "even" slaves for their masters, was "absolutely annihilated," jeopardizing, he surmised, the "majesty of the throne." Following the rebellion, he recalled,

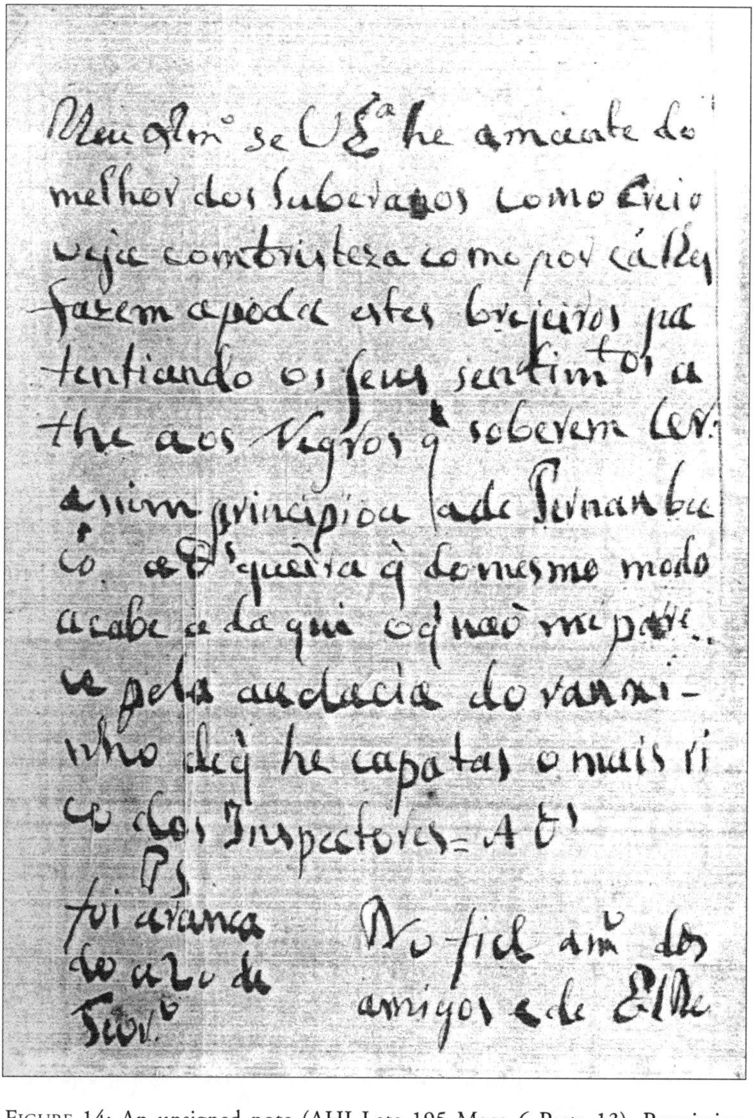

FIGURE 14: An unsigned note (AHI Lata 195 Maço 6 Pasta 13). Permission granted by the Arquivo Histórico do Itamaraty, Rio de Janeiro. An anonymous note denounced "rogues" who disseminated the message of constitutionalism "even to blacks who can read."

residents began to appear before Dom João not to request the grace of royal patronage, but rather to make demands "in the name of the people." Exhibiting what Pinheiro Ferreira judged an unnerving "presumption," they presented the king with a list of persons who should form a council to be consulted regarding all "public affairs."[55]

While the destruction of political hierarchies was advanced by constitutionalists in both Portugal and Brazil, in Rio de Janeiro such an affirmation of a more frank relationship between the king and "the people" resonated within the city's residents' claims to a new status before the crown following the transfer of the court, with what Gonçalves dos Santos described as the more equitable exercise of their "rights" previously denied by geographic distance. Local readings of a transatlantic constitutionalist discourse, in other words, perceived absolutism and the "old colonial system" as analogous. Both had usurped and "monstrously" distorted an original and just order of things. Absolutism obfuscated the people's own "nobility" and "deceptively" arrogated the power of the Cortes and "man's inalienable right to natural liberty," just as colonial monopolies undermined the "natural" practice of free trade and colonial government separated the city's residents from their monarch, making "the execution of [the royal] will impossible."[56]

These continuities and affinities between constitutionalism and the political discourse of the 1810s in Rio were both framed and authorized by the historic link between national politics and religion. While champions of the New World court claimed that Rio could be a bulwark against revolutionary impieties and a place for the monarchy's and the nation's political and moral renewal ordained by Providence itself, constitutionalists pledged to defend the "Holy Catholic Religion" and deliver it from the corruption of the old regime.[57] As the Portuguese pamphleteer José Joaquim Lopes de Lima argued, constitutionalism would end the church's subservience to a decadent papacy, for in the "servile system," he explained, a "bishop" was a "mere executor of the Pope's orders," whereas in the "liberal system" he recovered his position as "sovereign executor of the Law of God within his Diocese."[58] Eliminating aberrations and purifying the church then demanded the abolition of the "diabolical" Inquisition and, especially, of the "superfluous" hierarchy that had arisen out of the proliferation of ecclesiastical offices. Although, as the author of one constitutional sermon contended, "the Prelates [who] are and should be, men of God, vigilant judges" had nothing to fear, in pamphlets the *corcunda* (absolutist, literally "hunchback") clergy and members of religious orders were emblematic of the kind of corruption that had enabled the French invasion and then proliferated in its aftermath. "Friars" were, as Lima classified them, a "middle term between the two sexes, with the vices of one and the other."[59] Constitutionalism, in turn, like the transfer of the court, offered a restoration of piety and virtue.

As was the case in the political discourse of the transfer of the court, in constitutionalism religious principle and religious history also served to define and justify political change. If it were true, one pamphleteer argued, that "the King governs the Kingdom as God governs his Church," it followed, therefore, that such a government "should be with a Cortes, and a Constitution because God wrote the Decalogue which is a Constitution."[60] These religious foundations for constitutionalism, not surprisingly, were invoked even more clearly by members of the clergy who had adopted constitutionalist allegiances. "We give to the King what belongs to the King; that is we give him what our ancestors gave," the author of the constitutional sermon cited above explained, "and we take from him what was unfairly usurped." "None of this," he then reassured his listeners and readers, "infringes upon the Holy Religion, that we profess."[61] The clergy's public participation in the people's instruction in "recent reforms," solicited by the Lisbon Cortes and, in Rio de Janeiro, taken up by some who had ardently defended the monarchy and its move to Brazil during the Peninsular War, then further elucidated the connections between "political regeneration" and salvation.[62] More intimate modes of religious expression, in turn, provided a framework for the enunciation of constitutional allegiances. In one pamphlet, for example, when a group of constitutionalists convince a group of absolutists of the error of their ways, conversion and "regenerative" reconciliation are achieved through a formal penitence and an "Affirmation of the Constitutional Faith," followed by the recitation of the fifteen "Commandments of Constitutional Law," the "Articles of the Holy Constitutional Faith," the "Constitutional Creed," the "Our Constitutional Father," "Constitutional Ave Maria," and finally the "Save the Constitutional Queen."

This "constitutional catechism" integrated the foundations of constitutionalism and Catholicism. Thus, the commandments included not only "Honor God and the Roman Catholic Apostolic Religion," but also "Keep holy Sundays and the feast days that the Constitution declares." Similarly, the articles of the constitutional "faith" both recognized religion as "the Roman Catholic Apostolic" and declared that "liberty consists in each doing what the Law does not prohibit." The catechism also sacralized constitutionalism by placing references to constitutionalism within recognizably Catholic rites. The initial words of the Lord's Prayer thus became "Portuguese Constitution, which is in our hearts, hallowed be thy name," just as the Ave Maria became "Ave Constitution, full of grace, and wisdom . . . blessed is the fruit of your womb: Holy Constitution, Mother of the Portuguese."[63]

The ritualized pronouncement of constitutionalist allegiances, found as well in oaths and commemorative verses, also served as a point of departure for the integration of other religious and constitutional practices. As Maria Candida Proença has argued, commemorations of the anniversaries of the Porto and February rebellions were sacralized, just as religious festivals were constitutionalized in such acts as listening to a constitutional sermon during mass and the more extraordinary election of deputies that, as a draft of the constitution specified, was to take place on a Sunday, within a church and within a liturgical framework, preceded by a mass, followed by a *Te Deum*. Indeed, a meeting of the electoral junta in Rio de Janeiro in May

1821 was, Januário da Cunha Barbosa argued, "an act as religious as it was civil," one that "balanced religion and politics." "Who," he asked those gathered for the preceding mass, "would not unite within such an August Assembly, the glory of religion and the glory of the Pátria?"[64] While, as Lúcia Neves has argued, such uses of religious genres and contexts allowed constitutionalists "to reach a wider public,"[65] they were also an integral part of engendering the constitutional order itself. Just as the recitation of the traditional catechism called into being a community of Catholics, participating in the rituals of constitutionalism effectively created a recognizable community of patriotic, as well as pious, Portuguese. In this sense, even as the appropriation of Catholic rites attested to constitutionalism's recognition of tradition, the act of reformulating those rites, of substituting words and phrases with others, of adding "commandments," revealed that constitutionalists recognized that existing rituals and practices (those of Catholicism and monarchy) in and of themselves did not sufficiently express the constitutionalist ideal. Constitutionalists did not, to be sure, embark on the development of purely civic rituals, as was the case of revolutionaries in France. Yet they did recognize that constitutionalist politics entailed the creation of new political bonds.[66]

Notwithstanding their novelty, such bonds, like the new American court, were regarded by constitutionalists as the products of history. As Zilia Osório de Castro explains, Portuguese constitutionalism evinced an "historically based rationality"; it sought not to recover the past, but rather to use the past to make the present, including innovations, legitimate.[67] Thus, along with religion, constitutionalists on both sides of the Atlantic called on Portuguese history to prove constitutionalism's "truth" and reveal the foundations for a national regeneration. As one "glorious constitutionalist" explained to a "defeated corcunda" in a published "dialogue," the Cortes had the right to "make and unmake kings" because it had elevated Afonso Henriques, João I, and João IV to the throne.[68]

Historically, however, the rights and powers of the Cortes had not been so clearly defined. As it came to coexist with more recent political institutions associated with royal governance, its "juridical-constitutional foundation" became, as Pedro Cardim explains, "imprecise." By the eighteenth century the Cortes' privilege of convening to deliberate over "constitutional" questions and preside over royal succession clearly had eroded. Royal succession took place with the enunciation of an oath alone and even in moments of crisis—Dom João's assumption of the regency and the transfer of the court—and in spite of counsel and "opinion" to the contrary, the crown did not convene the Cortes. The challenge for constitutionalism thus became the recovery of what Cardim calls "the memory of [the Cortes'] elective capacities."[69] Indeed, emerging out of the political culture of the Napoleonic invasion and the transfer of the court in which the ideal of renewal was paramount and the meaning of history and tradition was both embraced and contested, constitutionalists defined strategically both the past and future of popular sovereignty. As one pamphleteer thus explained, the king had not "descended from the Heavens," but rather, as "the wisest, and most distinguished of Citizens," had been "elected" to serve as "trustee, and administrator of the Laws." Although hereditary succession then had replaced this original election, kingship, constitutionalists insisted, continued to be defined in this way. The king, therefore, was not a "Lord" or "Father," but rather the "first Magistrate of the Republic."[70]

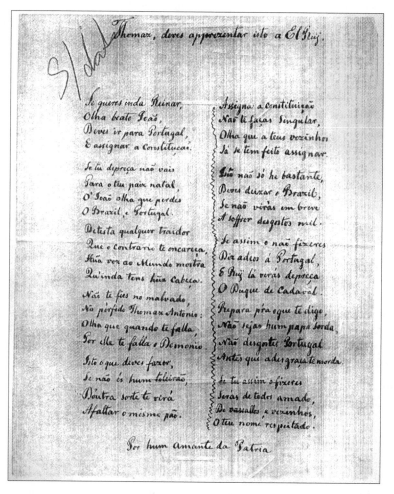

FIGURE 15: Anonymous, "Tomás, you should present this to the king," signed "By a lover of the pátria" (AHI Lata 195 Maço 6 Pasta 13). Permission granted by the Arquivo Histórico do Itamaraty, Rio de Janeiro. A satirical petition denounced the absolutist royal counselor Tomás António Vila Nova Portugal.

Rhetorically, this recovery of the history of the monarchy and political representation obscured by absolutism meant that constitutionalists then could assert that "the Kings are Kings when and where the Peoples want," without, as one pamphleteer explained, attacking "royal dignity" or the institution of monarchy per se.[71] Indeed, like royal officials who defended the new empire and United Kingdom, constitutionalists sought to achieve the monarchy's "salvation," a project that, in turn, came with its own historic legitimacy and heroism, having been manifest in the seventeenth-century war for independence from Spain and then most recently in the national struggle against Napoleon. Invoking a refrain used during the Peninsular War, one constitutionalist pamphleteer made these continuities explicit. In 1820, just as in 1808, he suggested, "To defend the Pátria / To give one's life for the King" was "for the valiant Portuguese / Character, Custom, and Law."[72]

The defense of monarchy and the invocation of religion, history, and tradition did not, however, preclude an embrace of change. Constitutionalism, after all, aimed not to "restore" an ancient order, but rather to "regenerate" politics. And this regeneration appeared, in certain moments, to depend on significant juridical-institutional transformations. As one pamphleteer explained, "the ancient method of convoking Cortes, while it is indeed legal, is not appropriate for the present epoch." "Laws are like everything else that with time grows old," he continued, "and as laws have the aim of regulating customs, it followed that if customs changed, the laws should change as well." The mandate of constitutionalism, therefore, was to make laws "more in agreement" with what one pamphleteer described as "the ideas of the century."[73]

Evoking "the ideas of the century," the pamphleteer also revealed the influence of the Enlightenment and the French Revolution in Portuguese constitutionalist discourse. As we have seen, in the late eighteenth and early nineteenth centuries royal officials sought to carefully limit, and in certain cases criminalized, engagement with French political thought and interest in French revolutionary politics and its spheres of influence. Constitutionalism and, most importantly, the press freedoms its supporters secured broke down these limits and, building on an earlier censored engagement with eighteenth-century thought and politics, allowed for a more open consideration of what the Enlightenment and the French Revolution meant in their own terms. Whereas royal officials in the 1790s and 1810s had sought to ensure the residents' allegiance to His Majesty, "Our Lord" and "Common Father," constitutionalists celebrated the triumph of contractual government over paternal rule; they praised the new political agency of "the people"; they hailed the rise of "the public" as the defeat of narrow, private interests associated with absolutism.[74] They proclaimed the inversion of existing political hierarchies that allowed the nation to assume its sovereignty. As one constitutionalist pasquinade declared:

From the people to the king, power is given,
Thus the people can legislate,
If upon this notice the king does yield,
To arms his inert power will be ceded.

Constitutionalists also grappled with two of the French Revolution's most emblematic principles: liberty and equality. As one pamphleteer contended, although liberty could not be construed as "absolute," it was "natural." Man was born "free" and this freedom then was circumscribed first by his relationship to God and then by his relationship with his wife, his children, and other men.[75] The "more relationships one has," he explained, "the more duties and obligations one has: and the more duties one has, the fewer freedoms one has." However limited, these liberties and rights were equally possessed by all. Adam and Eve themselves were "perfectly equal," he argued, in that they had not only "equal liberty," but also "equal relations" and "equal duties." In other words, liberty and equality were "always relative" to one another.[76] Or, as another pamphlet more succinctly explained, the "equality of the rights of all citizens" corresponded to the "equal weakness of all before the law." This kind of Rousseauian shorthand was used as well, as constitutionalists then explained the law or the "fundamental law" as the expression of "the general will of the people" and of the covenant, or constitution, through which equality and rights were established.[77]

These rights and "civil liberty," in turn, coincided with the "nobility of the Citizen,"[78] a "free vassal," as one constitutional catechism explained, born or naturalized "in the lands that belonged to the Crown of Portugal in any part of the world."[79] Citizen, in this sense, acquired the word vassal's designation of a national political identity, as in what the intendant referred to awkwardly in 1818 as "vassals of the United States of America."[80] Prior understandings of citizens as the well-regarded members of an urban community who fulfilled their duties to God and sovereign also expanded to include what the Visconde do Rio Secco referred to as both "respect for constituted authorities" and love of "Sovereign and Pátria." Indeed, as one pamphleteer contended, although the status of vassal initially qualified one to be a citizen, citizenship then displaced vassalage altogether, as the new order displaced the old.[81] Both citizens and vassals had "rights" and virtues. Yet a vassal was dependent on the crown, whereas a citizen was an equal member of the sovereign nation. In contrast to vassals, citizens thus retained the privilege of deliberating on the future of the political body. As a guide to the first constitutional elections explained, "a citizen of the people" was "circumspect," one who assumed responsibility for ensuring the "happiness of the Pátria" above individual interests.[82] Thus, several of those who petitioned the king to retain the court in Brazil added "citizen" to previously established identities—"Businessman and Citizen" or "Citizen and Knight of the Order

of Christ"—suggesting that the other title did not sufficiently express the civic nature of their gesture. The anonymous author of the April Assembly memoir concluded by signing "a citizen" as well, invoking both a sense of prerogative and
signaling that the account was the product of public, rather than personal, interest.[83]
Indeed, both the equitable and actively deliberative nature of citizenship had been
manifest in the April Assembly itself, as "barriers that separated the people from the
electors" were disregarded and residents who were once defined as spectators transformed themselves into orators.[84]

In calling attention to new terms and changing roles and identities, constitutionalists also promoted the idea that the creation of a new political order depended
on the creation of a self-consciously new political language, a rhetorical discourse
that sought not to simply reflect recent events, but rather to persuade and shape the
perception of interests as a way of reconstituting the political order itself, in this case
making "the nation," rather than the king, sovereign.[85] In other words, to be a constitutionalist was to speak as a constitutionalist. Consequently, pamphlets themselves
often served explicitly to translate the old absolutist language into a new constitutionalist one. A graphic juxtaposition, or "parallel," of political categories using a list
of synonyms and antonyms, for example, revealed that ambition and hypocrisy were
to "the corcunda" what virtue and reason were to "the liberal."[86] While, in this case,
readers were instructed in the meaning of words new to the Portuguese political lexicon ("the hunchback-absolutist" and "the liberal"),[87] José Joaquim Lopes de Lima's
"dictionaries," in turn, suggested that rather than a set of new vocabulary, constitutional language consisted of new meanings for old words. Rhetorically, however,
Lima presented these meanings not as "new," but as older meanings lost in more recent absolutist political discourse. Lima's task then, as he explained, was to identify
those "expressions transformed only to deceive" and "restore their genuine meaning." This recovery of original meanings became part of constitutionalism's recovery
of original political rights. To achieve this recovery, Lima provided a set of sardonic
translations of "phrases of the *carcundas*," a deconstruction, as it were, of the old political language that created a new one. Thus, he explained, what had formerly been
defined as "absurdities" were indeed "natural truths." "To abolish," in turn, was "to
reform, purify." "An offense" was a "truth" as in "To offend the Sovereignty . . . To
tell the truth to the King." This parody also continued, conversely, in Lima's corcunda definitions for Constitution— "a plan for disorder"—and Cortes—"irregular
association."[88]

This quest for a new, transparent language of politics, in opposition to the de-
ceptive one of the old regime, was itself a legacy of the French Revolution. In France,
as Lynn Hunt has argued, revolutionaries tore down past politics by embracing the
power of rhetoric even as they effaced representation itself. Words associated with

the old regime were forbidden because they were perceived as threatening the revolutionary transparency between citizens. Constitutionalists in Rio similarly purged from their vocabulary words that invoked absolutism, such as the royal title of "*Nosso Senhor*" (Our Lord). Thus, in September 1821, "Vivas" offered to Dom Pedro that included this "improper and unconstitutional title" were denounced as the sign of a "sinister attempt to promote the public's distrust and incite partisanship." Although an investigation then determined that the man who had made such an unsettling declaration was not politically motivated, but rather simply without "reason," the incident nevertheless provoked the "greatest possible sensation in the spirits of the well-intentioned residents of this capital." To restore the integrity of the constitutional order defiled by the lexical assault, the military officer from whose balcony the salute had been made was compelled to offer a public explanation of his conduct, published both as a broadside and as an article in the city's *Gazeta*.[89]

This displacement, as Joan Landes has described it, of an iconic and spectacular public life by a textualized symbolic order was itself the subject of one pamphlet published in Rio de Janeiro based on the rhetorical premise of a letter sent from Lisbon to a man named Braz Barnabé by his friend, André Mamede. Having spent time in a village where, as Mamede sensed, the public readings of old gazettes left him somewhat out of date, he took advantage of a trip to Lisbon to apprise himself of more recent events. While at a *casa de pasto* (eating house), he did hear about the Cortes' recent deliberations. Yet a new word used in the conversation had left him confused. Who were, he wondered, the corcundas to which the men at the eating house had referred? While, as he surmised, such a word apparently indicated a physical defect "of nature, or inclination," a subsequent exchange then led him to "suspect that the corcundas were not corporal but rather spiritual." Finally, as he discovered when one friend took the time to explain, a corcunda was an "Anti-Constitutional man," one who would do "anything to mislead public opinion from the true spirit of goodness." Happy for having learned this lesson, Mamede then set out to share the meaning of the word with others.[90] Thus using a narrative parody, the pamphleteer, in effect, confronted the complex workings of this new constitutionalist language within a social context. The remoteness of the village versus the crossroads of the city underscored the importance of the medium of print. Although Mamede's search for the meaning of new words arose from a sense of obliviousness, the keen interest in politics that motivated his inquiry in the first place also made the newness of constitutional language apparent: constitutional politics was so innovative that a brief period of disengagement could leave even a self-consciously politicized person ignorant. Mamede's search also uncovered the modes for the dissemination of this new language and politics: the conversation, the letter, and, above all, the letter's subsequent incarnation, the political pamphlet.

The concern with disseminating a transparent constitutional language, and
with enforcing its usage, was linked to constitutionalist understandings of the new
nature of politics and public life. "The Greatest good, which Liberal Governments
have given Society," explained the Visconde do Rio Secco, "is without a doubt the
faculty that each Citizen has to expound the truth in all its splendor and clarity.
Thus," he continued, "the use of masks and disguises was lost, and man appeared
just as the product of the chain of his actions. The law becomes the measure of all his
actions; and the general interest [becomes] the center, at which they converge; the
Public [becomes] the severe judge that condemns or rewards them, according to
their position in relation to the Society in which he lives. . . ." "All," he declared, "is
surrendered to the Empire of truth."[91] This vision of truthful collective judgment
was also described as "public opinion." Constitutionalists denounced "before the tribunal of Public Opinion, the errors and abuses" of absolutist government and
warned that "today Monarchs had the need not only to consult public Opinion, but
also to have their eyes always fixed on its Direction."[92]

The Portuguese crown, as we have seen, had also recognized public opinion
within its program of policing and with its sponsorship of pamphlets and newspapers in the 1810s. In the context of the constitutionalist movement achieving an understanding of public opinion and reshaping this opinion in the crown's favor
acquired a new urgency, for "silence," as the intendant Viana warned Vila Nova Portugal in 1821, would be "confused with pusillanimity." Assessing which of "the
classes of society" had taken up the "revolutionary spirit" marked the beginning of
this effort to be followed, as Viana then suggested, by the king's use of some "pretext" to elucidate "the way to think" and "to stop the people from searching for answers alone, and always, amid the evil that torments us." Pinheiro Ferreira too had
urged the crown to convoke the April assembly in order to "fix public opinion about
the true intentions of His Majesty, and close the door on the people's tumultuous intervention."[93]

While constitutionalists inherited and shared this sense of public opinion as
something that could be both gauged and engaged, they also declared its status
within the "constitutional system" to be fundamentally different. Absolutists, Andre
Mamede was told, sought to "mislead public opinion from the true spirit of goodness." Absolutist policing distorted opinion, pamphleteers also argued, "spying on
the most secret conversations, obliging citizens . . . to disguise their language; calling the day the night."[94] Constitutionalists, on the contrary, claimed to liberate public opinion, make it transparent, bring it out into the open, and place it at the center
of the exercise of national sovereignty. "Public opinion," one pamphleteer declared,
"expressed the vote of the people."[95] Thus, as Viana's successor in the office of intendant recognized, after 1821 it was for the "the public, impartial judge" to decide

whether officials themselves had properly observed the law.[96] As one pamphlet explained this process, in constitutional politics "words" and "printed discourses" were "thrown out, so to speak, into a vast stadium, where each citizen is allowed to enter and fight, having the whole nation as an arbiter who can freely pass judgment." The more open this confrontation was, the more legitimate its results would be. Such "freedom of discussion," he contended, was the only way to "make the truth known." It formed "the fundamental basis of the existence of civil and political liberty." Therefore freedoms of the press were crucial as well, for without them, the pamphleteer argued, any "national assembly . . . will always form an untrue representation." "[To] ask if the press should be free or enslaved," he declared, was "the same as to ask, in other words, if the monarchy should be constitutional or absolute."[97]

For constitutionalists this new publicly deliberative politics was to be not only free, but also educated. Education, the magistrate and resident of Rio José Albano Fragoso argued, was "the basis for public morality." Or, as one constitutional newspaper declared, to make "suitable excursions through the brilliant field of classic, ancient and modern Literature . . . to do so frequently, to reduce them to a few pages and put them within reach of the multitude, was to do an eminent service to the country and to civilization in general."[98] Along with this quest to edify, however, constitutionalists also called for an explicitly new and civic education. As Fragoso claimed, whereras previously education "had not sought to disseminate notions of interest to man in his capacity as citizen," indeed its aim should be "to form men and citizens with knowledge of the society and government in which they lived. . . ." Citing both Rousseau and Thomas Paine, Fragoso then argued that this education should be "public, uniform and universal." It was only thus that the constitutional government would be consolidated, for, as Fragoso further explained, education guarded against disorder and injustice. "When the people groan in ignorance and do not know their greatness," he wrote, "guided like a herd of animals," they voluntarily surrender "to the first dazzling usurper who asks them to obey."[99]

Such ignorance, constitutionalists sustained, indeed had allowed absolutism to corrupt the Portuguese monarchy. If the Portuguese nation had been instructed "as today it can be, in the principles of the eighteenth century," one pamphleteer asserted, "it would have never pacifically consented to the usurpation of its rights."[100] This same lesson, others argued, could also be learned by looking beyond the Portuguese world. Thus, in one instructive dialogue, when the Constitution encounters Despotism in the decidedly "Oriental" form it had taken in Constantinople, the correlation between education, "reason," civilization, and constitutional government was revealed. "Go and seek these enlightened Europeans," Despotism says to the Constitution, defending its imperious whims, "while I triumph in the vast regions of Asia and in the burning backlands of Africa." The Constitution faces the challenge and the encounter then comes to a happy end with both the defeat of Despotism and the universal triumph of enlightenment on the horizon. As the two separate, the Constitution departs for Brazil, "where for much time it had been desired."[101]

As pamphleteers juxtaposed an educated constitutionalism with an ignorant and barbaric absolutism, they also claimed that education distinguished their "regeneration," Portuguese public opinion, and its deliberative process from the French Revolution. "Those who executed the plan for revolution were not those distinguished philanthropists who had outlined it," wrote José António de Miranda shortly after arriving in Brazil.[102] Consequently, the French Revolution had become a moment of anarchy when "the People, who did not know what equality nor liberty were, undid everything, and created the most horrifying scenes. . . ."[103] In contrast, "the Greatest Triumph of Lusitania" was, one allegorical engraving suggested, "to take an oath to the Constitution / Without shedding blood."[104] Education then promised to fend off unbridled disorder in the Portuguese world in the future, even as the history of the French Revolution provided other lessons on how to avoid its "dishonorable and prejudicial excesses and losses." Indeed, one constitutionalist newspaper argued, what that "school of Revolutions" taught was that popular sovereignty was better expressed through representative institutions than in the "Jacobin usurpation of power by the people."[105] Although sovereignty resided in the nation, Portuguese constitutionalists contended, the nation could exercise this sovereignty only through legal representation. As one pamphleteer explained, "all of the nation elects, by way of a systematic means, a certain number of persons of their free choice, so that away from the excitement these may nominate the men that they judge to be capable of forming a congress, in which they should discuss the interests of that nation, and organize the laws that ensure its happiness."[106]

This quest to educate and "discipline new forms of popular power" in the wake of the French Revolution and the negotiation of a complex understanding of that revolution as both a model to be followed and an experience to be rejected[107] were also evident in the emerging image of the constitution itself. Both the power and virtue of the constitution derived from its very status as a written, printed, and disseminated text. As one pamphleteer explained, in an apparent gloss on Condorcet, "since the epoch in which the *art of printing* was invented, it is not by way of verbal discussion, nor theses, nor sermons, that nations can illuminate and instruct themselves." "Words pass and are forgotten," he continued, "and only writing fixes them, and gives them permanence."[108] Consequently, a written constitution, unlike custom and tradition, was not subject to change and erosion. As a consequence, it not only guaranteed the sovereignty of the nation in the present, but also guarded against its usurpation by either absolutists or a revolutionary assembly in the future. This promise of permanence indeed was at work during the April Assembly. As we have seen, for many who attended the meeting the Spanish Constitution appeared to embody the triumph of constitutional government in the present over the more illusive February allegiance and what one anonymous petitioner described as the uncertainty about "the new form of government" generated by the announcement of Dom João's departure. Adopting the Spanish Constitution until the Cortes' own constitution was completed, in other words, would disqualify absolutist attempts to derail constitutionalism in the meantime. Thus, prior to the Assembly, some residents purchased copies of the Spanish Constitution, and others openly campaigned for its immediate adoption.[109] And during the assembly the very presence of the Spanish Constitution within the praça was noted with interest. As José da Silva Lisboa, who attended the meeting as an elector, recalled, during the meeting Macamboa read from "a great book [that] he judged to be the Spanish Constitution."[110]

Yet in spite of its promise of indelibility, the meaning of the constitution as both icon and text was also open to debate within the Assembly. For some who gathered at the merchant's exchange to choose electors, as "the most ingenious work of the human spirit," and the acknowledged inspiration of both the Porto rebellion and of the Portuguese constitution's "Bases" adopted by the Cortes in March, the Spanish constitution was a symbol of the principle of popular sovereignty in general and its presence simply sanctioned the Assembly's demands. Others, however, insisted on citing passages from the constitution to debate the Assembly's own actions. Thus, one of the electors recalled, he had criticized the call for the nomination of ministers because "in article one hundred seventy one, it says that the ministers of state are nominated by the king." Similarly, even as some supported closing the city's port as an effort to stop an expropriation of the royal treasury and a defense of private property that the Spanish constitution upheld, recovering the "wealth of individuals" so that any transfer of funds could be accounted for and compensated, others saw the detention of ships as a violation of these property rights as they actually were defined.[111] Attempting to persuade both those who called for the closing of ports and the general assembly of this position, the elector Manuel Jacinto Nogueira da Gama requested a copy of the Spanish Constitution "that was found there on the ballot table, and looking for the relevant articles he made them read them once again and urged that they be read aloud to the people."[112]

There were thus two important effects of the February rebellion, the April Assembly, and constitutionalist pamphleteering for Rio de Janeiro's residents. On the one hand, like the transfer of the court, they presented the city's residents with opportunities to define the nature of local politics with terms that both accounted for history and recognized change. Invoking the principles of representative government and demanding allegiance to a written constitution, supporters of the rebellion and the Assembly's bid to define local government sought to safeguard the institution of monarchy as well as guarantee, or "fix," the enlarged and more equitable scope of political rights and economic freedoms that the city's residents had negotiated since the arrival of the Portuguese court in 1808.[113] On the other hand, both the rebellion and the Assembly also provided Rio's residents with the knowledge that the meaning of constitutionalism and the constitution were themselves open to interpretations that sought to further reconcile local circumstances with the principles that the constitution enshrined.

Indeed, in the wake of what Gonçalves dos Santos described as these extraordinary events, a great debate emerged on the subject of exactly who was "the nation" that the constitution called into being as sovereign. One draft of the constitution denominated the Portuguese nation as the "union of all Portuguese in both hemispheres," including "free men, born or residing in Portuguese territories, or their sons" and "slaves born in Portuguese territories who obtain freedom."[114] Yet, it was also the case, as Verdelho has noted, that "fraternity" was a keyword that constitutionalists did not substantially engage.[115] As Rio's residents discovered, the nation was not simply the embodiment of historic and civic unity and common interest that both their Peninsular War pamphlets and their constitutional catechisms celebrated, but also represented a site from which to enunciate differences and, as Gonçalves dos Santos observed, "interests difficult to reconcile." Even as constitutionalists celebrated equality before the law and popular participation in politics, they also claimed that the majority of the people were not "capable of profound deliberation." Accordingly, the election of deputies, as outlined in 1821 in the constitution's draft, would be restricted by age and the condition of stable residence.[116] While some constitutionalists envisioned ways to eradicate the hierarchies of slavery, others appropriated the empire's color hierarchies as matter-of-fact grounds for exclusion. In the face of a racist attack on Brazil written in Portugal, Gonçalves dos Santos both defended the political viability of "free pardos more or less light" who, together with "whites," constituted "the principal part of the population" and insisted that "blacks did not figure in the civil order."[117] Slavery, in turn, was condemned as an institution "contrary to the philosophy and lights of the present century," one to be abolished lest it further divide the nation and engulf Brazil in a Haitian-like war, yet also regarded as "an habitual evil" that could not, Miranda argued, be cured "suddenly" and therefore, as Maciel da Costa advised, needed to be further disciplined.[118]

Finally, constitutionalists left the relationship between the nation and imperial geography undefined. As one pamphleteer complained, "in the beautiful writings" of liberalism, the "essential component of our future greatness, which is the union of Portugal with Brazil" had generated only "some metaphysical speculations spread without any aim," rather than a decisive treatment.[119] This question was, of course, a crucial one, one that the crown and Rio's residents had sought to answer in the 1810s but that resurfaced in the Porto and February rebellions and in the April Assembly. Following Dom João's departure, speculation about the future grounds for union intensified. Was Brazil a place of natural inferiority and decadence or of promise and redemption? Were the nation and the United Kingdom coterminous, the products of history and tradition, language and law, as well as the noble will to live together as a political community? Or were they illusions that would succumb to perceptions of cultural, geographic, and racial difference and the idea that, as Viana speculated before his death in 1821, "that which is appropriate for Portugal may be inappropriate for Brazil, a land that encompasses various climates and colors of people"?[120] Did the United Kingdom represent a just recognition of Brazil's greatness and its residents' political allegiance, or was it an "oppressive" system that degraded Portugal and left it like a "dove in the clutches of an eagle?" "Would it be possible, as Gonçalves dos Santos declared, now writing anonymously as a "citizen" pamphleteer, to be "a Brazilian in every way Portuguese?"[121] In Rio de Janeiro, answers to these questions would lead to yet a further redefinition of monarchy and empire.

NOTES

1. Luiz Gonçalves do Santos, *Memórias para servir à História do Reino do Brasil* t. 2 (Belo Horizonte/São Paulo: Itatiaia/EDUSP, 1981), 273.

2. Valentim Alexandre, *Os sentidos do império: questão nacional e questão colonial na crise do antigo regime português* (Porto: Afrontamento, 1993), 452.

3. Copy of a proclamation issued August 24, 1820 in Porto, sent to Rio de Janeiro, August, 31, 1820, in "Cartas trocadas," BNRJ Ms. II-30,36,29, n. 3. As Alexandre explains, once convened the Cortes claimed to represent not only the now sovereign "nation," but also the absent king. Thus Dom João's portrait adorned the chamber where the Cortes convened and the constitution was announced as the salvation of "the preeminent attributes which are inherent to the royal decorum and the splendor of Majesty." See Alexandre, *Os sentidos*, 466–468.

4. Raymundo Faoro, "Folhetos da independência," in *O debate político no processo da independência*, ed. Raymundo Faoro (Rio de Janeiro: Conselho Federal de Cultura, 1973), 8.

5. *Memórias do Marquês de Fronteira e Alorna*, cited in Alexandre, *Os sentidos*, 452.

6. José da Silva Aréas to [Domingos António de Souza Coutinho], Rio de Janeiro, March 17, 1821, *DHI*, 238–242 (emphasis in original); and *Relação dos sucessos do dia 26 de Fevereiro de 1821 na Corte do Rio de Janeiro* (Bahia: Viuva Serva e Carvalho, [1821]). The royal counselor Silvestre Pinheiro Ferreira also noted demands for changes in the decree. See Carta 6 in "Cartas sobre a Revolução do Brasil," in Pinheiro Ferreira, *Idéias Políticas* (Rio de Janeiro: PUC/Conselho Federal de Cultura, 1976), 44. On the rebellion see also J.C. Fernandes Pinheiro, "Motins políticos e militares no Rio de Janeiro," *RIHGB* 37, pt. 2 (1874), 349; "Decreto," February 24, 1821; "Auto de Juramento," February 26, 1821, and "Lista de pessoas

nomeadas hoje para os empregos publicos," in *Código Brasiliense, Ou Collecção das Leis, Alvarás, Decretos, Cartas Régias, &c. Promulgadas no Brasil desde a feliz chegada de El Rey Nosso Senhor A Este Reino* (Rio de Janeiro: [Impressão Régia, 1811–1822]); and *Correio Braziliense,* May 1821, in *Antologia do Correio Braziliense,* ed. Barbosa Lima Sobrinho (Rio de Janeiro: Cátedra/Instituto Nacional do Livro, 1977), 311.

7. Bernardino Avellino Ferreira e Souza, *Versos que pelo Faustissimo Acontecimento do Maravilhoso Dia 26 de Fevereiro, Recitou no Real Theatro de S. João desta Corte . . .* (Rio de Janeiro: Impressão Régia, 1821), 3.

8. On the news of the Porto rebellion reaching Rio, see Sua Alteza Real to Vila Nova Portugal, October 17, 1820, *DHI,* 173. On subsequent news and rumors that circulated in Rio and elsewhere in Brazil, see Sua Alteza Real to Vila Nova Portugal, November 12, 1820, *DHI,* 177–178; Luiz do Rego Barreto to Vila Nova Portugal, December 19, 1820, AHI Lata 179 Maço 4 Pasta 2; and *Relação dos Sucessos,* 4.

9. Tomás António Vila Nova Portugal cited in Valentim Alexandre, *Os sentidos,* 496; Vila Nova Portugal to Sua Alteza Real, October 28, 1820, January 28 and 31, 1821, *DHI,* 174–175, 184–185, 217; and January 17, 1821, in Ângelo Pereira, *D. João VI, principe e rei* v. 3 (Lisbon: Empresa Nacional de Publicidade, 1956), 321–322. On Vila Nova Portugal's position see also Arnold B. Clayton, "The Life of Tomás Antônio Vilanova Portugal: A Study in the Government of Portugal and Brazil" (Ph.D. dissertation, Columbia University, 1977), 249–250. A facsimile edition of *Le Roi et la Famille Royal de Bragance Doivent-ils, dans les circonstances présentes, Retourner en Portugal, ou bien Rester au Brésil?* (Rio de Janeiro: A'l Imprimerie Royale: 1820) is included in Faoro, *Debate Político.* Letters between Dom João and Vila Nova Portugal in January 1821 refer to a manuscript by Cailhé and authorize its printing. See *DHI,* 180–181, including an editor's note. In correspondence with the police intendant Cailhé made references to "amusing" conjectures about the author of the "French pamphlet." See Cailhé to Viana, January 28, 1821, BNRJ Ms. II-33,22,54.

10. Pedro de Souza Holstein, Conde de Palmela (1781–1850) served as Portuguese representative at the Congress of Vienna, to the Cadiz government, and in London. On Palmela's position see Palmela to Sua Alteza Real, January 16, 1821, transcribed in Ângelo Pereira, *Os filhos de el-rei D. João VI* (Lisbon: Empresa Nacional de Publicidade, 1946), 289–290. For debates at court following the Porto rebellion see Pinheiro Ferreira, Cartas 1, 2, and 3, in *Idéias Políticas*; and Alexandre, *Os sentidos,* 490–510.

11. Acting as an informant, in letters to the police intendant Cailhé reported on the circulation of "public papers," the appearance of signs and constitutional slogans, and talk in the streets of Rio and Bahia and among courtiers and urged the crown to take action. See Cailhé to Viana, October 14, 24, and 25, 1820, summarized in *Dom João VI e o Império no Brasil, a Independência e a Missão Rio Maior,* ed. Marcos Carneiro de Mendonça (Rio de Janeiro: Biblioteca Reprográfica Xerox, 1984), 436–437, 445. On the situation in Rio after the arrival of news of the Porto rebellion see also Cailhé to Viana, January 2 and 28, February 18 and 23, 1821, BNRJ Ms. II-33,22,54; Vila Nova Portugal to Viana, n.d., with a note from Viana, November 9, 1820, BNRJ Ms. II-34,34,7; [Vila Nova Portugal?], [unsigned *parecer*], January 7, 1821, *DHI,* 215–217; and "Cartas anonymas denunciando os projectos de revolução," [ca. late 1820/ early 1821], *DHI,* 148–149. On the response to Cailhé's pamphlet see E. Thornton (British envoy) to Castlereagh, cited in Roderick Barman, *Brazil: The Forging of a Nation, 1798–1852*

(Stanford: Stanford University Press, 1988), 69; and *Relação dos Sucessos*, 4. Cailhé reported more diverse effects. See Cailhé to Viana, January 28, 1821, BNRJ Ms. II- 33,22,54.

12. Pinheiro Ferreira, Cartas 4 and 5, in *Idéias*, 39–41.

13. "Decreto," dated February 18, 1821, published February 22, 1821, in *Código Brasiliense*.

14. Barman, *Brazil*, 70; "Decreto," February 22, 1821, in *Código*.

15. According to Aréas, a draft of a decree had been shown to army officials so that a rebellion like that of Bahia would be avoided in Rio. Although their response was antagonistic, on February 22 the decree "appeared transformed" by Vila Nova Portugal "without the other ministers being heard." See Aréas to Souza Coutinho, March 17, 1821, *DHI*, 238–239; [Anonymous, ca. 1821], AHI, Lata 195 Maço 6 Pasta 13 (formerly Maço 7 Pasta 12); Marquês de Alegrete to Sua Alteza Real, February 25, 1821 (summary), and Cailhé to [Viana], February 24, 1821, in *Dom João VI*, ed. Carneiro de Mendonça, 445, 451. On the conflict between Vila Nova Portugal and Palmela, see Palmela to Sua Alteza Real, February 21, 1821, *DHI*, 217–219, including "the project for the decree" with references to the "the fundamental bases of the Constitutional Charter" and the "convocation of a *junta* of Cortes for the Kingdom of Brazil"; Vila Nova Portugal to Sua Alteza Real, February 22, 1821, *DHI*, 190–195; and Palmela to Sua Alteza Real, February 24, 1821, *DHI*, 220–221. In a letter to Vila Nova Portugal, Dom João indicated that to counter the hostility to the decree and meet the demand for "the Constitution of Portugal," the crown would seek to give "the hope that it would accept said Constitution with changes adopted for the Country (*País*) or give [its] bases." See Sua Alteza Real to [Vila Nova Portugal], February 24, 1821, *DHI*, 195. Planning for a new compromise apparently commenced, for according to Pinheiro Ferreira the text of the decree then issued in response to the rebellion had been drafted prior to February 26. A decision to publish a new decree was made by royal counselors on February 24, he explained, but Vila Nova Portugal succeeded in delaying publication. See Pinheiro Ferreira, Carta 6, in *Idéias*, 44.

16. Tobias Monteiro, *História do império. A elaboração da independência* (Rio de Janeiro: Briguiet, 1927), 302–313; Neill Macaulay, *Dom Pedro: The Struggle for Liberty in Brazil and Portugal, 1798–1834* (Durham: Duke University Press, 1986), 77–78; Barman, *Brazil*, 70; Aréas to Souza Coutinho, March 17, 1821, *DHI*, 239.

17. See *Relação dos Sucessos*, 10; and Cecilia Helena Lorenzini de Salles Oliveira, *A Astúcia Liberal: Relações de mercado e projetos políticos no Rio de Janeiro (1820–1824)* (Bragança Paulista: EDUSF/Ícone, 1999). The group to which she refers included Joaquim Gonçalves Ledo, Manuel Joaquim de Silva Porto, Januário da Cunha Barbosa, Clemente Pereira, and others with rural properties in the hinterland Recôncavo and Goiticazes, business interests in Rio, and positions within royal bureaucracy.

18. Aréas to Souza Coutinho, March 17, 1821, *DHI*, 240. Aréas identified the rebellion's leaders as Padre Goes, Padre Macamboa, Padre Cupertino, and Majors Pimenta, Padua e Almeida. The cleric Marcelino José Alves Macamboa was a native of Lisbon, trained in canon law at the University of Coimbra, who had served as a lawyer for the Court of Appeals. Goes was also born in Portugal and, according to Macaulay, was part of Dom Pedro's "circle of associates." See Macaulay, *Dom Pedro*, 78.

19. Pinheiro Ferreira, Carta 6, in *Idéias*, 42–43; and Salles Oliveira, *Astúcia*. According to Salles Oliveira, the "Brazilian party" to which Pinheiro Ferreira referred included members of

the emigrant Portuguese bureaucracy with interests in the Fluminense economy, linked to Paulo Fernandes Viana, Fernando Carneiro Leão, Manuel Jacinto Nogueira da Gama, José da Silva Lisboa, and Gonçalves dos Santos, men who were joined by their opposition to the radicalism of the constitutionalist movement in Portugal and by the idea that the king's departure and Dom Pedro's regency would provide for a more ordered and reformist constitutional regime in Brazil.

20. Aréas to Souza Coutinho, March 17, 1821, *DHI*, 240; and correspondence concerning the "Detenção de João Severiano Maciel da Costa . . . ," *DHI*, 268–276. The Visconde de São Lourenço, Francisco Bento Maria Targini, was president of the royal treasury. See the Appendix here for pasquinades denouncing Targini.

21. See decrees of March 7 and March 9, in *Código Braziliense*.

22. "Representações dirigidas a Dom João VI pedindo a sua permanência no Brasil," BNRJ Ms. II-43,30,61, including, "Representação dos negociantes e proprietários," March 30, 1821 (98 signatures); "Representação do Senado da Câmara," Rio de Janeiro, March 28, 1821 (352 signatures); "[Representação da] Corporação de Ourives" (99 signatures); "[Representação do] Corpo do Commércio desta Capital," March 20, 1821 (95 signatures). Similar arguments were advanced in "Carta anônima dirigida a Dom João VI, mostrando-lhe os inconvenientes do seu regresso ao Reino," BNRJ Ms. I-3,16,19. Although, as Barman notes, one British diplomat characterized the petitioners as from the "inferior class of Artisans and Tradesmen," the petitions also included the signatures of many of the city's wealthiest property owners. See Barman, *Brazil*, 71. Aréas reported that the king wept upon receiving the petitions. See Aréas to Souza Coutinho, March 31, 1821, *DHI*, 243.

23. Pinheiro Ferreira, Cartas 14, 21, 22, and 23, in *Idéias*, 65, 84–85.

24. Pinheiro Ferreira, Cartas 24 and 25, in *Idéias*, 89–91. On the *edital* see Monteiro, *História do império*, 333, note 2.

25. "Memoria sobre os acontecimentos dos dias 21 e 22 de Abril de 1821 na praça do commércio do Rio de Janeiro, escripta em maio do mesmo anno por uma testemunha presencial . . . ," *RIHGB* 27 (1864), 276; "Processo da revolta na praça do commércio do Rio de Janeiro, inquirição de testemunhas," *DHI*, 284, 290. The Itamaraty Archive contains a number of anonymous undated materials that appear to be from this period. See, for example, "Relação das pessoas que devião ser presos na intenção dos eleitores do novo governo do Rio de Janeiro," AHI Lata 195 Maço 7 Pasta 2. The list contains 49 names, in some cases followed by a description of offenses: the Marquês de Loule, "because all his servants are French"; the Conde de Palmela, "because he is of tyrannical sentiments"; and Paulo Fernandes Viana, Vila Nova Portugal, Almirante Rodrigo Pinto Guedes, the "French Colonel Cailhé," Fernando Carneiro Leão, and Amaro Velho Silva. This may be one of the unofficial documents drafted for the meeting of electors to which the memorialist referred, or it may have been produced earlier in the context of the February rebellion.

26. The Spanish Constitution of 1812 was drafted by the Spanish Cortes convened in Cadiz during the Napoleonic War. It declared that the nation was sovereign and established that the Cortes had legislative power. See Richard Herr, *An Historical Essay on Modern Spain* (Berkeley: University of California Press, 1971), 73.

27. Accounts of the meeting of parish electors in the praça do comércio used here are "Memoria sobre os acontecimentos," 271–289; Pinheiro Ferreira, Cartas 26 and 27, in *Idéias*,

91–105; and "Processo da revolta na praça do commércio," *DHI*, 277–325. In "Processo," see especially 281–284, 288–290, 293, 295.

28. "Processo," 284.

29. "Processo," 297, 301; Salles Oliveira, *Astúcia*, 171–172. According to one witness, this group made their presence known in the praça by unfurling a banner that read "The grateful Nation calls upon the Conde d'Arcos." At the meeting their plan may have been put into action by José Nogueira Soares, who, as one witnessed testified, waited for the reading of the original decree and then "said something to the people that appeared to him to be a signal" after which those gathered "began to shout 'down with despotisms and decrees'." Tobias Monteiro describes Nogueira Soares as a supporter of the Conde dos Arcos. See Monteiro, *História do império*, 335. This, however, did not prevent his later arrest. See also the Appendix here for another reference to Arcos in a pasquinade apparently drafted in February 1821.

30. "Processo," 284; Salles Oliveira, *Astúcia*, 173–177.

31. Pinheiro Ferreira, Carta 26, in *Idéias*, 94–95; "Processo," 293, 301. On Macamboa, Ramos, and Duprad, see "Processo," 282, 287, 289, 294, 298, and 322–324. During the inquiry Duprad emerged as the most curious and mysterious of those who attended the assembly. One witness identified him as "Monsieur Duprad" and claimed that it made the electors angry "as he was not Portuguese he had involved himself in such an affair," while others speculated "he was some Spaniard, because he was calling for the Spanish Constitution." As Duprad himself testified, however, he was born in Lisbon the son of a French merchant named Pedro Duprad and the Portuguese Joanna Duprad. In 1821 he was 20 years old. Recently, he had been nominated to a diplomatic post in the United States by Pinheiro Ferreira, according to Oliveira Lima. Oliveira Lima also reports that on returning to Portugal he studied law at the University of Coimbra and later practiced law with success until his death in 1843. See Albano da Silveira Porto, *Resenha das familias titulares e grandes de Portugal* v.1 (Lisboa: Francisco Arthur da Silva, 1883), 520–521; and Oliveira Lima, *O movimento da independência (1821–22)* (Fifth edition) (São Paulo: Melhoramentos, 1972), 57n. "Cavaquino" refers to a small guitar-like instrument and, as a nickname, to the person who plays it.

32. "Memoria," 284. According to Roderick Barman, the move to take over the assembly was plotted by some courtiers in "common cause with popular elements" in the city. Hence, the decision to open the meeting to residents. Both groups, Barman explains, "desired to retain the king in Rio, the first to establish its own supremacy and the other to set up a more democratic polity, which they hoped to dominate." Francisco Falcon and Ilmar Santos similarly characterize the assembly as the "culminating moment" of a growing movement to pressure the king to stay in Brazil. See Barman, *Brazil*, 71–72; Francisco Falcon and Ilmar Roloff Santos, "O Processo de Independência no Rio de Janeiro," in *1822: Dimensões*, ed. Carlos Guilherme Mota (São Paulo: Perspectiva, 1972), 295.

33. Aréas to Souza Coutinho, March 17, 1821, *DHI*, 239; "Memoria," 271–272; "Processo," 294, 296.

34. Pinheiro Ferreira, Carta 26, in *Idéias*, 101; "Processo," 297, 299, 322–325; "Memoria," 287–289. For decrees and the proclamation of April 22 and 23, see *Código Brasiliense*.

35. Macaulay, *Dom Pedro*, 86.

36. Gonçalves dos Santos, *Memórias* t. 2, 269–270, 273.

37. Aréas to Souza Coutinho, June 27, 1821, *DHI*, 245.

38. Salles Oliveira, *Astúcia*. Here Salles Oliveira analyzes the *Revérbero Constitucional Fluminense*, a newspaper published between September 1821 and October 1822, edited by Ledo, Clemente Pereira, and Januário da Cunha Barbosa.

39. The anonymity of early pamphlets and pasquinades makes an analysis of the social dimensions of constitutionalism difficult. The record of the "Processo da revolta na praça" includes references to the *povo miúdo* (small folk) as well as to artisans, merchants, property owners, and commercial clerks, all endorsing a constitutional sovereignty. Clerics and lawyers and both new and long-standing residents of Rio were also among those who publicly defended the new "constitutional system" in 1821. For a sociological analysis of pamphleteers in 1821–1822 see Lúcia Maria Bastos Pereira das Neves, "Corcundas, constitucionais e pes-de-chumbo: a cultura política da Independência 1820–1822" (Ph.D. dissertation, University of São Paulo, 1992), v. 1, 79–101.

40. Aréas to Souza Coutinho, March 17, 1821, *DHI*, 240. The end of certain restrictions on the press, promulgated by the Lisbon constitutionalists in 1820, was not applied in Rio until following the February rebellion. Although on March 2 a decree suspended the prior censorship of manuscripts, works printed in Rio and those imported from abroad could not contain "anything against Religion, Morality, and Good Customs, against the Constitution and Person of the Sovereign, or against public tranquility." Perhaps a violation of these standards led officials to "reprimand" José Anastacio Falcão, the author of a pamphlet entitled *O Alfaite Constitucional*. See João Ignacio da Cunha, "Registro do Ofício expedido ao Presidente do Erário," December 10, 1821, ANRJ Códice 323 v. 6, f101. On the end of censorship see "Decreto," March 2, 1821, in *Código Brasiliense*; Marcello de Ipanema, *Estudos de história da legislação de imprensa* (Rio de Janeiro: Aurora, 1949), 78–84; and Rubens Borba de Moraes, "A Impressão Régia no Rio de Janeiro: Origens e Produção," in Ana Maria de Almeida Camargo and Rubens Borba de Moraes, *Bibliografia da Impressão Régia do Rio de Janeiro* v. 1 (São Paulo: EDUSP/Kosmos, 1993), xxi.

41. *Constituição Explicada* (Reprint) (Rio de Janeiro: Impressão Régia, 1821). On its announcement in the *Gazeta*, see Neves, "Corcundas," v. 1, 38. The first pro-constitutional publication may have been in late 1820, a reprint of a hymn sung at the Royal Theater of São Carlos in Lisbon on September 18, 1820. See Camargo and Moraes, *Bibliografia*, v.1, 234. Between 1808 and 1820 the Royal Press published approximately 623 titles. Between 1821 and 1822, the number of titles was 531. See Cecilia Helena Lorenzini de Salles Oliveira, "O Disfarce do Anonimato: O Debate Político Através dos Folhetos (1820–1822)" (M.A. thesis, University of São Paulo, 1979), 22. Based on the titles registered in Camargo and Moraes, *Bibliografia*, in 1820 approximately 13 percent (6 of 45) of Royal Press titles concerned politics; in 1821 70 percent (191 of 273) of its publications were about politics, constitutionalism, and recent events.

42. *Gazeta do Rio de Janeiro*, November 10, 1821, transcribed in Renault, 74.

43. Paulo Martin, "Noticia" (Rio de Janeiro: Impressão Nacional, 1821). This announcement, published sometime after July 1821, advertised papers from Bahia, "all since February 10, day of the Fortunate Regeneration of that city until the end of July" and "Constitutional Pamphlets" from Lisbon. It included two lists and 129 titles. On print culture see also Laurence Hallewell, *Books in Brazil: a History of the Publishing Trade* (Metuchen, NJ: Scarecrow, 1982), 32–34; Neves, "Corcundas," v. 1, 41, 105–109; and Maria Beatriz Nizza da Silva, *Cul-*

tura e sociedade no Rio de Janeiro (1808–1821) (São Paulo: Companhia Editora Nacional, 1977), 7. Carla Hesse charted a similar shift in "the center of gravity in commercial printing" in France following the declaration of press freedom to what she described as "the democratic culture of the pamphlet, the broadside, and the periodical press." See Carla Hesse, *Publishing and Cultural Politics in Revolutionary Paris, 1789–1810* (Berkeley: University of California Press, 1991), 177.

44. Neves, "Corcundas" v. 1, 105–109, 126, 133; Cailhé to Viana, "Rapport sur la situation de l'opinion publique," Rio de Janeiro, November, 26, 1820, in Pereira, *D. João VI* v. 3, 306.

45. Faoro, "Folhetos," 7.

46. [Anonymous, ca. 1821], AHI Lata 195 Maço 6 Pasta 13 (formerly Lata 195 Maço 7 Pasta 12).

47. José Joaquim Lopes de Lima, *Supplemento ao Diccionario-Carcundatico . . .* (Rio de Janeiro: Imprensa Nacional, 1821), 7.

48. See the Appendix for a complete transcription of these and other verses.

49. *Pernicioso Poder dos Perfidos Validos e Conselheiros dos Reis Destruido Pela Constituição* (Reprint) (Rio de Janeiro: Impressão Nacional, 1821), 10; *A Regeneração Constitucional ou Guerra e Disputa entre Carcundas e os Constitucionaes . . .* (Rio de Janeiro: Impressão Nacional, 1821), 4.

50. Francisco Mai dos Homens Carvalho, *Oração de Acção de Graças que na Solemnidade do Anniversario do dia 24 de Agosto, Mandada Fazer na Real Capella desta Corte por Sua Alteza Real, o Principe Regente do Brazil . . .* (Rio de Janeiro: Impressão Nacional, 1821), 8, 20.

51. [João Pedro Fernandes], *Elogio Para se Recitar no Theatro de S.João no Faustissimo Dia Natalicio de Sua Alteza o Principe Real do Brazil . . .* (Rio de Janeiro: Impressão Nacional, 1821), 3.

52. *Constituição Explicada,* 1.

53. José Joaquim Lopes de Lima, *Diccionario Carcundatico ou Explicação das Phrazes dos Carcundas . . .* (Rio de Janeiro: Imprensa Nacional, 1821), 9.

54. João Severiano Maciel da Costa, *Memória sobre a necessidade de abolir a introdução dos escravos africanos no Brasil . . .* (1821), in *Memórias sobre a escravidão,* ed. Graça Salgado (Rio de Janeiro: Arquivo Nacional, 1988), 53.

55. Pinheiro Ferreira, Carta 6, 7, and Carta 23, in *Idéias,* 42–43, 46–47, 88–89. Pinheiro Ferreira was particularly disconcerted by the disregard for social hierarchy exhibited by an officer who demanded that he present himself in the rocio to assume his new post and take an oath to the constitutional regime. It signaled "a true revolution," he wrote, "if not in essence (if it were certain that His Majesty was in agreement) at least in the manner in which His will was manifest."

56. Mai dos Homens Carvalho, *Oração,* 8; *Dialogo entre a Constituição e o Despotismo* (Rio de Janeiro: Impressão Nacional, 1821), 3; Lima, *Supplemento,* 7.

57. *Cathecismo Constitucional,* 1.

58. Lima, *Diccionario,* 3.

59. Lima, *Supplemento,* 5; *Sermão Constitucional dirigido a Nação Portugueza e Proferido no Consistorio particular dos Verdadeiros Liberaes . . .* (Reprint) (Rio de Janeiro: Impressão Régia, 1821), 16.

60. *Dialogo entre o Corcunda Abatido e o Constitucional Exaltado*, 3–4.

61. *Sermão Constitucional*, 18.

62. "Decreto," February 28, 1821, cited in Camargo and Moraes, *Bibliografia*, v. 2, 146. Along with Mai dos Homens Carvalho, *Oração de Acção de Graças que na Solemnidade do Anniversario do dia 24 de Agosto*, there were at least two other commemorative sermons preached and published in 1821. See *Sermão Recitado na Real Capella no dia 24 de Agosto do Presente Anno* (Rio de Janeiro: Impressão Nacional, 1821); and *Sermão de Acção de Graças que, em Memoria dos Dias 24 de Agosto, e 15 de Septembro de 1820, o Senado, e os Cidadãos do Rio de Janeiro Solemnizarão no dia 15 de Septembro na Igreja de S. Francisco de Paula . . .* (Rio de Janeiro: Impressão Nacional, 1821), registered in Camargo and Moraes, *Bibliografia*, v. 1, 318. According to José Honório Rodrigues, the most ardent constitutionalist preachers were Frei Fransisco de Santa Teresa de Jesus Sampaio (1788–1830) and Januário da Cunha Barbosa (1786–1846). See his *Independência: revolução e contra-revolução* v. 4 (Rio de Janeiro: Francisco Alves, [1975–76]), 135–150.

63. *A Regeneração Constitucional ou Guerra e Disputa entre os Carcundas e os Constitucionaes*, 17–23. Along with the catechism included in *Regeneração Política* see also *Cathecismo Constitucional* and *Dialogo Instructivo, em que se explicão os fundamentos de Uma Constituição . . .* (Rio de Janeiro: Impressão Régia, 1821). Although there were "political catechisms" published in late eighteenth- and early nineteenth-century England and the United States, according to Ana Maria Ferreira Pina, the genre of the political catechism was imported into Portugal from France. See her *De Rousseau ao Imaginário da Revolução de 1820* (Lisbon: INIC, 1988), 104–105. The Rio Press had previously published a translation of a Spanish *Cathecismo Civil* (1809), an anti-Napoleonic tract, as well as an apparently more traditional catechism also entitled *Cathecismo Civil . . .* (1812). In 1822 the Royal Press also published *Cathecismo de Economia Política . . .* , a translation from a work in French, written by Jean Baptiste Say, published originally in 1815; and *Cathecismo dos Pedreiros Livres . . .* , a promasonic tract.

64. Maria Candida Proença, "1820: A 'Festa' da Regeneração: Permanências e Inovações," *RHI* 10, 375–384; *Constituição Politica da Monarquia Portuguesa Feita pelas Cortes Geraes, Extraordinarias, e Constituentes . . . Projeto para discussão...* (Lisbon: Impressão Nacional, 1821), 13–14; Januário da Cunha Barbosa, *Discurso, no Fim da Missa Solemne . . . em que Precedo ao Acto da Junta Eleitoral da Comarca, no Dia 15 de Maio de 1821* (Rio de Janeiro: Typografia Régia, 1821), 4, 6–7.

65. Neves, "Corcundas," v. 1, 39.

66. On political ritual and the creation of community see Lynn Hunt, *Politics, Culture and Class in the French Revolution* (Berkeley: University of California Press, 1984), 44, 49, 54.

67. Zilia Osório de Castro, "A Sociedade e a Soberania, Doutrina de um Vintista," *RHI* 1 (1979), 173, 176; Iara Lis Carvalho Souza, *Pátria Coroada: O Brasil como Corpo Político Autônomo, 1780–1831* (São Paulo: UNESP, 1998), 83–85. Valentim Alexandre has described Portuguese constitutionalism's traditionalism as "tactical." See *Os sentidos*, 468.

68. *Dialogo entre o Corcunda Abatido e o Constitucional Exaltado* (Rio de Janeiro: Impressão Nacional, [1821]), 3.

69. Pedro Cardim, "O quadro constitucional. Os grandes paradigmas de organização política: A coroa e a representação do reino. As cortes," in *História de Portugal: O Antigo*

Regime v. 4, ed. António Manuel Hespanha (Lisbon: Estampa, n.d.), 145–154. On the political theory of the Portuguese monarchy and the Cortes see also Carvalho Souza, *Pátria Coroada*, 21–38.

70. *Pernicioso Poder*, 11; *Dialogo entre a Constituição e o Despotismo*, 3.

71. *Pernicioso Poder, 8; Cathecismo Constitucional* (Rio de Janeiro: Impressão Régia, [1821]), 1.

72. [Ignacio José Correa Drummond], *Sonetos em Applauzo ao Feliz Succeso da Completa Regeneração da Nação Portugueza, Executado na Praça do Rocio da Corte e Cidade do Rio de Janeiro no memoravel dia 26 de Fevereiro de 1821* (Rio de Janeiro: Impressão Régia, 1821), 8, 10. The same "glosa" is also featured in Souza, *Versos pelo Faustissimo Acontecimento do Maravilhoso dia 26 de Fevereiro*. For the same refrain in an anti-Napoleonic pamphlet, see Chapter 3. Drummond, a member of the town council of Cidade do Funchal, Madeira was reportedly in Rio working in "favor of our Political Regeneration" and "forced" to leave for Lisbon in October 1821. See Camargo and Borba de Moraes, *Bibliografia*, v. 1, 319–320.

73. *Das Sociedades, e das Convenções, ou Constituições* (Reprint) (Rio de Janeiro: Impressão Régia, 1821), 4–5.

74. See Telmo dos Santos Verdelho, *As palavras e as idéias na revolução liberal de 1820* (Coimbra: INIC, 1981), 103–111, 116–119; Lima, *Diccionario*, 10. In contrast, José Honório Rodrigues concluded that pamphlets either attacked or defended the political predominance of Portugal or Brazil with "a few references to liberal principles." See Rodrigues, *Independência: revolução e contra-revolução* v. 1, 10.

75. See the Appendix for transcriptions in Portuguese. Pamphleteers also proclaimed that the "legislative power resided in the Nation." See, for example, *Dialogo Instructivo*, 4.

76. *Reflexões Filosoficas sobre a Liberdade, e Igualdade* (Rio de Janeiro: Impressão Régia, 1821), 2, 3–4. On rights, see also Lima, *Supplemento*, 4.

77. *Qualidades que se devem acompanhar os Compromissarios e Elleitores. Extrahido do Genio Constitucional N. 39* (Reprint) (Rio de Janeiro: Impressão Régia, 1821); *Dialogo Instructivo*, 5; Verdelho, *As palavras*, 48–50; 221–231. Another pamphleteer explained "the maintenance of liberty" as "the ability of each one to make manifest his ideas in word or in writing; and to do everything that the Law does not prohibit." See *Dialogo Instructivo*, 4. An early draft of the constitution similarly contended that "Liberty consists in the faculty of each Citizen to do all that the law does not prohibit." See *Constituição Politica da Monarquia Portuguesa . . . Projeto*, 4.

78. Mai dos Homens Carvalho, *Oração*, 20.

79. *Cathecismo Constitucional*, 4.

80. Viana, "Registro do Ofício expedido ao Ministro de Estado dos Negócios Marinhos," April 4 and 21, 1818, ANRJ Códice 323 v. 5, f55-f55v.

81. *Dialogo Entre o Corcunda Abatido e o Constitucional Exaltado*, 6; Joaquim José de Azevedo, Visconde do Rio Secco, *Exposição Analytica, e Justificativa da Conducta, e Vida Publica do Visconde do Rio Secco, desde o Dia 25 de Novembro de 1807 . . .* (Rio de Janeiro: Imprensa Nacional, 1821), 34. On prior understandings of citizen, see Fernando Teles da Silva Caminha e Meneses, Marquês de Penalva, *Dissertação sôbre as obrigações do vassalo* (Lisbon: Régia Officina Tipographica, 1804), 23; *Diccionario da lingua portuguesa, composta pelo Padre D. Rafael Bluteau, reformado e accrescentado por Antonio de Moraes Silva* (Lisbon: Simão Thaddeo Ferreira, 1779); and Maria de Fátima Silva Gouvêa, "Redes de Poder na América Por-

tuguesa—O Caso dos Homens Bons do Rio de Janeiro, ca. 1790–1822," *Revista Brasileira de História* 18, n. 36 (1998), 315.

82. See *Qualidades que se devem acompanhar os Compromissarios e Elleitores.*

83. Verdelho, *As palavras*, 235–237; 248–250. See "Memoria sobre os acontecimentos" and "Representações": Francisco José Pereira das Neves, "negociante e cidadão"; Ignacio Assis Saraiva e Fonseca, "cidadão e cavalheiro da Ordem de Cristo"; João José de Mello, "cidadão e negociante"; António Francisco Leite, "negociante e cidadão"; José António de Carvalho, "cidadão."

84. Pinheiro Ferreira, Carta 26, *Idéias*, 92.

85. On the notion of rhetorical political discourse, see Hunt, *Politics*, 20–24.

86. *Parallelo entre os Corcundas e Liberaes* (Rio de Janeiro: Impressão Régia, 1821). The defects of corcundas were also exposed in João Francisco Delgado, *As Amendoas dadas aos Corcundas, por hum Liberal, Inimigo de Golfinhos* (Rio de Janeiro: Imprensa Nacional, 1821), published in Lisbon the same year. Contemporary spellings of *corcunda* varied and included *carcunda*. Here I have transcribed these variations as they were originally printed.

87. On the shift in the meaning of "liberal" from "liberality" to defenders of "liberty" see Verdelho, *As palavras*, 69.

88. Lima, *Diccionario Carcundatico*, [introduction]. Lima referred to Rafael Bluteau (1638–1734), author of *Vocabulário portuguêz e latino* . . . (Coimbra: Collegio das Artes da Companhia de Jesus, 1712–28).

89. Hunt, *Politics*, 20–21, 45; Pedro Alvarez Diniz to João Ignacio da Cunha [intendant], September 25, 1821, and "Auto das perguntas feitas ao preso Manuel Luiz Nunes," October 2, 1821, ANRJ Ministério dos Negócios do Brasil Caixa 6J 86; António Luiz Pereira da Cunha to Luiz de Souza e Vasconcellos, September 26, 1821, ANRJ Códice 330 v. 1; João Ignacio da Cunha, "Ofício expedido ao Ministro e Secretário de Estado," October [11], 1821, ANRJ Códice 323 v. 6, f93; José de Almeida, Tenente Coronel Graduado do Batalhão de Caçadores da Corte, "[Anúncio] Havendo feito a maior sensação possivel nos animos bem intencionados dos habitantes desta Capital . . ." (Rio de Janeiro: Impressão Nacional, 1821).

90. Joan Landes, *Women and the Public Sphere in the Age of Revolution* (Ithaca: Cornell University Press, 1988); *Carta de André Mamede ao seu Amigo Braz Barnabé, na qual se Explica o que São Corcundas* (Rio de Janeiro: Impressão Régia, 1821), 3–5.

91. Rio Secco, *Exposição Analytica*, iii.

92. *O Português Constitucional Regenerado* 40 (September 18, 1821), cited in Pina, *De Rousseau*, 102; José António de Miranda, *Memoria Constitucional e Politica sobre o Estado Presente de Portugal, e Brasil* . . . (Rio de Janeiro: Impressão Régia, 1821), 50. A facsimile of the *Memoria* is found in *O debate*, ed. Faoro. See also Verdelho, *As palavras*, 103–110.

93. Cailhé to Viana, "Rapport," in Pereira, *D. João VI* v. 3, 304–307; Viana to Vila Nova Portugal, "Cartas trocadas . . . a respeito da Revolução Portuguesa de 1820," BNRJ Ms. II-30,36,29; Vila Nova Portugal to Sua Alteza Real, [February 24, 1821], in *DHI*, 195; Pinheiro Ferreira, Carta 24, *Idéias*, 90.

94. Lima, *Supplemento*, 7.

95. See *Qualidades*; Lúcia Maria Bastos P. Neves, "Leitura e leitores no Brasil, 1820–1822: o esboço frustrado de uma esfera pública do poder," *Acervo*, 8, n. 1/2 (December 1995), 123–138.

96. João Ignacio da Cunha, "Registro do Ofício dirgido ao Secretário de Estado dos Negócios de Guerra," December 8, 1821, ANRJ Códice 323 v. 6, f103.

97. *Quaes são os bens e os males que podem resultar da liberdade da imprensa; e qual he a influencia que elles podem ter no momento em que os Representantes da Nação Portugueza vão se congregar* (Reprint) (Rio de Janeiro: Impressão Régia, 1821), 1, 2. The author also contended that "the printed script" was "general, and as a consequence . . . capable of illuminating an entire people." Thus, with an engaged and free press the Cortes' deliberations could be made public and "the nation" could inform and instruct its representatives, renewing the "social pact" that existed "between the king and the people." On notions of the free press in Portuguese constitutionalism see also Pina, *De Rousseau*, 101.

98. José Albano Fragoso, "Plano de regeneração política e de renovação de ensino, elaborado por . . . ," December 29, 1821, ANRJ Códice 807 Livro 20, f71; *Português Constitucional Regenerado* 40 (September 18, 1821), cited in Pina, *De Rousseau*, 102.

99. Fragoso, "Plano," f64v, f67v, f70. See also Neves, "Corcundas," v. 1, 115.

100. *Quaes são os bens*, 9.

101. *Dialogo entre a Constituição e o Despotismo*, 1, 7.

102. Miranda, *Memoria*, 35.

103. *Reflexões Filosoficas*, 4.

104. "O Triumpho Maior da Luzitania," Instituto Histórico e Geográfico Brasileiro (Rio de Janeiro) Icon. Lata 47 n. 29.

105. *O Português Constitucional* 18 (October 12, 1820), cited in Pina, *De Rousseau*, 107.

106. *Dialogo Instructivo*, 3; José Esteves Pereira, "Identidade nacional: do reformismo absolutista ao liberalismo," in *A Memória da nação*, eds. Francisco Bethencourt and Diogo Ramada Curto (Lisbon: Livraria Sá da Costa, 1991), 433.

107. Hunt, *Politics*, 60; François-Xavier Guerra, "The Spanish American Tradition of Representation and its European Roots," *Journal of Latin American Studies* 26 (1994), 3.

108. *Quaes são os bens*, 2. See Condorcet, *Des conventions nationales* (1791) cited in Hesse, *Publishing*, 180: "The knowledge of printing makes it possible for modern constitutions to reach a perfection that they could not otherwise achieve. In this way a sparsely populated people in a large territory can now be free as the residents of a small city. . . ."

109. The sale of Spanish Constitutions is noted in Neves, "Corcundas," v. 1, 37. As one witness testified, before the April Assembly an elector named José Pedro Fernandes "urged many from the Candelária parish to call for the Spanish Constitution." At the entrance to the praça other residents reportedly distributed papers that amounted to "invitations to acclaim the Spanish Constitution and inaugurate a provisional junta." See "Processo," 284, 290, 301; "Memoria," 276.

110. "Carta anônima dirigida a Dom João VI. . . ," n.d. [ca. February 1821], BNRJ Ms. I-3,16,19; "Processo," 290.

111. "Processo," 285, 295, 301, 311; "Memoria," 282.

112. On the Spanish Constitution, see also "Processo," 284, 292–296, 302–303, 309–310.

113. The concern with the fixed nature of a written constitution stands in contrast to the political culture of constitutionalism in England where, as James Vernon explains, "the very word constitution itself conveys [a] lack of fixity, suggesting that meanings and identities were

never assumed as essential but were rather continually in the process of construction and (re-) constitution." See James Vernon, "Notes towards an introduction," in *Re-Reading the Constitution: New Narratives in the Political History of England's Long Nineteenth-century*, ed. James Vernon (New York: Cambridge, 1996), 2.

114. *Constituição Política . . . Projeto*, 8.

115. Verdelho, *As palavras*, 119.

116. *Qualidades que se devem acompanhar os Compromissarios e Elleitores.*

117. See *Dialogo Politico e Instructivo, entre os Dous Homens da Roça, Andre Rapozo, e seu Compadre Bolonio Simplicio, Á cerca da Bernarda do Rio de Janeiro, e novidades da mesma* (Rio de Janeiro: Impressão Régia, 1821), 7; [Gonçalves dos Santos], *Justa Retribuição Dada ao Compadre de Lisboa . . .* (1821) (Rio de Janeiro: Imprensa Nacional, 1822), facsimile in *O debate*, ed. Faoro, 22–23.

118. Miranda, *Memoria*, 62–69; Maciel da Costa, *Memória sobre a necessidade*, 37–38.

119. António D'Oliva de Souza Sequeira, *Projecto para o Estabelecimento Politico do Reino-Unido de Portugal, Brasil, e Algarves . . .* (Reprint) (Rio de Janeiro: n.p., 1821), 3.

120. See António de Moraes Silva, *Diccionario da lingua portuguesa, recopilado dos vocabulos impressos até agora . . .* (Lisbon: Typographia Lacerdina, 1813); Viana to Vila Nova Portugal, "Cartas trocadas . . . a respeito da revolução portuguesa de 1820," BNRJ Ms. II-30,36,29.

121. [Gonçalves dos Santos], *Justa Retribuição*, 32. On one round of debates see *Carta do Compadre de Lisboa em Resposta a Outra do Compadre de Belem, ou Juizo Critico sobre a Opinião Publica dirigida pelo Astro da Lusitania* (Lisbon, 1821) (Rio de Janeiro: Impressão Régia, 1821), transcribed in *Cartas de Compadres de Belém e Lisboa*, ed. Rosemarie Erika Horch (São Paulo: Revista de História, 1977), 40–42. This "carta" responded to another by [Manuel Fernandes Thomaz], *Carta do Compadre de Belem ao Redactor do Astro da Lustitania dada à Luz pelo Compadre de Lisboa* (Lisbon, 1820) (Rio de Janeiro: Impressão Régia, 1821), also transcribed in Horsh. It also elicited a number of responses including the one by Gonçalves dos Santos. An overview of these debates is provided in Horsh's introduction and in Camargo and Moraes, *Bibliografia* v. 1, 253–356. For an analysis of constitutionalism in Brazil as a whole that links the earliest readings of liberalism with the independence movement in 1822 see Salles Oliveira, "O Disfarce do Anonimato," where she first posed the links between economic interests and constitutionalist allegiances; and Neves, "Corcundas." On the question of political identity in the 1820s see Gladys Sabina Ribeiro, "'Brasileiros, vamos a eles!': identidade nacional e controle social no Primeiro Reinado," *Ler História* 27–28 (1995), 103–123; idem, "'Ser Português' ou 'Ser Brasileiro'? algumas considerações sobre o Primeiro Reinado," *Ler História* 25 (1994), 27–55; and Carvalho Souza, *Pátria Coroada*. On similar moments of inclusion and exclusion in the process of defining representation in Spanish America see Timothy Anna, "Spain and the Breakdown of the Imperial Ethos: The Problem of Equality," *Hispanic American Historical Review* 62 n. 2 (1982), 254–272; and Guerra, "Spanish American Tradition," 9.

Epilogue

In 1822, reflecting upon the thirteen years of Dom João's reign in Brazil, one anonymous critic concluded that the "invasion of the French in Portugal, and the consequent transfer of the Portuguese throne to Brazil, necessarily had to produce a revolution in the political and commercial system of the European and American continents. Whether this revolution was to be fortuitous or fatal for the Portuguese monarchy," he then explained, "depended entirely on the good or bad regime that the government adopted."[1] It was not, in other words, the transfer of the court itself but rather what happened in its wake—the ways in which the relocation of the court in Brazil was defined—that shaped the political and economic future of Portuguese on both sides of the Atlantic. More than in the royal family's departure from Lisbon, it was in the local and transatlantic politics of monarchy and empire in the 1810s that the Portuguese monarch's vassals saw obstacles to their fortune to be defeated and opportunities for transformation to be seized.

In Rio de Janeiro the creation of an American imperial capital appeared to embody a divinely, historically, and scientifically inspired rectification of the errors of an old colonial system that then ensured the renovation of imperial glory and prosperity. "In the year 1808 the Hand of Omnipotence," the bishop of Rio de Janeiro proclaimed with flourish in a pastoral letter published in 1822, "brought Lord Dom João VI to Brazil to open its closed ports to the commerce of nations, to raise it from the abject state of colony in which it was entombed, [and] with the sublime category of kingdom to place it on par with free and civilized peoples of Europe and America."[2] As they experienced these transformations, residents of the new royal court embraced, with a range of practices and discourses, what they beheld as their unprecedented full access to the traditional potential of vassalage and royal patronage and reckoned with the restorative innovations of political economy. Yet, the elevation of Brazil to "the degree of prosperity to which its physical circumstances made it disposed" was not, according to the anonymous critic cited above, the only task that the crown and its vassals faced. Equally important was the need to consolidate "by way of mystical political and economic interests, the union of diverse members of the monarchy, which nature put so distant from one another, spread out across the four parts of the globe."[3] This consolidation was made difficult, however, by the perception that Brazil's fortune had come at Portugal's expense. Whereas residents of Rio de Janeiro celebrated their new status, Portuguese in Portugal fought to expel the French and struggled against what many perceived to be the transformation of the old metropolis into a colony. In the 1810s, notwithstanding official and unofficial appeals to unity founded on the institution of monarchy (historic loyalties), the new commercial empire (unprecedented prosperity), and the nation (the renovation of virtue), tensions between the European and American experiences of a new royal court in Rio de Janeiro persisted.

As the decade of the 1820s commenced, constitutionalism then offered a resolution of these tensions by guaranteeing political and economic rights and freedoms (that Portuguese in Portugal perceived to be lost and Portuguese in Brazil claimed to have gained) through representation and national sovereignty. As rebels in Portugal set out to convoke the Cortes to draft a constitution, residents of Rio de Janeiro, joining constitutionalists in other parts of Brazil, took to the streets, witnessed and supported a rebellion, gathered for an assembly of representatives, and pamphleteered as part of an ultimately successful effort to guarantee Dom João's support for the new "constitutional system" for both Portugal and Brazil. In the months that followed the king's departure from Rio de Janeiro to return to Lisbon, his heir, the new prince regent Dom Pedro, assumed the crown's pledge to defend zealously the future constitution and respect the authority of the Lisbon Cortes.

Yet, even as Dom Pedro's defense of the future constitution and the Cortes appeared to favor Rio's residents' own demands for constitutional government as a guarantee of the rights and freedoms achieved since 1808, it also came to imply other foreboding consequences: that the new prince regent would return to Portugal, that Rio de Janeiro would be stripped of its status as a court and instead be made one of many provincial capitals, and that the exercise of political rights and the range of future economic exchange would be defined exclusively, as they were before 1808, by a distant government in Europe. In response, residents of the New World court used petitions, one of which included as many as 8,000 signatures, as well as newly achieved freedoms of the press to challenge these threats to their sovereignty and prosperity. Consequently, 1822 began with Dom Pedro's pledge to remain in Brazil: "tell the people I stay." As his presence proved to be irreconcilable with the Lisbon Cortes' claim of sovereignty over Brazil, a claim that the Cortes was willing to support with force, in Rio local campaigns for autonomy continued with placards, petitions, meetings, and public demonstrations. Before the year's end, on September 7, 1822, almost a year and a half after he bid his father good-bye, Prince Regent Dom Pedro then pledged to secure Brazil's independence from his native Portugal: "Independence or Death!"[4] As Rio's bishop proclaimed, the omnipotent "Hand, always constant and generous," now had worked to retain Dom Pedro in Brazil so as "to bring to a conclusion the act of its emancipation, and to crown the great work of its happiness," to proclaim and defend the "well-regarded independence of all of Brazilian territory."[5] Thus, the Empire of Brazil was created.

This contemporary claim, made with the advantage of hindsight, that independence finally brought to fruition the emancipation initiated during Dom João's residence in Rio effaced efforts, however assailable and ultimately short-lived, made throughout the 1810s in the new court to safeguard the unity of the Portuguese crown's dominions. Yet the claim also shaped, at least in part, the way in which independence would be defined in the months and years that followed. In designating the new polity as an "empire" the defenders of Dom Pedro and independence recognized what eighteenth-century Portuguese statesmen had characterized as Brazil's continental dimensions and copious resources. They reaffirmed, as the royal exiles and the city's residents had in the 1810s, that Brazil was a place where prosperity and political renovation could be achieved. Furthermore, this independent Empire of Brazil was built on the conviction that the monarch was a "protector" of rights, as well as of interests formerly denied or suppressed by the so-called old colonial system. By entrusting the monarch with maintaining "equilibrium and harmony" among other authorities, the Empire also affirmed that while defending certain privileges, the monarch could provide a defense against those privileges and interests. Following the transfer of the court to Rio de Janeiro, these professedly universal powers and responsibilities had been emblematically expressed within the city in Dom João's audiences and in acts of royal patronage and grace. On these occasions the sovereign both affirmed "the certainty that owners have that the state will always ensure the punishment of slaves" and defended slaves when undercutting their owners' authority enhanced the expression of his own power. The monarch, in other words, had shown that he would uphold social hierarchies, while also revealing the relative vulnerabilities of those hierarchies. Even as the monarch thus established the formal limits to the city's residents' political participation, he also constituted a forum in which they expressed their expectations and claimed their rights.

The new Empire of Brazil was proclaimed with the promise of a written constitution as well, one that would express the nation's sovereignty and define the political rights of the members of that nation. The political preeminence of the nation expressed a complex legacy of the transfer of the court. During the Peninsular War, the historic, heroic, and moral nation had served to reunite the divided Portuguese world. Having risen in 1808 to defend itself and its besieged sovereign, the nation then proclaimed its "regeneration" by assuming the role of sovereign itself in 1820 and 1821. The basis for unity, however, then became the basis for division, as the vision of a moral Portuguese nationhood expounded in the 1810s by exiles and long-standing residents of Rio de Janeiro collided fatally with nationalist discourse in Portugal that placed geography above all. As the Empire of Brazil then called into being a new nation "free and independent" from Portugal, the historic and heroic as well as the voluntary dimensions of nationhood would have to be formally rearticulated. In 1824 a constitution affirmed the nation's political representation to be both an Assembly and the Emperor himself, "unanimously acclaimed by the people."

The proclamation of the Empire of Brazil and its reception also revealed the local dimensions of imperial, monarchical, and constitutional politics. In the 1820s, as in the 1810s, certain understandings of monarchy and empire formed in Rio de Janeiro, and then projected beyond the city, were not necessarily shared or incorporated into other local contexts. Indeed, in 1824, as in 1817 and 1821, the northeastern provinces would rebel against the government in Rio, proclaiming their own, often republican, understandings of the end of the old colonial system. And across Brazil even among supporters of the new imperial, monarchical, and constitutional "system," conflicts and divisions surfaced. Questions of the status of slavery and the slave trade, the scope of economic liberties and open ports, relations with British merchants and their empire, and the conditions for civilization, order, and progress at the local level that emerged in the 1810s would continue to demand the attentions of residents of the empire throughout the nineteenth century.

And in the Empire of Brazil, the same imperative of a self-consciously postcolonial predicament that had led, for example, to attempts to metropolitanize slavery in Dom João's New World court, would yield similarly ambivalent readings of the liberal "ideas of this century." Liberals in nineteenth-century Brazil, along with their counterparts elsewhere in the Atlantic world, distinguished between "universal capacities" and "the conditions for their actualization" and therefore raised the bar for political inclusion.[6] Thus, popular sovereignty was both celebrated and targeted for discipline through education. Although citizenship was formally inclusive, the grounds for political participation were based on racialized understandings of difference: freedpersons (*libertos*) were citizens, but could not be electors. The Constitution of 1824 neither explicitly defended slavery nor decreed its demise. Consequently, the intendant's deliberations on the place of slaves at royal audiences and in judicial courts were followed by debates on the limits of imperial clemency for slaves and the further development of a complex, "ambiguous," and "peculiar" body of law that sought "to protect the master from the slave, the slave from the master, and the whole society from the institution of slavery itself."[7] These same tensions between ideals and realities, the imperial present and a colonial past, elite and popular practices and aspirations, Europe and Africa, which marked the transformation of Rio de Janeiro into the court and capital of the Portuguese empire in the 1810s, also shaped successive reformations and remodelations of the city, including twentieth-century quests to "civilize," once again, the built environment and the residents of the capital of a Brazilian republic.[8]

The transfer of the court had been a moment of incertitude and reckoning, of facing the consequences of and coming to terms with changing understandings of political legitimacy and empire. Rather than a simple reaction against these changes, the ways in which royal officials and vassals, exiles and residents in Rio de Janeiro and across the dominions of the Portuguese crown defined the meaning of monarchy and empire in the New World deepened an engagement already underway in eighteenth-century Portugal and Brazil with the "ideas of the century" that included political economy and representative government, liberty and equality, and renewed quests for social order and "civilization." While the transfer of the court alone did not determine that Brazilian independence would be its own outcome, an exclusively American empire both consecrated an earlier "emancipation," as it was defined by residents and officials in the new court of Rio de Janeiro, and reproduced its equivocations.

NOTES

1. Anonymous, "Considerações sobre o estado de Portugal e do Brasil desde a sahida d'el rei de Lisboa em 1807 até ao presente. Indicando algumas providencias para a consolidação do reino unido" [1822], *RIHGB* 26 (1873), 145–184.

2. [José Caetano da Silva Coutinho], *Carta Pastoral do Bispo do Rio de Janeiro . . .* (Rio de Janeiro: Silva Porto e Companhia, 1822), 3–4.

3. Anonymous, "Considerações."

4. Roderick Barman, *Brazil: The Forging of a Nation, 1798–1852* (Stanford: Stanford University Press, 1988), 83–96.

5. [Coutinho], *Carta Pastoral.*

6. Uday Singh Mehta, *Liberalism and Empire: A Study in Nineteenth-Century British Liberal Thought* (Chicago: University of Chicago Press, 1999), 49. On the North American revolutionary vanguard's exclusionary reactions to popular politics see Peter Linebaugh and Marcus Rediker, *The Many-Headed Hydra: Sailors, Slaves, Commoners, and the Hidden History of the Revolutionary Atlantic* (Boston: Beacon Press, 2000), 236–240.

7. Robert Edgar Conrad, *Children of God's Fire: A Documentary History of Black Slavery in Brazil* (University Park: The Pennsylvania State University Press, 1984), 236; Alexandra Kelly Brown, "'On the Vanguard of Civilization': Slavery, the Police, and Conflicts between Public and Private Power in Salvador da Bahia, Brazil, 1835–1888" (Ph.D. dissertation, University of Texas at Austin, 1998), 204–207; Manuela Carneiro da Cunha, "Silences of the Law: Customary Law and Positive Law on the Manumission of Slaves in 19th-Century Brazil," *History and Anthropology* v. 1 (1995), 427–443; and Keila Grinberg, *Liberata, a lei da ambigüidade: As ações de liberdade da corte de apelação do Rio de Janeiro no século XIX* (Rio de Janeiro: Dumará, 1994).

8. Jeffrey D. Needell, *A Tropical Belle Epoque: Elite culture and society in turn-of-the-century Rio de Janeiro* (New York: Cambridge University Press, 1987); Teresa A. Meade, *"Civilizing" Rio: Reform and Resistance in a Brazilian City, 1889–1930* (University Park: The Pennsylvania State University Press, 1997).

The Pasquinades of 1821

WHILE MOST OF THE PASQUINADES NOTED IN CORRESPONDENCE AND POLICE RECORDS have not survived, or are not systematically accounted for in archives, several notes and simple constitutionalist verses, transcribed on small sheets of paper, in varied and at times crudely executed handwriting, and with varied spelling and orthography, can be found in Rio's Itamaraty Archive.[1] Although these notes, or *poesias*, as they were labeled by an Itamaraty archivist, are not accompanied by clear references that attest to the context in which they were written, some feature annotations that suggest they were confiscated by royal officials who attributed their authorship to those identified as leaders of and participants in the February 1821 revolt. The connection between the pasquinades and the February rebellion is further suggested in a report written February 24, 1821 by the police informant Cailhé in which he transcribed similar verses and reported that they had been "circulating" within the city all day:

> Ás armas cidadões, ás armas peguem
> Nem um só momento se perder deveis
> Porque se a razão os reis não entendem
> As armas a farão ouvir os reis.[2]

Another resident also registered the impact of such slogans: "Beware of the insolent 'Long Live the Constitution, and death to all those who don't approve,'" he warned an unidentified confidant, "it is no longer the golden pearl of our beloved and good sovereign."[3] In his *Dom João VI no Brasil* Manuel de Oliveira Lima also recorded a pasquinade from 1821 denouncing royal counselors, although he did not indicate the archival location of the document:

> Excelso Rei,
> Se queres viver em paz
> Enforca Targini
> E degrada Thomaz . . . [4]

Here, the references are to royal minister Tomás António Vila Nova Portugal, a staunch absolutist, and to Francisco Bento Maria Targini, chancellor of the royal treasury, Barão (1811) and later Visconde (1819) de São Lourenço, known for his lavish lifestyle and the focus of a corruption scandal in 1820, which, as J. F. de Almeida Prado notes, inspired a number of similar satirical pasquinades, including:

> Quem furta pouco é ladrão,
> Quem furta muito é Barão,
> Quem mais furta e esconde,
> Passa de Barão ao Visconde.[5]

What follows are transcriptions of a selection of the verses referred to in Chapter 7. In some cases their brevity and small format suggest the possibility of memorization and concealed circulation. It is also possible that they were to be sung, as the drafting and later publishing of "hymns" suggests. In denouncing absolutist government many authors of the pasquinades refer, as do those above, to royal counselors and officials by name.

1. Untitled:

> Ás Armas Cidadãos! É tempo! Ás Armas
> Nenhum momento mais perder deveis
> Se a força da razão os Reis não cedem
> Das Armas ao poder se dão os Reis.[6]

2. "Aviso"

> Pelo povo ao Rei, o poder é dado,
> Ao povo por tanto legislar compete,
> Se a este aviso o Rei não cede,
> Ás armas cederá o seo poder inerte.
>
> Da Nação o Rei não é mais que Chefe,
> Para executar a Lei por ela imposta.
> Como é possível então que o Rei dite?
> Não! Não! Cidadãos! eis a resposta!!
>
> Vive o Rei que jurar
> A sabia Constituição,

Que pelas Cortes foi dada
Da Portuguesa Nação[7]

3. "Untitled"

Como pode o Rei ao Povo dar a Lei,
Se do Rei no Povo há o poder?
Pode haver Povo sem ter Rei,
E Rei sem ter Povo pode haver?

Demite, Rei, de ti esses malvados
Que de todo a Nação querem acabar
Chama homens de bem, desinteressados,
Se queres tantos males evitar.

Ao Povo compete dar a Lei
Ao Rei fazela executar.[8]

4. "Tomás, deves apresentar isto a El Rei," signed "Por um amante da Pátria"

Se queres ainda Reinar
Olha beato João,
Deves ira para Portugal,
E assinar a Constituição.

Se tu depressa não vais
Para o teu pais natal,
O' João olha que perdes
O Brasil, e Portugal.

Detesta qualquer traidor
Que o contrário te encareça,
Uma vez ao Mundo mostra
Qu'ainda tens uma cabeça.

Não te fies no malvado,
No pérfido Tomás António:
Olha que quando te fala,
Por ele te fala o Demônio.

Isto o que deves fazer,
Se não és um toleirão,
De outra sorte te virá
A faltar o mesmo pão.

Assina a Constituição
Não te faças singular,
Olha que a teus vizinhos
Já se tem feito assinar.

Isto não só é bastante
Deves deixar o Brasil,
Se não virás em breve
A sofrer desgostos mil.

Se assim o não fizeres
Diz adeus a Portugal,
E Rei lá verás depressa
O Duque de Cadaval.

Repara pr'a o que te digo,
Não sejas um papa sorda,
Não desgostes Portugal
Antes que a desgraça te morda.

Se tu assim o fizeres
Serás de todos amado,
De vassalos e vizinhos,
O teu nome respeitado.[9]

5. "Comemoração á cegueira desta Corte"

Levantai vos ludibriosos que estais dormindo na madorna do
pesado sono. Lembrai-vos que agora estais em tempo de pôr
esta corte em ordem, e se agora o não fazeis, tendes perdido
todo o vosso tempo vamos a consumar a vida a esta corja de
ladrões, que estão roubando os tesouros do rei; e os nossos vamos fazer as nossas obras em bom detalhe tanto para Deus,
como para com a medida dar merecimento a quem o [tem que]
pagar bem as nossas tropas finalmente. As armas [decidirão] a

questão. Viva El Rei Dom João, toda a Família Real, e a nova
Constituição, e morra tudo quanto é Ladrão.

6. "Himno"

> É vossa devira
> Leais Lusitanos,
> Amar os Soberanos
> A Pátria Salvar. __ P.voz.

> 1. Fiel patriotismo, . . . P.voz . . .
>   Da tropa briosa
>   Que a pátria ditosa
>   Veio salvar
> 2. Heroe filho ouvindo
>   Pai caro gemendo,
>   As armas correndo
>   O foi resgatar
> 3. E vós lusos, que os louros
>   Conquisteis altivos
>   Haveis de captivos
>   Ferros arrastar?
> 4. Brasil, não temas, arvora
>   Do luso império perdão[10]
>   Que teu rei já confirmou
>   A nossa constituição.
> 5. Realizou nossa esperança
>   Contra os votos dos malvados;
>   Vivam os lusos honrados
>   Reine a casa de Braganza
> 6. Astreia desça dos ceus
>   Alforea, paz, união,
>   A todos venham ditar
>   Luso império, constituição
> 7. De um lado esteja justiça
>   D'outro lado religião,
>   Firmando em bases d'ouro
>   Luso império de João
> 8. Em lugar mais eminente
>   Prezada em união

Lei divina, que inspira
A nossa constituição
9. Prestando o juramento
Curvados beijam a mão
Do pai, e filho, que durou
A nossa constituição
10. Ao mundo servindo
De pasmo, d' exemplo
Da glória no templo
Já temos lugar.
11. Viva o heroe sexto João,
Rei unido de Portugal,
Viva o jovem principe real,
Viva a nossa constituição.
12. Valor lusitanos
Liberdade oprimida
A custa da vida
Se deve salvar . . . P. voz pela

Por voz pela pátria
O sangue daremos
por glória so termos
vencer, ou morrer.

7. "Quadros"

1. Grande rei, feliz monarcha
Pejo o ditoso João;
Faça a tua, e nossa dita
Assina a Constituição
2. A mesma para o Brazil
Da de leal coração,
Não faças tua desgraça
Assig—
3. Vê que se perdes a Lizia
O Brasil perdes então;
Não tem mais p'ra onde fugir,
Assig—
4. Não quieram teus semelhantes
Arrastar sempre o grilhão,

Sê rei pela metade
Assig—

5. O valeroso Brazil
Ao norte vê o clarão
Teme o seu desespero
Assig—

6. Este mundo que habitas
É de outra geração
Se n'elle queiras reinar
Assig—

7. É muito tanto sofrer
Sempre em dura escravidão
Antes que os ferros quebrem
Assig—

8. Este rico continente
Está todo em convulsão
O teu mal é sem remédio
Assig—

9. Abre os olhos, que é tempo
De deixar à adulação
Lembra-te que és mortal
Assig—

10. Essa corja que te cerca
Urde a tua perdição
Manda enforca-la toda
Assina a Constituição.

8. Untitled

Temos tanta segurança
De cobrarmos liberdade
Que os Arcos do nosso templo
Somem-se na eternidade

Por tanto o [illegible] viçosa
Não te escusar protetor
Não suponhas ser loucura
Contra o barbaro opressor

Temos gente e temos armas

Temos dinheiro e valor
Temos um sabio marechal
Nosso amigo e diretor[11]

9. "Obra nova entitulada A Entrada do Careca pela Barra"

Tornastes a voltar filho da puta
Do país das araras, e coqueiros
O' mal hajam os bananas brasileiros
Que vivo te deixarão nessa luta.

Agora que Ulisea a paz disfruta
Agora que reluz com seus guerreiros
Não se precisa de chefes estrangeiros
E menos de tão pessima conduta

Visita a meretriz e vai te embora
Tu lá tens um signal de gratidão
Cabedal que bem falta faz agora.

Ah crê bife, soberbo beberão
que exaltando tudo só por ti chora
A Lacerda, o Filhinho, e o Cabrão.[12]

10. "Ás Armas Portuguezes ás Armas amantes da Vossa Nação"

Ás armas habitantes desta Cidade já é tempo de quebrares os
Grilhões em que a tanto tempo tendes Vivido enlaçados não
pelo nosso augusto Monarca mas sim pelos que o trazem en-
ganado e vendido esses nossos amantes [illegible] de povo; de-
tais as escamas dos vossos olhos fora e não percamos um só
momento por que Vos seguro que tereis quem Vos defenda e
Seja o nosso Grito em geral Viva El Rei Dom João 6o e toda a
família Real e vivão as cortes e para elas a Constituição do
[Reino] do [Rio] de Janeiro[13] aprecaivos quanto antes melhor
pois já é mais que tempo e retempo Vêde os nossos amantes da
nossa pátria o quanto tem feito na nossa Pátria; Grande Dia de
Glória para o nosso Reino não fiquemos atrás Vem sabeis que
somos os mesmos e devemos mostrarlhe que não ficamos atrás
pois o que tem obrado para nos [deve cá lhe?] Corresponder se

não ficaremos tidos e havidos por Covardes e indignos da Boa
União; Agora acabo de ver o decreto que ontem baixou em que
diz nomeara Sua Magestade os [Residentes?] então estavão [il-
legible] esses indevidos para que tornavão a ficar antes tin-
hamos o inferno dos Pobres de novo aceterado em fim Ás
armas Portuguesas Sem demora abrir os Olhos em quanto é
tempo. Ás armas amigos da nação Não tenhais medo; Viva El
Rei Dom João 6o e a Constituição do Rio de Janeiro"—"Na
Impressão Régia da N" [14]

11. Untitled:

> Iludido monarca os olhos abre
> encara e descortina o vasto abismo
> que do teu gabinete os vãos conselhos
> por alargar a [anocão?] noite e dia
>
> Repara que a origem da crueza
> augmenta mais, e mais o teu perigo
> Caga que o [illegible] exasperava
> cura muito melhor cheiroso balsamo
>
> Não é de Pernambuco tão somente
> o que [odias] crimes o mal abrange
> do famoso Brazil o corpo inteiro
> não creias possa haver Brasiliana
> que cedo veja com enxutos olhos
> em ferros seu irmão Pernambucano
> se o medo lhes [mascera] os sentimentos
> o medo tem limites; e dos males
> quando se enche amedida furiosa
> arrebenta a vingança e tudo involve.
>
> Ai do Rei insensato, que o provoca
> que podendo ter de pai o nome o doce nome
> prefer ser de povos o tirano[15]

The Biblioteca Nacional in Rio de Janeiro also retains at least one example of similar verses, labeled "Versos contra o governo de Dom João VI."

> Brasileiros decipai tudo o que pode servir

de Obstáculo do nosso socego, e os vossos inte—
resses, tirai de entre vos a prisão e fonte
donde tem manado todos os vossos des-
graças, e para segurar a Vossa feli-
cidade é necessario que—

Morra Francisco Lobato
Targini e Leão
Morra Frei Tomas António
Inimigo da Nação.

Paulo Fernandes Viana
Amaro Velho e Vieira
Rebelo, Filho e Carvalho
Tudo se faça em poeira.

O nosso Grão de Bico
Também deve ir desterrado
ou estar na Ilha das Cobras
Nove meses encerrado.

É preciso estar de molho
Porque ja é [Tanjão]¹⁶ velho
É por esta razão
Que eu dou este conselho.

O nosso Marquês de Loulé
Também ha de entrar na dança
Agora pagará o que fez
Quado se passou a França

O Conde de Parati
Vai tomar ares Emgola
E para distintivo traga
Em cada pe uma Argolá.¹⁷

Notes

1. AHI Lata 195 Maço 6 Pasta 13 (formerly Lata 195 Maço 7 Pasta 12).

2. Cailhé to [Viana?], February 24, 1821, transcribed in Marcos Carneiro de Mendonça, *Dom João e o Império no Brasil, a Independência e a Missão Rio Maior* (Rio de Janeiro: Biblioteca Reprográfica Xerox, 1984), 445.

3. [Anonymous], n.d., AHI Lata 195 Maço 6 Pasta 13 (formerly Lata 195 Maço 7 Pasta 12). The note begins ". . . depois do desoito nada se pode remediar."

4. Manuel de Oliveira Lima, *Dom João VI no Brasil, 1808–1821* (1908) (Rio de Janeiro: José Olympio, 1945), 964.

5. See J.F. de Almeida Prado, *D. João VI e o início da classe dirigente do Brasil, 1815–1889* (São Paulo: Companhia Editora Nacional, 1968). As early as 1812 Marrócos records a "pasquin" with references to Targini. See *Cartas de Luiz Joaquim dos Santos Marrocos* (Rio de Janeiro: Biblioteca Nacional/Ministério de Educação e Saude, 1939), 64.

6. See Chapter 7, Figure 13. A note on the back of this document reads: "É uma do [Major] Pimenta." The Itamaraty archive has three different copies of this verse. Two appear to have been written in the same handwriting.

7. The Itamarty Archive has two copies, in different handwriting, of this Aviso.

8. These verses appear transcribed on one copy of the above "Aviso."

9. See Chapter 7, Figure 15. Before the Porto rebellion there were rumors in Portugal that the Duque de Cadaval, a descendant of the second Duke of Braganza, was planning to claim the Portuguese throne. See Valentim Alexandre, *Os sentidos do império: questão nacional e questão colonial na crise do antigo regime português* (Porto: Afrontamento, 1993), 464; and José Anselmo Correa Henriques to Sua Alteza Real, Hamburg, October 26, 1820, in Ângelo Pereira, *D. João VI, principe e rei* v. 3 (Lisbon: Empresa Nacional de Publicidade, 1956), 293–296.

10. The word that appears to be "perdão" is barely legible, and could also be "pendão" from "pender."

11. A note on the back of the document reads "24 Fevereiro." The reference to "Arcos," underlined in the original, may be to the Conde dos Arcos. See Chapter 7 for his position within local constitutionalist politics in Rio de Janeiro.

12. These verses appear to refer to Dom João's return to Lisbon.

13. Here the text reads "do Ro do Ro de janeiro." This may be an erroneous repetition or the use of the same abbreviation to refer both to "Reino" and "Rio." See Maria Helena Ochi Flexor, *Abreviaturas: Manuscritos dos Séculos XVI ao XIX* (São Paulo: Secretaria da Cultura, 1979).

14. AHI Lata 195 Maço 7 Pasta 2.

15. A note on the back reads "20 de fev."

16. The word that appears to be "tanjão" is not completely legible. On the back of the document, in different handwriting, appears the annotation: "Macamboa, Goes, Pimenta."

17. BNRJ Ms. I-33-30-40.

REFERENCES

ARCHIVAL SOURCES

The primary manuscript source used here is a series of records from the general intendancy of the police, found at the Arquivo Nacional, Rio de Janeiro. Along with logbooks (*códices*), in which the intendant's correspondence with various superior and inferior authorities was transcribed, I consulted the documents relative to the police intendancy catalogued in the Arquivo Nacional, Rio de Janeiro as "Documentação identificada, GIFI." In most cases, this documentation consisted of original copies of the correspondence transcribed in the logbooks and, in many cases, the supporting documents that the intendant used to write his report, such as petitions and preliminary correspondence. In a few cases, this documentation also included records of interrogations of defendants and witnesses.

PUBLISHED PRIMARY SOURCES

A,B,C, poético, doutrinal e antifrancez, ou veni mecum. Para a utilidade e recreio dos Meninos Portuguezes. Reprint. Rio de Janeiro: Impressão Régia, 1810.

"Almanaque da cidade do Rio de Janeiro para o ano de 1792." *RIHGB* 266 (January–March 1965): 159–215.

"Almanaque da cidade do Rio de Janeiro para o ano de 1794." *RIHGB* 266 (January–March 1965): 218–287.

"Almanaque da cidade do Rio de Janeiro para o ano de 1811." *RIHGB* 282 (January–March 1969): 97–236.

"Almanaque da cidade do Rio de Janeiro para o ano de 1816." *RIHGB* 268 (July–September 1965): 179–330.

"Almanaque da cidade do Rio de Janeiro para o ano de 1817." *RIHGB* 270 (January–March 1966): 211–370.

"Almanaque histórico da cidade de S.Sebastião do Rio de Janeiro [1799]." *RIHGB* 267 (April–June 1965): 93–214.

Almeida, Manuel Antônio de. *Memórias de um sargento de milícias*. (1855) Rio de Janeiro: Ediouro, n.d.

Antonil, [Padre] André João, [João Antônio Andreoni]. *Cultura e opulência do Brasil*. (1711) Belo Horizonte/São Paulo: Itatiaia/EDUSP, 1982.

A.P.D.G. *Sketches of Portuguese Life, manners, costume and character*. London: George B. Whittaker, 1826.

Arago, J. *Narrative of a voyage round the world, in the Uranie and Physicienne corvettes, commanded by Captain Freycinet, during the years 1817, 1818, 1819, and 1820. . . .* London: Treuttel and Wurtz, 1823.

Autos da Devassa—prisão dos letrados do Rio de Janeiro. Niterói/Rio de Janeiro: Arquivo Público do Estado do Rio de Janeiro/UERJ, 1994.

"Autos de exame e averiguação sobre o autor de uma carta anônima escrita ao Juiz de Fora do Rio de Janeiro, Dr. Balthazar da Silva Lisboa (1793)." *ABN* 60 (1938): 260–313.

Azevedo, Francisco Ferreira de. *Oração de Acção de Graças que no dia 7 de Março de 1816 Anniversario da Chegada de El Rey Nosso Senhor ao Rio de Janeiro Recitou na Capella Real.* . . . Rio de Janeiro: Impressão Régia, 1816.

Barbosa, Januário da Cunha. *Sermão de Acção de Graças pela Feliz Restauração do Reino de Portugal Pregado na Real Capella do Rio de Janeiro na Manhãa de 19 de Dezembro de 1808.* Rio de Janeiro: Impressão Régia, 1809.

_____. *Oração de Acção de Graças Recitada na Capella Real do Rio de Janeiro, Celebrando-se o Quinto Anniversario da Chegada de S.A.R. Com Toda a Sua Real Familia a Esta Cidade.* Rio de Janeiro: Impressão Régia, 1813.

_____. *Oração de Acção de Graças que Celebrando-se na Real Capella do Rio de Janeiro, No Dia 7 de Março de 1818 o Decimo Anniversario da Chegada de Sua Magestade a esta Cidade.* . . . Rio de Janeiro: Impressão Régia, 1818.

_____. *Discurso. No fim da missa solemne do espirito santo celebrada na igreja dos terceiros minimos pelo reverendissimo doutor vigario geral deste bispado, e que precedeo ao acto da junta eleitoral da comarca, no dia 15 de Maio de 1821.* Rio de Janeiro: Impressão Régia, 1821.

Barros, João Jorge de. *Relação Panegyrica das Honras Funeraes que as Memórias do Muito Alto Poderoso Senhor Rey Fidelissimo D. João V consagrou a Cidade da Bahia, Corte da América Portuguesa.* . . . Lisbon: Régia Officina Sylvaniana, e da Academia Real, 1753.

Barrow, John. *A Voyage to Cochinchina, in the Years 1792 and 1793.* . . . London: Cadell and Davies, 1806.

Brackenridge, Henry. *Voyage to Buenos Aires, performed in the years 1817 and 1818, by order of the American Government.* London: Richard Phillips, 1820.

Burke, Edmund. *Reflections on the Revolution in France.* (1790) Indianapolis: Bobbs-Merrill, 1955.

_____. *Extractos das obras politicas e economicas de Edmund Burke por José da Silva Lisboa.* 2 v. Rio de Janeiro: Impressão Régia, 1812.

[Cabral, Luiz de Sequeira Oliva e Souza]. *Verdadeira Vida de Bonaparte, até a Feliz Restauração de Portugal.* . . . Reprint. Rio de Janeiro: Impressão Régia, 1809.

Campos, Francisco António de Novaes. *Príncipe Perfeito, Emblemas de D. João de Solórzano.* (1790) Lisbon: Instituto de Cultura e Lingua Portuguesa, 1985.

"Capitania do Rio de Janeiro. Correspondência de várias authoridades e avulsos." *RIHGB* 65, pt. 1 (1902), 71–335.

Carta de André Mamede ao seu Amigo Braz Barnabé, na qual se explica o que são Corcundas. Rio de Janeiro: Impressão Régia, 1821.

Carvalho, Francisco da Mãi dos Homens. *Oração de Acção de Graças que na Solemnidade do Anniversario do dia 24 de Agosto, Mandada fazer na Real Capella desta Corte por Sua Alteza Real, o Principe Regente do Brazil.* . . . Rio de Janeiro: Impressão Nacional, 1821.

Cathecismo Constitucional. Rio de Janeiro: Impressão Régia, [1821].

"Ceremonias religiosas em regozijo de se ter descoberto a conjuração." In *Autos da Devassa da Inconfidência Mineira* v. 6. Rio de Janeiro: Ministério da Educação, 1937.

Cevalhos, Pedro. *Política particular de Bonaparte, quanto á religião catholica; Ou Meios de que elle se vale para a estinguir; e subjugar os Hespanhões pela sedução, já que os não pode dominar pela força.* Rio de Janeiro: Impressão Régia, 1812.

Código Brasiliense, Ou Collecção das Leis, Alvarás, Decretos, Cartas Régias, &c. Promulgadas no Brasil Desde a Feliz Chegada de El Rey Nosso Senhor a Este Reino. Rio de Janeiro: [Impressão Régia, 1811–1820].

Confederação dos reinos, e provincias de Hespanha contra Bonaparte, N.III. Rio de Janeiro: Impressão Régia, 1809.

"Considerações sobre o estado de Portugal e do Brasil desde a sahida d'el rei de Lisboa em 1807 até ao presente. Indicando algumas providencias para a consolidação do reino unido." *RIHGB* 26 (1873): 145–184.

Constituição Explicada. Reprint. Rio de Janeiro: Impressão Regia, 1821.

Constituição política da monarquia portuguesa feita pelas Cortes Geraes, Extraordinárias, e Constituentes . . . Projeto para discussão. . . . Lisbon: Impressão Nacional, 1821.

Correio Braziliense, ou Armazem Literario. London: W. Lewis, 1808.

Costa, João Severiano Maciel da. *Memória sobre a necessidade de abolir a introdução dos escravos africanos no Brasil . . .* (1821). In *Memórias sobre a escravidão*, ed. Graça Salgado. Rio de Janeiro: Arquivo Nacional, 1988.

Costa, José Daniel Rodrigues da. *Portugal enfermo por vicios e abusos de ambos os sexos.* Lisbon: Impressão Régia, 1819.

Coutinho, Gastão Fausto da Camara. *Parabens ao Principe Regente Nosso Senhor, e á Pátria pelos Presagios Felices da Restauração de Portugal. . . .* Rio de Janeiro: Impressão Régia, 1808.

_____. *O Triunfo da America, Drama para se Recitar no Real Theatro do Rio de Janeiro. . . .* Rio de Janeiro: Impressão Régia, 1810.

_____. *O Juramento dos Numes. Drama. Para se representar na noite da abertura do Real Theatro de S. João em applauso ao Augusto Nome de Sua Alteza Real . . .* Rio de Janeiro: Impressão Régia, 1813.

[Coutinho, José Caetano da Silva]. *Carta Pastoral do Bispo do Rio de Janeiro. . . .* Rio de Janeiro: Silva Porto e Companhia, 1822.

Coutinho, José Caetano da Silva. *Memória Histórica da Invasão dos Francezes em Portugal no Anno de 1807.* Rio de Janeiro: Impressão Régia, 1808.

Coutinho, Rodrigo de Souza. *Composição e Regulação da Divizão Militar da Guarda Real da Polícia.* [Rio de Janeiro]: Impressão Régia, [1809].

_____. "Memória . . . sobre o Melhoramento dos Domínios de Sua Magestade na America." *Brasília* (Coimbra) 4 (1949): 383–422.

_____. *Textos políticos, económicos e financeiros (1783–1811)* 2 v. Lisbon: Banco de Portugal, 1993.

Cunha, Luiz da. *Instrucções inéditas de D. Luiz da Cunha a Marco António de Azevedo Coutinho.* (1736) Coimbra: Imprensa da Universidade, 1930.

Das Sociedades, e das Convenções, ou Constituições. Reprint. Rio de Janeiro: Impressão Régia, 1821.

Debret, Jean Baptiste. *Voyage Pittoresque et Historique au Brésil, sejour d'un Artiste Français au Brésil* 3 v. Paris: Firmin Didot Fréres, 1834–39.

_____. *Viagem Pitoresca e Histórica ao Brasil* 3 v. (1834–39) Belo Horizonte/São Paulo: Itatiaia/EDUSP, 1989.

Dialogo entre a Constituição e o Despotismo. Rio de Janeiro: Impressão Nacional, 1821.

Dialogo entre o Corcunda Abatido e o Constitucional Exaltado. Rio de Janeiro: Impressão Nacional, [1821].

Dialogo Instructivo, em que se Explicão os Fundamentos de uma Constituição e a Divisão das Autoridades que a formão, e executão. Rio de Janeiro: Impressão Régia, 1821.

Dialogo Politico e Instructivo, entre os Dous Homens da Roça, Andre Rapozo, e seu Compadre Bolonio Simplicio, Á cerca da Bernarda do Rio de Janeiro, e novidades da mesma. Rio de Janeiro: Impressão Régia, 1821.

Discurso Recitado na Abertura da Primeira Sessão das Cortes em Lisboa Copiado do Diario do Governo de 17 de Janeiro de 1821. Rio de Janeiro: Impressão Régia, 1821.

Discursos Extrahidos dos Numeros 10,11,12,25 e 16 do Genio Constitucional. . . . Rio de Janeiro: Impressão Régia, 1821.

Drummond, Ignacio José Correa. *Sonetos. Em Applauzo ao Feliz Succeso da Completa Regeneração da Nação Portugueza, Executado na Praça do Rocio da Corte e Cidade do Rio de Janeiro no memoravel dia 26 de Fevereiro de 1821.* Rio de Janeiro: Impressão Régia, 1821.

Ellis, Henry. *Journal of the Proceedings of the Late Embassy to China.* . . . (1817) Wilmington: Scholarly Resources, 1973.

Epanafora festiva, ou relação summaria das festas, com que na cidade do Rio de Janeiro, capital do Brasil se celebrou o feliz nascimento do Serenissimo Principe da Beira. . . . Lisbon: Miguel Rodrigues, 1763.

Ensaio Histórico, Político e Filosófico do Estado de Portugal, Desde o Mez de Novembro de 1807 até o Mez de Junho de 1808. Rio de Janeiro: Impressão Régia, n.d.

Faoro, Raymundo, ed. *O debate político no processo da independência.* Rio de Janeiro: Conselho Federal de Cultura, 1973.

[Fernandes, João Pedro]. *Elogio Para se Recitar no Theatro de S. João no Faustissimo Dia Natalicio de Sua Alteza o Principe Real do Brazil.* . . . Rio de Janeiro: Impressão Nacional, 1821.

Ferreira, Silvestre Pinheiro. "Documentos Annexos [ás Cartas]." *RIHGB* 51 (1888): 333–377.

_____. *Idéias Políticas.* Rio de Janeiro: PUC/Conselho Federal de Cultura, 1976.

Franco, Francisco Soares. *Reflexões sobre a Conduta do Principe Regente de Portugal.* Coimbra: Real Imprensa da Universidade, 1808.

Freitas, Frei Serafim de. *Do justo império asiático dos portugueses.* (1625) 2 v. Lisbon: Instituto Nacional de Investigação Cientítica, 1983.

Funchal, Marquêz do. *O Conde de Linhares.* Lisbon: Typografia Bayard, 1908.

Goes, José de. *Vozes do Patriotismo, ou Falla aos Portuguezes.* Rio de Janeiro: Impressão Régia, 1809.

Guimarães, Manuel Ferreira de Araújo. "Prospecto." Rio de Janeiro: Impressão Régia, 1812.

_____. *O Patriota.* Rio de Janeiro: Impressão Régia, 1813.

Hill, Henry. *Uma visão do comércio do Brasil em 1808/ A [v]iew of the commerce of Brazil.* [Salvador]: Banco da Bahia, n.d.

Homens, Francisco da Mãi dos. *Oração que na Real Capella desta Corte Celebrando-se as Acções de Graças pelas Noticias do Armisticio Geral no Dia 19 de Junho de 1814.* Rio de Janeiro: Impressão Régia, 1814.

Horch, Rosemarie Erika, ed. *Cartas dos compadres de Belém e Lisboa.* São Paulo: Revista de História, 1977.

Hymno Constiticional que appareceu e se cantou no Real Theatro de S. Carlos. . . . [n.p.]: Impressão Régia, [1821].

Hymnos Constitucionaes. [Rio de Janeiro]: Impressão Régia, 1821.

J. M. *Elegia á Sempre Saudosa e Sentidissima Auzencia de Sua Alteza Real de Lisboa para os seus estados do Brazil.* . . . Rio de Janeiro: Impressão Régia, 1808.

Keith, G.M. *A Voyage to South America and the Cape of Good Hope in His Majesty's Gun Brig, The Protector.* London: Richard Phillips, 1810.

Leitão, António José de Lima. *Ode ao Illustrissimo, e Excellentissimo Senhor Duque de Wellington, e da Victoria, Marechal General em Chefe dos Exercitos Britannicos.* . . . Rio de Janeiro: Impressão Régia, 1816.

_____. *Alfonsíada. Poema heroico da fundação da monarquia portugueza.* . . . Bahia: Manoel António da Silva Serva, 1818.

Leitão, Paulino Joakim. *Libambo. Metamorfose do Pão d'Assucar.* Rio de Janeiro: Impressão Régia, 1811.

Leite, António B. *A União Venturosa, Drama com Musica para se Representar no Real Theatro do Rio de Janeiro no Faustissimo Dia dos Annos de Sua Alteza Real.* . . . Rio de Janeiro: Impressão Régia, 1811.

L'Évêque, Henry. *Portuguese Costumes.* (1814) Lisbon: INAPA, 1993.

Lima, José Joaquim Lopes de. *Diccionario Carcundatico ou Explicação das Phrazes dos Carcundas.* . . . Rio de Janeiro: Imprensa Nacional, 1821.

_____. *Supplemento ao Diccionario-Carcundatico com Observações Acerca de Muitos Termos que Andão Hoje na Boca de Todos, o Outros que He Preciso que Andem.* Rio de Janeiro: Imprensa Nacional, 1821.

Lingham, Edward James. *Vindiciæ Lusitanæ, or an answer to a pamphlet entitled "The Causes and Consequences of the Late Emigration to the Brazils."* London: J. Budd, 1808.

Lisboa. Balthazar da Silva. *Annaes do Rio de Janeiro.* Rio de Janeiro: Seignot-Plancher, 1834–35.

Lisboa, Joaquim José. *A Protecção dos Inglezes: Versos.* . . . Rio de Janeiro: Impressão Régia, 1810.

Lisboa, José António. "Aula de Comércio." *RIHGB* 28 (July–September 1950), anexo IV: 172–185.

Lisboa, José da Silva. *Princípios de economia política* (1804). Rio de Janeiro: Pongetti, [1956].

_____. *Refutações das Reclamações contra o Commercio Inglez, Extrahida de Escriptores Eminentes.* Rio de Janeiro: Impressão Régia, 1810.

_____. *Memoria dos Beneficios Politicos do Governo de El-Rey Nosso Senhor D. João VI.* Rio de Janeiro: Impressão Régia, 1818.

_____. *Cairú: excertos da obra inédita "O Espirito de Cairú."* Rio de Janeiro: Arquivo Nacional, 1958.

Luccock, John. *Notes on Rio de Janeiro and the southern parts of Brazil; taken during a residence of ten years in that country, from 1808–1818.* London: Samuel Leigh, 1820.

Macedo, José Agostinho. *Justa Defeza do Livro Intitulado os Sebastianistas.* . . . Rio de Janeiro: Impressão Régia, 1810.

Machado, Joaquim José Pereira. *Promessas feitas ao Magnanimo e Sempre Invicto Rei o Senhor*

D. Affonso Henriques no Campo de Qurique, Realizadas nas Trez Vezes em que os Francezes Tem Sido Expulsados de Portugal pelo Exercito Anglo-Luso. Lisbon: Impressão Régia, 1811.

Manifesto, ou Exposição Fundada, e Justificativa do procedimento da Corte de Portugal a respeito da França desde o principio da Revolução até a epoca da Invasão de Portugal. . . . Rio de Janeiro: Impressão Régia, 1808.

Marrócos, Luiz Joaquim dos Santos. *Cartas de Luiz Joaquim dos Santos Marrocos*. Rio de Janeiro: Biblioteca Nacional/Ministério de Educação e Saude, 1939.

Mawe, John. *Travels in the Interior of Brazil part in the gold and diamond district of that country, by authority of the prince regent of Portugal*. . . . London/Boston: M. Carey/Wells and Tilly, 1816.

"Memória do exito que teve a conjuração de Minas e dos fatos relativos a ela. Acontecidos nesta cidade do Rio de Janeiro desde o dia 17 até 26 de abril de 1792." *Anuário do Museu da Inconfidência* (Ouro Preto) ano II (1953).

"Memória sobre os acontecimentos dos dias 21 e 22 de Abril de 1821 na praça do commércio do Rio de Janeiro, escripta em maio do mesmo anno por uma testemunha presencial. . . ." *RIHGB* 27 (1864): 271–289.

Memórias da Academia Real das Sciencias de Lisboa 1 (1797).

Memórias Econômicas da Academia Real das Sciencias de Lisboa para o Adiantamento da Agricultura, das Artes, e da Indústria em Portugal e Suas Conquistas 1–2 (1789–90).

Mendonça, Marcos Carneiro de, ed. *Dom João VI e o Império no Brasil, a Independência e a Missão Rio Maior*. Rio de Janeiro: Biblioteca Reprográfica Xerox, 1984.

M'Leod, John. *Voyage of His Majesty's Ship Alceste, along the coast of Corea, to the island of Lewchew, with an account of the subsequent shipwreck*. London: John Murray, 1818.

[Moniz, Nuno Álvarez Pereira Pato]. *A Gloria do Oceano, Drama que se Representou no Theatro Nacional da Rua dos Condes, em Obsequio do Fausto Dia Natalicio de S.M. Britanica El Rei Jorge III*. . . . Reprint. Rio de Janeiro: Impressão Régia, 1810.

_____. *A Queda do Despotismo: Drama Dedicado a Sua Alteza Real o Principe Regente Nosso Senhor*. Reprint. Rio de Janeiro: Impressão Régia, 1810.

Montesquieu, Charles de Secondat, Baron de. *The Spirit of the Laws*. (1748) New York: Cambridge University Press, 1989.

Neves, José Acúrsio das. *Manifesto da Razão Contra as Usurpações Francezas. Offerecido á Nação Portugueza, aos Soberanos, e aos Póvos*. Rio de Janeiro: Impressão Régia, 1809.

_____. *História geral da invasão dos franceses em Portugal e da restauração deste reino*. (1810) 2 v. Porto: Afrontamento, n.d.

O'Neill, Thomas. *A concise and accurate account of the proceedings of the squadron under the command of Rear Admiral Sir William Sidney Smith, K.C., in effecting the escape, and escorting the royal family of Portugal to the Brazils, on the 29th of November, 1807*. London: R. Edwards, 1809.

Parallelo entre os Corcundas e Liberaes. Rio de Janeiro: Impressão Régia, 1821.

Penalva, Fernando Teles da Silva Caminha e Meneses, Marquês de. *Dissertação sôbre as obrigações do vassalo*. Lisbon: Régia Officina Tipographica, 1804.

Pernicioso Poder dos Perfidos Validos e Conselheiros dos Reis Destruido Pela Constituição. Reprint. Rio de Janeiro: Impressão Nacional, 1821.

Pereira, Ângelo. *Os filhos de el-rei D. João VI.* Lisbon: Empresa Nacional de Publicidade, 1946.

_____. *D. João VI, principe e rei.* 4 v. Lisbon: Empresa Nacional de Publicidade, 1953–1958.

Planta da Cidade de S.Sebastião do Rio de Janeiro Levantada por Ordem de Sua Alteza Real o Principe Regente Nosso Senhor no anno de 1808. Feliz e Memoravel Epoca da Sua Chegada Á Esta Cidade. Rio de Janeiro: Impressão Régia, 1812.

O Plutarco Revolucionario, na Parte que Contém as Vidas de Madama Buonaparte, e Outros desta Familia. Traduzido do Inglez. Rio de Janeiro: Impressão Régia, 1810.

Pope, Alexander. *Ensaio sobre a Critica de Alexandre Pope traduzido em Portuguez pelo Conde de Aguiar.* Rio de Janeiro: Impressão Régia, 1810.

_____. *Ensaios Moraes de Alexander Pope em Quatro Epistolas a Diversas Pessoas traduzidas em Portuguez pelo Conde de Aguiar.* Rio de Janeiro: Impressão Régia, 1811.

Portugal, Luiz de Almeida, Marquês de Lavradio. "Relatório . . . entregando o governo a Luiz de Vasconcellos e Souza, que o succedeu no vice-reinado." *RIHGB* 16 (January 1843): 409–486

Prior, James. *Voyage along the eastern coast of Africa, to Mosambique, Johanna, and Quiloa; to St. Helena; to Rio de Janeiro, Bahia, and Pernambuco in Brazil, in the Nisus Frigate.* London: Richard Phillips and Co., 1819.

"Prohibição do uso da imprensa no Brasil nos tempos coloniais." *RIHGB* 47, pt. 1 (1884): 167–168.

Protecção à Franceza. Reprint. Rio de Janeiro: Impressão Régia, 1809.

Quaes são os bens e os males que podem resultar da liberdade da Imprensa; e qual he a influencia que elles podem ter no momento em que os Representantes da Nação Portugueza vão se congregar? Reprint. Rio de Janeiro: Impressão Régia, 1821.

Qualidades que se devem accompanhar os Compromissarios e Elleitores. Extrahido do Genio Constitucional n. 39. Rio de Janeiro: Impressão Régia, [1821].

Queiros, Joaquim José de. "Mappa da população da côrte e província do Rio de Janeiro em 1821." *RIHGB* 33, pt. 1 (1870): 135–142.

Ratton, Jacome. "Lettres de Jacques Ratton a António de Araújo de Azevedo, Comte da Barca (1812–1817)." *Bulletin des Etudes Portugaises* (nouvelle série) 25 (1964): 137–256.

_____. *Recordações de Jacome Ratton, sobre occorrências do seu tempo em Portugal de Maio de 1747 a Setembro de 1810* (1813). Lisbon: Fenda, 1992.

Receita Especial para Fabricar Napoleões Traduzida de hum Novo Exemplar. . . . Reprint. Rio de Janeiro: Impressão Régia, 1809.

Reflexões Filosóficas Sobre a Liberdade, e Igualdade. Rio de Janeiro: Impressão Régia, 1821.

A Regeneração Constitucional ou Guerra e Disputa entre Carcundas e os Constitucionaes. . . . Rio de Janeiro: Impressão Nacional, 1821.

Relaçam da Aclamação que se fez na Capitania do Rio de Janeiro do Estado do Brasil, & nas mais do Sul, ao Senhor Rey Dom João IV por verdadeiro Rey, & Senhor do seu Reyno de Portugal. . . . Lisbon: Jorge Rodrigues, 1641. Facsimile published in *Boletim Internacional de Bibliografia Luso-Brasileira* 6, n. 2 (1965): 433–447

Relação da entrada que fez o excellentissimo, e reverendissimo D. F. António do Desterro Malheyro, bispo do Rio de Janeiro. Rio de Janeiro: António Isidoro da Fonseca, 1747.

Relação das festas que se fizerão no Rio de Janeiro quando o Principe Regente Nosso Senhor e toda a sua Real Familia chegarão pela primeira vez a'quella Capital. . . . Lisbon: Impressão Régia, 1810.

Relação dos sucessos do dia 26 de Fevereiro de 1821 na Corte do Rio de Janeiro. Bahia: Viuva Serva e Carvalho, [1821].

"Rellação dos livros aprehendidos ao bacharel Mariano José Pereira da Fonseca." *RIHGB* 63 (1901): 15–18.

Rio Secco, Joaquim José de Azevedo, Visconde de. *Exposição Analytica, e Justificativa da Conducta, e Vida Publica do Visconde do Rio Secco, Desde o Dia 25 de Novembro de 1807, em que Sua Magestade Fidelissima o Incumbio dos Aranjamentos Necessarios da Sua Retirada para o Rio de Janeiro.* . . . Rio de Janeiro: Imprensa Nacional, 1821.

Rylance, Ralph. *A Sketch of the Causes and Consequences of the Late Emigration to the Brazils.* London: Longman, Hurst, Rees and Orme, 1808.

Sá, José António. *Defeza dos Direitos Nacionaes e Reaes da Monarquia Portugueza.* Lisbon: Impressão Régia, 1816.

Santa Anna, José Joaquim. *Memória sobre o Enxugo Geral Desta Cidade do Rio de Janeiro.* . . . Rio de Janeiro: Impressão Régia, 1815.

Santa Gertrudes Magna, Francisco de Paula de. *Sermão em Memoria do Faustissimo Dia em que Sua Alteza Real Dezembarcou Nesta Cidade da Bahia.* . . . Rio de Janeiro: Impressão Régia, 1816.

[Santos, Luiz Gonçalves dos]. *Justa Retribuição Dada ao Compadre de Lisboa* . . . (1821). Rio de Janeiro: Imprensa Nacional, 1822.

Santos, Luiz Gonçalves dos. *Memórias para servir à História do Reino do Brasil.* (1825) 2 v. Belo Horizonte/ São Paulo: Itatiaia/EDUSP, 1981.

São Carlos, Francisco de. *Oração de Acção de Graças recitada no dia 7 de Março de 1809 na Capella Real, Dia Anniversario da Feliz Chegada de Sua Alteza Real a Esta Cidade.* Rio de Janeiro: Impressão Régia, 1809.

_____. *Oração Sagrada, que na Solemne Acção de Graças pelo muito Feliz e Augusto Nascimento da Serenissima Senhora D. Maria da Gloria.* . . . Rio de Janeiro: Impressão Régia. 1819.

São Payo, Duarte Mendes de. *Oração Sagrada Que em Acção de Graças pelo feliz transito de Sua Alteza Real, e Sua Serenissima Familia, da Europa Portugueza para os Seus Estados do Brazil, foi recitada na Santa Igreja Cathedral do Rio de Janeiro estando presente o mesmo Senhor.* Rio de Janeiro: Impressão Régia, 1808.

Seixas, Romualdo António de. *Sermão de Acção de Graças que no Dia 13 de Maio Celebrou o Senado da Camara desta Capital do Pará pela Feliz Acclamação do Muito Alto e Poderoso Senhor D. João VI.* . . . Rio de Janeiro: Impressão Régia, 1818.

Sequeira, António D'Oliva de Souza. *Projecto para o Estabelecimento Politico do Reino-Unido de Portugal, Brasil, e Algarves, Offerecido aos Illustres Legisladores, em Cortes Geraes e Extraordinarias.* Reprint. Rio de Janeiro: n.p., 1821.

Sequeira, João de Nossa Senhora da Porta. *Escola de política ou tratado pratico da civilidade portuguesa, com as regras e exemplos do estylo epistolar em todo o genero de cartas.* Lisbon: Typografia Rollandia, 1833.

Sermão Constitucional Dirigido a Nação Portugueza, e proferido no Consistorio particular dos ver-

dadeiros Liberaes amantes, e defensores da Patria. . . . Reprint. Rio de Janeiro: Impressão Régia, 1821.

Silva, António de Moraes. *Diccionario da lingua portuguesa, composta pelo Padre D. Rafael Bluteau, reformado e accrescentado por.* . . . Lisbon: Simão Thaddeo Ferreira, 1779.

_____. *Diccionario da lingua portuguesa, recopilado dos vocabulos impressos até agora.* . . . Lisbon: Typographia Lacerdina, 1813.

Silva, Hélio. *As Constituições do Brasil.* Rio de Janeiro: Globo, 1985.

Silva, João Pereira da. *Sermão de Acção de Graças, Rendidas ao Ceo na Feliz Chegada de Sua Alteza Real o Principe Regent Nosso Senhor.* . . . Rio de Janeiro: Impressão Régia, 1809.

Silva, Manuel Viera da. *Reflexões sobre Alguns dos Meios Propostos por mais Conducentes para Melhorar o Clima da Cidade do Rio de Janeiro.* Rio de Janeiro: Impressão Régia, 1808.

Smith, Adam. *An Inquiry into the Nature and Causes of the Wealth of Nations.* (1776) New York: Modern Library, 1994.

_____. *Compendio da Obra da Riqueza das Nações de Adam Smith traduzida do Original Inglez, por Bento da Silva Lisboa.* . . . Rio de Janeiro: Impressão Régia, 1811.

Sobrinho, Barbosa Lima, ed. *Antologia do Correio Braziliense.* Rio de Janeiro/Brasília: Cátedra/Instituto Nacional do Livro, 1977.

[Souza], Bernardo Avellino Ferreira e. *Relação dos Festejos, que a Feliz Acclamação do Muito Alto, Muito Poderoso, e Fidelissimo Senhor D. João VI.* . . . Rio de Janeiro: Impressão Régia, 1818.

Souza, Bernardo Avellino Ferreira e. *Versos que pelo Faustissimo Acontecimento do Maravilhoso Dia 26 de Fevereiro, Recitou no Real Theatro de S. João desta Côrte.* . . . Rio de Janeiro: Impressão Régia, 1821.

Souza, Luiz António da Silva. *A Discordia Ajustada, Elogio Dramatico para Manifestação do Real Busto do Senhor D. João VI.* . . . Rio de Janeiro: Impressão Régia, 1819.

Souza, Luiz de Vasconcellos. "Officio . . . com a cópia da relação instructiva e circunstanciada, para ser entregue ao seu successor. . . ." *RIHGB* 13 (April 1842): 3–42 and 14 (July 1842): 129–167.

Staunton, George. *An authentic account of an embassy from the King of Great Britain to the Emperor of China.* . . . London: Robert Campbell, 1799.

Trinidade, Bento da. *Sermão de Acção de Graças pela Feliz Vinda do Principe Regente Nosso Senhor para os Estados do Brazil, Pregado na Igreja do Sacramento do Recife de Pernambuco em 1808.* Rio de Janeiro: Impressão Régia, 180[9].

Tuckey, J.H. *An Account of a voyage to establish a colony at Port Philip in Bass's Strait, on the south coast of New South Wales, in his Majesty's Ship Calcutta, in the years 1802–3–4.* London: Longman, Hurst, Rees and Orme, 1805.

"Ultimos momentos dos Inconfidentes de 1789, Pelo Frade Que os assistio de confissão." *Anuário do Museu da Inconfidência* (Ouro Preto) ano II (1953).

Valle, Joaquim Rafael do. *Manifesto Juridico, e Político A favor da Conducta do Principe Regente N.S., e dos Direitos da Caza de Bragança, contra as usurpações Francezas desde a Epoca da injusta invasão de Portugal.* Rio de Janeiro: Impressão Régia, 1811.

Vasconcellos, António Luiz de Brito Aragão. "Memórias sobre o Estabelecimento do Império do Brazil, ou novo Imperio Lusitano." *ABN* 43–44 (1920–21): 1–48.

Vaz, António José. *A Sua Alteza Real, o Principe Regente, Nosso Senhor, em o Faustissimo dia 7 de*

Março de 1810, Anniversario da sua Plausivel, e Feliz Entrada neste Porto do Rio de Janeiro. Rio de Janeiro: Impressão Régia, s.d.

Viana, Paulo Fernandes, "Abreviada demonstração dos trabalhos da polícia." *RIHGB* 55, pt. 1 (1892): 373–380.

Vieira, António. *Obras Escolhidas* v. 10. Lisbon: Livraria Sá da Costa, 1954.

Wilson, James. *A missionary voyage to the southern Pacific Ocean, performed in the years 1796, 1797, 1798, in the Ship Duff, commanded by Captain James Wilson, Compiled from journals of the officers and missionaries. . . .* London: Chapman, 1799.

[Wolcot, John]. *The Fall of Portugal; or The Royal Exiles, A Tragedy in Five Acts.* London: Longman, Hurst, Ress and Orme, 1808.

PRINCIPAL BOOKS, DISSERTATIONS, AND ARTICLES

Adams, Christine, Jack R. Censer, and Lisa Jane Graham, eds. *Visions and Revisions of Eighteenth-Century France.* University Park: The Pennnsylvania State University Press, 1997.

Adelman, Jeremy. *Republic of Capital: Buenos Aires and the Legal Transformation of the Atlantic World.* Stanford: Stanford University Press, 1999.

Aguiar, Manuel Pinto. *A abertura dos portos, Cairu e os inglêses.* Salvador: Progresso, 1960.

Alden, Dauril. *Royal Government in Colonial Brazil, with Special Reference to the Administration of the Marquis of Lavradio, Viceroy, 1769–1779.* Berkeley: University of California Press, 1968.

_____, ed. *Colonial Roots of Modern Brazil.* Berkeley: University of California Press, 1973.

Alexandre, Valentim. "O nacionalismo vintista e a questão brasileira: esboço de análise política." In *O liberalismo na península ibérica na primeira metade do século XIX* v. 1, ed. Miriam Halpern Pereira. Lisbon: Livraria Sá da Costa, 1982.

_____. *Os sentidos do império: questão nacional e questão colonial na crise do antigo regime português.* Porto: Edições Afrontamento, 1993.

Alexandrowicz, C.H. "Freitas Versus Grotius." In *Theories of Empire, 1450–1800,* ed. David Armitage. Brookfield: Ashgate/Variorum, 1998.

Algranti, Leila Mezan. *O feitor ausente: estudos sobre a escravidão urbana no Rio de Janeiro, 1808–1822.* Petrópolis, Rio de Janeiro: Vozes, 1988.

_____. "Costumes afro-brasileiros no corte do Rio de Janeiro: um documento curioso." *Boletim do Centro de Memória UNICAMP* 1, n. 1 (January/June 1989): 17–21.

_____. *Honradas e devotas: mulheres da colônia, condição feminina nos conventos e recolhimentos do Sudeste do Brasil, 1750–1822.* Rio de Janeiro: José Olympio, 1993.

Álvarez, Fernando Bouza. "Lisboa *Sozinha, Quaze Viúva.* A Cidade e a Mudança da Corte no Portugal dos Felipes." *Penélope: Fazer e Desfazer a História* 13 (1994): 71–93.

Alves, Ana Maria. *Iconologia do poder real no período manuelino, à procura de uma linguagem perdida.* Lousã: Imprensa Nacional, 1985.

Alves, José Augusto dos Santos. "A Revolução Francesa no Discurso de *O Portuguez* (Londres—1814–1826)." *RHI* 10 (1988): 509–517.

_____. *Ideologia e Política na Imprensa do Exílio, "O Portuguez" (1814–1826).* Lisbon:

Imprensa Nacional/Casa da Moeda, 1992.

Anderson, Benedict. *Imagined Communities: Reflections on the Origin and Spread of Nationalism.* (1983) New York: Verso, 1991.

Anna, Timothy. "Spain and the Breakdown of the Imperial Ethos: The Problem of Equality." *Hispanic American Historical Review* 62, n. 2 (1982): 254–272.

Annino, A., L. Castro-Leiva, and F.X. Guerra, eds. *De los Imperios a las Naciones Iberoamerica.* Zaragoza: Ibercaja, 1994.

Araújo, Ana Cristina. "As Invasões franceses e a afirmação das idéias liberais." In *História de Portugal: O Liberalismo* v. 5, ed. Luiz Reis Torgal and João Lourenço. Lisbon: Estampa, n.d.

——————. "Revoltas e Ideologias em Conflito durante as Invasões Francesas." *RHI* 7 (1985): 7–90.

——————. "Ruína e Morte em Portugal no Século XVIII, A Propósito do Terramoto de 1755." *RHI* 9 (1987): 327–365.

——————. "O 'Reino Unido de Portugal, Brasil e Algarves' 1815–1822." *RHI* 14 (1992): 233–261.

Araújo, Elysio de. *Estudo histórico sobre a polícia da capital federal de 1808–1831.* Rio de Janeiro: Imprensa Nacional, 1898.

Armitage, David, ed. *Theories of Empire, 1450–1800.* Brookfield: Ashgate/Variorum, 1998.

Arquivo Nacional, Rio de Janeiro. *Os Franceses Residentes no Rio de Janeiro, 1808–1820.* Rio de Janeiro: Arquivo Nacional, 1960.

Arruda, José Jobson. *O Brasil no comércio colonial.* São Paulo: Ática, 1980.

Aufderheide, Patricia Ann. "Order and Violence: Social Deviance and Social Control in Brazil, 1780–1840." Ph.D. dissertation, University of Minnesota, 1976.

Azevedo, Francisca L. Nogueira de. "Carlota Joaquina, a Herdeira do Império Espanhol na América." *Estudos Históricos* 10, n. 20 (1997): 251–274.

Baecque, Antoine de. "The Allegorical Image of France, 1750–1800: A Political Crisis of Representation." *Representations* 47 (Summer 1994): 111–143.

Baker, Keith Michael. "Politics and Public Opinion Under the Old Regime: Some Reflections." In *Press and Politics in Pre-Revolutionary France*, ed. Jack R. Censer and Jeremy Popkin. Berkeley: University of California Press, 1987.

Barman, Roderick. *Brazil: The Forging of a Nation, 1798–1852.* Stanford: Stanford University Press, 1988.

Barreto Filho, Mello, and Hermeto Lima. *História da polícia do Rio de Janeiro, aspectos da cidade e da vida carioca, 1565–1831* v. 1. Rio de Janeiro: S.A.A. Noite, [1939].

Bebiano, Rui. *D. João V: poder e espectáculo.* Aveiro: Livraria Estante, 1987.

Bernardino, Teresa. *Sociedade e atitudes mentais em Portugal (1777–1810).* Vila da Maia: Imprensa Nacional, 1986.

Bethell, Leslie, ed. *Colonial Brazil.* New York: Cambridge University Press, 1987.

——————, ed. *The Independence of Latin America.* New York: Cambridge University Press, 1987.

Bethencourt, Francisco, and Diogo Ramada Curto, eds. *A Memória da nação.* Lisbon: Livraria Sá da Costa, 1991.

Bittencourt, Gean Maria. *A missão artística francesa de 1816.* Petrópolis: Museu de Armas Ferreira da Cunha, 1967.

Blake, Augusto Victorino Alves Sacramento. *Diccionário bibliographico brazileiro.* (1883) Nendeln, Liechtenstein: Krause Reprint, 1969.

Boxer, Charles R. *The Golden Age of Brazil, 1695–1750, Growing Pains of a Colonial Society.* Berkeley: University of California Press, 1962.

_____. *The Portuguese Seaborne Empire, 1415–1825.* London: Hutchinson, 1969.

Brandão, Raul. *El-rei Junot.* (1912) Lisbon: Imprensa Nacional/Casa da Moeda, 1982.

Brown, Alexandra Kelly. "'On the Vanguard of Civilization': Slavery, the Police, and Conflicts between Public and Private Power in Salvador da Bahia, Brazil, 1835–1888." Ph.D. dissertation, University of Texas at Austin, 1998.

Brown, Larissa. "Internal Commerce in a Colonial Economy: Rio de Janeiro and Its Hinterland, 1790–1822." Ph.D. dissertation, University of Virginia, 1986.

Brown, Laura. *Alexander Pope.* Oxford: Blackwell, 1985.

Buescu, Ana Isabel. "Um mito das origens da nacionalidade: o milagre de Ourique." In *A Memória da nação*, ed. Francisco Bethencourt and Diogo Ramada Curto. Lisbon: Livraria Sá da Costa, 1991.

Burke, Peter. *The Fabrication of Louis XIV.* New Haven: Yale University Press, 1992.

Burns, E. Bradford. "The Enlightenment in Two Colonial Brazilian Libraries." *Journal of the History of Ideas* 25, n. 3 (July–September 1964): 430–438.

Calmon, Pedro. *História do Brasil* v. 4. Rio de Janeiro: José Olympio, 1963.

Camargo, Ana Maria de Almeida, and Rubens Borba de Moraes. *Bibliografia da Impressão Régia do Rio de Janeiro* 2 v. São Paulo: EDUSP/Kosmos, 1993.

Cañeque, Alejandro. "The King's Living Image: The Culture and Politics of Viceregal Power in Seventeenth-Century New Spain." Ph.D. dissertation, New York University, 1999.

Cardim, Pedro. "O quadro constitucional. Os grandes paradigmas de organização política: A coroa e a representação do reino. As cortes." In *História de Portugal: O Antigo Regime* v. 4, ed. António Manuel Hespanha. Lisbon: Estampa, n.d.

Cardoso, José Luiz. *O pensamento económico em Portugal nos finais do século XVIII, 1780–1808.* Lisbon: Estampa, 1989.

_____. "Economic thought in late eighteenth-century Portugal: physiocratic and Smithian influences." *History of Political Economy* 22 n. 2 (1990): 429–441.

Cardoso, Tereza Maria Rolo Fachada Levy. "A Gazeta do Rio de Janeiro: Subsídios para a História da Cidade (1808–1821)." M.A. thesis, Federal University of Rio de Janeiro, 1988.

Carvalho, José Murilo de. "Political Elites and State Building: The Case of Nineteenth-Century Brazil." *Comparative Studies in Society and History* 24, n. 3 (1982): 378–399.

_____. *A formação das almas: o imaginário da República no Brasil.* São Paulo: Companhia das Letras, 1990.

Castro, Zilia Osório de. "A Sociedade e a Soberania, Doutrina de um Vintista." *RHI* 1 (1979): 171–230.

Censer, Jack R., and Jeremy Popkin, eds. *Press and Politics in Pre-Revolutionary France.* Berkeley: University of California Press, 1987.

Chartier, Roger, ed. *The Culture of Print: Power and the Uses of Print in Early Modern Europe.* Princeton: Princeton University Press, 1989.

_____. *The Cultural Origins of the French Revolution*, trans. by Lydia G. Cochrane, Durham: Duke University Press, 1991.

Clayton, Arnold B. "The Life of Tomás Antônio Vilanova Portugal: A Study in the Government of Portugal and Brazil." Ph.D. dissertation, Columbia University, 1977.

Coelho, Jacinto Prado, ed. *O Rio de Janeiro na literatura portugueza*. Lisbon: Commissão Nacional das Commemorações do IV Centenario do Rio de Janeiro, [1965].

_____. *Dicionário de Literatura*, 3a. ed. Porto: Figueirinhas, 1979.

Cohen, Thomas. *The Fire of Tongues: António Vieira and the Missionary Church in Brazil and Portugal.* Stanford: Stanford University Press, 1998.

Coimbra, Álvaro da Veiga. "Noções de Numismática. Condecorações (III)." *Revista de História* 26, n. 53, ano 14 (1963): 219–264.

_____. "Noções de Numismática. Condecorações (IV)." *Revista de História* 26, n. 56, ano 14 (1963): 457–471.

Conrad, Robert Edgar. *Children of God's Fire: A Documentary History of Black Slavery in Brazil.* University Park: The Pennsylvania State University Press, 1984.

Costa, Emilia Viotti da. *The Brazilian Empire: Myths and Histories.* Chicago: University of Chicago Press, 1985.

Costa, J.A., "Napoléon I au Brasil." *Revue de monde latin* (Paris) v. 8 (1883–89): 205–216.

Cunha, Alcingstone de Oliveira. "The Portuguese Royal Court and the Patronage of Sacred Music in Rio de Janeiro, 1808–1821." Ph.D. dissertation, Southwestern Baptist Theological Seminary, Fort Worth, Texas, 1998.

Cunha, Manuela Carneiro da. "Silences of the Law: Customary Law and Positive Law on the Manumission of Slaves in 19th-Century Brazil." *History and Anthropology* v. 1 (1985): 427–443.

_____. *Antropologia do Brasil: mito, história, e etnicidade.* São Paulo: Brasiliense, [1988].

Cunha, Rui Viera da. "A vida do Rio de Janeiro através dos testamentos: 1815–1822." *RIHGB* 282 (January–March 1969): 46–64.

Curto, Diogo Ramada. "Ritos e cerimónias da monarquia em Portugal." In *A Memória da nação*, eds. Francisco Bethencourt and Diogo Ramada Curto. Lisbon: Livraria Sá da Costa, 1991.

D'Alcochete, Nuno Daupias. "Les Pamphlets Portugais Anti-Napoléoniens." *Arquivos do Centro Cultural Portugues.* (Paris, Fundação Calouste Gulbenkian) 11 (1977): 507–515.

Darnton, Robert. *The Forbidden Best-Sellers of Pre-Revolutionary France.* New York: Norton, [1995].

Dean, Warren. *With Broadax and Firebrand: The Destruction of the Brazilian Atlantic Forest.* Berkeley: University of California Press, 1995.

Delson, Roberta Marx. *New Towns for Colonial Brazil: Spatial and Social Planning of the Eighteenth Century.* Ann Arbor: University Microfilms International/Dellplain Latin American Studies, 1979.

Dias, Maria Odila da Silva. "Aspectos da Ilustração no Brasil." *RIHGB* 278 (January–March 1968): 105–170.

_____. "A Interiorização da Metrópole." In *1822: Dimensões*, ed. Carlos Guilherme Mota. São Paulo: Perspectiva, 1972.

_____. "The Establishment of the Royal Court in Brazil." In *From Colony to Nation:*

Essays on the Independence of Brazil, ed. A.J.R. Russell-Wood. Baltimore: The Johns Hopkins University Press, 1975.

Donovan, Bill M. "Changing Perceptions of Social Deviance: Gypsies in Early Modern Portugal and Brazil." *Journal of Social History* 26, n. 1 (Fall 1992): 33–53.

Edmundo, Luiz. *A côrte de D. João no Rio de Janeiro, 1808–1821*. Rio de Janeiro: Imprensa Nacional, 1939.

_____. *O Rio de Janeiro no tempo dos vice-reis* 2 v. Rio de Janeiro: Editôra Aurora, 1951.

Elliott, J.H. "A Europe of Composite Monarchies." *Past and Present* 137 (November 1992): 48–71.

Farge, Arlette. *Subversive Words: Public Opinion in Eigtheenth-Century France*. University Park: The Pennsylvania State University Press, 1995.

Ferguson, Stephen. "The Código Brasiliense: Brazil's First Official Legal Code." *Inter-American Review of Bibliography* 24, n. 2 (April–June 1974): 129–134.

Feros, Antonio. "'Vicedioses, pero humanos': el drama del Rey." *Cuadernos de Historia Moderna* (Madrid): 103–131.

Ferreira, Ana Maria. "'Mare Clausum, Mare Liberum': Dimensão Doutrinal de um Foco de Tensões Políticas." *Cultura e História* 3 (1984): 315–357.

Ferreira, Manuel Rodrigues, and Tito Lívio Ferreira. *A Maçonaria na Independência Brasileira* v. 1. São Paulo: Gráfica Biblos, 1962.

Ferreira, Marieta de Moraes. "A nova 'velha história': o retorno da história política." *Estudos Históricos* 10 (1992): 265–271.

Ferrez, Gilberto. *O Paço da Cidade do Rio de Janeiro*. Rio de Janeiro: Fundação Nacional Pró-Memória, 1985.

Florentino, Manolo Garcia. *Em Costas Negras: Uma História do Tráfico Atlântico de Escravos entre a África e o Rio de Janeiro (Séculos XVIII e XIX)*. Rio de Janeiro: Arquivo Nacional, 1995.

Fragoso, João Luiz Ribeiro. *Homens de Grossa Aventura: Acumulação e Hierarquia na Praça Mercantil do Rio de Janeiro (1790–1830)*. Rio de Janeiro: Arquivo Nacional, 1991.

Fragoso, João, and Manolo Florentino, *O Arcaísmo como Projeto: Mercado Atlântico, Sociedade Agrária e Elite Mercantil no Rio de Janeiro, c.1790–c.1840*. Rio de Janeiro: Diodorim, 1993.

França, José Augusto. *Lisboa Pombalina e o Iluminismo*. Lisbon: Livraria Bertrand, 1977.

Francis, David. *Portugal, 1715–1808, Joanine and Rococo Portugal as Seen by British Diplomats and Traders*. London: Tamesis, 1985.

Furtado, Celso. *The Economic Growth of Brazil, A Survey from Colonial to Modern Times*, trans. Ricardo W. de Aguiar and Eric Charles Drysdale. Berkeley: University of California Press, 1965.

Galvão, Benjamin Franklin Ramiz. "O Pulpito no Brasil." *RIHGB* 92 (1922): 9–160.

Gates, David. *The Spanish Ulcer: A History of the Peninsular War*. New York: Norton, 1986.

Gerbi, Antonello. *The Dispute of the New World, The History of a Polemic*. Pittsburgh: University of Pittsburgh Press, 1993.

Gerson, Brasil. *História das Ruas do Rio de Janeiro*. Rio de Janeiro: Editôra Souza, n.d.

Gomes, Angela Castro. "Política: História, Ciência, Cultura, etc." *Estudos Históricos* 17 (1996): 59–84.

Gomes, Flávio dos Santos. *Histórias de Quilombolas: Mocambos e Comunidades de Senzalas no Rio de Janeiro, Século XIX.* Rio de Janeiro: Arquivo Nacional, 1995.

Gomes, Maria Eugénia Reis. *Contribuição para o estudo da festa no antigo regime.* Lisbon: Instituto Português de Ensino a Distancia, 1985.

Gouvêa, Maria de Fátima Silva. "Redes de Poder na América Portuguesa—O caso dos Homens Bons do Rio de Janeiro, ca. 1790–1822." *Revista Brasileira de História* 18, n. 36 (1998): 287–330.

Graham, Lisa Jane. "Crimes of Opinion: Policing the Public in Eighteenth-Century Paris." In *Visions and Revisions of Eighteenth-Century France,* ed. Christine Adams, Jack R. Censer, and Lisa Jane Graham. University Park: The Pennsylvania State University Press, 1997.

Grinberg, Keila. *Liberata, a lei da ambigüidade: as ações de liberdade da corte de apelação do Rio de Janeiro no século XIX.* Rio de Janeiro: Dumará, 1994.

Guenther, Louise Helena. "The British Community of Bahia, Brazil, 1808–1850." Ph.D. dissertation, University of Minnesota, 1998.

Guerra, François-Xavier. "The Spanish American Tradition of Representation and Its European Roots." *Journal of Latin American Studies* 26 (1994): 1–35.

Hallewell, Laurence. *Books in Brazil: a History of the Publishing Trade.* Metuchen, NJ: Scarecrow, 1982.

Hamnett, Brian R. "Process and Pattern: A Re-examination of the Ibero-American Independence Movements, 1808–1826." *Journal of Latin American Studies* 29, pt. 2 (May 1997): 279–328.

Helgerson, Richard. *Forms of Nationhood: The Elizabethan Writing of England.* Chicago: University of Chicago Press, 1992.

Herbert, Christopher. *Culture and Anomie: Ethnographic Imagination in the Nineteenth Century.* Chicago: University of Chicago Press, 1991.

Hespanha, António Manuel. *La gracia del derecho: economia de la cultura en la edad moderna.* Madrid: Centro de Estudios Constitucionales, 1993.

_____. "A punição e a graça." In *História de Portugal: O Antigo Regime* v. 4, ed. António Manuel Hespanha. Lisbon: Editorial Estampa, n.d.

_____, ed. *História de Portugal: O Antigo Regime* v. 4. Lisbon: Estampa, n.d.

Hesse, Carla. *Publishing and Cultural Politics in Revolutionary Paris, 1789–1810.* Berkeley: University of California Press, 1991.

Higgs, David. "Unbelief and Politics in Rio de Janeiro During the 1790s." *Luso-Brazilian Review* 21, n. 1 (1984): 13–31.

_____. "Nota sobre um documento acerca da história político-religiosa do Rio de Janeiro no periodo da revolução francesa." *RHI* 9 (1987): 439–449.

_____, ed. *Portuguese Migration in Global Perspective.* Toronto: Multicultural History Society of Toronto, 1990.

_____. "'A Luceferina Assembleia': Rio de Janeiro nos anos 1790 [Sumário contra José Luiz Mendes, boticário, morador na cidade do Rio de Janeiro e outros]," manuscript, April 2000.

Holanda, Sérgio Buarque de. "A herança colonial—sua desagregação." In *História Geral da Civilização Brasileira* tomo 1, v. 1, ed. Sérgio Buarque de Holanda. São Paulo: DIFEL, 1985.

_____. *Raízes do Brasil.* (1936) Rio de Janeiro: José Olympio, 1989.

Holloway, Thomas H. *Policing Rio de Janeiro: Repression and Resistance in a Nineteenth-Century City.* Stanford: Stanford University Press, 1993.

Holston, James. *The Modernist City: An Anthropological Critique of Brasília.* Chicago: University of Chicago Press, 1989.

Hunt, Lynn. *Politics, Culture and Class in the French Revolution.* Berkeley: University of California Press, 1984.

_____, ed. *The New Cultural History.* Berkeley: University of California Press, 1989.

"Hygiene da cidade do Rio de Janeiro." *ABN* 1 (1876): 187–190.

Instituto Brasileiro de Geografia e Estatística. *Estatísticas históricas do Brasil.* Rio de Janeiro: IBGE, 1990.

Ipanema, Marcello de. *Estudos de história da legislação de imprensa.* Rio de Janeiro: Aurora, 1949.

Jancsó, István. "A sedução da liberdade: cotidiano e contestação política no final do século XVIII." In *História da Vida Privada no Brasil* v. 1, ed. Fernando Novais and Laura de Mello e Souza. São Paulo: Companhia das Letras, 1997.

Jouhaud, Christian. "Readability and Persuasion: Political Handbills." In *The Culture of Print: Power and the Uses of Print in Early Modern Europe*, ed. Roger Chartier. (1987) Princeton: Princeton University Press, 1989.

Kaminsky, Amy K. *Reading the Body Politic: Feminist Criticism and Latin American Women Writers.* Minneapolis: University of Minnesota Press, 1993.

Karasch, Mary. *Slave Life in Rio de Janeiro, 1808–1850.* Princeton: Princeton University Press, 1987.

Keith, Henry, and S.F. Edwards, eds. *Conflict and Continuity in Brazilian Society.* Columbia, SC: University of South Carolina Press, 1969.

Kendrick, T.D. *The Lisbon Earthquake.* Philadelphia/New York: Lippincott, n.d. [1955].

Kilian, Norbert. "New Wine in Old Skins? American Definitions of Empire and the Emergence of a New Concept." In *Theories of Empire, 1450–1800*, ed. David Armitage. Brookfield: Ashgate/Variorum, 1998.

Kraay, Hendrik. "The Politics of Race in Independence-Era Bahia, The Black Militia Officers of Salvador, 1790–1840." In *Afro-Brazilian Culture and Politics, Bahia, 1790s–1990s*, ed. Hendrik Kraay. New York: M.E. Sharpe, 1998.

Ladner, Janet. "John VI of Portugal: Contemporary of Napoleon and Wellington." In *Consortium on Revolutionary Europe. Proceedings* 20 (1990): 869–892.

Landes, Joan. *Women and the Public Sphere in the Age of the French Revolution.* Ithaca: Cornell University Press, 1988.

Langley, Lester. *The Americas in the Age of Revolution, 1750–1850.* New Haven: Yale University Press, 1996.

Lara, Silvia Hunold. "Signs of Color: Women's Dress and Racial Relations in Salvador and Rio de Janeiro, ca. 1750–1815." *Colonial Latin American Review* 6, n. 2 (1997): 205–224.

_____. "Significados Cruzados: as embaixadas de congos no Brasil colonial." Paper delivered at the meeting of the Latin American Studies Association, April 1997.

La Vopa, Anthony. "Conceiving a Public: Ideas and Society in Eighteenth-Century Europe." *Journal of Modern History* 64 (March 1992): 79–116.

Leão Filho, Joaquim de Souza. "O Rio de Janeiro de Dom João (1808–1821)." *RIHGB* 276 (July–September 1967): 74–89.

Lemos, Carlos, José Roberto Teixeira Leite, and Pedro Manuel Gismonti. *The Art of Brazil.* New York: Harper & Row, 1983.

Leonzo, Nanci. "Oliveira Lima: o dramaturgo da independência." *Revista da Sociedade Brasileira de Pesquisa Histórica* (São Paulo) 2 (1984–85): 53–58.

Levenson, Jay, ed. *The Age of the Baroque in Portugal.* Washington, DC/New Haven: The National Gallery of Art/Yale University Press, 1993.

Lima, Manuel de Oliveira. *Dom João VI no Brasil (1808–1821)* (1908) 3 v. Rio de Janeiro: José Olympio, 1945.

Linebaugh, Peter and Marcus Rediker. *The Many-Headed Hydra: Sailors, Slaves, Commoners, and the Hidden History of the Revolutionary Atlantic.* Boston: Beacon Press, 2000.

Lobo, Eulalia Maria Lahmeyer. *História do Rio de Janeiro (do capital comercial ao capital industrial financeiro)* 2 v. Rio de Janeiro: IBMEC, 1978.

Lyra, Maria de Lourdes Viana. *A Utopia do Poderoso Império, Portugal e Brasil: Bastidores da Política, 1798–1822.* Rio de Janeiro: Sette Letras, 1994.

Macaulay, Neill. *Dom Pedro: The Struggle for Liberty in Brazil and Portugal, 1798–1834.* Durham: Duke University Press, 1986.

Machado, António Pires. *D. Sebastião e O Encoberto.* Lisbon: Fundação Calouste Gulbenkian, [1969].

Magnoli, Demétrio. *O corpo da pátria: imaginação geográfica e política externa no Brasil, 1808–1912.* São Paulo: UNESP, 1997.

Malerba, Jurandir. "A corte no exílio. Interpretação do Brasil joanino, 1808–1821." Ph.D. dissertation, University of São Paulo, 1997.

_____. "Instituições da monarquia portuguesa decisivas na fundação do império brasileiro." *Luso-Brazilian Review* 36, n. 1 (Summer 1999): 33–48.

Manchester, Alan K. *British Preëminence in Brazil, Its Rise and Decline. A Study in European Expansion.* (1933) New York: Octagon, 1964.

_____. "The Transfer of the Portuguese Court to Brazil." In *Conflict and Continuity in Brazilian Society,* ed. Henry Keith and S.F. Edwards. Columbia, SC: University of South Carolina Press, 1969.

_____. "The Growth of Bureaucracy in Brazil, 1808–1821." *Journal of Latin American Studies* 4, n. 1 (1972): 77–83.

Marques, A.H. Oliveira. *A History of Portugal,* 2nd ed. New York: Columbia University Press, 1976.

Martinho, Lenira Menezes, and Riva Gorenstein. *Negociantes e Caixeiros na Sociedade da Independência.* Rio de Janeiro: Secretaria Muncipal de Cultura, 1992.

Mauro, Frédéric, ed. *Nova História da Expansão Portuguesa. O Império Luso-Brasileiro, 1620–1750* v. 7. Lisbon: Estampa, 1991.

Maxwell, Kenneth R. *Conflicts and Conspiracies: Brazil and Portugal, 1750–1808.* New York: Cambridge University Press, 1973.

_____. "The Generation of 1790s and the Idea of Luso-Brazilian Empire." In *Colonial Roots of Modern Brazil,* ed. Dauril Alden. Berkeley: University of California Press, 1973.

_____. *Pombal: Paradox of the Enlightenment.* New York: Cambridge University Press, 1995.

McClintock, Anne. *Imperial Leather: Race, Gender and Sexuality in the Colonial Contest.* New York: Routledge, 1995.

Meade, Teresa A. *"Civilizing" Rio: Reform and Resistance in a Brazilian City, 1889–1930.* University Park: The Pennsylvania State University Press, 1997.

Meghreblian, Caren Ann. "Art, Politics and Historical Perception in Imperial Brazil, 1854–1884." Ph.D. dissertation, University of California, Los Angeles, 1990.

Mehta, Uday Singh. *Liberalism and Empire: A Study in Nineteenth-Century British Liberal Thought.* Chicago: University of Chicago Press, 1999.

Monteiro, George. *The Presence of Camões: Influences on the Literature of England, America and Southern Africa.* Lexington: University of Kentucky Press, 1996.

Monteiro, Nuno Gonçalo. "Poder senhorial, estatuto nobiliárquico e aristocracia." In *História de Portugal: O Antigo Regime* v. 4., ed. António Manuel Hespanha. Lisbon: Estampa, n.d.

Monteiro, Tobias. *História do império. A elaboração da Independência.* Rio de Janeiro: Briguiet, 1927.

Moreira, Ariadna Gonçalves. "The Influence of the Portuguese Royal Court on the Development of Opera, The Opera Nova, and the Real Teatro São João in Rio de Janeiro from 1808–1824." Doctoral Essay, Doctor of Musical Arts, University of Miami, 1998.

Morris, Marilyn. *The British Monarchy and the French Revolution.* New Haven: Yale University Press, 1998.

Mota, Carlos Guilherme. "Presença francesa em Recife em 1817." *Extrait des Cahiers du Monde Hispanique et Luso-Brésilien* caravelle 15 (1970).

_____, ed. *1822: Dimensões.* São Paulo: Perspectiva, 1986.

Mota, Carlos Guilherme, and Fernando Novais. *A Independência Política do Brasil.* São Paulo: Moderna, 1983.

Mott, Luiz R.B. "A Escravatura: o propósito de uma representação a El-rei sobre a escravatura no Brasil." *Revista do Instituto de Estudos Brasileiros* 14 (1973): 127–136.

_____. "A Revolução dos Negros do Haiti e o Brasil." In *História: Questões e Debates* (Revista da Associação Paranaense de História, Curitiba) 3, n. 4 (June 1982): 55–63.

Moura, Carlos Francisco. *Os chineses do Rio de Janeiro requerem a D. João VI um consul e intérprete.* Macau: Imprensa Nacional, 1974.

Museu Nacional de Belas Artes. *Memória da independência, 1808/1825.* Rio de Janeiro: Museu Nacional de Belas Artes, 1972.

Myscofski, Carole A. *When Men Walk Dry: Portuguese Messianism in Brazil.* Atlanta: Scholars Press, 1988.

Naro, Nancy. "Leitores e Reformadores: alguns aspectos comparativos da cultura do livro em relação à independência do brasil e da américa inglesa." *Revista da Sociedade Brasileira de Pesquisa Histórica* 3 (1986–87): 17–28.

Naves, Rodrigo. *A forma difícil: ensaios sobre a arte brasileira.* São Paulo: Editora Ática, 1996.

Needell, Jeffrey D. *A Tropical Belle Epoque: Elite Culture and Society in Turn-of-the-Century Rio de Janeiro.* New York: Cambridge University Press, 1987.

Neves, Guilherme Pereira das. "Del Imperio Luso-Brasileño al Imperio del Brasil (1789–1822)." In *De los Imperios a las Naciones Iberoamerica*, ed. A. Annino, L. Castro-Leiva, and F.X. Guerra. Zaragoza: Ibercaja, 1994.

Neves, Lúcia Maria Bastos Pereira das. "Comércio de livros e censura de ideias: A actividade dos livreiros franceses no Brasil e a vigilância da Mesa do Desembargo do Paço (1795–1822)." *Ler História* 23 (1992): 61–78.

_____. "Corcundas, constitucionais e pes-de-chumbo: a cultura política da independência, 1820–1822" 2 v. Ph.D. dissertation, University of São Paulo, 1992.

_____. "Leitura e leitores no Brasil, 1820–1822: o esboço frustrado de uma esfera pública do poder." *Acervo* 8, n. 1/2 (December 1995): 123–138.

Nicoulin, Martin. *A Gênese de Nova Friburgo. Emigração e colonização suíça no Brasil (1817–1827)*. Rio de Janeiro/Nova Friburgo: Biblioteca Nacional/Prefeitura Municipal de Nova Friburgo, 1996.

Norton, Luiz. *A côrte de Portugal no Brasil*. São Paulo: Companhia Editora Nacional, 1938.

Novais, Fernando. *Portugal e Brasil na Crise do Antigo Sistema Colonial (1777–1808)*. São Paulo: Hucitec, 1979.

Novais, Fernando, and Laura de Mello e Souza, eds. *História da Vida Privada no Brasil* v. 1. São Paulo: Companhia das Letras, 1997.

Oliveira, Cecilia Helena Lorenzini de Salles. "O Disfarce do Anonimato: O Debate Político Através dos Folhetos (1820–1822)." M.A. thesis, University of São Paulo, 1979.

_____. "A Astúcia Liberal. Relações de mercado e projetos políticos no Rio de Janeiro (1820–1824)." Ph.D. dissertation, University of São Paulo, 1986.

_____. *A Astúcia Liberal: Relações de Mercado e Projetos Políticos no Rio de Janeiro (1820–1824)*. Bragança Paulista: EDUSF/Ícone, 1999.

Olwell, Robert. *Masters, Slaves and Subjects: The Culture of Power in the South Carolina Low Country, 1740–1790*. Ithaca: Cornell University Press, 1998.

Pagden, Anthony. "The 'Defense of Civilization' in Eighteenth-Century Social Theory" (1988). In Anthony Pagden, *The Uncertainties of Empire*. Norfolk, G.B.: Variorum, 1994.

_____. *Spanish Imperialism and the Political Imagination: Studies in European and Spanish-American Social and Political Theory, 1513–1830*. New Haven: Yale University Press, 1990.

_____. *Lords of All the World: Ideologies of Empire in Spain, Britain and France, c.1500–c.1800*. New Haven: Yale University Press, 1995.

Paim, António. *Cairu e o liberalismo econômico*. Rio de Janeiro: Tempo Brasileiro, 1968.

Palmer, R.R., *The Age of Democratic Revolution: A Political History of Europe and America, 1760–1800* 2 v. Princeton: Princeton University Press, 1959–64.

Parker, John David. "The Tridentine Order and Governance in Late Colonial Brazil, 1792–1821." Ph.D. dissertation, University of Washington, 1982.

Paulson, Ronald. *Representations of Revolution (1789–1820)*. New Haven: Yale University Press, 1983.

Pereira, José Esteves. "Identidade nacional: do reformismo absolutista ao liberalismo." In *A Memória da nação*, ed. Francisco Bethencourt and Diogo Ramada Curto. Lisbon: Livraria Sá da Costa, 1991.

Pereira, Miriam Halpern, ed. *O liberalismo na península ibérica na primeira metade do século*

XIX v. 1. Lisbon: Livraria Sá da Costa, 1982.

Pijning, Ernst. "Controlling Contraband: Mentality, Economy and Society in Eighteenth-Century Rio de Janeiro." Ph.D. dissertation, The Johns Hopkins University, 1997.

Pimentel, António Felipe. "Absolutismo, Corte e Palácio Real—Em torno dos palácios de D. João V." In *Arqueologia do Estado, Jornadas sobre Formas de Organização e Exercício dos Poderes na Europa do Sul, S.XVII–S.XVIII.* (special issue) *História e Crítica* (Lisbon) (1988): 685–710.

Pina, Ana Maria Ferreira. *De Rousseau ao Imaginário da Revolução de 1820.* Lisbon: INIC, 1988.

Pinheiro, Lígia. "Portuguese Court Festivities and Dance in Early Nineteenth-Century Monarchical Brazil." M.A. thesis, Ohio State University, 1998.

Pinto, Teixeira. *A maçonaria na independência do Brasil (1812–1823).* Rio de Janeiro: Salogan, 1961.

Pocock, J.G.A. *Politics, Language and Time: Essays in Political Thought and History.* New York: Atheneum, 1971.

_____. *Virtue, Commerce, and History: Essays on Political Thought and History, Chiefly in the Eighteenth Century.* New York: Cambridge University Press, 1985.

Pontifícia Universidade Católica do Rio de Janeiro. *Uma Cidade em Questão I: Grandjean de Montigny e o Rio de Janeiro.* Rio de Janeiro: PUC, 1978.

Porto, Albano da Silveira. *Resenha das Famílias Titulares Grandes de Portugal.* Lisboa: Francisco Arthur da Silva, 1883–90.

Prado, J.F. de Almeida. *D. João e o início da classe dirigente do Brasil (depoimento de um pintor austríaco no Rio de Janeiro).* São Paulo: Companhia Editora Nacional, 1968.

Prado, Maria Lígia. "Lendo Novelas no Brasil Joanino." In Prado, *América Latina no Século XIX: Tramas, Telas e Textos* (São Paulo: Edusc/EDUSP, 1999).

Prado, Caio, Jr. *Evolução Política do Brasil, Colônia e Império* (1933). São Paulo: Brasiliense, n.d.

Prakash, Gyan, ed. *After Colonialism: Imperial Histories and Postcolonial Displacements.* Princeton: Princeton University Press, 1995.

Pratt, Mary Louise. *Imperial Eyes: Travel Writing and Transculturation.* New York: Routledge, 1992.

Proença, Maria Candida. "1820: A 'Festa' da Regeneração: Permanências e Inovações." *RHI* 10: 375–384.

Rama, Angel. *The Lettered City.* trans. and ed. John Charles Chasteen. Durham: Duke University Press, 1996.

Reis, João José. *Slave Rebellion in Brazil: The Muslim Uprising of 1835 in Bahia.* Baltimore: The Johns Hopkins University Press, 1993.

Reis, Marcos de Freitas. "A intendência geral da polícia da corte e do estado do Brasil: os termos de bem viver e a ação de Paulo Fernandes Viana" In *Anais da II Reunião da Sociedade Brasileira de Pesquisa Histórica (SBPH).* São Paulo: SBPH, 1993.

Reis Filho, Nestor Goulart. *Contribuição ao estudo da evolução urbana do Brasil (1500–1720).* São Paulo: Livraria Pioneira/EDUSP, 1968.

Renault, Delso. *O Rio antigo nos anúncios de jornais, 1808–1850.* Rio de Janeiro: Francisco Alves, 1984.

Ribeiro, Maria Eurydice de Barros. *Os símbolos do poder. Cerimônias e imagens do Estado monárquico no Brasil.* Brasília: Editora UnB, 1995.

Rocha-Trinidade, Maria Beatriz. "Portuguese Migration to Brazil in the Nineteenth and Twentieth Centuries: An International Cultural Exchange." In *Portuguese Migration in Global Perspective*, ed. David Higgs. Toronto: Multicultural History Society of Toronto, 1990.

Rodrigues, José Honório. *Independência: revolução e contra-revolução* 5 v. Rio de Janeiro: Francisco Alves, 1975–76.

Roseberry, William. "Hegemony and the Language of Contention." In *Everyday Forms of State Formation: Revolution and the Negotiation of Rule in Modern Mexico*, ed. Gilbert Joseph and Daniel Nugent. Durham: Duke University Press, 1994.

Russell-Wood, A.J.R. *Fidalgos and Philanthropists: The Santa Casa da Misericórdia da Bahia, 1550–1755.* Berkeley: University of California Press, 1968.

――――――, ed. *From Colony to Nation: Essays on the Independence of Brazil.* Baltimore: The Johns Hopkins University Press, 1975.

――――――. "Iberian Expansion and the Issue of Black Slavery: Changing Portuguese Attitudes, 1440–1770." *American Historical Review* 83, n. 1 (February 1978): 16–42.

――――――. *The Portuguese Empire, 1415–1808: A World on the Move.* Baltimore: The Johns Hopkins University Press, 1998.

――――――. "'Acts of Grace': Portuguese Monarchs and their Subjects of African Descent in Eighteenth-Century Brazil." *Journal of Latin American Studies* 32 (2000): 307–332.

――――――. "Ambivalent Authorities: The African and Afro-Brazilian Contribution to Local Governance in Colonial Brazil." *The Americas* 57, n. 1 (July 2000): 13–36.

Salgado, Graça, ed. *Memórias sobre a escravidão.* Rio de Janeiro: Arquivo Nacional, 1988.

Santos, Afonso Carlos Marques dos. *No rascunho da nação: inconfidência no Rio de Janeiro.* Rio de Janeiro: Secretaria Municipal de Cultura, 1992.

Santos, Célia Galvão Quirino dos. "As sociedades secretas e a formação do pensamento liberal." *Anais do Museu Paulista* 19 (1965): 51–59.

Santos, Corcino Medeiros dos. *Relações comerciais do Rio de Janeiro com Lisboa (1763–1808).* Rio de Janeiro: Tempo Brasileiro, 1980.

Schwartz, Stuart B. "The Voyage of Vassals: Royal Power, Noble Obligations, and Merchant Capital before the Portuguese Restoration of Independence, 1624–1640." *American Historical Review* 96, n. 3 (June 1991): 735–762.

――――――. "Somebodies and Nobodies in the Body Politic: Mentalities and Social Structures in Colonial Brazil." *Latin American Research Review* 31, n. 1 (1996): 113–134.

Seoane, Carmen Sylvia Sicoli. "Aquarelas do Brasil. Estudo iconografico e textual da natureza do indio em Debret e Rugendas (1816–1831)." M.A. thesis, Fluminense Federal University, 1990.

Serrão, Joaquim Veríssimo. *Do Brasil filipino do Brasil de 1640.* São Paulo: Companhia Editora Nacional, 1968.

Silva, Ana Cristina Nogueira da, and António Manuel Hespanha. "A identidade portuguesa." In *História de Portugal: O Antigo Regime* v. 4, ed. António Manuel Hespanha. Lisbon: Estampa, n.d.

Silva, Innocencio Francisco da. *Diccionário bibliográfico portuguez.* Lisbon: Imprensa Nacional, 1858–1923.

Silva, José Luiz Werneck da. "A polícia na corte e no distrito federal, 1831–1930." *Estudos PUC/RJ* 3 (1981).

Silva, Maria Beatriz Nizza da. *Análise de estratificação social (o Rio de Janeiro de 1808 a 1821).* São Paulo: Faculdade de Filosofia, Letras e Ciências Humanas da Universidade de São Paulo, 1975.

_____. *Cultura e sociedade no Rio de Janeiro (1808–1821).* São Paulo: Companhia Editora Nacional, 1977.

_____. *Sistema de casamento no Brasil colonial.* São Paulo: Queiroz/EDUSP, 1984.

_____. "A Intendência-Geral da Polícia: 1808–1821." *Acervo* 1, n. 2, (July– December 1986): 187–204.

_____, ed. *Nova História da Expansão Portuguese. O Império Luso-Brasileiro, 1750–1822* v. 8. Lisbon: Estampa, 1986.

_____. *Vida Privada e Quotidiano no Brasil. Na época de D. Maria e D. João VI.* Lisbon: Estampa, 1993.

Simon, William. *Scientific Expeditions in the Portuguese Overseas Territories (1783–1808) and the Role of Lisbon in the Intellectual-Scientific Community of the Late Eighteenth Century.* Lisbon: Instituto de Investigação Científica Tropical, 1983.

Soares, Carlos Eugênio Líbano. *A negreada instituição: os capoeiras no Rio de Janeiro.* Rio de Janeiro: Prefeitura do Rio de Janeiro, 1994.

Souza, Antônio Cândido de Mello e. "Dialética da Malandragem (caracterização das *Memórias de um sargento de milícias*)." *Revista do Instituto de Estudos Brasileiros* (São Paulo) 8 (1970): 67–89.

Souza, Iara Lis Carvalho. *Pátria Coroada: O Brasil como Corpo Político Autônomo, 1780–1831.* São Paulo: Editora UNESP, 1998.

Souza, J. Galante de. *O Teatro no Brasil* 2 v. Rio de Janeiro: Ministério de Educação e Cultura/INL, 1960.

Souza, Laura de Mello e. *Desclassificados do ouro: a pobreza mineira no século XVIII.* Rio de Janeiro: Graal, 1982.

_____. *Inferno Atlântico: demonologia e colonização, séculos XVI–XVIII.* São Paulo: Companhia das Letras, 1993.

Stoler, Ann Laura, and Frederick Cooper, eds. *Tensions of Empire: Colonial Cultures in a Bourgeois World.* Berkeley: University of California Press, 1997.

Strong, Roy. *Art and Power, Renaissance Festivals, 1450–1650.* Berkeley: University of California Press, 1984.

Subrahmanyam, Sanjay. *The Portuguese Empire in Asia, 1500–1700, A Political and Economic History.* London: Longman, 1993.

Subtil, José. "Os poderes do centro: governo e administração." In *História de Portugal: O Antigo Regime* v. 4., ed. António Manuel Hespanha. Lisbon: Estampa, n.d.

Taunay, Afonso de E. *A Missão Artística de 1816.* [Rio de Janeiro]: Dirétorio do Patrimônio Histórico Nacional, 1976.

Tavares, Luiz Henrique Dias. *História da sedição intentada na Bahia em 1798: ("A Conspiração dos Alfaiates").* São Paulo: Pioneira/Ministério da Educação e Cultura, 1975.

Torgal, Luiz Reis. *Ideologia Política e Teoria do Estado na Restauração* 2 v. Coimbra: Biblioteca Geral da Universidade, 1981.

Torgal, Luiz Reis, and João Lourenço. *História de Portugal: O Liberalismo* v. 5. Lisbon: Estampa, n.d.

Underwood, David Kendrick. "The Pombaline Style and International Neo-classicism in Lisbon and Rio de Janeiro." Ph.D. dissertation, University of Pennsylvania, 1988.

_____. "Alfred Agache, French Sociology, and Modern Urbanism in France and Brazil." *Journal of the Society of Architectural Historians* 50, n. 1 (March 1991): 130–166.

Vainfas, Ronaldo. *Ideologia e escravidão: os letrados e a sociedade escravista no Brasil colonial.* Petrópolis: Vozes, 1986.

Valladares, Clarival do Prado. *Rio, análise iconográfica do barroco e neoclássico remanentes no Rio de Janeiro* 2 v. Rio de Janeiro: Bloch Editores, 1978.

Verdelho, Telmo dos Santos. *As palavras e as idéias na revolução liberal de 1820.* Coimbra: INIC, 1981.

Verger, Pierre. "Uma rainha africana mãe de santo em São Luiz." *Revista USP* (June–August 1990): 151–158.

Wahrman, Dror. "The New Political History: A Review Essay." *Social History* 21, n. 3 (October 1996): 343–354.

Weinstein, Barbara. "Not the Republic of Their Dreams: Historical Obstacles to Political and Social Democracy in Brazil." *Latin American Research Review* 29, n. 2 (1994): 262–273.

Williams, Alan. *The Police of Paris, 1718–1789.* Baton Rouge: Louisiana State University Press, 1979.

Winius, G.D. "Millenarianism and Empire: Portuguese Asian Decline and the 'Crise de Conscience' of the Missionaries." In *Theories of Empire, 1450–1800,* ed. David Armitage. Brookfield: Ashgate/Variorum, 1998.

Wood, Gordon. *The Radicalism of the American Revolution.* New York: Vintage, 1993.

Yates, Frances. *Astraea: The Imperial Theme in the Sixteenth Century.* London: Ark Paperbacks, 1975.

INDEX